The Latin American Casebook

Traditionally relegated because of political pressure and public expectations, courts in Latin America are increasingly asserting a stronger role in public and political discussions. This casebook takes account of this phenomenon, by offering a rigorous and up-to-date discussion of constitutional adjudication in Latin America in recent decades. Bringing to the forefront the development of constitutional law by Latin American courts in various subject matters, the volume aims to highlight a host of creative arguments and solutions that judges in the region have offered.

The authors review and discuss innovative case law in light of the countries' social, political, and legal context. Each chapter is devoted to a discussion of a particular area of judicial review, from freedom of expression to social and economic rights, from the internalization of human rights law to judicial checks on the economy, from gender and reproductive rights to transitional justice. The book thus provides a very useful tool to scholars, students, and litigants alike.

Juan F. Gonzalez-Bertomeu is Assistant Professor of Law at Instituto Tecnológico Autónomo de México (ITAM). He specializes in constitutional law, constitutional adjudication, empirical studies, and legal theory. He received his first law degree from Universidad Nacional de La Plata (1999), and obtained an LL.M. degree (2003) and a J.S.D. degree (2012) at NYU. Between 2004 and 2007, he worked for Asociación por los Derechos Civiles (ADC), a leading NGO based in Buenos Aires devoted to civil rights protection, strategic litigation, and justice reform. Mr. Gonzalez-Bertomeu has taught constitutional law and legal philosophy at Universidad de Palermo, Universidad Nacional de La Plata, Universidad de San Andrés and Universidad de Buenos Aires.

Roberto Gargarella is currently Professor of Constitutional Law, Universidad de Buenos Aires, since 1998, and Professor of Constitutional Law and Legal Philosophy, Universidad Di Tella, since 1995. He has also been Visiting Researcher at Harvard University (2010), Visiting Professor at Columbia University (2003, 2007–8), Central European University (2007), University of Bergen (2005), and Universidad Pompeu Fabra, Barcelona, (1993–9). He has won numerous awards, including: Tinker Scholarship (2007), First Prize, National Contest of Essays, organized by Argentina's Supreme Court (2007), Fulbright Scholarship (2006), Harry Frank Guggenheim Fellow (2002–2003) and John Simon Guggenheim Fellow (1999–2000).

The Latin American Casebook

Courts, constitutions, and rights

Juan F. Gonzalez-Bertomeu and Roberto Gargarella

Routledge
Taylor & Francis Group
LONDON AND NEW YORK

First published 2016
by Routledge
2 Park Square, Milton Park, Abingdon, Oxon OX14 4RN

and by Routledge
711 Third Avenue, New York, NY 10017

First issued in paperback 2017

Routledge is an imprint of the Taylor & Francis Group, an informa business

British Library Cataloguing in Publication Data
A catalogue record for this book is available from the British Library

Library of Congress Cataloging-in-Publication Data
The Latin American casebook : courts, constitutions and rights / by Juan F. Gonzalez-Bertomeu and Roberto Gargarella.
pages cm
Includes bibliographical references and index.
ISBN 978-1-4094-6969-8 (hardback) — ISBN 978-1-4094-6970-4 (epub)
1. Constitutional law—Latin America—Cases. 2. Civil rights—Latin America—Cases. I. González Bertomeu, Juan F. editor. II. Gargarella, Roberto, 1964– editor.
KG548.L38 2016
342.808'0264—dc23
2015029340

ISBN 13: 978-1-138-48384-2 (pbk)
ISBN 13: 978-1-4094-6969-8 (hbk)

Typeset in Times new Roman
by Apex CoVantage, LLC

Contents

Cases

Argentina

Supreme Court of Argentina

"E.F.E." (Decisions 310:1081), 1987.
"Camps, Ramón Juan Alberto y otros," June 22, 1987 (Decisions 310:1162).
"Riveros, Santiago Omar y otros," May 22, 1988 (Decisions 311:734).
"Repetto, Inés M. c/ Provincia de Buenos Aires s/ Acción de Inconstitucionalidad," November 8, 1988 (Decisions 312:1902).
"Ekmekdjian, Miguel A. c/ Neustadt, Bernardo y otros s/amparo," December 1, 1988.
"Ekmekdjian, Miguel A. c/ Sofovich, Gerardo y otros," July 7, 1992.
"Giroldi, Horacio David y otro s/recurso de casación," April 7, 1995.
"Dessy s/habeas corpus," October 19, 1995 (D. 346:XXIV).
"Monges, Analía M. c/ U.B.A.," December 26, 1996.
"Calvo y Pesini, Rocío c/ Córdoba, Provincia de s/ amparo," February 24, 1998 (Decisions 231:194).
"Suárez Mason, Carlos Guillermo s/ homicidio, privación ilegal de la libertad," August 13, 1998 (Decisions 321:2031).
"Asociación Benghalensis y otros c/ Ministerio de Salud y Acción Social—Estado Nacional s/ amparo ley 16.986," June 1, 2000 (A. 186. XXXIV).
"Smith, Carlos Antonio c/ Poder Ejecutivo Nacional O Estado Nacional S/ Sumarísimo," February 1, 2002.
"Mignone, Emilio H. s/habeas corpus," April 9, 2002 (M. 1486. XXXVI. / M. 1491. XXXVI).
"Franco, Blanca Teodora c/ Provincia de Buenos Aires," June 27, 2002 (Decisions 313:1513).
"Domínguez, Amparo Carmen c/ ANSES s/ reajustes por movilidad" April 24, 2003 (Decisions 326:1436).
"Cantos, José María c/ Santiago del Estero," August 21, 2003.
"Lifschitz, Graciela Beatriz c/ Estado Nacional," June 15, 2004 (Decisions 327:2413).
"Arancibia Clavel, Enrique Lautaro y otros s/ homicidio calificado y asociación ilícita y otros," August 24, 2004.
"Yofre de Vaca Narvaja, Susana c/ M° del Interior," October 14, 2004 (Decisions 327:4241).
"Hooft, Pedro C.F. v. Provincia de Buenos Aires," November 16, 2004 (Decisions 327:5118).
"Maldonado, Sergio Adrián s/ recurso de amparo," November 23, 2004 (Decisions 327:5210).
"Espósito, Miguel Ángel s/ incidente de prescripción de la acción penal promovido por su defensa," December 23, 2004.

"Romero Cacharane, H.A. s/ejecución penal," March 9, 2005 (R. 230. XXXIV).
"Verbitsky s/habeas corpus," May 3, 2005 (V. 856. XXXVIII).
"Bussi Antonio Domingo c/ Estado Nacional (Congreso De La Nacion—Camara De Diputados) s/ Incorporacion A La Camara De Diputados," May 31, 2005 (B. 903. XL. REX).
"Recurso de hecho deducido por la defensa de Julio Héctor Simón en la causa Simón, Julio Héctor y otros s/ privación ilegítima de la libertad, etc.—causa No. 17,768," June 14, 2005 (Decisions 328:2056).
"Mendoza, Beatriz y otros c/ Estado Nacional y otros y otro s/daños y perjuicios (daños derivados de la contaminacion ambiental del Río Matanza-ria-chuelo)," June 20, 2006. (Decisions 331:1622).
"Gottschau, Evelyn Patrizia c/ Consejo de la Magistratura de la Ciudad Autónoma de Buenos Aires s/ amparo," August 8, 2006 (Decisions 329:2986).
"Mazzeo, Julio Lilo y otros s/rec. de casación e inconstitucionalidad," July 13, 2007 (Decisions 330:3248).
"Bussi, Antonio Domingo c/Estado Nacional (Congreso de la Nación—Cámara de Diputados) s/ incorporación a la Cámara de Diputados," July 13, 2007 (Decisions 330:3160).
"Defensor del Pueblo de la Nación v. Estado Nacional y otra (Provincia del Chaco)," September 18, 2007.
"Badaro, Adolfo Valentín c/ ANSES s/ reajustes varios," November 26, 2007 (V. 856. XXXVIII).
"Reyes Aguilera c. Estado Nacional," December 4, 2007 (Decisions 330:3853).
"Patti, Luis Abelardo s/ promueve acción de amparo c/ Cámara de Diputados de la Nación," April 8, 2008 (Decisions 331:548).
"Salas, Dino y otros c/ Provincia de Salta y Estado Nacional," March 26, 2009 (V. 1144. XLIV) (Decisions 332:663).
"Bustos Alberto Roque y otros c/ Poder Ejecutivo Nacional o Estado Nacional s/ sumarisimo," October 26, 2004.
"Derecho, René Jesús s/ incidente de prescripción de la acción penal—Case No. 24,079," November 29, 2011.
"Comunidad Mapuche Mellao Morales c/ Corporación Minera del Neuquén S.E s/ Acción Procesal Administrativa," December 20, 2011.
"F.A.L. s/ Medida autosatisfactiva," March 13, 2012.
"Comunidad Aborigen de Santuario Tres Pozos otros el Jujuy, Provincia de otros s/ amparo," December 18, 2012 (C. 1196. XLVI).
"Comunidad Indígena Toba La Primavera—Novogoh c. Provincia de Formosa y otros s/ medida cautelar", March 9, 2013.

National Court of Cassation in Criminal Matters

"Schifrin, Marina", Decision of July 3, 2002.
"Alais, Julio alberto y otros s/recurso de casación," April 23, 2004.

Córdoba Court of Appeals in Civil and Commercial Matters

"Vera de Casih, Blanca S. vs. Casih, Carlos E," September 11, 2006.

High Court of Buenos Aires City

"Asociación por los Derechos Civiles c/ GCBA s/ acción declarativa de inconstitucionalidad," September 6, 2013.

National Federal Court in Criminal and Correctional Matters No. 4

"Simón, Julio, Del Cerro, Juan Antonio s/sustracción de menores de 10 años," March 6, 2001 (8686/2000).

Neuquén Province Higher Court

"Caso Comunidad Mapuche Mellao Morales v. Corporación Minera del Neuquén", Resolución Interlocutoria 6943/09, September 29, 2009.

Chaco Province Judicial Administrative Appellate Court

"Consejo Qompi—Lqataxac Nam Qompi v. Provincia del Chaco", Decision on the merits, April 21, 2006.

Appeals Court on Civil, Commercial, Labor, and Mining Matters, Zapala

"Comunidad Mapuche Paichil Antriao v. Provincia de Neuquén s/acción de amparo", Decision of October 12, 2004.

Penal and Misdemeanors District Court no. 26, Buenos Aires City (Juzgado en lo Penal, Contravencional y de Faltas No. 26 de la Ciudad de Buenos Aires)

Decision by judge María Cristina Nazar, March 1, 2011.

Bolivia

Plurinational Constitutional Court of Bolivia

Decision 2008–17547–36-RAC, October 25, 2010.
Decision 300–2012, June 18, 2012.
Decision 0206/2014, February 5, 2014.
Constitutional Declaration 0003–2013, April 25, 2013.

Brazil

Supreme Federal Court of Brazil

Decision ADPF 153, April 29, 2010.
Decision ADI 1949-0-RS, November 11, 1999.
Decision ADI 4277, July 22, 2009.

Chile

Constitutional Court of Chile

Decision 46/1987, December 21, 1987.
Decision 519/2007, June 5, 2007.
Decision 1340/09, September 29, 2009.
Decision 1710/10, August 6, 2010.

Supreme Court of Chile

Decision 469-98, September 9, 1998.
Decision 559-2004, December 13, 2006.
Decision 907/2004, March 13, 2007.
Decision 4183/2006, April 18, 2007.

Court of Appeals of Copiapó

"Comunidad de Chañaral v. Codeco División el Saldor," June 23, 1988, File No. 2052.

Colombia

Constitutional Court of Colombia

Decision T-409/92, June 8, 1992.
Decision T-429/92, June 24, 1992.
Decision T-456/92, July 14, 1992.
Decision C-574/92, October 28, 1992.
Decision T-596/92, December 10, 1992.
Decision T- 092/93, February 19, 1993.
Decision C-071/93, February 25, 1993.
Decision C-295/93, July 29, 1993.
Decision T-097/94, March 7, 1994.
Decision T-324/94, July 14, 1994.
Decision C-350/94, August 4, 1994.
Decision T-539/94, November 30, 1994.
Decision C-225/95, May 18, 1995.
Decision T-447/95, October 23, 1995.
Decision C-098/96, March 7, 1996.
Decision C-139/96, April 9, 1996.
Decision T-406/96, August 23, 1996.
Decision SU-039/97; February 3, 1997.
Decision T-523/97, October 15, 1997.
Decision T-622/97, November 27, 1997.
Decision T-101/98, March 24, 1998.
Decision T-153/98, April 28, 1998.
Decision SU-224/98, May 20, 1998.
Decision C-481/98, September 9, 1998.
Decision T-652/98, November 10, 1998.

Decision T-568/99, August 10, 1999.
Decision T-823/99, October 21, 1999.
Decision C-010/00, January 19, 2000.
Decision T-999/00, August 2, 2000.
Decision C-093/01, January 31, 2001.
Decision C-169/01, February 14, 2001.
Decision T-606/01, June 7, 2001.
Decision SU-623/01, June 14, 2001.
Decision C-814/01, August 2, 2001.
Decision T-1319/01, December 7, 2001.
Decision T-595/02, August 1, 2002.
Decision C-891/02, October 22, 2002.
Decision C-150/03, February 25, 2003.
Decision C-152/03, February 25, 2003.
Decision C-551/03, July 9, 2003.
Decision C-1017/03, October 30, 2003.
Decision C-1058/03, November 11, 2003.
Decision T-025/04, January 22, 2004.
Decision C-038/04, January 27, 2004.
Decision T-304/04, March 29, 2004.
Decision T-615/04, June 26, 2004.
Decision T-642/04, July 1, 2004.
Decision T-654/04, July 8, 2004.
Decision T-666/04, July 9, 2004.
Decision T-697/04, July 22, 2004.
Decision C-754/04, August 10, 2004.
Decision T-827/04, September 29, 2004.
Decision C-931/04, September 29, 2004.
Decision T-447/05, May 2, 2005.
Decision T-1090/05, October 26, 2005.
Decision T-349/06, May 5, 2006.
Decision C-355/06, May 10, 2006.
Decision C-370/06, May 18, 2006. Decision T-896A/06, November 2, 2006.
Decision C-075/07, February 7, 2007.
Auto 109/07, May 4, 2007.
Decision T-391/07, May 22, 2007.
Decision C-811/07, October 3, 2007.
Decision C-030/08, January 23, 2008.
Decision T-209/08, February 28, 2008.
Decision T-760/08, July 31, 2008.
Decision C-336/08, April 16, 2008.
Decision C-070/09, February 12, 2009.
Decision C-307/09, April 29, 2009.
Decision T-388/09, May 28, 2009.
Decision C-488/09, July 22, 2009.
Decision T-544/09, August 6, 2009.
Decision C-376/10, May 19, 2010.
Decision T-585/10, July 22, 2010.

Decision C-914/10, November 16, 2010.
Decision T-129/11, March 3, 2011.
Decision C-577/11, July 26, 2011.
Decision T-636/11, August 25, 2011.
Decision T-841/11, November 3, 2011.
Decision C-715/12, September 13, 2012.

District Court no. 56, Bogotá City (Juzgado 56 Penal del Circuito de Bogotá)

Acción de tutela 2012–0158, January 30, 2013.

Costa Rica

Supreme Court of Costa Rica, Constitutional Chamber (Sala Constitucional)

Decision 239–90, 1990.
Decision 709–91, October 4, 1991.
Decision 3705–93, "Carlos Roberto Mejía Chacón," July 30, 1993.
Decision 5934–97, 1997.
Decision 1175–98, December 3, 1998.
Decision 2306–2000, March 15, 2000.
Decision 7484–00, August 25, 2000.
Decision 8377–03, 2003.
Decision 2792–04, March 17, 2004.
Decision 8383–04, July 30, 2004.
Decision 7980–05, June 22, 2005.
Decision 2773–09, "XXX c. Universidad San Isidro Labrador," February 20, 2009.
Decision 2249–09 "Delroy Morgan González c. la Municipalidad de Guácimo," February 13, 2009.
Decision 3419–09 "Johnny Chinchilla Barboza c. la Municipalidad del Paraíso," February 27, 2009.
Decision 17942–10, October 29, 2010
Decision 4621–13, April 13, 2013.

Ecuador

Constitutional Court of Ecuador

Decision No. 222–2004-RA, June 9, 2004.
Decision No. 4 0020–09-IC, September 9, 2008.
Decision No. 001–10-SIN-CC, March 18, 2010.
Decision No. 002–10-SIC-CC, September 9, 2010.
Interpretative Decision No. 002–10-SIC-CC, September 9, 2010.

Provincial Court of Loja

Case 11121–2011–0010, "Richard Frederick Wheeler vs. Director de la Procuraduría General del Estado de Loja."

El Salvador

Constitutional Chamber of the Supreme Court of Justice of El Salvador

Decision 24–97/21–98, September 26, 2000.
Decision 18/98, November 20, 2007.
Decision 310–2013, May 28, 2013.

Guatemala

Constitutional Court of Guatemala

File 3878–2007, December 21, 2009.
File 2643–2008, August 16, 2010.

Honduras

Supreme Court of Honduras

File SJCSJ-RH0159, Decision of March 7, 2007.
Decision "RI20–99—Unconstitutionality of Decree No. 199–87 and Decree No. 87–91," June 27, 2000.

Mexico

Supreme Court of Mexico

Amparo Directo en Revisión 502/2007, November 21, 2007.
Acción de Inconstitucionalidad 146/2007 and 147/2007, August 28, 2008.
Acción de Inconstitucionalidad 2/2010, August 16, 2010.
Contradicción de Tesis 268/2010, May 3, 2011.
Amparo directo en revisión 1464/2013, November 13, 2013.

Federal Electoral Tribunal of Mexico

Decision SUP-JRC-604/2007, December 23, 2007

Nicaragua

Supreme Court of Justice of Nicaragua

Judgment No. 504. Dossier No. 602–09 of the Constitutional Chamber, October 19, 2009.

Peru

Constitutional Court of Peru

File No. 895/02–2002-PA/TC, August 19, 2002.
File No. 1429–2002, November 19, 2002.

File No. 2488–2002-HC/TC, March 18, 2004.
File No. 3283–2003, June 15, 2004.
Process of Unconstitutionality, Judgment of June 3, 2005.
"Santiago Martín Rivas," Extraordinary Appeal, File No. 4587–2004-AA/TC, November 29, 2005.
File No. 4677–2004-PA/TC, December 5, 2005.
File No. 0022–2009-PI/TC, June 9, 2010.
"Cinco Mil Trescientos Noventaitres [sic] Ciudadanos," File No. 00012–2008-PI/TC, July 14, 2010.
File No. 06111–2009-PA/TC, March 7, 2011.

Puerto Rico

Supreme Court of Puerto Rico

"Juan Mari Bras y otros c. Juan F. Castañas," May 10, 1968.
"Heirs of Victoria Capella v. Pentecostal Church of God", 21 February 1974.
"Soto v. Secretario de Justicia," 112 DPR 477, 485 (1982).
"Colón Cabrera v. Caribbean Petroleum," 170 DPR 582, 590 (2007).

Uruguay

Supreme Court of Justice of Uruguay

"Sabalsagaray Curutchet Blanca Stela—Denuncia de Excepción de Inconstitucionalidad," Decision No. 365, October 19, 2009.

United States

Supreme Court of the United States

"Hague v. Committee of Industrial Organization," 307 U.S. 496 (1939).
"Linmark Associates, Inc. v. Township of Willingboro," 431 U.S. 85 (1977).
"BG Group, PLC v. Republic of Argentina." 134 S. Ct. 1198, 1203 (2014).

Inter-American Court of Human Rights

Decisions

"Aloeboetoe v. Suriname," September 10, 1993 (Reparations and Costs).
"Neira-Alegría et al. v. Peru," January 19, 1995.
"Street Children (Villagrán-Morales et al.) v. Guatemala," November 19, 1999.
"Barrios Altos (Chumbipuma Aguirre et al.) v. Peru," March 7, 2000.
"Bámaca Velásquez et al. v. Guatemala," February 22, 2001.
"Barrios Altos (Chumbipuma Aguirre et al.) v. Perú," March 14, 2001 (Merits).
"The Mayagna (Sumo) Awas Tingni Community v. Nicaragua," August 31, 2001 (Merits, Reparations, and Costs).

"Barrios Altos (Chumbipuma Aguirre et al.) v. Peru," September 3, 2001 (Interpretation of the Decision on the Merits).
"Cantoral Benavídez v. Peru," December 3, 2001 (Reparations and Costs).
"Trujillo Oroza v. Bolivia," February 27, 2002 (Reparations and Costs).
"Cantos v. Argentina," November 28, 2002 (Merits, Reparations, and Costs).
"Bulacio v. Argentina," September 18, 2003 (Merits, Reparations, and Costs).
"Myrna Mack Chang v. Guatemala," November 25, 2003.
"Gómez Paquiyauri Brothers v. Peru," July 8, 2004.
"Juvenile Reeducation Institute v. Paraguay," September 2, 2004.
"Tibi v. Ecuador," September 7, 2004.
"Yakye Axa Indigenous Community v. Paraguay," June 17, 2005.
"Yatama v. Nicaragua," Preliminary Objections, June 23, 2005 (Merits, Reparations, and Costs).
"Girls Yean and Bosico v. Dominican Republic," September 8, 2005.
"Sawhoyamaxa Indigenous Community v. Paraguay," March 29, 2006 (Merits, Reparations, and Costs).
"Montero-Aranguren et al. (Detention Center of Catia) v. Venezuela," July 5, 2006.
"Claude Reyes y otros v. Chile," September 19, 2006.
"Almonacid Arellano v. Chile," September 26, 2006.
"Miguel Castro-Castro Prison v. Peru," November 25, 2006.
"Zambrano Vélez et al. v. Ecuador," July 4, 2007.
"Albán Cornejo et al. v. Ecuador," November 22, 2007.
"Saramaka People v. Suriname," November 28, 2007 (Merits, Reparations, and Costs).
"Saramaka People v. Suriname," August 12, 2008 (Interpretation of the Judgment of Preliminary Objections, Merits, Reparations, and Costs).
"Perozo and others v. Venezuela," January 28, 2009.
"Ríos and others vs. Venezuela". Decision of January 28, 2009.
"Anzualdo Castro v. Peru," September 22, 2009 (Preliminary Objection, Merits, Reparations, and Costs).
"Radilla Pacheco v. United States of Mexico," November 23, 2009.
"Gomes Lund et al. (Guerrilha do Araguia) v. Brazil," November 24, 2010 (Preliminary Objections, Merits, Reparations, and Costs).
"Gelman v. Uruguay," February 24, 2011 (Merits and Reparations).
"Atala Riffo and Daughters v. Chile," February 24, 2012.
"Pacheco Teruel et al. v. Honduras," April 27, 2012."K*ichwa Indigenous People of Sarayaku v. Ecuador,"* June 27, 2012 (Merits and Reparations).
"Artavia Murillo et al. (In Vitro Fertilization) v. Costa Rica," November 28, 2012.

Advisory Opinions

OC-4/84, January 19, 1984, "Proposed Amendments of the Naturalization Provisions of the Constitution of Costa Rica."
OC-9/87, October 6, 1987, "Judicial Guarantees in States of Emergency (Arts. 27(2), 25 and (8) American Convention on Human Rights)."
OC-17/02, August 28, 2002, "Juridical Condition and Human Rights of the Child."
OC-18/03, September 17, 2003, "Juridical Condition and Rights of Undocumented Migrants."

Inter-American Commission on Human Rights

Report 28/92, Cases 10,147, 10,181, 10,240, 10,262, 10,309 and 10,311, Argentina, October 2, 1992.
Report 30/93, Case 10,804, October 12, 1993.
Report 1/99, Case 10,480, January 27, 1999.
Report 21/00, Case 12,059, February 29, 2000.
Report 28/00, case 11,528, "Barrios Altos v. Peru", March 7, 2000.

United Nations Human Rights Committee

"K.N.L.H. v. Peru," Communication No. 1153/2003, UN Document CCPR/C/85/D/1153/2003, October 24, 2005.

International Centre for Settlement of Investment Disputes

"Compañía de Aguas Del Aconquija SA and Compagnie Générale Des Eaux v Argentina, Award," No. ARB/97/3, November 21, 2000.
"Compañía de Aguas Del Aconquija S.A. and Vivendi Universal S.A. v. Argentine Republic, Decision of the Ad Hoc Committee on the Application for Annulment of the Award," No. ARB/97/3 (Viviendi I), July 3, 2002.
"Compañía de Aguas Del Aconquija S.A. and Vivendi Universal S.A. v Argentine Republic," No. ARB/97/3, August 20, 2007.
"Compañía de Aguas Del Aconquija S.A. and Vivendi Universal S.A. v. Argentine Republic, Decision of the Ad Hoc Committee on the Application for Annulment of the Award," No. ARB/97/3 (Viviendi II), October 8, 2010.

Notes on contributors

Martín Aldao: Research fellow, School of Law, Universidad de Buenos Aires.

Marcelo Alegre: Professor of Law, Universidad de Buenos Aires; JSD, New York University School of Law.

Ramiro Álvarez Ugarte: JSD candidate and Herman N. Finkelstein Memorial Fellow, Columbia Law School.

Fernando Basch: Lecturer in Law, Universidad de Palermo and Universidad de San Andrés, Argentina; Partner at Governance Latam; LLM in Legal and Political Theory, University College London.

Paola Bergallo: Adjunct Researcher at Argentina's Consejo Nacional de Investigaciones Científicas y Técnicas (CONICET), and Global Fellow at the Center for Law and Social Transformation, CMI Bergen. LL.B., Universidad de Buenos Aires; LL.M., Columbia Law School; J.S.M. and J.S.D. Stanford Law School.

Agustín Cavana: Lawyer for the office of the *Procuración Penitenciaria de la Nación*, Argentina; LLB, Universidad de Buenos Aires.

Laura Clérico: Professor of Law, Universidad de Buenos Aires; researcher, Consejo Nacional de Investigaciones Científicas y Técnicas (CONICET).

Jorge Contesse: Assistant Professor of Law, Rutgers School of Law, Newark; LLB, Diego Portales University, Chile; LLM and JSD, Yale University.

Leonardo Filippini: Lecturer in Law, Universidad de Buenos Aires; LLB, Universidad de Buenos Aires; LLM, Universidad de Palermo and Yale Law School; JSD candidate, Yale Law School.

Roberto Gargarella: Professor of Constitutional Law, Universidad de Buenos Aires; Professor of Constitutional Law and Legal Philosophy, Universidad Di Tella; LLB, Universidad de Buenos Aires (1985); BA in Sociology, Universidad de Buenos Aires (1987); LLM (1992) and JSD (1993), University of Chicago Law School; JSD, Universidad de Buenos Aires (1991).

Camila Gianella: Post-doctoral fellow at the Department of Comparative Politics, University of Bergen; Associate Researcher at the Chr. Michelsen Institute; MSc, PhD, University of Bergen.

Juan F. Gonzalez-Bertomeu: Assistant Professor, ITAM Law School; LLB, Universidad Nacional de La Plata (1999); LLM (2003) and JSD (2012), New York University.

Agustin Grijalva: Professor of Law, Universidad Andina Simon Bolivar; member of the Higher Council for University Education in Ecuador; LLB, Catholic University, Quito, Ecuador; PhD in Political Science, University of Pittsburgh.

Elsa Guerra Rodríguez: Lecturer in Law, Universidad Andina Simón Bolívar; LLB, Universidad Central del Ecuador; LLM in Constitutional Law, Universidad Andina Simón Bolívar.

Nahuel Maisley: Lecturer in Public International Law, Universidad de Buenos Aires; LLB and PhD candidate, Universidad de Buenos Aires; doctoral scholar, Consejo Nacional de Investigaciones Científicas y Técnicas (CONICET).

Dunia Martínez Molina: Lecturer of Law, Universidad de las Américas and Universidad Andina Simón Bolívar, Quito, Ecuador; LLB, Azuay University, Cuenca; LLM in Economic Law and PhD candidate, Universidad Andina Simón Bolívar.

Mariana Mota Prado: Associate Professor (tenured) and Associate Dean (Graduate) at the University of Toronto Faculty of Law. LLB, University of São Paulo; LLM and JSD, Yale University.

Oscar Parra-Vera: MSc Candidate in Criminology and Criminal Justice, University of Oxford. Former Senior Legal Officer, Inter-American Court of Human Rights. LLB and LLM, Universidad Nacional de Colombia.

Silvina Ramírez: Assistant Professor of Law (Constitutional Law), Universidad de Buenos Aires; Lecturer of Law (Legal Pluralism), Universidad de Palermo.

Agustina Ramón Michel: Assistant Professor of Law and Co-coordinator of the Public Interest Law Clinic, Universidad de Palermo School of Law; LLB (silver medal award), Universidad de Tucumán; LLM, University of Texas at Austin; PhD, Universidad de Palermo.

Liliana Ronconi: Doctoral Fellow, Consejo Nacional de Investigaciones Científicas y Técnicas (CONICET); PhD candidate, Universidad de Buenos Aires.

Pedro Salazar Ugarte: Director of Instituto de Investigaciones Jurídicas, Universidad Nacional Autónoma de México; LLB, Instituto Tecnológico Autónomo de México; PhD in Political Philosophy, Università di Torino.

María Florencia Saulino: Faculty Director of the Center for Studies on Environmental Law and Policy (CEDEPA) and Professor of Law at Universidad de Palermo School of Law; Global Clinical Associate Professor of Law at New York University School of Law; LLM, New York University School of Law.

Luis José Torres Asencio: Lecturer, Inter-American University of Puerto Rico Faculty of Law and University of Puerto Rico Graduate School of Planning. LLM, Harvard Law School; JD, University of Puerto Rico School of Law.

René Urueña: Associate Professor and Director of the International Law program at the Universidad de Los Andes, Bogotá; LLB, Los Andes; LLM and LLD, Helsinki.

Bruce M. Wilson: Professor of Political Science, University of Central Florida; Associate Senior Researcher at Chr. Michelsen Institute, Bergen, Norway; PhD in Political Science, Washington University in St Louis.

Introduction

This collective work, which we have had the pleasure to edit, grew out of a straightforward concern—courts in Latin America[1] are playing an increasingly relevant role in constitutional and human rights adjudication,[2] but their work goes largely unnoticed in the English-speaking world. This volume is thus an attempt to bring to the forefront the development of constitutional law (and, to a considerable degree, human rights law) by Latin American courts on various subject matters, with the hope of triggering discussions in the classroom and putting the region on the agenda of constitutional scholars. Our aim is to highlight a host of often-creative arguments and solutions that courts in the region have offered. As far as we are concerned, the book is the first to do so.

With few exceptions, it seems that comparative constitutional scholars working in English have focused their attention either on case law from countries that share that language (Canada, South Africa and India) or on case law translated into English from a small set of non-English speaking developed countries (Germany and Israel). This emphasis is justified, since courts and scholars in some of these countries have had a leading role in constitutional discussions. But this means that Latin American courts, as well as courts from much of the rest of the world, are most often overlooked. We consider this to be unfortunate. Although it is still developing and in many ways wanting, constitutional adjudication in Latin America is at times also innovative and the discussion around it is stimulating. Courts have been dealing for decades with pressing issues pertaining to the countries' social and political problems and transformations. While commentators may find some of their answers unsatisfactory or even ineffective, we believe that, overall, they are worth exploring.

The lack of scholarly focus on Latin America is understandable. One reason that may be cited for it is the language barrier, although, as pointed out, case law from some countries outside the English-speaking world has been translated into English. A more important factor may be that courts in Latin America are creatures of democratic systems that, though with differences among countries, are still in the process of consolidation, with a legacy of authoritarianism and the ever-present powerful executives, corruption, and patronage. Courts in the region have been relegated because of political pressure, which has impacted upon their independence,[3] but also because of low public expectations about their role and legal formalism (and, in some cases, because of deliberate institutional design).[4] Yet ignoring what courts in the region have been doing entails a cost for constitutional scholars, since, in at least some of these countries, courts have been having a significant role in political and constitutional discussions. Another reason for the scarcity of publications may be the relative difficulty of accessing court materials in Latin America, since courts' publication systems often lack systematization and are not always available to everyone.

The missing focus on Latin American courts is not exclusive to the English-speaking world. Curiously enough, we believe that this book will also be useful within Latin America, since at present there is a striking paucity of works that take account of decisions made by courts in the region. Perhaps comparative constitutionalism should begin at a regional level but, in the case of Latin America, it has not done so yet, at least not in a systematic way.

The book's 13 chapters review a selection of case law and constitutional arguments in the region and discuss them in light of the countries' social, political, and legal contexts. Each of the chapters is devoted to a particular subject matter of constitutional law (and human rights law): equal protection of the laws, religious freedom, abortion rights, LGBTI rights, prisoners' rights, the right to protest, transitional justice, social and economic rights, the protection of the environment, the rights of indigenous groups, limits to the executive, economic regulation, and the link between domestic law and international human rights law. The book mostly revolves around decisions taken by high courts in the last decades, but it also reviews quite a few decisions from the Inter-American system of human rights.

To stress a point hinted at above, nothing in the book suggests either that the decisions that courts make are largely "adequate" (whatever the interpretation of this standard) or that they always prove effective. Indeed, while the book remarks upon the implementation of some of the decisions, the topic is not its main focus, so the question remains whether the intervention of courts overall has teeth. The issue is a complex one, but to the extent that we editors have a rough, ill-defined view about the issue, we would submit that Latin American courts are perhaps neither completely effective nor ineffective. Courts, we believe, cannot radically change an unjust reality, but they can provide much-needed redress in many cases, and help shape political discussions around constitutional values. Of course, the issue is far too complicated to be adjudicated by such an impressionistic stance.

The remainder of this introduction briefly presents the book's plan and structure, reflects on some common traits in adjudication, and acknowledges the book's collaborators.

Book plan and structure

Who will benefit from reading this book? Our target in editing it was twofold. We tried to build a casebook to be of use in the classroom—mainly for comparative constitutional law courses. But, apart from students, we think that the book will be of interest to researchers concerned with Latin American constitutional adjudication. Not only is this the case due to the scarcity of resources on the topic but also because we believe that the book offers quite relevant material for analysis.

Typically, the chapters begin by introducing the reader to the main questions being discussed and by placing them within the broader social and political context, and go on to present the way in which some courts in the region have dealt with those questions. This is done either by transcribing relevant passages of decisions or by describing them. Also, the chapters often include some reflections both on the decisions' "appropriateness" (from one or more points of view) and, in a handful of cases, on their impact. A short section at the end of each chapter poses some questions that can be used to trigger debate.

Since this is a collaborative project, it was only natural that authors would bring their own perspectives to their work, and we editors did nothing to prevent it. The authors had freedom to strike what they saw as the right balance between description and evaluation. However, we tried to ensure that the chapters left issues as open as possible for fruitful discussion. We believe that the resulting texts allow for such discussion, but the reader will obviously be the ultimate judge.

The book's chapters are much more selective than exhaustive in their treatment of court decisions but, as suggested, the choice of subject matters was intended to cover most of what is relevant in constitutional adjudication and human rights law. The chapters do not review all decisions (perhaps not even all relevant decisions) in the chosen subject matters, and this selective character is mainly due to two reasons. The first is fairly obvious—it is the only possible way to go about writing a casebook. A single book could not possibly attempt to cover what is a broad and ever-growing field. Secondly, and perhaps most importantly, the project was guided by the aim of highlighting significant, while at the same time possibly controversial, contributions of courts in the region rather than offering a comprehensive view of constitutional (and human rights) adjudication. It should be clear, then, that this is not an exhaustive or even an unbiased view of adjudication in the region. We asked authors to employ a purposely loose criterion for case selection—the case's "relevance"—so everything the authors did not consider relevant was left out. We believe that the authors did quite a nice job of identifying decisions that seriously dealt with the issues involved and that their treatment of the subject matters was rich.

The decisions featured in the chapters typically come from the countries' highest courts—be that a supreme court or, as in the case of Colombia, a constitutional court. Decisions from Argentina, Colombia, and Costa Rica are more prevalent than decisions from other countries, but the book also analyzes cases from such countries as Bolivia, Brazil, Chile, Ecuador, El Salvador, Guatemala, Honduras, Mexico, Nicaragua, Peru, Puerto Rico, and Uruguay. A significant number of decisions also come from the bodies in charge of interpreting the American Convention of Human Rights, mainly the Inter-American Court but also the Commission—an entire chapter, the book's last, is devoted to the interaction and dialogue between these bodies and some domestic judiciaries.

Common threads

Latin America's rich constitutional life roughly extends over two centuries. While, as a trend, courts have been more positively asserting their role as constitutional guardians in the last decades,[5] this by no means implies that courts or more generally constitutional law were irrelevant before. Since the turn of the twentieth century, countries in the region have faced pressing political and legal challenges, including such issues as the strength, and possible abuses, of the executive, the role of courts under and after authoritarian rule, the state's intervention in the economy, and the judicialization of social rights. Courts, politicians, and constitutional scholars have had to confront these issues at a quite early stage, or with a sense of urgency that is not so usual elsewhere. Again, while this does not mean that courts have always risen to the occasion, it does suggest that their decisions deserve to be the focus of analysis.

With the purpose of giving the reader some background information, in this section we provide a very rough sketch of common features across the region. We start by pointing out some key social and political facts that, we believe, do not need much elaboration. While the region is anything but uniform, since the social and political situation varies, often dramatically, from one country to the next, we can generalize with some confidence.

The region has only recently recovered from decades of fierce political turmoil, including military coups and widespread political repression, in some cases through forced disappearances and systematic torture.[6] Serious political problems persist. Among others, corruption and the personalization of power are still not exceptional in most of the countries, and largely unaccountable security forces often resort to excessive violence,[7] sometimes to silence the opposition.[8]

An apparent trait of Latin American societies is their striking social and economic inequality and their inability to eradicate poverty. Also, many of the states in the region have faced recurrent cycles of economic crises that severely hit their societies, particularly the worst-off.[9] Latin American states have a very uneven reach, which often means that starkly different realities coexist within a single state. Again with variation, countries feature "brown areas," in which extreme personalism, prebendalism, and clientelism replace the rule of law[10]—or, as scholars have recently described with reference to Colombia, an "institutional apartheid."[11] Also, prejudice against ethnic minorities[12] and gender-based discrimination have been quite predominant.[13] Finally, states and societies in the region have been, and to some degree still are, much influenced by the Catholic Church, which has entailed that social conservative perspectives about individual morality have been fairly dominant, and that the church's views have been privileged over others (including those of nonreligious individuals).[14]

These features have been present in constitutional discussions, since in one way or another they have often demanded the attention of courts. To them can be added a set of traits more specifically related to adjudication that are prevalent in the region, which we present in the next paragraphs. The extremely important issue of the institutional variation that one finds in the region in terms of systems of constitutional adjudication is not reviewed here, since it largely exceeds the purposes of this work.[15]

New constitutions, the rise of so-called "New Constitutionalism," and social rights

Over the last decades, most countries in the region have either amended their constitution or enacted an entirely new one.[16] Among other issues, this entailed the incorporation of several new rights clauses, both negative and positive, and in some cases new legal tools for their protection, with the result that adjudication skyrocketed. In countries such as Colombia, a paradigm shift regarding constitutional interpretation also took place, from a legal formalist stance to a more evolving and flexible approach to interpretation. A number of scholars have regarded this development as the rise of a "new constitutionalism."[17] Although we believe this phrase is not entirely appropriate or useful, the phenomenon itself is, on the whole, real.

Some of the new, or newly reformed, constitutions feature socioeconomic rights provisions (an issue that Latin America pioneered with their inclusion in the 1917 Mexican constitution), with the resulting ever-pressing question of whether these provisions should be enforceable by courts.[18] Though still hesitant, courts are increasingly more willing to recognize the justiciability of social rights, which is not tantamount to saying that this is always a positive development. As in jurisdictions outside Latin America, arguments against justiciability typically revolve around three issues: courts should not decide questions with heavy budgetary implications, judges lack expertise to meddle with what often are systemic problems and, perhaps more important in a region with very high inequality and poverty rates, courts' intervention not always benefits the worst-off.[19] Defenders of some form of justiciability—we can be counted among them—attempt to deflect some of these claims by replying that traditional "negative" liberties also are costly, that allowing courts to take part in cases involving social rights does not mean that they should have leeway to redefine entire public budgets, and that their intervention can be crucial for a discussion of budgetary priorities.[20] As in other parts of the world, this is still an open discussion.

The writ of amparo and the vertical and horizontal effect of the constitution

In Latin America, constitutional adjudication can hardly be grasped without considering the *amparo*, a special writ for the protection of rights.[21] Either under this name or similar ones (like the Colombian *tutela*), the *amparo* is used ubiquitously in adjudication. Depending on the jurisdiction, it can be filed only against public officials or, at least in some cases, also against individuals or private entities.

The *amparo* evolved from its early use in nineteenth-century Mexico and has been expanding ever since. One of the main reasons explaining its prevalence, or even its existence, is that judiciaries in Latin America have been traditionally slow-moving and bureaucratic, heavily dependent as they are on weighty written procedures, so ordinary litigation can take years. The need for a summary process for the protection of rights was thus perceived, and so the writ was created (which does not mean that *amparo* procedures are always as summary as they promise to be). Depending on the jurisdiction, individuals face varying legal and financial hurdles to file an *amparo*, the decisions of which only have effect on the individual case at hand. In Colombia, for instance, the *tutela* seems to be much more flexible than most of its counterparts, and something similar happens in Costa Rica. A number of jurisdictions have also adopted the "collective" *amparo*, or similar legal actions, to bring groups of petitions (or classes) to courts.

The widespread and ever-growing use of the writ of *amparo* entails, at least in some countries, that the constitution's effect is becoming more horizontal.[22] Accordingly, individuals (as in Argentina, and in Colombia with the *tutela*) can file a writ of *amparo* against certain private persons, including, though not only, a person who is under a quasi-official function. This means that, more and more, the constitution is governing interactions among private individuals. This coexists, however, with a traditional perception—the source of which one can probably trace back to the continental European legal tradition inbred in Latin America—that civil and commercial codes are paramount within the legal system. Only recently has this perception begun to erode, under the notion that the constitution radiates also to private law.

New grounds in litigation

A noteworthy development in the last two decades in Latin America is that of so-called public interest litigation and, more particularly, structural reform litigation. Concerned with social and institutional change on a larger scale than is individual litigation, the latter has experienced significant growth. This development is the result of the creation of new legal tools and new uses for old ones (e.g. class actions and the collective *amparo*), but also to the strengthening of the "support structure" for rights advocacy by way of better-funded NGOs and public ombudsmen, among other factors.[23]

This development goes hand in hand with a second one—the also-increasing disposition on the part of courts to avoid command-and-control orders to the government in cases in which they have found a constitutional violation with structural implications.[24] Courts are often willing to either totally or partially defer to the government regarding the implementation of a remedy to such a violation (sometimes by setting a timeframe within which the government must comply) in a way that, according to some scholars, better respects the separation of powers and democracy, recognizes the limits of judicial capabilities, and invites compliance.[25] Now, if the respect for constitutional rights is deemed of central importance, allowing the government considerable leeway as to how (or when) to comply may not always be the best way to minimize rights violations.

The legal standing of human rights and the Inter-American System

Any commentary on the state of affairs regarding constitutional and human rights adjudication in Latin America would be incomplete if it did not acknowledge the impact on it of the

Inter-American Court of Human Rights and the Inter-American Commission of Human Rights. These bodies have exerted enormous influence over the development of human rights in the region in general and of constitutional law in particular.[26]

The court has undergone different periods. Since it first decided a case in 1987, and for years, the court devoted itself almost entirely to the pressing issues of the transgression of civil and political rights by authoritarian regimes and transitional justice. As years went by, the court started to show interest in other subject matters, ranging from the right to privacy to social rights.[27] Since the court is the final interpreter of the American Convention, which is part of the law of the land within Latin American countries, its decisions are binding for the state that is party to a case. However, they more generally serve as (something resembling) case law for the remaining countries' courts.

A phenomenon that complements this trend is that some countries in the region (including Argentina, Colombia, Brazil and, more recently, Mexico), and with differences among them, have assigned to a number of human rights treaties or human rights provisions the same legal standing as the constitution. So, for instance, in Argentina, those human rights treaties are since 1994 part of the constitution. Sometimes, as in Colombia, those treaties are identified as composing a "constitutional bloc."

These last trends have not escaped criticism. Some scholars claim that the alleged democratic deficits that are present in any case in which a domestic court declares a statute unconstitutional are only exacerbated when a court seated outside the relevant country decides matters that are significant to it, thus potentially foreclosing political debate and even ignoring democratic decisions taken at the domestic level.[28] Yet, few would argue that the inter-American organs have not had a positive role in the consolidation of Latin American democratic societies after authoritarian rule, or that their role is not central as a way to force domestic governments to show themselves faithful to their alleged commitment to human rights.

The book's collaborators

We have had the great fortune of enrolling as authors many leading constitutional scholars in the region (a brief section details their current affiliations). They brought their expertise in identifying relevant subtopics and judicial decisions as well as offering very interesting viewpoints. This was a long process and they had to endure us, so we are extremely thankful to all of them for both their patience and generosity.

Apart from the authors, this book would not have seen the light of day had it not been for the disinterested assistance of a host of students and young lawyers who contributed their time to it. Among them stand out Ana Liz Chiban, Cathy Greene, and Mariana Acevedo Nuevo. Ana Liz had a quite prominent role leading a group of students who edited several of the chapters, and editing for herself. Her availability, generosity and professionalism are to be highly commended. Ana Liz took over from Cathy Greene, who had a similar role in the early stages of the project, with a comparable level of commitment, competence, and generosity. Mariana joined the project at a later stage but, similarly, her work editing chapters proved extremely reliable and helpful. We are very much indebted and thankful to the three of them.

We are also obliged to the following, both students and professionals, who kindly offered their time to edit early manuscripts (the chapters' authors also acknowledge the assistance they received): Johanna Hardwich, Brian Burton, José Maria Saravia, Roberto Coutenceau, Macarena Obligio, Jimena Baez Breard, Georgina Timossi, and Aurea María Fuentes. Paula Arturo translated some of the chapters into English—her contribution is duly acknowledged in each of them.

The idea for this book came from a conversation between Paola Bergallo and Roberto Gargarella. Paola played a crucial part during the first stages of the project. The book just would not have been possible without her and, for this, we are extremely grateful.

The editors

Notes

1 By "Latin America" we refer to the sovereign countries of the Americas where Romance languages are predominant. This does not mean that the book discusses cases of all countries. Also, our use of the category is admittedly loose, since it extends to non-sovereign Puerto Rico.

2 By "constitutional adjudication" we generally refer to a court's authorization to protect the constitution, either by directly interpreting its provisions (even when a legal rule is not said to violate it) or by halting as unconstitutional a legal rule that is considered to violate it. The expression is used fairly interchangeably with "judicial review," although the latter is often employed to mean the review of statutes and other rules vis-à-vis the constitution.

3 Gretchen Helmke and Julio Ríos-Figueroa, *Introduction: Courts in Latin America*, in Courts in Latin America, at 1–26 (Gretchen Helmke and Julio Ríos-Figueroa eds, 2011).

4 Javier Couso, Alexandra Huneeus, and Rachel Sieder, Cultures of Legality (2010).

5 Rachel Sieder, Line Schjolden, and Alan Angell (eds), The Judicialization of Politics in Latin America (2005); Roberto Gargarella, Siri Gloppen, and Elin Skaar (eds), Democratization and the Judiciary: The Accountability Function of Courts in New Democracies (2004); Gretchen Helmke and Julio Ríos-Figueroa (eds), Courts in Latin America (2011).

6 See chapter 7 on transitional justice.

7 Daniel M. Brinks, The Judicial Response to Police Killings in Latin America: Inequality and the Rule of Law (2007).

8 See, e.g., Belén Domínguez Cebrían, *Amnesty International denounces torture of opposition protestors in Venezuela*, El País, April 1, 2014.

9 Augusto de la Torre, Eduardo Levy Yeyati, Guillermo Beylis, Tatiana Didier, Carlos Rodríguez Castelán, and Sergio Schmukler, Inequality in a Lower Growth Latin America, (The World Bank 2014).

10 Guillermo O'Donnell, *On the State, Democratization and Some Conceptual Problems. (A Latin American View with Glances at Some Post-Communist Countries)*, 21 World Development (1993).

11 Mauricio García Villegas and José Rafael Espinosa R., *El derecho al Estado. Los efectos legales del apartheid institucional en Colombia*, DeJusticia (2013).

12 Martín Hopenhayn and Alvaro Bello, Discriminación étnico-racial y xenofobia en América Latina y el Caribe (United Nations Economic Commission for Latin America and the Caribbean (ECLAC–CEPAL) 2001).

13 Luisa Cabal and Cristina Motta (eds), Más Allá del Derecho: Justicia y Género en América Latina (2005).

14 See chapter 2.

15 Patricio Navia and Julio Ríos-Figueroa, *The Constitutional Adjudication Mosaic of Latin America*, 38, No. 2, Comparative Political Studies, 189–217 (2005).

16 Gabriel Negretto, *Replacing and Amending Constitutions: The Logic of Constitutional Change in Latin America*, 46/4, Law & Society Review, 749–79 (December 2012).

17 Miguel Carbonell (ed.), Teoría del neoconstitucionalismo (2007); Leonardo García Jaramillo and Miguel Carbonell (eds), El canon neoconstitucional (2010).

18 Christian Courtis, *Judicial Enforcement of Social Rights: Perspectives from Latin America*, in Courts and Social Transformation in New Democracies: An Institutional Voice for the Poor? (Roberto Gargarella, Pilar Domingo and Theunis Roux eds, 2006); Rodolfo Arango, El concepto de derechos sociales fundamentales (2005); Varun Gari and Daniel M. Brinks (eds), Courting Social Justice. Judicial Enforcement of Social and Economic Rights in the Developing World (2010); Siri Gloppen and Alicia Yamin (eds), Litigating Health Rights (2011). See also Paola Bergallo, *Courts and Social Change: Lessons from the Struggle to Universalize Access to HIV/AIDS Treatment in Argentina*, 89 Texas Law Review, 1611 (2011); César Rodríguez-Garavito, *Beyond the Courtroom: The Impact of Judicial Activism on Socioeconomic Rights in Latin America*, 89 Texas Law Review, 1669 (2011).

19 Devoted to social rights, chapter 8 of this volume elaborates on this issue. See also Octavio Luiz Motta Ferraz, *Harming the Poor through Social Rights Litigation: Lessons from Brazil*, 89 Texas Law Review (2011); Daniel M. Brinks and William Forbath, *Commentary: Social and Economic Rights in Latin America: Constitutional Courts and the Prospects for Pro-poor Interventions*, 89 Texas Law Review (2011); Daniel M. Brinks and Varun Gauri, The Law's Majestic Equality? The Distributive Impact of Litigating Social and Economic Rights (World Bank Policy Research Working Paper No. 5999, 2012).
20 Victor Abramovich and Christian Courtis, Los derechos sociales como derechos exigibles (2002).
21 Allan Brewer-Carías, Constitutional Protection of Human Rights in Latin America (2009).
22 The literature on the topic is still scarce. See Willmai Rivera Perez, International Human Rights Law and the Horizontal Effect of Constitutional Rights in Latin America: A Look at the Direct Application of Constitutional Rights in Argentina, Colombia, and Puerto Rico (2010).
23 Charles Epp, The Rights Revolution (1998); Catalina Smulovitz, *La política por otros medios. Judicialización y movilización legal en la Argentina*, 48 Desarrollo Económico (2008).
24 Paola Bergallo, *Justicia y experimentalismo: la función remedial del poder judicial en el litigio de derecho público en Argentina* (SELA, 2005); Roberto Gargarella, *Dialogic Justice in the Enforcement of Social Rights*, in Litigating Health Rights (Siri Gloppen and Alicia Yamin eds, 2011).
25 Ibid.
26 See chapter 13, on the dialogue between the inter-American system and domestic courts.
27 Víctor Abramovich, *From Massive Violations to Structural Patterns: New Approaches and Classic Tensions in the Inter-American Human Rights system*, 6/11, Sur International Journal on Human Rights (January 2009).
28 Roberto Gargarella, *No Place for Popular Sovereignty? Democracy, Rights, and Punishment in Gelman v. Uruguay*, (SELA, 2013), available at www.law.yale.edu/documents/pdf/sela/SELA13_Gargarella_CV_Eng_20121130.pdf.

1 Equal protection

Laura Clérico, Liliana Ronconi, and Martín Aldao

Introduction

A large number of academic studies and reports by international human rights organizations, non-governmental organizations, and community-based organizations deliver the same diagnosis: Latin America exhibits profound traces of social, economic, and political inequality, which can be construed in terms of redistribution, as well as a lack of recognition. This inequality lingers in spite of all efforts (large or small) made through public policies addressing the more severe forms of inequality. As two social scientists have stated,

> [t]he available data show that development has been erratic and has not reached the expected parameters, and that the jobs created have not been sufficient or of good enough quality to have the expected social impact. In this context, neither has poverty been diminished in a structural form, nor has social vulnerability been tackled by social security programs, nor has the social exclusion to which indigenous people and afro-descendants have been historically subjugated been significantly reduced.[1]

Several current scenarios of inequality in Latin America evidence structural problems that cannot be resolved on a case-by-case basis but rather require affirmative action measures aimed at providing a remedy or transforming reality. Therefore the application of the principle of formal equality, or even the principle of non-arbitrary discrimination under strict scrutiny, has proven unsuccessful in guaranteeing actual equal conditions for the exercise of legal rights and has begun to be supplemented by the notion of equality in terms of anti-subordination, construed as redistribution and recognition. The aim of this chapter[2] is to explore how the decisions of the superior courts and constitutional courts of the region may be constructed to trace the level of acknowledgment of the structural inequality perspective.

The chapter begins by presenting to the reader some general themes concerning the equality test (the concept of formal and substantive equality in terms of anti-subordination and the perspectives of redistribution and recognition). It then reviews decisions from a number of Latin American countries' high courts, the Inter-American Commission on Human Rights and the Inter-American Court of Human Rights[3] related to discrimination based on nationality, age, disability, and sexual orientation. Analyzing the cases will contribute to determine the concept of equality that prevails in each decision (as evidenced in the grounds provided by the court, as well as in the remedies awarded). Finally, we attempt to draw some conclusions as to the prevailing regional trend concerning equality.

Models of equality

The principle of equality was originally designed to prevent arbitrary acts by authorities. Over time it acquired a restorative function against long-lasting and far-reaching social inequality, which was profoundly connected, first, to the development of social rights and then to economic, social, and cultural rights. This involved the need to extend the restricted model of formal analysis of inequality, which responded to a liberal conception of society, towards a material analysis that could account for a more egalitarian idea of democracy.

The formal equality model is limited to verifying that all those who belong in the same classification made by the legislator are treated in the same way. This is the weakest version of the test for equality since it does not examine the grounds for classification or how the individuals must be treated under certain circumstances.

The inadequacy of this form of equality has led to the development of the formula of substantive legal equality, which considers the legitimacy of the classification criteria, and the reasoning behind the selection made by the legislator. Accordingly, the principle of equality is fulfilled "as long as all individuals who are under the same circumstances are treated in the same manner." As the Inter-American Court has repeatedly stated, a difference in treatment is only discriminatory "when it has no objective and reasonable justification."[4]

The regional trend shows that the justification test is connected to the proportionality test.[5] A more elaborate version is the integrated test, which combines the principle of proportionality used by European case law with the American courts' approach of a higher or lower intensity of control (scrutiny tests: mere rationality test, intermediate scrutiny test, and strict scrutiny test which applies to suspect classifications). This integrated test analyzes suitability, necessity, and proportionality in its narrow sense, while including the intensity of control addresses the reasoning behind the classification, and weighs up the importance of the grounds on which the challenged laws or regulations were approved.

Despite the fact that substantive legal equality has developed elements of strict scrutiny, these are far from being useful argumentative tools powerful enough to challenge a status quo of inequality. The anti-discriminatory principle operates in specific cases of discrimination but has failed to overcome inequality that responds to a systematic practice of domination, which is firmly rooted in the colonial origin of the countries in the region. This inequality is not spontaneous; it emerges from a given social structure and strikes at disadvantaged groups. In order for these disadvantaged groups to be able to exercise their rights under equal conditions, the state should not only refrain from taking action that could increase the marginalization of these groups, but also take affirmative action measures.[6] These measures involve, under certain conditions, the redistribution of economic and social assets, with the purpose of breaking the vicious circle by which those who have less access to material resources have fewer chances to question the distribution of those assets. Under different circumstances, these measures also entail recognition. In this respect, inequality should not be understood (solely) as the gap between the rich and the poor, but rather as the gap between dominant and dominated identities.[7] This form of discrimination, practiced historically over women, afro-descendants, indigenous people, migrants, and members of the LGBT community, among other groups, demands positive action that entails recognizing the existence of these diverse identities—which are altogether invisible to the dominant perspective of society. No form of the equality principle may be validly achieved, within a democratic context, without the involvement of those who are in actual situations of disparity.

The role of courts

Even if some of the most common forms of discrimination in the Latin American region are specifically analyzed throughout this chapter, it is worth pointing out that, in a large number of cases, discrimination does not arise in relation to a single feature, but rather from a plurality of factors.[8] As stated by the Children's Rights International Network: "Most people have multiple identities; for example, a child may also be a boy with a disability who is gay. Multiple—or 'intersectional'—discrimination describes discrimination that occurs as a result of how these different identities or circumstances interact."[9] The *Yean and Bosico* case[10] clearly illustrates the idea of multiple discrimination—like most children, these two girls were discriminated against: because of their age, because they were immigrants, and because they were poor.

Hence, "[a] single ground approach to addressing discrimination confines people's identity to this one ground and fails to see people as multi-faceted."[11] In this way, the discriminated person suffers a complex situation encumbering different angles of her life (social, educational, and working areas, among others), which are not likely to be reverted by unidirectional public policies (those that only address a single cause of discrimination). Therefore, integrated public policies are required if the goal is to eradicate all forms of inequality.

Case law analysis shows that, in a large number of cases requiring structural remedies, the group concerned suffered from extreme poverty, and this situation was worsened by one or several situations of discrimination. Thus, poverty becomes a transversal source of discrimination aggravating other forms of discrimination. The Constitutional Court of Colombia set an example by issuing Decision T-025/04, in which the category of "unconstitutional state of affairs" was used to describe the living conditions of more than 3 million internally displaced people because of violence in Colombia:

> . . . there is a need for the state to intervene and confront structural inequality because . . . unless the restrictions and circumstances of inequality that ordinary individuals face daily are effectively fought by means of positive and focused action taken by the authorities, freedom and equality amongst human beings shall remain an abstract utopian concept. For this reason, in many cases, it has been settled that freedom and equality require the adoption of measures and the provision of services and benefits that individuals are unable to secure by themselves.[12]

The court held that the state's lack of ability to prevent the massive, generalized, and systematic violation of rights entailed a situation of domination contrary to the standards of a democratic state under the rule of law. The court not only dismissed the notion of formal equality, but also analyzed the actual conditions required to allow an individual to lead a dignified life.

Scrutinizing classifications based on national origin: some examples and questions

Latin America shows a variety of scenarios in relation to the migration of individuals through the territory of the different countries—foreigners," or "migrating" people. At the end of the nineteenth century and the dawn of the twentieth century, Argentina, Uruguay, Brazil, and the United States of America received massive immigration and, in the exercise of their sovereignty, passed laws that restricted the rights of foreign individuals who resided in their territory.[13] In this context especially, claims were raised by aliens involved in discrimination disputes. In Argentina, the traditional jurisprudence of the Supreme Court of Justice concerning the status of aliens residing in the country, set forth by the precedents in *Repetto*,[14] *Calvo y Pesini*,[15] *Gottschau*,[16] and *Hooft*,[17] analyzes norms which contain classifications that are detrimental to the rights of aliens. The court resorted, to different degrees, to the strict scrutiny test in order to establish the unconstitutionality of the challenged norms.

Nonetheless, since the complainants mostly belonged to the upper classes, the court did not address, in any of these cases, the most relevant issues behind the status of the migrants residing in Argentina, most of whom often face situations of structural discrimination.[18]

The Constitutional Court of Colombia, following a similar trend, rendered Decision C-1058/03 regarding the constitutionality of a law that allowed only Colombian nationals to act as agents of a foreign company which exploited public utilities.

These were specific and isolated cases and, as a rule, these types of cases were not related to groups affected by structural inequality.[19]

While the process of south–north migration has become evident, Latin American and Caribbean countries have not only "exported" over 25 million people, but some of them have also received more than 6 million people, which represents intra-regional migration, leaving aside asylum seekers, African or Asian refugees, and Central American residents in transit to the United States.[20] This involves a different aspect of discrimination, based on nationality, experienced by members of intra-regional migrant groups residing in recipient or transit countries. Pursuant to the structural nature of the matter, the Inter-American Court held that, as a general principle:

> . . . the regular situation of a person in a State is not a prerequisite for that State to respect and ensure the principle of equality and nondiscrimination, because, as mentioned above, this principle is of a fundamental nature and all States must guarantee it to their citizens and to all aliens who are in their territory. This does not mean that they cannot take any action against migrants who do not comply with national laws. However, it is important that, when taking the corresponding measures, States respect human rights and ensure their exercise and enjoyment to all persons who are in their territory, without any discrimination owing to their regular or irregular residence, or their nationality, race, gender or any other reason.[21]

In these cases, equality must be understood in terms of anti-subordination. The need to identify the actual circumstances that place a social group at a disadvantage with respect to their peer citizens of the recipient state arises as the only path for developing more appropriate strategies to compensate for situations of inequality.[22] In this sense, it is proper to wonder about the ways in which local courts are fit to channel claims for equality.

An example is the discrimination suffered by Haitian people and their descendants, usually sugarcane workers, currently living in the Dominican Republic. The Inter-American Court addressed this issue in the case of *Yean and Bosico v. Dominican Republic*. To understand the cause of action, it must be mentioned that Haitian women who reside in the Dominican Republic often give birth to their children at their homes, since it is extremely difficult for them to travel from the *bayetes*[23] to a city clinic, plus they lack economic resources and fear being deported by hospital authorities, the police, or the local civil registry. This has led many Haitian parents and Haitian descendants to notify the authorities of the birth of their children on Dominican soil later in life. The case was brought by the children Yean and Bosico, based on the fact that the Dominican state had refused to grant them Dominican nationality, which they had requested by means of the late declaration of birth procedure. The Dominican authorities had denied the petition despite the fact that these children had been born in Dominican territory. The fact that recognition of their nationality had been denied placed the girls in imminent danger of being deported, plus they had no access to school or healthcare services and were not eligible for welfare assistance because they had no identity documents. The Inter-American Court held that the Dominican state, by refusing to issue their birth certificates, had violated their rights to equal protection and to non-discrimination, to nationality, to a juridical personality, and to a name, therefore being prevented from exercising their citizenship rights, all on account of their Haitian origin. The Inter-American Court argued that "the importance of nationality is that [it] is a requirement for the exercise of specific rights."[24] As a result, the court ordered the state to adopt measures to revert the longtime situation of discrimination concerning the procedure for birth registration and access to education and, more importantly, to enforce a simple, accessible, and reasonable procedure for Dominican children born to Haitian parents to obtain their birth certificate. Correspondingly, the court held that, when establishing the requirements for late registration of birth, the state:

> . . . should take into consideration the particularly vulnerable situation of Dominican children of Haitian origin. The requirements should not constitute an obstacle for obtaining Dominican nationality and should be only those essential for establishing that the birth occurred in the Dominican Republic. In this regard, the identification of the father or the mother of the child cannot be restricted to the presentation of the identity card; rather, for this purpose, the State should accept another appropriate public document, since the said identity cards are only held by Dominican citizens.[25]

This is a paradigmatic case for two reasons. On the one hand the Inter-American Court not only recognized the situation of subordination that Haitian or Dominican children of Haitian origin suffered, but also ordered the state to adopt affirmative action measures. Moreover, the forms of redress (section C of the judgment) evidence how the judgment was also concerned with reversing a situation of subjugation. The Inter-American Court required the state to guarantee free access to primary education to all children, regardless of their origin or parentage. These became measures that transformed reality and aimed to dismantle the scenario of inequality in which these children are immersed. On the other hand, the Inter-American Court pointed out how the lack of nationality and the lack of equal recognition of rights to citizens and aliens (in spite of the constitutional guarantees whereby citizens and aliens are granted equality before the law, no prior nationalization being required) prevent the exercise of other rights necessary to comply with what the Inter American Court has called "conditions of dignified existence."[26]

Reyes Aguilera[27] is another paradigmatic case brought before the Supreme Court of Justice of Argentina, although it is not considered a prevailing precedent among local case law. The case involved a girl of Bolivian origin who resided in Argentina and suffered from a disability that affected her motor skills and communicative skills and prevented her from self-feeding. Her parents applied for a disability pension. The Argentinian government denied such a benefit in pursuance of the regulation set forth by Decree 432/1997, which established a requirement of a minimum 20-year residence period prior to granting disability pensions. This case evidences the great discrimination suffered by immigrants from neighboring countries, who are also in a vulnerable situation, in this case a little girl, born in Bolivia in extreme poverty and enduring a severe disability. The court argued that the period of residence required was unconstitutional, given that the other requirements were met (disability and poverty). Yet, each of the justices' votes followed a reasoning based on a different aspect of discrimination. Justices Fayt and Zaffaroni stated that the 20-year residence requirement implied denying social security, and that social security rights are directly connected to the right to life "which must be guaranteed by positive actions, since it is a pressing obligation public authorities are meant to comply with,"[28] and also made reference to the "conditions of dignified existence" for children as set out by the paradigmatic case *Villagrán Morales*, heard by the Inter-American Court. Justices Petracchi and Argibay, on the other hand, applied a strict scrutiny test of equality. They stated that, since the norm was based on prohibited criteria of classification, a suspect classification (Section 1 of the American Convention of Human Rights), it should be presumed unconstitutional. They concluded that:

> The reasonableness of the norm . . . should be studied under a strict scrutiny test. This evaluation implies the inversion of the burden of proof, in such a way that the party that claims the constitutionality of the decree (in this case, the state) must carefully demonstrate what *interests* it sought to protect and the *means* it used to achieve this purpose. The protected interest must be compelling and not merely a convenient one. Then, when studying the means set forth by the challenged norm, the state should not only establish that the norm is 'adequate' to achieve the compelling interests, but also must prove that the norm in question is effective, and that there are no other less restrictive means to achieve the interests at stake.[29]

The justices concluded that the defense presented by the state failed to establish what compelling interest the norm intended to protect and why the means chosen to do so were either more effective or less restrictive than any other measure. It is worth noting that these justices' votes upheld the presumption of unconstitutionality of any norm that makes a distinction between citizens and aliens regarding the exercise of rights, including social rights.

By contrast—although admitting the child's cause of action—Justice Maqueda argued that the state can make a distinction based on national origin concerning access to social rights, but required the distinction to be based on "a . . . reasonable cause that is proportional to the purpose sought by the state."[30] Thus:

> . . . the requirement of a continuous period of residence in the country, for both citizens and aliens alike, is deemed a minimum requirement considering the rights at stake, and constitutes a constitutionally valid requirement to guarantee, in terms of formal and substantive equality, equal access to assistance services.[31]

In this case, the extent of the residence period (20 years) was unreasonable since no child could ever be eligible to receive assistance benefits on account of a severe disability. Justice Maqueda argued that:

> The unreasonableness of the 20-year period established by the law entails in fact that the law, upon its enforcement, becomes indirectly discriminatory since the actual consequence is that a disability pension would be inaccessible to aliens who have certified residence in Argentinian soil.[32]

It can be construed, then, that discrimination based on national origin is a criterion of classification subject to an intensive scrutiny test of equality when the classification violates migrants' access to civil rights. It is also possible to speak of an emerging intense scrutiny test, where nationality-based discrimination affects social rights of certain vulnerable alien residents. The

Reyes Aguilera and *Yean and Bosico* case developments made clear that the existence of a disadvantageous impact on migrants' right to a "dignified existence" does suffice to evoke a heightened review.

Age classifications

The anti-discriminatory principle as a tool to analyze individual cases can still be seen to be used by, for example, the Constitutional Court of Colombia[33] or the Supreme Court of Argentina.[34] Most actions deal with laws and regulations that imposed restrictions of a minimum or maximum age to practice a profession, develop a career, or occupy a position.

However, the prevailing trend can be overturned when analyzing judgments related to children. In this sense, the Supreme Court of Argentina has held that judges should have special consideration for the circumstances surrounding the case of children who claim their rights, and has therefore revoked decisions from lower courts and ordered medical treatments or the provision of medication for children who have had no access to them given their economic or social status. The court has argued that:

> . . . this court has repeatedly decided that when a child's higher interest is at stake, the judges must find solutions consistent with the urgency and nature of the claim, to prevent any delay and to avoid mere formalisms which would frustrate the exercise of a constitutionally guaranteed right.[35]

Several Latin American countries have ratified the Convention on the Rights of the Child, and have included, in their constitutions and laws, regulations concerning children's rights. Some have enforced affirmative action measures towards their protection (the family allowance per child, *plan bolsa* (family benefit plan), among others). However, these positive steps are still insufficient to achieve actual equal conditions. The echo of the statement made by the Inter-American Court in the paradigmatic case *Villagran Morales*, addressing the situation of street children, still reverberates throughout the region. The court held that rights (mainly the rights to life and to physical integrity) were violated not only by an omission by the state, but also by the state's breach of its obligation to implement positive measures which would generate conditions for a dignified life. In relation to how the absence or the failing of affirmative actions denotes inequality, Judges Cançado Trindade and Abreu-Burelli added:

> 6 . . . In the last years, the living conditions of large segments of the population of the States Parties to the American Convention have deteriorated notoriously, and an interpretation of the right to life cannot make an abstraction of this reality, above all when dealing with children at risk in the streets of Latin American countries.
>
> 8 We believe that the project of life is consubstantial of the right to existence and requires, for its development, dignified living conditions and conditions that ensure security and integrity of the human person.
>
> 9 A person who lives his childhood in humiliating misery, as happens in so many Latin American countries, without even the minimal possibility of carrying out his or her own project of life, experiences a state of suffering which amounts to a spiritual death; the physical death which follows is, in such circumstances, the culmination of the total destruction of the human being. These offences render victims not only those who suffered them directly in body and in spirit; they project themselves painfully into the people dear to them, particularly into their mothers, who usually also endure that state of abandonment.[36]

The Inter-American Court based its decision on arguments that took into account the structural inequality problems that affected street children, and also laid out guidelines for analyzing similar cases. There is, at least in this case, a recognition of the fact that the actions that states must take should not be specific but should contemplate all the difficulties children face that place them in a position of greater vulnerability. A similar path is taken by the Constitutional Court of Colombia in the Decision T-447/05, on the age limit to access or remain in the public education system. The case dealt with the problem of children in rural areas, where secondary educational facilities are scarce and usually very far from children's homes. Their only possibility of continuing their education is to be admitted to the SAT (Distance Learning Program). However, due to their age, these children were not admitted. Even if they had passed the fifth grade of primary school, they still had not reached the age of 15 as required by the program. The court ordered the admission of the children to the program after having analyzed the regulations under a strict scrutiny test of equality. The ruling focused on structural equality, which can also be perceived in the redress awarded: it forced the state to take affirmative action measures to improve access to secondary school to all children living in poor rural areas. The court ordered the Colombian Department of Education to carry out educational programs providing continuous and complete secondary school education consistent with the geography and living conditions of the potential student body. Furthermore, the court stated that, until these changes were enforced, the children would have to be admitted by the only viable alternative to continue their learning process. Clearly, the court expressed, both in the grounds for the decision and in the remedy imposed, that it considered the cause of discrimination to be a structural problem. It is worth noting that, despite the fact that the complaint was filed by just two children, the court reached further and ordered the state to provide an overall solution to the general problem that affected all children in the region.

Discrimination based on disability

Based on recent reports, more than one billion people live with some form of disability, of whom nearly 200 million experience considerable difficulties in functioning. This is partly because people with disabilities experience barriers in accessing services that many of us have long taken for granted, including health, education, employment, and transport, as well as information. These difficulties are exacerbated in the case of less advantaged communities.[37]

Under these circumstances, the challenge in terms of equality is to "empower people living with disabilities."[38] The Constitutional Court of Colombia has laid down interesting precedents in relation to this concept, when stating that:

> . . . this court has recognized the situation of social marginalization that disabled people have endured throughout history, and has pointed out that such recognition entails an obligation to make decisions directed to remove the obstacles that bar disabled people from an adequate integration in society, under actual and effective conditions of equality.[39]

In a case concerning the elimination of structural obstacles, the Supreme Court of Justice of Costa Rica set an important example in the decision issued on February 27, 2009 in a writ of *amparo*[40] brought by Johnny Chinchilla Barboza, a visually impaired person, against the Municipality of Paraíso. The action was based on the violation of his right to equality and freedom of movement. The claimant requested an improvement of the urban infrastructure, since there were no ramps or pathways from sidewalks to streets, nor were there traffic lights for the blind or bus stops. The court admitted the complaint based on the notion that

> [t]he state and society as a whole have an obligation to progressively eliminate all 'architectural barriers' that may make it difficult or prevent a disabled person's mobility . . . these circumstances only deny a part of the population a possibility to naturally integrate to society and adequately comply with their everyday activities.[41]

The court added that fundamental rights of persons with disabilities were being violated (especially the right to self-determination and to independent living), and thus a solution must be given immediately since the exercise of these rights could not be subject to budget issues.[42]

Similarly, the Constitutional Court of Colombia issued Decision T-595/02, in which it addressed access to public transportation for a person with a disability who depended on a wheelchair. The court ordered Transmilenio S.A. to design a plan which would guarantee full access for people with disabilities to Bogota's basic public transport system. The court based its decision on the fact that

> . . . a disabled person's right to mobility entails the possibility of accessing the basic public transport system of the city in equal conditions to the rest of the citizens . . . without having to endure limitations that impose severe hardship.[43]
>
> [P]ublic services protected by a right require the adoption of public policies, planning and programs directed to advance gradually towards the effective enjoyment of rights by all members of the community and, especially, the enjoyment by certain social groups, such as the disabled population.[44]

This right is violated ". . . every time there is not even a plan that leads to the progressive, committed and continuous guarantee and protection of these rights".[45]

This case law states that measures taken towards the removal of these obstacles lead to structural equality, even when those measures are taken in response to a particular complaint. Furthermore, achieving equal access to public services entails imposing obligations on the service providers that operate in the region.

Concerning access to higher education, Decision 2773/09 of the Supreme Court of Justice of Costa Rica is representative. An *amparo* action was brought against the Universidad de San Isidro Labrador by a hearing-impaired student (who used a hearing aid device and sign language to communicate), because the university had refused to enroll him again due to his hearing problems.[46] The university had granted the claimant a full scholarship in exchange for 40 hours of community work per term (four months). However, given that the university failed to assign community work consistent with his disability, the claimant had only completed 19 hours of community work. Based on his breach, the university had refused to enroll him for the second term. The court ordered the university to register the claimant, based on its obligation to guarantee "equal opportunities by eliminating all obstacles of a physical, economic, social or psychological nature that may limit or exclude him from full integration to society."[47]

The court considered that the authorities of the university must have known about the claimant's condition since it could be easily noticed and it had granted the claimant a full scholarship, and thus "the learning center should have provided in due course support and technical assistance as well as an adaptation of the curricula."[48] Therefore, the court ordered the university to adopt the necessary measures and execute the pertinent changes to guarantee the claimant equal access to education.

Despite the fact that Argentina has a large record of cases related to the health rights of people with disabilities, these are mostly concerned with providing an answer to a specific complaint and, even when the court does address the issue of structural inequality, the remedies ordered only apply to that specific case. To set an example, in the *Lifschitz* case,[49] the court ordered the Argentinian state to pay a monthly allowance to cover the education and transport expenses of a child with a disability, because his parents couldn't afford them and the local public schools could not admit the child or provide special school transport. By making a structural analysis, the court argued that it was obvious that the public transport system could not meet the needs of a student with disabilities. In addition, it was established by the court that the burden of proof in showing that the local public school (the closest school) could admit the claimant's child with disability lies on the state. Finally, the court decided to sentence the state to pay an allowance regularly until it was able to prove that the child's parents had sufficient means to support the expenses or that the local school for children with special needs could receive the child and provide adequate transportation.

The court noted that the child was not under the same conditions as other children who had access to private health care or received state benefits through a monthly allowance paid to the private special school. Sadly, and much in the same way as with the cases of age discrimination, the Argentinian court failed to see that the vast number of claims are born of a structural problem rather than being mere singled-out cases.

However, the principle of equality construed as non-domination has begun to gain strength in the region, at least concerning this form of discrimination. Thus, for example, in the field of inclusive education, the Constitutional Court of Colombia issued Decision T-429/92. The case was about a girl whose admission to the third year of high school was conditional upon the prior presentation of an EEG and a neurological diagnosis, because her teachers believed she suffered from a learning disability and needed special education. The first-instance judge allowed the complaint, but decided that the girl's father had to demonstrate within four months that his daughter did not need special education. The Constitutional Court decided that the girl's education could not be subject to her parents presenting any evidence to certify she did not need any kind of special care. It held that a child's right to education was a fundamental prevailing right and therefore "the state must guarantee the necessary conditions to secure students access and continuity in the educative system."[50]

In this case, the court additionally considered that the girl was entitled to an educational program in accordance with the principle of integration that includes her in the whole educational system, since the segregation of children with some type of limitation (social, mental, emotional, cognitive, or physical) in special education schools implies discrimination, either directly or indirectly. Further, the court warned that:

> From the beginning, [disabled children] are placed in the center of the normal-abnormal paradigm, where they experience a great level of discrimination, much of which comes from the labeling itself. This creates a disparity that shall have a positive or negative effect in all of the opportunities that may be presented to the child, depending on whether the child is included in the normal or abnormal category respectively . . . Ordinary education, on the other hand, is offered to all children regardless of their limitations or special needs. This entails having access and continuity to what is considered ordinary, that is to say, to what is 'normal' daily living. Procedures and teaching skills are, then, those required to educate a 'normal' child . . . Equality of opportunities is not only a precondition of today's constitutional democracy but also a substantial element of the Social State based on the

> rule of law into which Colombia has evolved . . . This requires not only the absence of discrimination but also the provision of effective aid so that those who are in a situation of need or disparity may find an effective solution.[51]

In both cases, the courts provided specific remedies, but the grounds behind their judgment addressed the broad context of inequality experienced by these complainants, and the state's liability towards this group, by recognizing that affirmative action measures must be taken in order to guarantee these children's right to education.

In relation to disabled people's rights to employment, courts in Latin America have developed a vast amount of case law, especially in relation to employment injuries, sick leave, and unjustified dismissal, among others. A decision of the Constitutional Court of Bolivia issued on July 3, 2000, dealt with a claim against the municipal authority of the City of Oruro filed by a dismissed public servant who suffered from partial paraplegia. The claimant requested that the court order his reinstatement and the payment of the pertaining damages. The claimant alleged that he had received discriminatory treatment on account of his disability. The court's majority vote understood that the claimant's petition should be admitted because

> . . . the effects of a disability on a person depend mainly on his social background; this means that a disability is not only the problem of an individual but of society as a whole. This implies that a negative and rough social background may turn a disability into an impairment and, to the contrary, a positive and inviting social environment contributes decisively to alleviate and facilitate the life of the disabled person . . . the purpose of the state is to enforce the protection of citizens' rights and guarantees and to provide the means for a better life within their limits; as such, it must be understood as a social obligation to be undertaken by both public and private institutions alike.[52]

Overall, case law on inequality for people with disabilities evidences the adoption of the principle of non-discrimination with intensive scrutiny, while simultaneously including the perspective of structural inequality. Thus, the case law not only focuses on the importance of taking measures of affirmative action—typically the responsibility of legislative or administrative agencies—but also stresses the indispensability of access to justice, which is often a requirement to ensure not only the enforcement but also the improvement of these measures.

In this sense, courts' decisions may be construed as part of the state's affirmative action policies directed at accomplishing actual equality for persons with disabilities in the exercise of their rights. Furthermore, this extensive case law provides sufficient grounds to nourish class action claims on behalf of people with disabilities.

Scrutinizing classifications based on sexual orientation

In the last decade, courts in the region have issued cutting-edge judgments in terms of equality. Despite the fact that, as a whole, the region's case law is still hesitant, and some cases of discrimination based on sexual orientation are still being solved using the classic concept of equality,[53] the seed of equality in the form of recognition has begun to grow. It must be noted that discrimination on account of sexual orientation or identity is not only a problem of redistribution but also a problem of recognition. Thus, not only is the mere approximation of patrimonial rights an insufficient remedy, but granting rights while denying recognition of the group's identity aggravates the situation of inequality. The Colombian Constitutional Court has applied a new analysis towards recognition in Decision C-577/11, where it held that:

> There are no sustainable legal grounds to determine that there is no affection, respect and solidarity to inspire a stable life in common among the members of a same sex couple, or that these personal affairs only deserve the protection of the law when they involve heterosexual couples and not when a homosexual couple is concerned.[54]

Following the same path, the Supreme Court of Justice of Mexico went a step further when deciding an unconstitutionality action brought in February 2010. The Legislative Assembly of the Federal District in Mexico amended Section 146 of the civil code on December 21, 2009. This section's statement that "marriage is the free union of a man and a woman" was thereby replaced by "marriage is the free union of two people." This amendment would later be challenged by the Office of the Mexican Attorney General on the grounds that the amendment was against the traditional concept of family, and was not reasonable or supported by adequate legal grounds.[55] The Supreme Court, for its part, had already stated on the principle of equality that:

> The highest value that this principle sustains consists, then, in preventing legislation that, while aimed at governing situations of actual equality, undermines this same equality as a result of its enforcement and leads to discriminatory treatment in similar situations, or a similar effect on persons who are in a situation of disparity, which would be understood as legal inequality.[56]

The 2010 decision analyzes the principle of equality beyond the legal concept of family, regarding it as a social reality: ". . . [the legal protection of the family] must cover all forms and expressions in current reality to protect all families that are established by marriage, by common law marriages, single parent families or even by any other type of family that denotes a similar bond."[57]

On the other hand, the court rejected straightforward alternatives to marriage, by arguing that, to the contrary,

> the decision made by the Legislative Assembly of the Federal District, by which the right of same sex couples to join in matrimony given their sexual orientation is recognized, corresponds to the recognition of several fundamental rights . . . and allows these couples to effectively acquire judicial protection, reinforced by their union or bond, in the same way as it happens with heterosexual couples, since both types of relationships exhibit similar features (love, sexuality, solidarity, stability, continuity, common expectations etc.). Therefore, and contrary to the Attorney General's opinion, marriage is the suitable form for recognizing the equality of this group, irrespective of them being heterosexual or homosexual, since they are all motivated by the same reasons to join in matrimony, which is mainly the desire to unite in lawful wedlock to lead a life in common, acquire the rights and obligations that derive from such bond and have social recognition of their union. It is not valid to argue that these couples may resort to other legal formulas: this would entail denying them access to real judicial protection on account of their sexual orientation, or to consider that those unions are less important.[58]

In this way, the court points out the lack of recognition and the need for it, while excluding intermediate alternatives that would resolve redistributive aspects (for example, civil unions) but not symbolic aspects of discrimination, which would remain unaddressed. This line of analysis has been followed by other courts in the region.

The Brazilian courts have also explored the area of recognition by means of an *Action of Unconstitutionality* [ADI] and a series of lawsuits filed by same-sex couples demanding to be recognized with the same rights as heterosexual unions. The Supreme Federal Court of Brazil held that homo-affective relationships are to be recognized as family entities and must therefore be legally recognized under equal conditions. The court based its decision on the fact that the constitution does not contain any provision concerning sexual choice, and on the principle of legality. The court concluded that Section 1723 of the civil code could not deny same sex couples the attribute of a family without infringing the principle of equality, with the constitutional protection available to families and their rights being applicable.[59]

Finally, a great advance towards the recognition of equal rights for same-sex couples came from the judgment issued by the Inter-American Court in the case of *Karen Atala v. Chile*. The case fell under international jurisdiction when the Supreme Court of Chile decided to grant a father of three minor girls full custody because their mother (and ex-wife) had started a relationship with a woman with whom she lived. Having set aside several reports that considered that living in a homosexual home caused no harm to children, as well as reports that had been presented during the proceedings which gave evidence of the good living conditions of the girls while living with their mother, the Supreme Court of Chile decided to give full custody to their father and take them away from their mother.

The Inter-American Court made a broad interpretation of the anti-discriminatory principle by arguing that, according to Section 1(1) of the American Convention, the specific criteria by virtue of which discrimination is prohibited does not constitute an exhaustive or limiting list, but is merely illustrative. Indeed, the wording of said article leaves open the criteria with the inclusion of the term "another social condition," allowing for the inclusion of other categories that have not been explicitly indicated. Consequently, the court should interpret the term "any other social condition" of Section 1(1) of the convention in the context of the most favorable option for human beings and in light of the evolution of fundamental rights in contemporary international law.[60]

The court concluded that the Inter-American Court accepts that the sexual orientation of persons is a category protected by the convention. Therefore, any regulation, act, or practice considered discriminatory based on a person's sexual orientation is prohibited. Consequently, no regulation, decision, or practice of domestic legislation, whether by state authorities or individuals, may diminish or restrict, in any way whatsoever, the rights of a person based on their sexual orientation (Section 91)

The case has a double importance: first, the judgment issued by the Inter-American Court clearly states that the parents' homosexuality does not affect the child's welfare, and, secondly, this being the first case of its kind to reach the court's jurisdiction, it gave the court the opportunity to set not merely a precedent but to achieve an act of recognition by restoring the voice of thousands of individuals who suffer different levels of discrimination in the region.

Conclusion

The case law of many Latin American courts clearly supports the idea that the model of equality in terms of non-arbitrary discrimination is firmly rooted in the region. There is a certain trend which shows that it is possible to consider local courts as forums, where claims of inequality in terms of non-domination can be brought and solutions to tackle structural problems can be obtained.

The following trends can be established:

Concerning discrimination on account of nationality, there seems to be a development of the model used to address the issue where the application of the old principle of equality in liberal terms has been complemented by a greater understanding of the terms of recognition of structural inequality, especially in the case of migrating persons.

Concerning discrimination based on age, case law seems to be taking similar steps, by recognizing structural inequality, especially that which involves children.

However, in the case of discrimination based on disabilities, it seems that the model by way of which the cases were addressed has been changed, and the courts interpret equality in terms of non-subjugation. Those resolutions are still focused on certain individuals or certain groups, not taking into account that those who suffer a situation of discrimination require broader remedies. Thus, the positive or inverse discrimination that measures efficiency is blunted, because they were designed to address a single case.

Case law concerned with discrimination based on sexual orientation has clearly evolved, supported by an application of the principle of equality in terms of recognition. In this sense

> . . . in a pluralist society, respectful of differences, it is not enough to formally recognize equal rights to different social groups. It is necessary to further attend to the consequences of a segregationist treatment. It is unacceptable and indignant, because it creates an environment of humiliation and inferiority in the heart of those who suffer discrimination.[61]

With exceptions, there have been high expectations whenever a case of sexual orientation-based discrimination has been heard by the Inter-American Court of Human Rights. Thus, the potential emancipating power of law has begun to be employed.

Questions

1 Name the constitutionally valid conditions under which differences between nationals and aliens may be established. Who must determine compliance with those conditions?

2 As shown by the decisions analyzed in this chapter, an intensive scrutiny test of equality is applied to cases concerned with migrants' access to civil rights. Taking this into consideration, provide grounds to justify the application of that standard in cases involving restrictions on the access to social rights imposed on vulnerable migrant groups.

3 In Sentence T-1090/05, regarding discrimination on the basis of race, the Constitutional Court of Colombia:

> accepted the action for protection filed by a black female youth who was denied entry to a disco in the city of Cartagena de Indias (Colombia) because she was black. The court recalled that under the definition of suspect classifications, the country's authorities accept that the Afro-Colombian community has been subjected to historical subjugation, cultural denigration and social abandonment.[62]

Which kind of equality test did the court apply? Compare this decision with three decisions analyzed in this chapter related to discrimination based on disability, age, and sexual orientation, in order to establish the similarities and differences.

4 In the same ruling, the court further argued that:

> . . . equality is a fundamental component of the state and society and consequently any discriminatory or differential treatment that is not fully in line with the principles of the Colombian constitution should be rejected. . . . Discrimination not only affects the fundamental rights of the plaintiff but also ignores and excludes directly the existence of the Afro-Colombian community.[63]

Can you establish the relationship between equality and democracy contained in this paragraph? Which kind of equality is it concerned with: equality in terms of redistribution of socioeconomic wealth or equality in terms of redistribution of recognition?

Notes

1 Carlos Barba Solano and Néstor Cohen, Perspectivas críticas sobre la cohesión social. Desigualdad y tentativas fallidas de integración social en América Latina 11–12 (CLACSO 2011). On the other hand, most constitutions and international human rights instruments now enforceable in the region identify the "disadvantaged groups" which suffer a situation of inequality caused by the asymmetrical distribution of power. Several of these instruments even recognize—expressly or impliedly—that escaping from a situation of structural dominance requires taking affirmative action measures to repair and transform reality in order to achieve real equality conditions for the exercise of rights.

2 Research project *UBACyT* (2012–15): "Judges' credentials: profiles and suitability in relation to an egalitarian society model," Ambrosio Lucas Gioja Institute Law School, Universidad de Buenos Aires.

3 Research on jurisprudence was made using the snowball and multiplicity sampling methods.

4 Inter-American Court of Human Rights, Advisory Opinion OC-18/03 (2003), September 17, 2003, 89; Advisory Opinion OC-17/02 (2002), August 28, 2002, 46; and Advisory Opinion OC-4/84, January 19, 1984, 56.

5 Regarding the fairness of the challenged classification, several tests have been developed in order to reduce judicial discretion by providing common formulae and criteria. The proportionality test, originating in the jurisprudence of the German constitutional court, aims to discern the correct balance between the goal pursued by the state and the intervention and the equality principle. On the other hand, the scrutiny test, originating in American case law, establishes the extent of the judicial review based upon rationales such as the rights involved, suspect classifications, etc.

6 Marcelo Alegre and Roberto Gargarella (comps), El derecho a la igualdad: aportes para un constitucionalismo igualitario (2007).

7 Nancy Fraser and Axel Honneth, Redistribution Or Recognition? A Political-Philosophical Exchange (2003).

8 Kimberley Crenshaw, *Mapping the Margins: Intersectionality, Identity Politics, and Violence Against Women of Color*, in The Public Nature of Private Violence (Martha Fineman and Roxanne Mykitiuk eds, 1994), available at www.hsph.harvard.edu/Organizations/healthnet/WoC/feminisms/crenshaw.html, 93–118.

9 Child Rights International Network, *Briefing on multiple discrimination*, September 2, 2009, available at www.crin.org/resources/infodetail.asp?id=20801.

10 Inter-American Court of Human Rights, case of "Girls Yean and Bosico v. Dominican Republic," September 8, 2005.

11 Child Rights International Network, *Briefing on multiple discrimination*, September 2, 2009, available at www.crin.org/resources/infodetail.asp?id=20801.

12 Constitutional Court of Colombia, Decision T-025/04, November 2, 2006.

13 Despite the fact that some constitutions guarantee equal rights to all aliens who live in their territory (e.g. Section 20 of the Argentinian national constitution).

14 Supreme Court of Argentina, case of "Repetto, Inés M. c. Provincia de Buenos Aires s/ Acción de Inconstitucionalidad," November 8, 1988 (Decisions 312:1902).

15 Supreme Court of Argentina, case of "Calvo y Pesini, Rocío c/ Córdoba, Provincia de s/ amparo," February 24, 1998 (Decisions 231:194).

16 Supreme Court of Argentina, case of "Gottschau, Evelyn Patrizia c/ Consejo de la Magistratura de la Ciudad Autónoma de Buenos Aires s/ amparo," August 8, 2006 (Decisions 329:2986).

17 Supreme Court of Argentina, case of "Hooft, Pedro C.F. v. Provincia de Buenos Aires," November 16, 2004 (Decisions 327:5118).

18 Migrants from neighboring countries (Bolivia, Brazil, Chile, Paraguay, and Uruguay) and other Latin American countries (Peru) are often victimized by the dominant discourse; see WALDO VILLALPANDO et al., LA DISCRIMINACIÓN EN ARGENTINA: DIAGNÓSTICO Y PROPUESTAS 168 (2006).

19 In this sense, these cases may be referred to as "customized" proceedings, since they involve members of society's strongest groups (middle- and upper-class society members, professionals, and immigrants from central countries). An exception is the case of the Supreme Court of Argentina, case of "Reyes Aguilera c. Estado Nacional," December 4, 2007 (Decisions 330:3853).

20 Pablo Asa and Pablo Ceriani Cernadas, *Migrantes, derechos sociales y políticas públicas en América Latina y el Caribe: La universalidad en juego*, in DERECHOS SOCIALES: JUSTICIA, POLÍTICA Y ECONOMÍA EN AMÉRICA LATINA, at 334 (Pilar Arcidiácono et al. coords, 2010).

21 Inter-American Court of Human Rights, Advisory Opinion OC-18/03, 118.

22 Pablo Asa and Pablo Ceriani Cernadas, *Migrantes, derechos sociales y políticas públicas en América Latina y el Caribe: La universalidad en juego*, in DERECHOS SOCIALES: JUSTICIA, POLÍTICA Y ECONOMÍA EN AMÉRICA LATINA, at 334 (Pilar Arcidiácono et al. coords, 2010).

23 Sugarcane plantations.

24 Inter-American Court of Human Rights, case of "Girls Yean and Bosico v. Dominican Republic," September 8, 2005, cons. 240.

25 Ibid.

26 Inter-American Court of Human Rights, case of "Street Children (Villagrán-Morales et al.) v. Guatemala," (Merits), November 19, 1999.

27 Supreme Court of Argentina, case of "Reyes Aguilera, D. c. Estado Nacional," December 4, 2007, vote of Justices Fayt and Zaffaroni.

28 IA Court HR, *Case of the "Street Children" (Villagrán-Morales et al.) v. Guatemala*, Merits. Judgment of 19 November 1 1999.

29 "Supreme Court of Argentina, case of "Reyes Aguilera, D. c. Estado Nacional," December 4, 2007, paragraph 11 (quotations of "Gottschau", Decision 329:2986, paragraph 5).

30 Ibid., vote of Justice Maqueda, paragraph 7.

31 Ibid., vote of Justice Maqueda, paragraph 15.

32 Ibid.

33 Constitutional Court of Colombia, Decisions C-071/93, SU-224/98, and C-093/01.

34 Supreme Court of Argentina, cases of "Domínguez, Amparo Carmen c/ ANSeS s/ reajustes por movilidad," April 24, 2003 (Decisions 326:1436) and "Franco, Blanca Teodora c/ Provincia de Buenos Aires," June 27, 2002 (Decisions 313:1513).

35 Supreme Court of Argentina, cases of "Maldonado, Sergio Adrián s/ recurso de amparo," November 23, 2004 (Decisions 327:5210) and "Lifschitz, Graciela Beatriz c/ Estado Nacional," June 15, 2004 (Decisions 327:2413).

36 Inter-American Court of Human Rights, case of "Street Children (Villagrán-Morales et al.) v. Guatemala," (Merits), November 19, 1999, joint concurring opinion of Justices A.A. Cançado Trindade and A. Abreu-Burelli.

37 WORLD HEALTH ORGANIZATION, WORLD REPORT ON DISABILITY (2011), available at www.who.int/mediacentre/news/releases/2011/disabilities_20110609/en/.

38 Ibid.

39 Constitutional Court of Colombia, Decision T-595/02, August 1, 2002; Decision T-823/99, October 21, 1999.

40 The writ of *amparo* [*acción de amparo*] is a judicial remedy/action developed in Latin America to provide an effective, urgent, and inexpensive instrument for the protection of constitutional rights. While originally thought of as an exceptional remedy, it has been increasingly used in order to protect economic, social, and cultural rights. See Article 25 of the American Convention of Human Rights.

41 Supreme Court of Justice of Costa Rica, Constitutional Chamber, Decision 3419–09, case of "Johnny Chinchilla Barboza c. la Municipalidad del Paraíso," February 27, 2009.

42 A similar judgment was entered on February 13, 2009, in the claim brought by a disabled person, Delroy Morgan González against the Municipality of Guácimo, on mobility freedom due to the bad shape of the sidewalks and the lack of ramps. Supreme Court of Justice of Costa Rica, Constitutional Chamber, Sentence 2249–09, case of "Delroy Morgan González c. la Municipalidad de Guácimo," February 13, 2009.
43 Constitutional Court of Colombia, Decision T-595/02, section III.
44 Ibid., section II, 5.3.
45 Ibid., section II, 5.4.
46 Supreme Court of Justice of Costa Rica, Constitutional Court (Decision 2773–09), case of "XXX c. Universidad San Isidro Labrador," February 20, 2009.
47 Ibid.
48 Ibid.
49 Supreme Court of Argentina, case of "Lifschitz, Graciela Beatriz c/ Estado Nacional," June 15, 2004. (Decisions 327:2413).
50 Constitutional Court of Colombia, Decision T-429/92, June 24, 1992.
51 Ibid., section II.5; see, for use as precedent, 036/93 and 884/96, among others.
52 Constitutional Court of Bolivia, "César Huanca Matías c. Edgar Bazán Ortega" Decision N° 638/2000 of July 3, 2000.
53 The Constitutional Court of Colombia's traditional case law is a clear example: after having dismissed several claims by the LGBT community, the court issued Decision C-075/07, reaffirming the precedent according to which, while the constitution forbids any type of discrimination on account of sexual orientation, there are differences between homosexual couples and heterosexual couples that cannot be overlooked and therefore there's no constitutional order to grant equal treatment to either. In this case, where diverse issues related to cohabitation were discussed, the court decided that in fact the restrictions were discriminatory. However, the court went no further, and would not do so in Decision C-336/08, concerning the scope of the property system that applies to common law marriages of heterosexual couples, which was intended to apply to homosexual couples.
54 Constitutional Court of Colombia, Decision T-429/92, section IV.3.
55 Supreme Court of Justice of Mexico, *Acción de Inconstitucionalidad 2/2010*, available at www2.scjn.gob.mx/juridica/engroses/cerrados/207/10000020.019.doc.
56 *Semanario Judicial de la Federación y su Gaceta*, Ninth Era, vol. V, June, 1997, thesis P./J. 42/97, 36.
57 Supreme Court of Justice of Mexico, *Acción de Inconstitucionalidad 2/2010*, 235, available at www2.scjn.gob.mx/juridica/engroses/cerrados/207/10000020.019.doc.
58 *Acción de Inconstitucionalidad 2/2010*, 275.
59 Supreme Federal Court of Brazil, *Ação Direta de Inconstitucionalidade* [ADI] *4277*, available at www.stf.jus.br/portal/peticaoInicial/verPeticaoInicial.asp?base=ADIN&s1=4277&processo=4277.
60 Inter-American Court of Human Rights, case of "Atala Riffo and Daughters v. Chile," February 24, 2012.
61 *Rodolfo Arango, Diversidad étnica, igualdad y derechos humanos,* 14/1 Revista de Antropología y arqueología, 27–31 (2003).
62 Constitutional Court of Colombia, Decision T-1090/05, available at: http://english.corteconstitucional.gov.co/sentences/T-1090–2005.pdf.
63 Ibid.

References

Rodolfo Arango, *Diversidad étnica, igualdad y derechos humanos,* 14/1 Revista de Antropología y Arqueología, 27–31 (2003).

Pablo Asa and Pablo Ceriani Cernadas, *Migrantes, derechos sociales y políticas públicas en América Latina y el Caribe: La universalidad en juego*, in Derechos Sociales: justicia, política y economía en América Latina at 334 (Pilar Arcidiácono et al. coords, 2010).

Carlos Barba Solano and Néstor Cohen, Perspectivas críticas sobre la cohesión social. Desigualdad y tentativas fallidas de integración social en América Latina (CLACSO 2011).

Kimberley Crenshaw, *Mapping the Margins: Intersectionality, Identity Politics, and Violence Against Women of Color*, in The Public Nature of Private Violence (Martha Fineman and Roxanne Mykitiuk eds, 1994), available at www.hsph.harvard.edu/Organizations/healthnet/WoC/feminisms/crenshaw.html, 93–118.

Nancy Fraser and Axel Honneth, Redistribution or Recognition? A Political-Philosophical Exchange (2003).

Waldo Villalpando et al., La discriminación en Argentina: diagnóstico y propuestas (2006).

World Health Organization, World Report on Disability (2011), available at www.who.int/mediacentre/news/releases/2011/disabilities_20110609/en/.

Child Rights International Network, *Briefing on multiple discrimination*, September 2, 2009, available at www.crin.org/resources/infodetail.asp?id=20801.

Semanario Judicial de la Federación y su Gaceta, Ninth Era, vol. V, June, 1997, thesis P./J. 42/97, 36.

Further reading

Marcelo Alegre, and Roberto Gargarella (coords), El Derecho a la igualdad. Aportes para un constitucionalismo igualitario (2012).

Bernal Pulido, Carlos, "El principio de proporcionalidad como criterio para la aplicación del derecho fundamental a la igualdad," in Gustavo Beade and Laura Clérico (eds), Desafíos a la Ponderación (Bogotá: Universidad del Externado, 2011).

Bogdandy A. von, Piovesan F. and Morales Antoniazzi M. (eds), Igualdad y Orientación Sexual. El Caso Atala de la Corte Interamericana de Derechos Humanos y su Potencial (México: Editorial Porrúa, 2012).

Clérico, Laura and Martín Aldao, "Nuevas miradas de la igualdad en la jurisprudencia de la Corte Interamericana de Derechos Humanos: la igualdad como redistribución y como reconocimiento," *Revista Estudios Constitucionales* (2011): 141–179.

Sergio Costa, *Researching Entangled Inequalities in Latin America: The Role of Historical, Social and Transregional Interdependencies.* desiguALdades.net working paper series, No. 9, Berlin: desiguALdades.net Research Network on Interdependent Inequalities in Latin America, available at www.desiguALdades.net.

de Sousa Santos, Boaventura, Sociología jurídica crítica. Para un nuevo sentido común en el derecho (Madrid: Trotta/ILSA, 2009).

Nancy Fraser, Scales of Justice: Reimagining Political Space in a Globalizing World (2008).

Nancy Fraser, *Injustice at Intersecting Scales: On 'Social Exclusion' and the 'Global Poor,'* 13/3 European Journal of Social Theory, 363–71 (2010).

Roberto Gargarella, The Legal Foundations of Inequality: Constitutionalism in the Americas, 1776–1860 (2010).

Manuel Eduardo Góngora-Mera, *Transnational Articulations of Law and Race in Latin America. A Legal Genealogy of Inequality.* desiguALdades.net working paper series, No. 18, Berlin: desiguALdades.net Research Network on Interdependent Inequalities in Latin America, available at www.desiguALdades.net.

Pecheny Mario and Rafael de la Dehesa, "Sexualidades y políticas en América Latina: el matrimonio igualitario en contexto" in M. Aldao and L. Clérico, Matrimonio Igualitario: perspectivas sociales, políticas y jurídicas (Eudeba: Buenos Aires, 2010).

Saba, Roberto, "El principio de igualdad en el diálogo entre el derecho constitucional y el derecho internacional" in Griselda Capaldo, Jan Sieckmann and Laura Clerico (comps), Internacionalización del Derecho Constitucional, constitucionalización del Derecho Internacional (EUDEBA: Buenos Aires, 2012).

Hilda Sabato, *Political Citizenship, Equality, and Inequalities in the Formation of the Spanish American Republics.* desiguALdades.net working paper series, No. 16, Berlin: desiguALdades.net Research Network on Interdependent Inequalities in Latin America, available at www.desiguALdades.net.

Rodrigo Uprimny Yepes, *The Recent Transformation of Constitutional Law in Latin America: Trends and Challenges*, 89 Texas Law Review, 1587, available at www.texaslrev.com/wp-content/uploads/Uprimny-89-TLR-1587.pdf.

2 Religious freedom

*Marcelo Alegre and Pedro Salazar Ugarte**

Introductory note: freedom of religion and from religion

This chapter refers to the challenging relationship between religion and the state. The constitutional conflicts that will be analyzed can be roughly classified into two groups. On the one hand, there are the disputes regarding freedom *of* religion; on the other, there are the disputes regarding freedom *from* religion. Conflicts of the first kind occur every time that the obligations imposed by one's own worship clash with those imposed by the state. In these cases, the discussion revolves around how far the legal system is willing to go to accommodate the demands imposed by the various religions practiced by its citizens. Problems of the second group emerge when the state identifies itself with a particular worship to the disadvantage of other religious and non-religious conceptions. In these cases, the discussion comes down to the necessity and importance of the separation between religion and the state.

The distinction between cases of freedom of religion and freedom from religion should not be taken as comprehensive or complete. It may be argued that when the state imposes or endorses, whether directly or indirectly, a religious practice, symbol or belief, it impacts negatively on the religious freedom of those who do not share the belief in question. In addition, it may be claimed that some obligations, allegedly secular, actually contradict a particular religious mandate in order to disguise the state's preference for a certain religion (usually the one practiced by the majority of the population).

Another way of making clear the questions posed by these disagreements is through the idea of equality as a value. In each of these cases, and in the ones we have chosen for this chapter, equal treatment, which is the primary duty of a democratic state, is at stake. One of the main aspects of equality is the equality of conscience—or moral equality—which demands that the state does not favor or indulge a certain view in terms of religious values. When the state trespasses this limit, there is a perceptible (to a smaller extent) risk of creating or reinforcing a sort of stratification of first-class and second-class citizens. A constitutional democracy requires that every citizen is equally allowed to device, cultivate, and express autonomously her own vision of the ultimate values that give meaning to her life and her own perspective of the universe.

In light of these considerations, located at the very foundation of the idea of constitutionalism, the cases that we include in this study display different reasonings that support some form of state favoritism towards a religious belief. The three main arguments are the following: a) The argument that the state's position on religious matters should be the one held by the majority. This argument states that it is legitimate for the state to adopt the religion of the majority, as part of the democratic aim of reaching collective preferences that are sensitive to the number and content of individual ones. b) The moral argument, according to which religiosity must be encouraged as the only, or at least the most privileged, way of constructing a minimal public morality. A variation of this argument starts from the values of social order and social cohesion and defends religiosity as a crucial tool to achieve these values. And c) the argument based on tradition and culture. This argument values the existence of active policies that support one or more religions as part of the state's duty to maintain inter-generational bonds or to foment a society's culture and roots.

On the one hand, the majority argument has the weakness (following Ronald Dworkin[1]) of not distinguishing between internal preferences (for one's own life or person) and external ones (over other people's lives). On the other hand, would it not be appropriate, in the context of religious hegemony, to make special efforts to protect all other religious views? The moral argument expresses an opinion that was dominant up to the early nineteenth century, but has lost applicability: today it is accepted that morality and religion are separable spheres and that people and societies do not need religion to be decent and civilized. It would be offensive toward non-religious people to say otherwise. Lastly, the tradition or culture argument underestimates just how much a democratic state can do to ensure conditions for cultural development in a diverse society without reaching the extreme of interfering with people's ethical equality. In other words, it is certainly disputable that the state (as an expression of society), besides guaranteeing public freedoms and access to necessary resources for cultural development, can assume a religion as its own and impose it, directly or indirectly, upon the entire aggregate.

Historical and political context

The relationship between the Catholic Church and the different states has been of great relevance in Latin American history. As Ernesto Bohoslavsky notes, after the several independence wars that took place during the nineteenth century, and facing the configuration of new states, political forces in the region had to solve some fundamental issues. An important matter was the definition of the "legal and constitutional structure that should be adopted, or the creation of a public (and private) sphere; each of which would have its own characteristics, rules and competences; and finally, the role the Catholic Church should play in both the political system and the social environment of each country."[2] Thus, each state adopted a different structure. Some countries adopted one whose constitutional and political design openly favored the Catholic Church (for example, Peru and some Central American countries); others combined some preference for Catholicism with an ample protection of freedom of conscience (for example, Argentina); others declared themselves non-religious (Mexico and Uruguay).

This close relationship between the state and the Catholic Church was a crucial subject in the constitutional, political, and social agenda of the newly established Latin American states. Roberto Blancarte affirms that true independence could not be achieved until the state was autonomous from the Catholic Church.[3] He makes this statement specifically about Mexico, but it is also true for every country in the region. The separation of church and state and, most importantly, the acquiescence of the former to secular laws represented a decisive challenge towards the construction of modern Latin American states.

Topics and issues

In order to analyze the relationship between the churches and states in Latin America, several issues must be noted: a) there is a religion that historically has been, and still is, predominant in

Latin America: the Catholic Church; b) this is an institution that has had, and continues to have, a strong political weight; c) thus, identifying the degrees of separation and autonomy between the states and this church is of great importance; d) it is also important to reflect on the capacity of the state to impose its authority and its laws on that church; and, lastly, e) it is important to consider that each state in the region shows differences in this particular area.

There is, however, another relevant dimension to this matter. If rather than looking at the institutional relationship between state and church from a formal point of view we focus our attention on social reality, we will notice some interesting features. One of them relates to the presence of different beliefs and religions that coexist within Latin American societies. The Catholic Church continues to be dominant in practically every Latin American country, but it is not the only religion followed by Latin Americans. Here are a few figures collected by Ernesto Bohoslavsky:

> In Chile, evangelicals went from 3 percent to 15 percent of the population between 1992 and 2002; and Catholics descended from 76 percent to 69 percent. The census taken by the Brazilian Institute of Geography and Statistics in 2000 showed that 74 percent of the population identified themselves with Catholicism, while 18 percent declared to be Protestants, and mainly evangelicals. A survey taken in Honduras in 2007 showed that 47 percent of its population identified himself or herself as Catholic, and 36 percent as Protestant. The information provided by the National Statistics Institution in Uruguay in 2007 showed that 45 percent of its population was Catholic, 10 percent Christian but not Catholic, and nearly 28 percent expressed that they were 'believers but had no religion.' In Nicaragua, a study developed in 2005 by the Nicaraguan Institute for Statistics and Census stated that 58 percent of its population was Catholic and 21 percent Protestant. In 2007, 81 percent of Peruvians claimed to be Catholic and 12 percent Protestant (mainly evangelicals). The census performed in Bolivia in 2001 identified the 78 percent of its population as Catholic and 16 percent as Protestant (in some rural areas those numbers went up to 20 percent).[4]

These statistics show the extent to which Latin American states are also facing the challenges that come along with religious pluralism.

The secular agenda also manifests itself on this practical dimension; it relates to a requirement of tolerance at two levels. On the one hand, the issue is assessed from a vertical perspective, in which finding out whether the state is granting privileges to a specific religion and consequently adopting discriminatory policies on the matter is relevant. On the other hand, the horizontal perspective demands an answer to the concerns brought by the coexistence of people with different beliefs. This dimension of the religious issue has been studied in depth in societies where religious plurality is a historic element, but this is not the case in Latin America, historically considered a Catholic continent. This phenomenon is similar to what is happening in some European countries, such as Italy, Spain, or France, which now face a great challenge on this particular subject as a consequence of the waves of migration that took place during the last decades of the twentieth century and which, despite the economic crisis in most parts of the continent, continue to exist.

All these aspects are involved in the human rights agenda. Just as the relationship between the state and the different churches (in plural), the relationship between believers of different religions, and between believers and those who do not profess any religion, depend to a great extent on an aggregate of freedoms. These are, at the least, freedom of thought (which transcends the religious field), liberty of ethical convictions (which includes non-believers), freedom of conscience (which also includes non-religious matters), and freedom of religion. These aggregated freedoms have both a public and a private dimension, and they are expressed in very different ways. In the analysis of the social relevance of this ensemble of rights, it is common to encounter this issue in discussions about the family, education, sexual and reproductive rights, expressions by the media, scientific research, and so on, but there is yet another issue which impacts on the equality agenda, not only in terms of equality as non-discrimination, but also in terms of equality as non-domination, when an effective recognition of rights is denied to underprivileged groups precisely for religious reasons. That said, when studying judicial decisions associated with the relationship between the state and the different religious institutions in Latin America, it is important to take into consideration two kinds of questions: a first one, that ultimately implies a constitutional political decision (to what extent does religion and/or its church influence politics? What is their impact on social life? What is the limit to the state's intervention in religious matters? etc), and a second one, related to human rights (equality, freedom, sexual and reproductive rights, etc.). We should always bear in mind that there is not a consistent and uniform trend in the way judges handle the subject in every country. Therefore, in this chapter we analyze several cases that provide a general picture of the discussions and decisions related to the relationship between the state and the different churches, but that do not set a general tendency.

Constitutional provisions matter

In Latin America there are different ways in which constitutions regulate the relationships between the state, religions and their churches; and constitutional courts' decisions involve interpretations of what constitutions say. Below, we outline some examples of this from a normative perspective.

Article 2 of the Argentinian constitution states that "The Federal Government supports the Roman Catholic Church."[5] Yet Article 14 grants to all citizens the right "to freely profess their religion,"[6] and Article 19 acknowledges a strong right to autonomy and privacy: "The private actions of men which in no way offend public order or morality, nor injure a third party, are only reserved to God and are exempted from the authority of judges."[7] The first article contrasts in a significant way with what the Mexican constitution states in its recently modified Article 40: "It is the will of the Mexican people to constitute itself in a representative, democratic, secular, and federal republic . . ."[8] Accordingly, in another article (Article 130), the constitution not only abstains itself from adopting an official religion, but also imposes strong limits when it comes to the participation of religious authorities in political life. Here are some excerpts from Article 130:

> The historic principle of separation of the state from the different churches guides the provisions established in this Article. Churches and any other religious groups shall observe the law.
>
> . . . d) Religious ministers shall not perform any governmental employment. However, as Mexican citizens, they shall be entitled to vote and those who have finished their religious activities according to the law, shall be entitled to be elected to public posts as well; e) Religious ministers shall refrain from objecting to any of the country's laws through any religious meetings or publicity. They shall also refrain from attacking the national symbols . . . The naming of a political association using any religious reference shall be forbidden. Political gatherings shall never take place at temples of any sort . . .[9]

Other dispositions in the Mexican constitution reinforce the secular nature of the state on matters such as public education which, under the terms of Article 3, "will be secular and, therefore, free from any religious orientation;"[10] it will also be oriented by "scientific progress and will fight against ignorance, ignorance's effects, servitude, bigotry, and prejudice." This does not imply that there is no religious freedom in Mexico (which is acknowledged in Article 24), or that the state discriminates against people because of their religious preferences (which is prohibited by Article 1), but it does mean that, contrary to what happens in Argentina and other countries, Mexico affirms its absolute secularism.

That said, there are also constitutions that were enacted "invoking God Almighty"[11] like the constitution of Peru. Article 50 of the Peruvian constitution establishes that: "Within a regime of independence and autonomy, the state acknowledges the Catholic Church as an element of great importance in the historical, cultural and moral background of Peru, and lends it its cooperation."[12] In the same article, it declares that "the state respects other denominations and may establish forms of cooperation with them"[13] but there is a clear preference for the Catholic religion over others. Regardless, Article 2 of the same constitution states that among every person's fundamental rights is the right to not be discriminated against for religious reasons and also "freedom of conscience, individually or as a member of a group" because "no one may be persecuted for his ideas or beliefs."[14] The constitution contemplates the possibility of religious education in these terms: "Ethical and civic training and the teaching of the Constitution and human rights are compulsory in all civil or military educational processes. Religious education is provided with respect for freedom of conscience."

Another country with relevant rules on the subject is Colombia. The country's constitution forbids discrimination based on religion and, whilst recognizing freedom of religion, claims that "every individual has the right to freely profess his/her religion and to disseminate it individually or collectively."[15] Contrary to the legislation in Peru, it also states that "all religious faiths and churches are equally free before the law."[16] Therefore, it chooses an intermediate path between the countries that grant a privilege to the Catholic religion and the Mexican example, which adopts a clear secular stance. In Colombia, there is also a vast amount of case law on the subject. Leonardo García Jaramillo claims that "more than a consecration of principles and rights on the constitution, the influx that determines the principle of secularism is due to jurisprudential practices."[17]

Some relevant cases and decisions

Resisting the hegemony of Catholicism

In this section, we begin with a series of cases in which certain rules or actions were challenged for implying an excess of religiosity and becoming an imposition of the majority's religious values (which are those of Catholicism in these cases in particular) on minorities.

Colombia's classification

The Constitutional Court of Colombia, in an interesting judgment, declared a law (the First Law of 1952) to be unconstitutional because it required the president or his agents to be part of a yearly religious ceremony at the national capitol, in which the Republic's consecration to the Sacred Heart was to be renewed. The court suggested the following classification of types of states when it comes to their relationship with religion:[18]

(1) Confessional States, which establish an official religion whose contents are mandatory by law without religious tolerance. They prohibit or discriminate against any religion other than the official one. Some examples of this kind of states are Christian medieval states, absolutist monarchies, and some Muslim countries . . .
(2) Tolerant confessional states, where there is an official religion and the others are not discriminated against. The existence of an official religion does not imply that the normative religious contents are obligatory for everyone. There are two variations: (2.1) where non-official religions are tolerated; for example, the Albertine Italian Statute of 1870 stated that the Catholic religion was 'the only state religion. The others are tolerated by the law'; (2.2) where the governmental nature of a religion coexists with full freedom of religion and absence of discrimination. Examples: the Anglican religion is the official one in England but there is complete freedom of religion. Israel is also a tolerant religious nation because, while Judaism is its official religion, it protects religious freedom of all confessions . . .
(3) States with a confessional orientation or a special protection to a specific religion where, whilst the state does not necessarily establish an official religion, it endeavors to acknowledge the social and historical fact that one religion is much more recurrent in the population than others. Examples: the current constitutional regulation in Spain and Italy grant complete religious freedom and do not establish an official religion, but they favor Catholicism . . .
(4) Secular states with complete religious freedom. There is not an official religion and the legal system does not have any influence on religious institutions. There is a strict separation of the different churches and the state because their constitutions and laws establish equality between every religious confession. Examples: United States of America and France . . .
(5) Atheist states that tolerate religious practices that are not opposed to secular or official practices, but where religious or cult freedom is not guaranteed by the law. To some extent, there can be hostile manifestations against religious phenomena.[19]

This classification is useful to understand the meaning of some judicial decisions from this and other tribunals or constitutional courts in Latin America in cases related to freedom of religion.

The prohibition of alcohol in Peru

An interesting case took place in Peru, where a ban on the sale of alcoholic drinks during a religious holiday was put into question. In 2001, an ordinance was passed in the Province Municipality of Huancayo, Peru, a place inhabited by a large Catholic community, according to which the sale and consumption of alcohol in bars, night clubs, and similar businesses was banned from 12:00pm on Good Friday until 6:00pm on Holy Saturday. The owner of a discotheque argued against this regulation because of the negative impact on his business, on the basis that this ordinance imposed an alcohol prohibition for religious reasons.

The Constitutional Court decided against the challenge, since the restriction was not based on religious reasons but on reasonable criteria for security matters, stating that:

> Neither in the *ratio decidendi*, nor in the findings and conclusions of Municipal Ordinance No. 039-MPH-CM, issued by the Provincial Municipality of Huancayo, was the invocation or justification of the religious customs of the area given as the basis of the prohibition of the consumption of liquor during Holy Week. To the contrary, the *ratio juris* of said provision is based upon the protection of public order; . . . the justifying element of the referred prohibition is preserving order and public security during the celebration of a religious rite that brings thousands of people out into the street, since it has taken into account the fact that, as was expressed above, the Catholic religion is the one held by the majority in our country. In short, the underlying public interest is closely related to maintaining public order, but not to a requirement of a conduct imposed by a determined religion.[20]

The court also formulated some considerations related to the link between the state and the church in a "non-religious state." The court expressed that the relationship between the state and religion must be governed by the "principle of reciprocal incompetence,"[21] meaning that, on the one hand, the state recognizes the existence of "spheres" in people's lives which it is forbidden to regulate and, on the other, churches accept a legal limit to institutional intervention in matters that are strictly of the state. The tribunal recognized the deeply rooted importance of Catholic traditions in Peruvian society,[22] but affirmed that, even though religious customs were ingrained in the population, that does not entitle the state to establish prohibitions on conducts that are not compatible with Catholic dogmas and rites. The court maintained that "if some organ of the state forbade people to act according to the demands deriving from their religious customs, it would be violating the principle of immunity from coercion and, therefore, breaching the freedom of conscience and of religion."

Mary Law in Colombia

We present next the case of the Ley María—or Mary Law—in Colombia. In 2002, the Colombian Congress passed Law 755, which modified the regime for paternity and maternity leave. This law was called the "Mary Law" on account of three different reasons: to pay tribute to Colombian mothers, to the "eternal mother," and to the daughter of a renowned journalist who, in the days after her birth, promoted the passing of a paternity leave law.

Aside from the reasons for which this law was passed, the court observed that the use of the name "Mary" in this case brought up constitutional matters that had to be addressed—particularly whether it infringed the principles of pluralism and cultural diversity or freedom of religion and worship. Even though the court's decision was to uphold the statute, the doctrine established is interesting.[23]

The interpretation of the principle of equality and of the principle of separation between the state and religion result in two normative consequences: the impossibility for the state to grant preferential treatment to a church or religious confession, and that both principles require neutrality by state authorities towards religious manifestations.

The first consequence is that any discriminatory treatment that privileges a particular religion or worship over others should not exist. Even though the court itself has admitted a favorable legal treatment of churches and religious confessions, it only did so in order to offer equal access to those benefits to all religious institutions that fulfilled the requirements of the law.

The second consequence, on the other hand, relies on the idea that there is a separation of state and religion. The court stated that the criteria for drawing a line between state actions in religious matters that are constitutionally allowed and those that are unconstitutional are related to the purpose or ends sought by the intervention of public authorities, and that this would be violated, for example, in a situation where the state discriminated between different religions by granting advantages to some churches without offering equal opportunities for others. However, "the fact that a decision with a secular purpose and an event of 'religious nature' coincide does not breach those principles, as long as every person can worship freely and profess the faith that they choose." [24]

With these considerations, the court analyzed the case and expressed that, in naming the law "Mary," no advantage in favor of a determined church or religion was created, that the Colombian state does not formally and explicitly identify with one religion or belief, that it does not adhere officially to any religious faith, and that the name "Mary" has no single or necessary connotation that could, because of its title, imply that the law is a vehicle for promoting a determined religious faith.

In fact, regarding the purposes of paying tribute to all mothers of Colombia and the girl named Mary, the court understood that they did not violate constitutional precepts. The first, given its degree of generality—a tribute to all Colombian mothers—respects the equality of all before the law. Moreover, a tribute to a particular person does not present constitutional conflicts either: the intention of paying tribute to a specific natural person was not the exclusive or principal objective of the law, rather it was a way to promote that person through identification with a common name within the Colombian population which was easy to remember and was associated to the ultimate purpose of that law, which was the welfare of newborns in Colombia. Concerning the tribute to the "eternal mother" allegedly sought by the law, it was not a deliberate mention of the "mother of Christ," from the Christian religion. In fact, the name "eternal mother" is not at all common when referring to the Virgin Mary within that tradition. Instead, for many people, it is associated with cosmovisions which see the Earth as their eternal mother, or which at least acknowledge the land as the birth mother of everything that exists on this planet.

There was a dissenting opinion by Beltrán Sierra, Araujo Rentería, and Vargas Hernández which suggested that the independence of the state with regards to religion was in fact being affected, given that such principle insists that "the state may not adopt a decision of any sort that identifies its own actions with a certain religion."[25] It also stated that it was not plausible to defend the argument that the law was named after the daughter of the journalist who promoted its passing, given that was contrary to Article 150 of the constitution.[26] Lastly, the opinion makes clear that naming a law "Mary" as a "tribute to all Colombian mothers" could not be defended either, given that it was not true that all Colombian women that are mothers are named "Mary," neither was it true that a "tribute" was being paid with that designation, "when it is true that the best that could be offered to them would be the creation of legal norms that allow them the full realization of their freedom and effective use of their rights, all of which we are still far from doing."[27]

The need for the state to act with neutrality, which would supposedly require the removal of these symbols, or their absence, in certain specially regulated activities such as elections and official acts, is a frequent argument. However, some defenders of using or displaying these symbols officially deny that a secular stance by the state is a neutral one: if the presence of these symbols could offend non-Catholics, in the same manner, their removal could offend Catholics.[28] It is doubtful that both types of "offenses" (those towards members of religious minorities that must accept a religious symbol they do not consider their own, on the one hand, and those towards the hegemonic majority forced to interact in public spaces "not devoted" to religious imagery, on the other) have the same moral impact.

Religious votes in Mexico

As we know, Mexico (following the Colombian court's classification) is a secular state with complete religious freedom, and constitutional judges have adopted a few decisions that confirm it. An interesting electoral case confirms the strict separation between the political and the religious sphere. In 2007, the Electoral Tribunal confirmed a decision that came from the Supreme Court of the State of Michoacan. This decision annulled a municipal election because the winner had used religious symbols during his campaign.[29] In particular, he attended two religious ceremonies as part of his campaign, he rode an automobile with religious motifs, and he thanked "all social and religious structures"[30] for their support. These reasons were enough for the judges in Michoacan to annul the election, in spite of the fact that the law did not explicitly contemplate the annulment of elections for those reasons.

The judges' argument was that Article 130 of the Mexican constitution is clear when it requires that the separation of the state from the churches be "absolute" and that there is no way that one "can contaminate the other."[31] From their point of view, the acts of political campaigning that used religious symbols affected the "freedom and authenticity of the elections;" moreover, they posed a "direct violation of constitutional norms."[32] It is interesting to note that the judgment was approved by a unanimous vote and served as a precedent for the annulment of other elections.

The Peruvian case

In March 2011, a Peruvian citizen demanded that the president of the Supreme Court of Justice order the removal of all crucifixes and Bibles from the court's premises. He also asked for the parties and witnesses in a trial to be no longer requested to state their religion, basing his claim on the right to equal and non-discriminatory treatment on a religious or any other basis.

The Constitutional Court said that "freedom of religion is not only expressed positively, through our right to believe, but also through our right to practice our religion."[33] On the other hand, that freedom is to be exercised in a secular environment provided by the state, but taking into account national culture and history. According to the court, Peru is a secular state with "autonomy and independence"[34] from the Catholic Church and other religions; but, as we already know, the Catholic Church enjoys a special recognition. As stated by the court, religious pluralism and non-adherence to a particular faith by the state are compatible with a special recognition of the Catholic Church because "the radical incompetence of the state towards faith does not imply that, within the context of secularism, it may adopt an agnostic or atheist attitude, or rest on a passive indifference towards the religious element."[35] In the court's words, "the constitution, along with the principle of secularism, considers the religious element to be important in society."[36] The court said that the presence of "religious symbols in a public space such as the judiciary responds to the influence of the Catholic Church and its cultural, historical, and social roots"[37] and does not suggest any violation to the equality and non-discrimination principles. The worth of a Bible or crucifix in a court is merely "cultural, related to the country's history or traditions."[38] Thus, the interpretation of fundamental rights and the definition of the secular state are historically and culturally influenced.

Consequently, the court decided that the Bible and crucifix could still be exhibited in the court. However, it ruled in favor of the claimant on the second point and banned the question of what religion the witnesses practiced. In this case, an unjustified violation to religious freedom was deemed present. In fact, asking the particular religion of the parties and witnesses seems unreasonable, given its irrelevance regarding the aims of the judicial process.

The virgin of the courts

In 2002, the Supreme Court of Justice of Argentina, exercising its administrative powers, authorized the exhibition of an image of the *Virgin Mary Queen Medjugorje* in the lobby of the court's building. The alleged Virgin of the Courts should have only stayed on exhibition for two months, but instead it stayed there indefinitely.[39] As a result of this situation, an association named ADC[40] requested that the image be removed, arguing, above all, that its presence in the court infringed the principle of equal treatment to every person regardless of their religious preferences. The court dismissed the claim, since it understood that this was within its powers of supervision and that it responded to considerations of a historical, regulatory, cultural, and sociological order. Further, it rejected the possibility that the presence of the image in the lobby could affect the equal treatment of people in terms of the provision of justice without religious discrimination.

The organization filed a writ of *amparo* against this decision, requesting that the Supreme Court's decision that authorized the installation of the image, and any other symbol of a religious nature, be declared contrary to the constitution and other international human rights treaties.

After a district judge granted the writ, a group of Catholic lawyers appealed to the decision, and an appeals court overturned it. ADC took the case back to the Supreme Court. The court said that it had already withdrawn the image. Arguing that placing or removing the image was under its purview, it overturned the appeals court decision, denied appellant standing and declared the issue moot.

Protection of religious minorities

The three cases outlined below discuss the extension of the duty to adjust the law and the law's institutions to accommodate minorities' religious requirements.

The first case, in the area of family law, confirms that, in spite of a strict separation between state and church, the Mexican judicial system acknowledges and protects religious freedom. The father of a five-year-old girl, after getting a divorce, asked that, since he was a Jew, the custody calendar take into account Jewish festivities, especially because his former wife was not Jewish. With this request, he made clear that he had the intention of initiating his daughter in his religion. The court[41] that first heard the case denied the request because it was based on religious grounds. The judges' explanation was that Mexico is a secular state and therefore judges are forbidden to base their decisions on religious arguments. The court said that "courts cannot determine what is pertinent regarding the subjective right to religious freedom and therefore impose a regime of custody in order for the child to attend Jewish festivities and celebrations." In response to this decision, the father appealed to the Supreme Court of Justice of Mexico.[42]

The court's First Chamber reviewed the case and, contrary to the local court, accepted the religious arguments. In fact, the Supreme Court stated that the local court had violated the law because, in order to protect "the child′s best interests . . . the court should have made clear [the child's] own opinion about her religious instruction,"[43] in accordance with what is stated by the Convention on the Rights of the Child and a series of clauses from laws that protect children against discrimination. The court decided that the child should be directly heard before issuing any decisions. In his concurrent opinion, Justice Cossío said that the greatest challenge was harmonizing secularism with religious freedom: "The principle of state secularism demands, on one hand, that all state agents are impartial and agnostic when it comes to the beliefs of others; and, on the other, respect for the ideological and religious freedom of people, rights that are grounded in the constitution of Mexico."[44]

For this justice, "the lower court understands in a radically incorrect way what secularism or state neutrality in a liberal democracy is" because "refraining from action, on occasion, validates an asymmetrical reality from a rights and freedoms perspective."[45] According to Justice Cossío, a secular state "must refrain from backing or promoting the beliefs of individuals within its institutions, in a direct or indirect way."[46] It must also "regulate the different issues related to religious life."[47] The latter should be done with the aim of securing the right to freedom of religion, in this case, that of the five-year-old child first and, then, that of her parents.

Special concessions for religious minorities

The case 895/02, from Peru, concerns the adaptation of labor requirements to the demands of religious minorities. Lucio Valentín Rosado Anaque was a member of the Adventist Church of Peru ("Iglesia Adventista del Séptimo Día"). One of the central obligations of his religion is not to work on Saturdays (identified as a day dedicated to worship, as it is the "Day of the Lord" or "Day of Christian Rest"). Since 1988, Rosado Anaque had worked at National Hospital Almanzor Aguinaga Asenjo. Since that time, aware of his religious affiliation, his employee excluded him from the list of those who had to work on Saturdays. Yet, in 2001, after an internal restructuring, he was asked to work on that day. Rosado disputed this modification because "he would be forced to fail to meet the terms of his religious precepts or to generate a series of absences that could cause his dismissal." The defendant declared that the reorganization responded, above all, to equal treatment regarding working hours; and that "religious practices cannot force public institutions to modify, in favor of one worker, the distribution of labor shifts."

After his claim was denied by two courts because of formal matters, the case reached the Constitutional Court of Peru, which decided it on August 19, 2002. The majority vote affirmed:

> Freedom of conscience and freedom of religion . . . are two rights with different content. The right to freedom of conscience supposes the right . . . to build freely one's own conscience, in such a way that said formation is free from any type of interference. The free development of an individual's personality implies that the person keeps forming the values or principles that give rise to her own creation of criteria and ideas throughout her life. The constitutional rule of law protects the forging of one's own conscience from disturbance or impositions of any type, not even those ethical or moral notions that have forceful or widely shared social support, since, for exactly that reason, an intrinsic condition of the democratic ideal is guaranteeing respect for the values of the minority. On the other hand, freedom of religion entails every individual's right to form part of a determined religion, to believe in the dogma and doctrine proposed by that religion, to manifest publicly and privately the consequent religious convictions, and to worship. As with all rights to freedom, the right to religious freedom has a negative aspect, which guarantees the freedom of every person to decide consciously that they do not want to partake in acts of the nature described above. To put it clearly, freedom of conscience is related to freedom of ideas; whilst freedom of religion is linked to freedom of belief.[48]

How, then, could the court strike a balance between the right to conscientious objection and the state's interests at stake (the regular provision of the health service)? The court focused on the reasonableness of the modification of the work schedules and demanded that the defendant provide reasons to justify the sudden change in the way of providing services. In this particular case, the defendant did not prove that he had a valid reason. Thus, the court stated that "[t]he vague reference to 'reasons of institutional necessity' made by the defendant in its written submission would appear to be, from any point of view, ambiguous and insufficient."[49]

In this way, the majority opinion concluded that the conscientious objection to the duty of going to work on Saturdays by Rosado Anaque was justified, since the defendant had not offered objective reasons that would allow the court to conclude that the change in its work schedule followed institutional interests that were compatible with the sacrifice of the plaintiff's rights.

On the other hand, the minority opinion of Justice Revoredo Marsano favored the dismissal of the lawsuit with four arguments: a) that the plaintiff, when choosing a medical career, should have known of the sacrifices that it imposes, particularly those related to personal freedom and rest; b) that the plaintiff never stated that his work was at stake due to his failure to attend on Saturdays; c) that health services, because of their particularities, cannot be interrupted for considerations such as the plaintiff's; and d) that accepting the plaintiff's claim would imply a violation of the principle of equality towards his work colleagues.[50]

Are these arguments convincing? Regarding the first one, it seems to beg the question, since precisely what the plaintiff did was to question that he had a duty to accept the sacrifice of breaking his religious mandates. Regarding the second one, it seems to contradict the hospital authority's conduct, which, for a long time, accommodated this very restriction. As for the third argument, it incorrectly assumes that adapting to the plaintiff (who is part of a small minority) implied the interruption of the health services provided by the hospital, without any evidence that such an adaptation was impossible or difficult. The last argument turns the principle of equality upside down: it was the plaintiff who saw his right to equality affected by being forced to choose between his work and his faith, unlike the majority of his colleagues, who did not face that terrible dilemma.

A third case on the scope of the "compromise" required by the respect for religious freedom is "Heirs of Victoria Capella v. Pentecostal Church of God, 102 D.P.R. 20 (1974)," from Puerto Rico. The Constitution of the Commonwealth of Puerto Rico, in its Article II (Bill of Rights), Section 3, Freedom of Religion and Establishment Clause, reads: "No law shall be made respecting an establishment of a religion or prohibiting the free exercise thereof. There shall be complete separation of church and state."[51]

Some neighbors from the corner of Sol and Cruz streets in San Juan, Puerto Rico, were disturbed by the activities of the Pentecostal Church of God during their worship. These practices took place three or four times a week, from 7:00pm to 10:00pm, as well as during the day on Sundays and public holidays. The neighbors filed a lawsuit against this practice in the trial court of Puerto Rico. The court ordered the Pentecostal Church to take the necessary measures to insulate the noises that came from the church during worship. The church appealed the decision.

The claimants' legal arguments were that they were protected by Section 7 of Article II of the Constitution of the Commonwealth of Puerto Rico and that they had a right to privacy in their home without being interfered with by the loud noises made by the Pentecostal Church of God that was nearby. The defendant argued that they had been in the neighborhood before the claimants moved there, and that the corner where they had established was already noisy, from people crossing and cars moving.

The court held that the state cannot interfere with the worship and religious beliefs of a citizen, but that it can with the methods used when they affect the right to privacy of the family. Otherwise, the government would be neglecting its obligation to guarantee the equal protection of the law. In the "sanctuary" called home, a citizen is not required to endure the practices and unwanted noises caused by the activities of a church that interfere with and destroy the right to privacy in his home, causing torture and extreme moral suffering.[52] The decision from the trial court was confirmed by the Supreme Court of Puerto Rico.

Religion and freedom of speech: the León Ferrari case

We said that the border that separates freedom of religion and freedom from religion is tenuous. The next case is an example of this idea, by showing how some people see their religious freedom as threatened by a display of secular art, while others see their freedom of expression endangered by the demands of religious persons. León Ferrari was born in Buenos Aires, Argentina, in 1920 (he died in 2013). He was a famous artist with a well-known career, during which he developed a characteristic artistic language. In 2004, the city of Buenos Aires put on a retrospective exhibition of all his life's work, which attracted over 70,000 spectators between 2004 and 2005. A part of this exhibition contained certain works that could be regarded as offensive to Christian beliefs,[53] held by the majority in Argentina. For this reason, the government had put up some signs warning that the display could hurt spectators' feelings and emotions.

After a few months, the situation took an important public turn: Catholic organizations presented petitions signed by citizens to different state agencies demanding that the exhibition be shut down. However, most of the local artistic scene expressed itself in favor of the exhibition and of León Ferrari.

In addition to this, a Catholic association filed a writ of *amparo*, aimed at forcing the city of Buenos Aires to abstain from displaying this exhibit, considering that it affected the religious sentiments of the Catholic community.[54]

A first-instance judge, by way of a preliminary measure, ordered the local government to suspend the exhibition.[55]

The Court of Appeal, after formulating an interesting conceptualization of religious freedom and the limitations to artistic expression, overturned this decision and ordered the continuation of the exhibition.

First, it held that there was no link between the right to profess freely a religious faith and the continuance of the exhibition, since the city´s cultural activity did not affect the right of each individual to choose their beliefs, whether religious, aesthetic or of any other type. Accordingly, the Court of Appeal added that even though it was unquestionable that Ferrari had a clear aesthetic–political stance regarding the Catholic religion, it could not automatically be deduced that the government, by organizing the exhibition, discriminated against members of that religion.[56]

Secondly, it emphasized that the existence of a Catholic majority does not necessarily imply the automatic existence of identical ideas, judgments, and concrete feelings within that majority.[57]

Thirdly, it inquired about the particular characteristics that imply recognizing a substantial normative protection to artistic expressions. The Court of Appeal explored the idea that art, as an expression, has two main features: it is essentially critical and, consequently, annoying and irritating;[58] but it is also ambiguous and, therefore, subject to multiple interpretations:[59]

> These last reflections, which have their starting point in Ferrari's sculpture, reveal a particular quality of art: its ambiguity. A piece of art is open to diverse readings, various interpretations. It does not say something clearly determined, but rather it expresses a multiplicity of senses. Because of that, a piece of art does not provoke univocal feelings, it generates a multitude of sensations, impressions and feelings in the viewer, emotions that, at the same time, cannot be separated from cognitive aspects, ideas or thoughts, that are also diverse.[60]

This is something that must be dealt with by the legal system, because

> it is in respecting the freedom of that form of art that a democratic society demonstrates what value it gives to artistic freedom of speech. That is when genuine tolerance is satisfied, when society deals with and accepts the existence of a work of art that annoys, irritates, disturbs or degrades . . . when such types of expression are forbidden, censorship presents itself, which is another way of violating freedom of conscience and, ultimately, of imposing a particular belief, an idea, or a value upon another.[61]

Finally, the court held that the separation of state and religion affects the way in which the state's cultural policies must be understood: as a kind of pluralist activity that embraces aesthetic diversity without incurring in discrimination. On this point, the fact that the government had included signs that warned of the possible effects on the spectator was a sufficient caution statement. Also, the court dealt with the matter of the public funding of the art work, and considered it to be a part of the design and execution of a comprehensive cultural public policy that ensured the pluralistic demands of a democratic system:[62]

> The decision by the local state to assign spaces for the expression of ideas—artistic ideas in this case—should have as an objective the enrichment of collective debate. As such, it is expected that the government act democratically by way of an equal and plural distribution of opportunities for expression when conceding spaces for expressing opinions (Opinion of Justice Carlos Balbin).

Conclusion

The cases discussed in this chapter map out the enormous diversity in the area of religious freedom in Latin America. However, an ubiquitous feature is worth noticing: the huge influence of Catholicism as the majority religion. Even in countries that are theoretically secular, social practices and legal institutions are under huge cultural and political pressure to impose the predominant religious worldview upon the whole of society. Sometimes, a court is the forum in which such hegemony is questioned, with varying outcomes. In the future, we must expect new and stronger debates over the requirements of religious equality.

Questions

a Which of the arguments in favor of an official endorsement of a religion do you find most compelling, if any?

b What is your opinion regarding the absolute prohibition that Mexican law imposes on the religious expression of political candidates?

c Do you find the display of religious symbols in courts problematic? Why? Does it make any difference if the symbols are displayed in a public classroom?
d Would you defend any limits to the exercise of the right to conscientious objection in the case of medical doctors?
e Would you have solved the *León Ferrari* case differently? How?
f Do you recall any similar case in your country? Identify differences and similarities with the cases discussed above.

Notes

* With the invaluable assistance of Paulina Barrera, UNAM; Pablo Ignacio Cattaneo, UBA; Federico Orlando, UBA; and Paola García Rivera, Universidad de Puerto Rico, UBA. Johanna Hardwick and Tamara Tenenbaum (UBA) collaborated with the edition of the chapter's English version.
1 Ronald Dworkin, Taking Rights Seriously (1977).
2 Ernesto Bohoslavsky, *Laicidad y América Latina*, Colección de cuadernos "Jorge Carpizo." Para entender y pensar la laicidad, Cuaderno No. 11, 3 (2013).
3 Roberto Blancarte, Los retos de la secularización y de la laicidad en el mundo contemporáneo (2008).
4 Ernesto Bohoslavsky, *Laicidad y América Latina*, Colección de cuadernos "Jorge Carpizo." Para entender y pensar la laicidad, Cuaderno No. 11, 35 (2013).
5 Constitución de la Nación Argentina (Constitution of Argentina), August 22, 1994, Article 2.
6 Ibid., Article 14.
7 Ibid., Article 19.
8 Constitución Política de los Estados Unidos Mexianos (Political Constitution of the United States of Mexico), February 5, 1917, Article 40.
9 Ibid., Article 130.
10 Ibid., Article 3.
11 Constitución Política del Peru (Political Constitution of Peru), December 29, 1993.
12 Ibid., Section 50.
13 Ibid.
14 Ibid.
15 Constitución Política de Colombia (Political Constitution of Colombia), July 4, 1991.
16 Ibid.
17 Leonardo García Jaramillo, *Laicidad y Justicia Constitucional*, Colección de cuadernos "Jorge Carpizo." Para entender y pensar la laicidad, Cuaderno No. 34, 32–4 (2013).
18 Until 1994, the Republic of Colombia was consecrated to the Sacred Heart of Jesus in a yearly official commemoration, which took place at the national capitol. Decision C-350/94 (lead by Judge Alejandro Martínez) analyzed the subject and declared the First Law of 1952 to be unconstitutional. This law forced the president or his agents to renew the country's commemoration.
19 Constitutional Court of Colombia, Decision C-350/94, August 4, 1994.
20 Constitutional Court of Peru, Decision No. 3283–2003, June 15, 2004.
21 Ibid.
22 One cannot avoid the fact that the Catholic religion has been, and continues to be the traditional faith of the Peruvian people—which, for various reasons, is articulated with their very concept of nation—and has meant that Article 50 of the constitution establishes, as a recognition of its institutional roots, that "[w]ithin an independent and autonomous regime, the state recognizes the Catholic Church as an important element in the historical, cultural and moral formation of Peru, and provides it with full state collaboration."
23 Constitutional Court of Colombia, Decision C-152/03, February 25, 2003.
24 Ibid.
25 Ibid.
26 Article 150, paragraph 15 of the constitution authorizes the Congress of the Republic to decide, by means of a law, "to issue honors to those citizens who have provided a service to the nation."
27 Ibid.
28 Joseph Weiler, *Lautsi: a reply*, 11/1 International Journal of Constitutional Law, 230–33 (2013).
29 Electoral Tribunal of the Federal Judiciary of Mexico, Decision SUP-JRC-604/2007, December 23, 2007.

30 Ibid.
31 Ibid.
32 Ibid.
33 Constitutional Court of Peru, Decision 06111–2009-PA/TC, March 7, 2011.
34 Ibid.
35 Ibid.
36 Ibid.
37 Ibid.
38 Ibid.
39 Roberto Saba, *Laicidad y símbolos religiosos*, Colección de cuadernos "Jorge Carpizo." Para entender y pensar la laicidad, Cuaderno No. 7 (2013).
40 Asociación de los Derechos Civiles (ADC).
41 A circuit court.
42 Supreme Court of Mexico, Amparo Directo en Revisión 502/2007, November 21, 2007.
43 Ibid.
44 J.R. Cossío, *Laicidad del Estado y libertad religiosa: cómo armonizarlas*, 112 Letras Libres, 62 (2008).
45 Ibid., 64.
46 Ibid.
47 Ibid., 65.
48 Constitutional Court of Peru, Decision 895/02–2002-PA/TC, August 19, 2002.
49 Ibid.
50 Ibid.
51 Constitución del Estado Libre Asociado de Puerto Rico (Constitution of the Commonwealth of Puerto Rico), Article 3, March 3, 1952.
52 Supreme Court of Puerto Rico, Decision R-69–306, February 21, 1974.
53 For example, one piece—perhaps one of the most controversial—showed an image of Christ crucified in a US bomber plane.
54 It held, literally, that "the artist belongs to the Club of the Impious, Heretics, Apostates, Blasphemers, Atheists, Pagans, Agnostics and Infidels, in formation." The text of the decision says, literally: "[The plaintiffs] [a]dd that the artist belongs to . . ." That is to say, that there can be no doubt as to what they said in the complaint.
55 High Court of Buenos Aires City, Decision 14194/1, December 27, 2004.
56 Ibid.
57 Ibid.
58 The court noted: "There can be no doubt that one of the facets of artistic activity is its critical dimension. Art is a critical medium in many senses. It is (or could be) critical of customs and habits. Bear in mind, for example, the classic studies of formalist literary theory from the beginning of the last century, developed by artists such as Sholovski, for whom art is a means for breaking with automatized forms of perception (because of that, he refers to Aristotle, for whom, as is outlined, 'art should have a strange, surprising character.' See 'El arte como artificio,' essay included in '*Teoría de los formalistas rusos*,' Siglo XXI editores, 1997, p. 69, edited by Tzvetan Todorov). Art is also critical of deeply-rooted ideas, of beliefs (both of the majority and the minority) and, on another level, of political and social situations. In fact, there are aesthetic theories according to which, when given the painful characteristics of reality, the critical dimension is an unavoidable part of art. It is for that reason that, for example, Adorno quotes the following text by Brecht, which is without a doubt eloquent: What kind of times are they, when / A talk about trees is almost a crime / Because it implies silence about so many horrors? Theodor W. Adorno 'Teoría Estética' Hyspamérica, 1983, p. 60." (High Court of Buenos Aires City, Decision 14194/1, December 27, 2004)."
59 The court further held that: "These last reflections, which have their starting point in Ferrari's sculpture, reveal a particular quality of art: its ambiguity. A piece of art is open to diverse readings, various interpretations. It does not say something clearly determined, but rather it expresses a multiplicity of senses. Because of that, a piece of art does not provoke univocal feelings, it generates a multitude of sensations, impressions and feelings in the viewer, emotions that, at the same time, cannot be separated from cognitive aspects, ideas or thoughts, that are also diverse" (High Court of Buenos Aires City, Decision 14194/1, December 27, 2004).
60 Ibid.

61 Ibid.
62 Ibid.

References

Roberto Blancarte, Los retos de la secularización y de la laicidad en el mundo contemporáneo (2008).

Ernesto Bohoslavsky, *Laicidad y América Latina*, Colección de cuadernos "Jorge Carpizo." Para entender y pensar la laicidad, Cuaderno No. 11 (2013).

José Ramón Cossío, *Laicidad del Estado y libertad religiosa: cómo armonizarlas*, 112 Letras Libres, 62 (2008).

Ronald Dworkin, Taking Rights Seriously (1977).

Leonardo García Jaramillo, *Laicidad y Justicia Constitucional*, Colección de cuadernos "Jorge Carpizo." Para entender y pensar la laicidad, Cuaderno No. 34 (2013).

Roberto Saba, *Laicidad y símbolos religiosos*, Colección de cuadernos "Jorge Carpizo." Para entender y pensar la laicidad, Cuaderno No. 7 (2013).

Further reading

Theodor W. Adorno, Teoría Estética (1980).

Marcelo Alegre, *Laicidad y ateísmo*, Colección de cuadernos "Jorge Carpizo." Para entender y pensar la laicidad, Cuaderno No. 9 (2013).

Jean-François Bayart, *Laicidad e Islam*, Colección de cuadernos "Jorge Carpizo." Para entender y pensar la laicidad, Cuaderno No. 24 (2013).

Daniel Gutiérez-Martínez, *Laicidad y Multiculturalismo*, Colección de cuadernos "Jorge Carpizo." Para entender y pensar la laicidad, Cuaderno No. 19 (2013).

Julieta Lemaitre, *Laicidad y resistencia*, Colección de cuadernos "Jorge Carpizo." Para entender y pensar la laicidad, Cuaderno No. 6 (2013).

Valentina Pazé, *Laicidad y Sociedad*, Colección de cuadernos "Jorge Carpizo." Para entender y pensar la laicidad, Cuaderno No. 27 (2013).

Jesús Rodríguez Zepeda, *Laicidad y discriminación,* Colección de cuadernos "Jorge Carpizo." Para entender y pensar la laicidad, Cuaderno No. 18 (2013).

Alfonso Ruiz Miguel, *Laicidad y Constitución,* Colección de cuadernos "Jorge Carpizo." Para entender y pensar la laicidad, Cuaderno No. 11 (2013).

Laura Saldivia, *Laicidad y diversidad*, Colección de cuadernos "Jorge Carpizo." Para entender y pensar la laicidad, Cuaderno No. 4 (2013).

Tzvetan Todorov (ed.), Teoría de la literatura de los formalistas rusos (1997).

Juan Vaggione, *Laicidad y sexualidad*, Colección de cuadernos "Jorge Carpizo." Para entender y pensar la laicidad, Cuaderno No. 16 (2013).

3 Abortion

Paola Bergallo and Agustina Ramón Michel[*]

Introduction

Latin American estimates of unsafe abortions and of deaths associated to them are still shameful.[1] Restrictive criminal regulations partially account for such estimates. Even if the voluntary termination of a pregnancy is a safe procedure when conducted legally, by 2015 the criminal laws of the region continue to push women to bear the risks of backstreet abortions. For most of the twentieth century, these restrictive abortion laws and policies have remained untouched. Only recently have some changes begun to take place, especially in the context of important developments in the expansion of constitutional and human rights arguments. Against such a backdrop, this chapter offers an overview of the constitutionalization of abortion disputes throughout Latin America. With that goal in mind, this chapter surveys the main decisions adopted by the high courts of Argentina, Bolivia, Colombia, Costa Rica, El Salvador, and Mexico in the last decade.[2]

Starting in the early 2000s, supreme and constitutional courts of different Latin American countries have had the opportunity to assess the constitutionality of criminal laws regulating abortion. The new judgments reflect a gradual shift in the framing of constitutional discussions about reproductive rights. Although Latin American judges have adopted more conservative positions than their counterparts in the Global North, the new decisions do show an increasing maturity in the approach of one of the most sensitive issues for the Catholic cultures of the continent.

To begin with, the constitutionalization of abortion disputes has implied the establishment of limits on the extent to which congresses have been deemed authorized to use criminal law to restrict abortions. Although criminal law continues to be the preferred tool for the regulation of abortion, its use has been constrained through limits hard to imagine in the past. As a result of these limits, in the countries studied in this chapter, abortion arguments no longer revolve around the constitutional and categorical mandate of totally criminalizing abortion, a mandate that used to be interpreted as a default rule in most of the region's past debates. Instead, current conversations on the use of criminal law have been reoriented towards the definition of situations in which punishment is waived, or situations in which abortions are considered legal under what is known as a model of indications. Moreover, most of the region's high courts have understood that constitutional and human rights treaty provisions mandate the adoption of, at least, a model of indications that should contain certain legal grounds for abortion.

Secondly, another trait in the constitutionalization of the region's legal discourse on abortion stems from decisions such as those from Argentina or Colombia, where the constitutions have been found to require not a mere model of formal requirements, but rather a regulatory framework that effectively ensures access to and provision of legal abortion services. In these decisions, Latin American courts have made original contributions regarding the institutional context of the supply of abortions services, as well as the individual duties of healthcare professionals and public officials for ensuring the right to a legal abortion. Finally, the constitutionalization of the criminal treatment of abortion has also yielded more complex judicial arguments about the constitutional status of unborn life and the duty to balance it against increasingly elaborate conceptions of dignity, autonomy, and equality between the sexes.

The rest of the chapter discusses these features of the constitutionalization of abortion debates across Latin America. The first section presents a brief overview of the evolution of the limits established by the courts with regard to the use of criminal law in regulating abortion. In order to illustrate the development of increasing demands for redesigning and implementing current criminal rules in several Latin American countries, this first part of the text systematizes judgments from the courts of Argentina,[3] Bolivia,[4] Colombia,[5] Costa Rica,[6] El Salvador,[7] and Mexico.[8] The second part of the chapter focuses on the diverse characterizations of the duty to protect unborn life adopted in judicial framings of the abortion issue. The third part underscores the diverse uses of dignity, autonomy, and equality applied by the courts in the context of abortion rights arguments. The chapter concludes with a brief review of the main changes experienced in the constitutional framing of abortion across the region.

From the categorical mandate to criminalize abortion to the identification of the institutional dimension of rights

By 2004, 10 years after the agreements reached in Cairo, few constitutional and supreme courts in Latin America had had the chance of ruling on the criminalization of abortion. Moreover, in the rare instances in which judges faced abortion claims, courts issued highly restrictive judgments, following an extended conservative public consensus on the practice. In Mexico, for example, in a decision issued by the Supreme Court in 2002, the justices failed to agree about the legal status of the indications for abortion introduced in 2000 after a reform of the Federal District's criminal code. In that case, the judges were not able to reach a consensus on the status of the indications. The court could not agree on whether the indications for abortion were instances that fell under the *causas de justificación* (justifications), in which case abortions were to be considered legal and thus legally provided for.[9]

A similar situation happened in Colombia, a country that in 1980 eliminated the provisions of the criminal code where abortion was permitted. In spite of its progressive reputation, when the constitutionality of this total ban on abortion was disputed for the case of rape, the Constitutional Court of Colombia was not able to reach an agreement on the constitutional status of certain grounds for abortion.[10] In the case of Argentina, the Supreme Court had dodged the debate on the permission of abortion in cases of anencephalic fetuses. In a lawsuit brought to the court in 2001, the judges authorized the termination of a pregnancy, arguing that, given the delay in the court proceedings, the termination was not an abortion but an "induction of labor."[11] Lastly, another group of courts, headed by the Constitutional Chamber of the Supreme Court of Costa Rica in 2000 and then followed by the highest courts of Argentina and Ecuador, also considered unconstitutional a set of allegedly "abortive" practices, such as the manipulation of embryos in the deployment of assisted human reproduction techniques or the authorization to distribute a particular brand of emergency contraception (the "morning after pill").[12]

In these early judgments, Latin American judges were obsessed with the scope of the constitutional mandate to protect the human person, the definition of the right to life of the unborn, and the alleged duty to protect it after conception. Most of these early decisions on abortion revolved around the parameters for defining the beginning of life. In the decisions of the Costa Rican and Argentinian supreme courts, after recognizing the right to life of the embryo, a right that existed, for the courts, even before implantation, the judgments revealed a categorical conception regarding an absolute mandate to protect life after conception. Moreover, in the rulings of the courts of these countries, references included citation of dubious scientific knowledge and junk science, as well as quotations from papal encyclicals. The judges of both the Argentinian and the Costa Rican supreme courts understood that Article 4.1 of the American Convention on Human Rights, and other rules that explicitly or implicitly protected the right to life in the constitutions, mandated the protection of the right to life through legal rules.[13] As a result, any balancing against other rights or interests in conflict had to be dismissed. At the same time, references to sexual and reproductive rights or gender-based reproductive injustices were completely absent from the judgments.

Starting in 2004, this categorical and simple-minded framing was to experience some changes, especially in the context of a new set of cases discussing the constitutionality of various criminal laws on abortion. Since that year, the high courts of Costa Rica, Colombia, El Salvador, Mexico, Argentina, and Bolivia—in that order—began to adopt approaches that took into account the collision of values emerging from the clash between the right to prenatal life and the rights of women. Courts began to appeal to proportionality tests or the need to balance interests and rights and thus they became the starting point of the new constitutional framing of abortion in several countries. From the decisions in countries with more restrictive rules, such as El Salvador, to those of the progressive Constitutional Court of Colombia that applied a more rigorous proportionality test, all courts were encouraged to apply a balancing test to assess the constitutionality of the various models of criminal regulation of abortion that had been in effect since 2004. Although, for over three decades, courts in North America and Europe had assumed the existence of a conflict of interests and rights and the need to apply a balancing test or proportionality analysis, it was only in 2004 that Latin American judges began to apply such a balancing approach to the conflict regarding the rights or interests posed by the regulation of abortion.

To these very precarious beginnings two other traits were added to the courts' framing of the constitutional debate over abortion in the new generation of decisions which will be studied in the following pages. On the one hand, in the decisions issued by the six courts since 2004 and considered in this chapter, the judges agreed upon the utility of the criminal regulation as a tool to protect unborn life, and they did so without questioning whether criminal law was an effective tool to achieve that goal. Moreover, the judges also agreed that it was the duty of democratic legislators to define the extent of the use of criminal law towards abortion. Therefore, in the six judgments analyzed in the following pages, Latin American courts focused, first, on the definition of the scope of the mandate to protect unborn life, in order to establish, later, what range of discretion was awarded by the constitutions to lawmakers for choosing or rejecting the employment of criminal punishment over abortion.

These shared premises yielded different results in the arguments of the Latin American courts studied in this chapter.[14] This was in part a consequence of the fact that the cases brought to the courts confronted different regulatory frameworks regarding abortion. In Colombia and El Salvador, for instance, the litigants were requesting the adoption of a model of indications for abortion, given the fact that both countries had abandoned such a style of regulation to adopt a total ban on abortion (in the case of Colombia in the late 1970s, and in the case of El Salvador at the end of the 1990s).[15] In other countries, such as Argentina, Bolivia, and Costa Rica, judges confronted longstanding rules which established a model of indications for abortion that had been operating ambiguously, either as *excusas absolutorias* (excuse defense) or *causas de justificación*, and which in practice had led to the total prohibition of abortion.[16] That is, in these countries, the courts were facing a model of indications "on the books," that "in practice" operated as a model of total criminalization. Finally, the Supreme Court of Mexico had to deal with a case in which a conservative person was challenging the constitutionality of the trimester regulation, approved in 2007 by the legislature of Mexico City, which authorized voluntary abortions performed before the twelfth week.

Yet the cases studied in the following pages differ not only in the style and extent of the criminal regulations being challenged, but also in the diversity of the interests represented by the stakeholders challenging the constitutionality of the abortion laws at stake. While some cases involved women objecting to restrictive rules, as in the claims filed in Colombia, El Salvador, Argentina, and Bolivia, on other occasions, such as Mexico City's, the litigation was confronting what was perceived as too liberal regulations.

The increase in the number of high courts' decisions on abortion studied in this chapter clearly reflects the significant activation of the confrontation about abortion rights experienced in the last decade across Latin America. Such an increase also reveals the development of civic organizations and their interest in using courts as a battlefield in which to fight for rights or resist changes, both from liberal and conservative perspectives.[17] In that context of changes, the courts studied here reached different conclusions regarding the constitutionality of abortion regulations. Decisions differed fundamentally on two levels. On one level, courts differed in their interpretation of the extent to which they understood that the legislative branches were mandated or authorized by their constitutions to resort to the criminalization of abortion. On another level, courts also disagreed in their understanding of the constitutional mandate to reduce uncertainties and to warrant access to the type of abortions considered legal under the model of indications.

In the variety of judicial responses given by the courts in these two dimensions of the judicial debate over abortion, it is also possible to observe how women and their rights have finally become key visible actors. This new presence of women in the judicial consideration of the abortion controversy has oscillated, however, between the recognition of their mere presence in the conflict and the understanding that visibility is only the first step on the road to guaranteeing women's rights, which will require important commitments in order to achieve even a minimum degree of implementation. The following paragraphs, therefore, trace the stages of this transformation process regarding the constitutional framing of abortion and exhibit the move from the increased visibility of women towards the recognition of the importance of guaranteeing the supply of abortion services while fighting uncertain regulations and barriers to access.

A minimum demand: women enter the scene, but guaranteeing their rights can wait

The constitution establishes that criminal law will not be used regarding certain types of abortions, but it does not provide a specific body of rules to provide legal certainty to women seeking abortions under those exceptions. This sentence summarizes the views expressed by the supreme courts of Costa Rica and El Salvador while evaluating the constitutionality of criminal abortion laws in their judgments from 2004 and 2007, respectively. Those judgments were announced by judges willing to accept the existence of a conflict between women's rights and the rights of the fetuses, but they were the result of cautious views about the role of judges in establishing constitutional limits on legislative discretion in the use of criminal law on abortion.

In its 2004 decision, the Constitutional Chamber of the Supreme Court of Costa Rica undertook the abstract review of the constitutionality of standards decriminalizing abortion when the health of the woman was at risk. The case was brought to the court by a conservative litigant who objected to the constitutionality of the unequal treatment granted to born and unborn life in a series of private and criminal law rules. With quotes from a judgment of the same chamber that, in 2000, had found assisted reproduction techniques unconstitutional for violating the right to life of embryos, the plaintiff demanded the repeal of the indications for abortion in cases of rape or where the life or health of a woman was compromised.

The Costa Rican judges dismissed the claim and found that:

> (. . .) the concrete variables cannot and should not be considered in the abstract by the Chamber, but should be verified and reported by the relevant courts with jurisdiction to rule—it is neither misguided nor unconstitutional that the legislature has refrained from punishing abortion in cases of risk to the woman's health, if she is going to be seriously injured by the pregnancy to the degree of seriously affecting her dignity as a human being and ultimately her life.[18]

As the foregoing paragraph makes clear, the Costa Rican justices were willing to accept the constitutional status of the model of indications established by the criminal code. Their acknowledgment of the health risk and the dignity of women is a recognition of the role of women when dealing with the abortion issue. However, the justices held that the authorization of an abortion had to be done by a court on a case-by-case basis.

A few years later, the Constitutional Chamber of the Supreme Court of El Salvador had to evaluate an abstract review request filed by two litigants challenging the constitutionality of the lack of exceptions to the criminalization of abortion in the country's new criminal code, approved in 1997. In its decision from November 2007, the Supreme Court of El Salvador dismissed the petition. For these judges, "the legislature has chosen not to establish a model of indications under the belief that the cases that could arise under each of such indications could be treated with the general excuses provided in Article 27 of the criminal code."[19] The generic definition of the circumstances authorizing the defense of necessity and the general excuses from criminalization were sufficient to satisfy the constitutional duty to balance the right to life of unborn persons against the rights of women in the specific situations identified by the plaintiffs in the case.

According to the Salvadoran court, the absence of express grounds authorizing abortion in certain circumstances did not constitute an unconstitutional omission. The provisions of Article 27 of the Salvadoran criminal code contained "exemptions from illegality (*causas de justificación* [justifications]) and exemptions from the personal liability of the perpetrator (*causas de inculpabilidad* [exculpation defense])."[20] The legislature did not fully criminalize or absolutely decriminalize abortion, but the legislature was not obligated to provide clarification on the status of cases in which abortion was justified or exempted from punishment. Moreover, as the "general provisions of criminal law" provided both unspecific grounds of justification as well as exceptions to the criminalization of abortion, the judges did not see any problem in the uncertainty that stemmed from the fact that the legality of supplying abortions for the cases of the indications was not clarified in the legislation.

In this respect it should be taken into account that the Salvadoran judges recognized that there was a partial failure "to regulate beforehand instead of as a result of a criminal proceeding"[21] how to face the controversy over the rights of the woman and the unborn child. In this regard, the court found that:

> . . . the legislature is constitutionally obligated to establish, within legal standards, which state agency has to afford jurisdiction to hear and decide on the situation, the requirements laid out and the conditions under which it will be decided if certain grounds are admissible or not, prior to the criminal prosecution of the conflict. Relying solely on the criminal

system is another failure of a state that focuses only on the effects of social problems and not their causes.[22]

In this 2007 decision, the Salvadoran Constitutional Chamber showed minor concern over the need to regulate when non-punishable abortions should be allowed for. A few years later, however, the judges gave up even this very basic concern. In fact, when, in 2013, the same chamber faced the case of *Beatriz*[23], where a woman was requesting access to an abortion due to the life-threatening risk posed by an anencephalic fetus, the judges overtly failed to consider the claimant's allegations about the uncertainties caused by the lack of medical guidelines regulating cases such as hers, and, thus, denied the abortion in question.

The road towards a model of indications implemented without prior judicial authorization

The constitution demands or permits the regulation of abortion through a model of indications. The indications derive from the understanding that abortions are justified in certain circumstances and, therefore, permitted abortions are authorized by law and do not require prior judicial authorization. The courts of Colombia, Argentina, and Bolivia arrived at this conclusion in a new generation of abortion controversies decided after 2006. In these very moderate and conservative set of judgments, the courts continued to show their main concern about the protection of prenatal life. At the same time, however, women's rights began to gradually occupy some room in the new decisions, a place they had totally lacked in previous judgments on abortion.

In 1979, Colombia was the first country in the region to eliminate the indications for abortion provided in its criminal code. Twenty-five years later and, despite the widespread tolerance for the practice of abortion in the country,[24] "on the books," Colombian law continued to deny explicit exceptions to the criminalization of abortion. Against that legal backdrop, and after having rejected several lawsuits filed in the nineties, the Constitutional Court issued in 2006 its renowned ruling C-355/06.[25] In the judgment, the court recognized an objective interest in the protection of fetal life under the 1991 constitution. However, the court also understood the need to perform a proportionality test that took into consideration the interest in protecting unborn life and the various women's rights that could clash with it, and that came from considerations of equality, autonomy and dignity. Unlike the Salvadoran judges, the Colombian court concluded that the legislature's margin of appreciation regarding the use of criminal law to regulate abortion required providing at least four specific indications for abortion: when there was a risk to the woman's life, or a risk to her physical or mental health, in the case of rape, and when there were malformations "incompatible with life." The judges accepted the need for balancing and applied a test of proportionality that highlighted the obligation to provide grounds of justification for abortion, i.e. situations where the behavior of women and other participants would not be unlawful and therefore would not require prior judicial authorization. In addition, in defining these grounds, the court provided certain minimum demands for the regulation of the supply of abortions in the cases of the indications. The court specified, for instance, that in the case of risk to the mental or physical health of the woman the risk should be confirmed by only one doctor rather than by a committee. Other requirements included the need to previously report the rape in order to access an abortion for that cause, and still others concerned the regulation of conscientious objectors.

The Constitutional Court recognized the conflict between an objective interest in protecting fetal life and the various rights of women, accepted the need for a proportionality test, and excluded from legislative discretion a regulation model that totally banned abortions.[26] The court thus laid out the foundations of a constitutional framing that judges from Argentina and Bolivia were to expand and develop in the course of the following decade.

In the context of *F.A.L.*,[27] a lawsuit decided in March 2012, the Supreme Court of Argentina, for the first time since 1922, considered the constitutionality of the model of indications established in the criminal code. In that case, a teenager who had been raped by her mother's husband approached a court in the province of Chubut seeking authorization to terminate her pregnancy. The case was decided in 2010 in her favor by the supreme court of the province, but the General Public Defender of Minors appealed the decision before the national Supreme Court, arguing that the judgment violated the right to life that the constitution and human rights treaties protected after conception.

After a detailed analysis of both the constitutional and conventional—i.e. pertaining to the American Convention on Human Rights—rules in play, the Argentinian court concluded in *F.A.L.* that the rule of the criminal code that allowed abortion in the case of rape was constitutional and conventional. It was a regulatory option that democratic lawmakers had made within the boundaries of their discretion as defined by the constitution, which did not call for the total criminalization of abortion. Due to the debate that arose because of this "permission," the justices went on to state that all victims of rape, and not only those with a mental disability, could demand a legal abortion.

Unlike their Colombian counterparts, the Argentinian justices chose not to expressly address whether the indications for abortion provided in Article 86 of the criminal code were to be treated as *causas de justificación* [grounds for a justification defense] or *excusas absolutorias* [excuse defense]. However, other references and conclusions of the judgment suggest that their interpretation was that the indications should be considered *causas de justificación* [justification], and, hence, the conduct of the women seeking the abortions and those performing them should be understood as legal. First, the justices emphasized that there was no need for prior judicial authorization in order to perform abortions requested by rape victims. Secondly, they expressly recognized a right to the abortions provided for in Article 86 of the criminal code and urged authorities in the health system to regulate and to ensure access to such legal abortions. Moreover, the Argentinian court clarified that the only requirement to be posed to rape victims as a precondition to accessing a legal abortion was the demand of an affidavit notifying the rape. In this point, the Argentinian court diverged from its Colombian counterpart, which had specifically requested that abortions in the case of rape be performed once evidence of their report had been provided.

The Plurinational Constitutional Court of Bolivia considered a partially similar debate in 2014. In 2008, the constitution of the Plurinational State of Bolivia had incorporated several provisions recognizing the reproductive rights of women. Appealing to these constitutional innovations, Congresswoman Patricia Mansilla Martínez requested the Constitutional Court of Bolivia to adjust various articles of the criminal code which preceded the enactment of the new constitutional text. Congresswoman Mansilla Martínez argued, first, that the new constitution and the international human rights treaties signed by Bolivia demanded that abortion be regulated through a trimester law decriminalizing abortion before the twelfth week, for which it was also necessary to regulate "the conditions of the healthcare system and the health facilities where the abortions were to take place."[28] Secondly, the litigant requested the court to remove special requisites that had become a precondition in order to access non-punishable abortions. She focused, in particular, on the practice of requesting prior judicial authorization to access decriminalized abortions, the need to begin proceedings against the alleged perpetrator in the case of rape, and the threat of punishment for those providing legal abortions. In their extensive judgment, the justices of the Constitutional Court understood that there was a duty to:

> . . . assess whether the criminalization of abortion was an appropriate and necessary tool for protecting life and restoring the balance and harmony that supports the new paradigm of 'good living' [*suma qamaña*].[29]

After tracing the roots of the protection of prenatal life and the treatment of abortion in prior centuries, the court concluded that:

> While it is true that the Supreme Norm [the constitution] guarantees the sexual and reproductive rights of all its citizens, its Article 66 does not establish that reproductive rights include abortion; therefore, the exercise of sexual and reproductive rights does not imply recognition of a right to have an abortion.[30]

Ultimately, the court rejected the constitutional challenge arguing that the plurinational constitution required the legislature to also protect the fetus through criminal law before the twelfth week. In spite of their conclusion, the judges admitted the request to establish certain rules in order to guarantee access to legal abortions and concluded that: a) no prior judicial authorization need be requested in order to provide a legal abortion, and b) no rape report could be demanded from victims seeking access to a legal abortion. In that sense, the justices found that:

> . . . the phrase 'provided that criminal proceedings are initiated' in the first paragraph of Article 266 of the criminal code and the phrase 'judicial authorization where applicable' in the last paragraph of that same article are understood to constitute provisions that are incompatible with the rights to physical, psychological and sexual integrity, the rights not to be tortured, not to suffer cruel, inhumane, degrading or humiliating treatments, the right to physical health and the right to dignity with respect to the free development of personality and empowerment of women enshrined in Articles 15, 18, and 22 of the constitution.[31]

The request for a previous judicial authorization in order to obtain a legal abortion and the demand that criminal proceedings have opened before performing an abortion to rape victims were construed by the Bolivian court as instances of torture and cruel treatment. The Bolivian judges were finally joining their Argentinian and Colombian peers in eliminating the prerequisites to implementing a model of indications for abortion that would begin to gradually imply the actual supply and accessibility of certain abortion services.

Individual and institutional duties resulting from the right to a legal abortion

The judgments discussed in the preceding article laid out the groundwork for a new interpretation of the prerequisites that, according to the courts, regulated abortion in Argentina, Bolivia, or Colombia.[32] Yet the judges also advanced a constitutional reading of abortion that would incorporate a number of central innovations to ensure the practical decriminalization of abortion on several grounds, innovations that show some of the more interesting and creative features of the recent Latin American case law on abortion. A comprehensive review of all the original considerations made in this regard would exceed the scope of this chapter. Therefore, the following paragraphs highlight three important contributions that evidence the courts' central concern regarding the implementation of their decisions.

A first interesting contribution by the Argentinian court was the identification of certain contextual dynamics that were hindering the actual supply of legal abortions. The justices clearly understood that the delay or lack of supply of abortion services in fact resulted in an "implicit total prohibition"[33] and, therefore, in a *contra legem* practice that restricted access to legal abortions. The court also reminded healthcare professionals, as well as national and provincial judicial actors, that the legality principle demanded that a practice that was not prohibited at a national level could not be restricted. At the same time, the justices recognized that there was "a significant degree of misinformation" and a context of "general confusion"[34] regarding the requirements that the health system could demand in order to provide legal abortions. Such confusion revolved around issues like the need to require a judicial authorization, a prerequisite established nowhere in the applicable laws. In addition to these broader contextual references to the operation of the model of indications in action, the court also underscored that the illegal practice of denying non-punishable abortions was "encouraged by health professionals and validated by different judicial players"[35] who requested additional formalities to those established by law. The irregular practices generated by the imposition of these requirements, which were not stipulated by existing rules, and their potential to thwart the right of access to legal abortions, could be interpreted, according to the judges, as an act of institutional violence under the provisions of the "Law for the Integral Protection, Prevention, Punishment and Eradication of Violence against Women in Interpersonal Relationships."[36] For the judges, these practices also had the potential to expose the country to international liability given its duty to fight gender violence arising from different international human rights treaties. Moreover, the court also pointed out the risk of individual criminal, civil, and administrative liabilities that could result from the illegal obstruction to the health services requested by women seeking legal abortions.

A second type of innovation contained in the Argentinian and Colombian cases stems from the clarifications offered by the courts on the institutional responsibilities of different public offices in order to ensure access to legal abortions. In this sense, the Argentinian court emphasized: a) the duty to provide medical and sanitary conditions for the performance of legal abortions; b) the duty to implement and make operational hospital guidelines regulating the supply of those abortions; c) the duty to regulate the exercise of conscientious objection; and d) the duty to implement information campaigns.[37] More specifically, the Colombian court developed a detailed set of standards for regulating the exercise of conscientious objection by medical workers. According to the Constitutional Court:

> (i) Conscientious objection is a fundamental constitutional right that, as every right within a regulatory framework that is open to guaranteeing protection and fostering cultural diversity (Article 1 and Article 7 of the constitution), cannot be exercised in an absolute fashion. (ii) The exercise of the fundamental constitutional right to conscientious objection is in the private sphere, by way of Article 18, a very extensive protection that can only be limited in the event that its implementation interferes with the third parties' exercise of rights.[38]
>
> Conscientious objection is individual, not collective, or institutional, or judicial, or of public officials. Regarding the voluntary termination of pregnancy, it can only be exercised by health professionals directly involved in the process.[39]
>
> Only medical personnel whose role involves direct participation in the intervention aimed at terminating the pregnancy can claim conscientious objection; thus, this is a nonexistent possibility for administrative staff, medical personnel who perform preparatory work only and medical personnel involved in the patient's recovery phase.[40]

Finally, a third type of innovative considerations consisted in underlining the different liabilities that could potentially arise from the lack of supply and access to legal abortions. As we mentioned earlier, the Argentinian court warned public officers and health professionals about potential professional, civil, administrative, and criminal liabilities to which they could be open by impeding access to legal abortions. The Colombian justices went even further when in concrete cases they applied fines for the obstruction of access to the abortions deemed constitutional under judgment C-355/06.

The legislative margin of appreciation neither demands nor excludes a trimester model in the regulation of abortion

Most of the abortion decisions discussed so far have dealt with regulatory frameworks adopting a model of indications where both the constitutional status of the regulation and its implementation were at stake. In deciding such claims, courts have moved slowly from the elementary recognition of the constitutional status of the indications to the specification of certain regulatory and institutional duties required to increase access to legal abortions. Yet, at least in the case of two courts, Latin American judges have also considered the margin that legislative bodies have to establish a model of periods, allowing for abortion on demand in the early stages of pregnancy.

In Decision C-355/06, the Colombian justices evaluated the existence of a constitutional duty to establish a trimester model and they concluded that the margin of legislative appreciation encompassed the capacity to provide for the decriminalization of abortion, authorizing abortion on demand for certain cases. However, the court also understood that this was one of the options available to legislators, who could choose between a model of trimester or indications, depending on their policy goals.[41]

In Mexico, judges also addressed this question, but they did so in the context of an abstract petition ("unconstitutionality action") challenging the constitutionality of the regulation of abortion in Mexico City. In 2007, Mexico City's legislators had amended the criminal code in order to incorporate a periodic regulation decriminalizing first-trimester abortions. The constitutionality of such rules had been immediately challenged in two cases filed by the Attorney General of Mexico and the president of the National Human Rights Commission. For the plaintiffs it was clear that the legislators had stepped outside the rules of the separation of powers by approving a regulation that harmed the right to life of the unborn, discriminated against the male parent and embryos less than three months of age, and infringed the principle of legality.

In a judgment questioned for its minimalist approach, the Mexican justices, as most of their peers in the region, began by clarifying the constitutional mandate to protect the value of life as it was entrenched in the Mexican legal tradition. After that clarification, the justices went on to scrutinize the duties, prohibitions, and powers of democratic lawmakers to criminalize and decriminalize behaviors, and concluded that the challenged rules were within the scope of optional criminalization, and therefore could not be deemed in violation of the constitution. For the justices of the Supreme Court of Mexico:

> [t]he Legislative Assembly of the Federal District has the power to determine, by a majority of its members and through open debate, which behavior should or should not be reproached by criminal law, and in the absence of an express constitutional obligation, it has the duty to weigh the various events, issues and rights that may be in conflict.[42]

As Francisca Pou has noted,[43] in this case the judges missed a valuable opportunity to further develop a constitutional reading of women's rights and reproductive rights as enshrined in the constitution. However, even conceding that the court lost the chance to expand the constitutional interpretation of women's rights, the court's assertion that the legislative margin of appreciation encompassed the option to eliminate the criminalization of abortion in the early stages of pregnancy constituted the most permissive approach to the constitutionalization of abortion across Latin America.

The constitutional status of gestational life

Discussions of the legal status of unborn life have been at the core of most contemporary confrontations regarding abortion. The duty to protect fetal life was at the heart of pioneer decisions such as *Roe v. Wade* or the famous German Supreme Court rulings. In our region, the definition of the legal status of unborn life has also occupied a central place in the drafting of the American Convention on Human Rights as well as in several of the constitutional assemblies held in recent decades. The inter-American human rights system has also participated in the debate on the status of gestational life through two specific rulings on abortion: the opinion of the Inter-American Commission on Human Rights in *Baby Boy*[44] and the recent decision of the Inter-American Court of Human Rights in *Artavia Murillo v. Costa Rica*.[45]

As we have already mentioned, the clarification of the legal status of gestational life has also monopolized domestic constitutional debates in the region's courts. In spite of the recent contributions of certain judgments underscoring women's rights, and a duty to balance potential conflicts, the issue remains at the heart of the interpretive disputes surrounding abortion.

When it comes to the judicial assessment of the legal status of fetal life, it is possible to place the conclusions reached by the courts of Costa Rica and El Salvador, which have recognized the personhood of unborn children, at one end of the spectrum. Other courts, such as the Supreme Court of Mexico and the Constitutional Court of Colombia have understood that unborn life should be considered, respectively, a constitutionally protected right or a constitutional value. Moreover, the justices of the Plurinational Constitutional Court of Bolivia have recognized an imperfect right to life of the unborn. Finally, the Argentinian court has avoided expressly ruling on the status of the unborn but concluded that neither the constitution nor the human rights treaties incorporated to it mandated the total criminalization of abortion as a tool to realize the right to life of the unborn.[46]

The courts of Costa Rica and El Salvador have arrived at the most conservative reading of their constitutional provisions, recognizing prenatal legal personhood and the unborn's right to life. The Costa Rican court arrived at this conclusion through an unsophisticated interpretation of the international human rights instruments and the constitution. For the Costa Rican justices, the law did not distinguish between born and unborn life:

> . . . once conceived, a person is a person and, as such, a living being, who is entitled to protection by law, as demonstrated below. This second conclusion is in line with the rules of international law of human rights in force in Costa Rica.[47]

The Salvadoran court reacted similarly, although with a somewhat higher degree of sophistication. The justices embraced a literal interpretation of the constitutional text, in which Articles 1 and 2 refer to life as a fundamental right guaranteed to "every person," and concluded that those provisions referred to a right recognized to "every human being from the moment of conception."[48] For the court, "the view of the Salvadoran drafters of the constitution implied that there was a human life from the moment of conception," and, therefore, "the state and other subjects were obliged to guarantee life from that moment."[49] This determination of the status of prenatal life did not prevent the court from accepting the need to address the issue, as mentioned above.

In the judgment of the Constitutional Court of Bolivia, the reasoning about the legal status of unborn life dealt with different dimensions of its constitutional protection. First, the court devoted several paragraphs to the description of the different conceptions of life and death of indigenous nations and peoples, from a perspective of the plurality not only of cultures but also of lives (as expressed in the preamble to the constitution). For centuries, life has been viewed by the majority of the country's indigenous communities as part of the cosmos and *pacha* (Mother Earth), i.e. not as an isolated event, but as a creation of *pacha*. Hence, humanity is connected to other living beings and deities. According to the court, most indigenous and peasant communities identify with a dynamic culture of life, where nothing is irreparable and abortion is seen as part of the cycle of life.[50]

Then, the court set aside these philosophical and cultural considerations and went on to focus on the dimension of international human rights law and domestic regulations and the treatment granted by them to unborn life. In doing so, the judgment quoted several provisions on the right to life from the Inter-American Convention and reproduced a central passage of the opinion in the *Baby Boy* case, concluding that: "Article 4.1 of the convention cannot be read as a recognition of an absolute right to life from conception."[51] The ruling also pointed out that the country's constitutional assembly had discussed two proposals on the right to life and had chosen one that omitted to specify that life begun "from conception."

At this point, however, the court started to recede and explicitly concluded that the mandate to protect human life is gradual: the more it seems like a cell, the less protection it will have, but it will never be fully unprotected. To the extent that it develops and begins to resemble a human being, the protection of the right to life increases. In other words, the fetus is constitutionally and legally protected, but to a lesser extent than a person born alive (an imperfect right to life). This legal determination allowed the court to dismiss the challenge of unconstitutionality of criminal laws punishing abortion generically, while still answering positively the request to improve the conditions of access to abortion in cases of rape.

The Constitutional Court of Colombia, on the other hand, relied on an extensive menu of arguments including references to comparative law, interpretations of international human rights law, and conceptual developments surrounding the evolution of intrauterine life, to interpret the constitution of 1991 as granting life the status of a fundamental value and right. This generic protection of life means that the state has an obligation to protect life in both a positive and negative sense. The court distinguished between life as constitutionally protected property and the right to life as a subjective right of a fundamental nature. In its reading of the constitution and international human rights instruments—construed as constituting a *bloque de constitutionalidad* (constitutional bloc) in Colombia—the court did not recognize a constitutional right to life of the unborn. This conclusion, according to the court, was compatible with recognizing that the state has an obligation to protect unborn life, precisely because life in the Colombian constitutional system is—in addition to a right—a fundamental value. In this way, the court argued that the protection of unborn life does not have the same degree and intensity as the protection of the human person, but both must be protected. On the other hand, the court saw a constitutional duty to apply a balancing test, and thus asked if the absolute protection of unborn life (through the absolute criminalization of abortion) was constitutional in light of other constitutional rights (of women). The court answered its question by recognizing that it could not be alleged that the right to life of the unborn or the duty to take legislative action by the state was absolute and concluded that the constitution requires a model of indications to regulate abortion.[52]

Lastly, the Supreme Court of Mexico found that life is a constitutionally protected right. While this implies a duty to protect unborn life, according to the court, it does not necessarily translate into an explicit mandate obliging states to criminalize abortion; instead, there is a discretionary margin for defining the type and scope of the regulation of abortion.

In all the cases cited, references to international human rights law occupied a prominent place in the judicial reasoning concerning the definition of the legal protection of gestational life. However, not all the courts arrived at the same conclusion or shared the same reading of the central rule in dispute: Article 4.1 of the American Convention on Human Rights. In November 2012, the Inter-American Court extensively ruled on the interpretation of this article in the case of *Artavia Murillo v. Costa Rica*, in which a group of couples objected to the decision of the Constitutional Chamber of the Supreme Court of Costa Rica, which in 2000 had considered unconstitutional the decree regulating in vitro fertilization in the country. In its judgment, the judges of the Inter-American Court devoted lengthy paragraphs to offering an interpretation of the scope of Article 4.1 that is likely to impact future domestic decisions on abortion.

The status of intrauterine life has a decisive influence in shaping our understanding of the constitutional status of abortion regulations. As suggested by Alejandro Madrazo in describing the conflict over abortion as a narrative:

> the status of prenatal life determines who is the main character of such narrative and, in doing so, it determines how the situation is framed, which is the conflict at stake, which are the acceptable answers, and over all, who are the opposing players in the story. Basically, all the elements upon which the narrative is built.[53]

Even if this has often been the case in Latin American confrontations over abortion, it is feasible to imagine a world in which the definition of the legal status of unborn life, including the recognition of a right to life of the unborn, would not be the factor fatally defining constitutional answers on abortion.[54]

Dignity, autonomy, and equality as tools to constrain the use of criminal law

The decisions studied in the prior sections also exhibit an incipient but incremental development in the consideration of the rights of women in constitutional deliberations across Latin America. Although this consideration has reached different degrees of complexity, that women and their rights have become visible in the constitutional arguments of the region's courts is definitively a sign of progress. In this section we emphasize in particular the presence of dignity, privacy, and equality, three rights and values that have occupied a place of increasing relevance in the treatment of abortion by Latin American high courts. Although it would exceed the analysis we can offer in these pages, it should be noted that the decisions studied here have also included references to the right to health, while making certain progress in the articulation of the concept of sexual and reproductive rights, a realm in which the debate is still lacking argumentative quality.

References to dignity have been prominent in recent constitutional arguments recognizing women's rights as well as protecting unborn life. Privacy, however, has still not been accepted as a substantial part of the argumentative toolkit in the constitutional field of abortion, but it has appeared in some marginal references. Moreover, equality-based arguments have not yet deployed their full potential, despite equality being one of the most frequently invoked values in Latin American constitutional debates. However, with varying degrees of presence, the three notions can be currently identified as part of the set of rights-based arguments of the constitutional narrative on abortion in the region.

Dignity has been an ambivalent ideal in the field of abortion rights. As already mentioned, this concept has been used from very different perspectives, including some conflicting ones.[55] In fact, local and international human rights forums on reproductive rights have invoked dignity both to rank the status of prenatal life as well as to defend the rights of women. For some authors, such as Reva Siegel, it is precisely this open texture, its permeability to future constructions of meaning, which makes it an interesting notion.[56]

Dignity has considerable abstract weight in most constitutional systems of the Western tradition. At least four human rights conventions contain explicit references to human dignity.[57] Based on these instruments, both the universal human rights system and the inter-American system have interpreted dignity in their legal analysis of reproductive rights and abortion. National courts have also recurrently appealed to the argument of dignity.[58]

Among the examined rulings, Colombian judgment C-355/06 is the one that most overwhelmingly and densely resorts to the idea of dignity.[59] It is likely that, in contemporary comparative constitutional jurisprudence, this is the decision on abortion that best develops the analysis of this value. For this court, dignity must be understood as a limit to the discretionary margins of the legislator. The absolute criminalization of abortion violates the dignity of women, for even in the worst situations the legislator would be imposing on women the role of reproductive instrument. The idea of supererogatory burdens as conceptual implications of dignity appear in the analysis of proportionality made by the court in considering the position of women in view of certain events (the danger to the health of the pregnant woman or the case of rape). According to the court, in such cases "it is clearly excessive to demand sacrificing a developed life to protect a life in development . . ."[60]

This reading of dignity as an anti-instrumentalist principle can also be seen in the discourse of the Supreme Court of Argentina:

> from human dignity . . . stems the principle that persons are ends in themselves and their utilitarian treatment is prohibited . . . In fact, the attempt to demand from all other victims of sexual crimes to carry a pregnancy to term . . . is, clearly, disproportionate, and contrary to the postulate . . . that prohibits demanding that people make sacrifices, for the benefit of others or for the greater good, of immeasurable magnitude.[61]

In the judgments of Colombia and Argentina, the dignity argument also appears embodied as the right to freedom from torture and mistreatment, which is based on the decision of the United Nations Committee on Human Rights in the case of *K.L. v. Peru*, which found that the lack of regulation of abortion in case of anencephaly violated several articles of the Covenant on Civil and Political Rights.[62]

The judges of Bolivia also appealed to this dignity-based argument. To declare unconstitutional the requirement of filing criminal proceedings for accessing abortion in cases of rape, the court relied especially on the right not to be tortured, or suffer cruel, inhuman, or degrading treatment, the right to physical health, and the right to dignity and its components, the free development of personality and autonomy of women. Moreover, besides this classic formulation, the Bolivian court also used dignity in a slightly different way. It indicated that this principle, combined with plurality, precludes the imposition of "a certain type of morality or a conception of good and bad," because that should be determined by each person.[63]

In a similar vein, though occupying a marginal place in the argumentation, dignity has also been employed by the Constitutional Court of Colombia as regards the right to autonomy—understood as the free development of personality—which prohibits "assigning women stigmatized gender roles or deliberately subjecting them to moral suffering."[64]

Lastly, the ambiguity of the possible uses of dignity seems clear in the courts of El Salvador and Costa Rica, which resorted to this notion both as a conservative argument to confirm the constitutionality of restrictive regimes and to justify the existence of grounds for exemption from punishment. The court of El Salvador noted the incidence of the dignity of the human person as a constitutional value and the recognition of personhood (expressed in the preamble and Article 1) in the controversy over abortion. In fact, the court combined a concept centered on fetal personality with dignity to stress that "the human person is not only the object and purpose of any state activity, but also the legitimizing element of that activity."[65] At the same time, the decision outlines the use of dignity as a limit to the exploitation of women. The justices considered that:

> . . . the law may not require heroic behavior or, in any case, cannot impose a decision when in extreme situations someone prefers to perform an unlawful act before sacrificing their own life, physical integrity, or other personal rights.[66]

In this case, the appeal to the dignity argument was used to justify the requirements for abortion. However, as in the famous judgments of the German Supreme Court, the principle of dignity also seems to translate into positive state obligations, a kind of duty of care towards the most vulnerable. According to the court:

> [human dignity has the] ability to determine the orientation of the goals or tasks of the state towards institutional policies . . . and to secure the help of public authorities against attacks or actions from entities of that nature or private actors.[67]

From this perspective, the court interpreted that resorting to "the criminal punishment of certain conducts" is ultimately constitutional when ensuring human dignity. However, the court later made an effort to weigh in and claimed that "the drafters of the constitution clearly intended to extend state protection to prenatal life;" lawmakers have the duty "to also regulate other interests at stake, to which the pregnant woman is entitled."[68] This interpretative line allowed the court to conclude that the existing framework, encompassing a general rule of criminalization and requirements for abortion (as a necessity defense exempting from, or diminishing, liability), is consistent with the duty of lawmakers to enhance the rights "both of the mother and the unborn."

Finally, of all the judgments analyzed, that of Costa Rica is the one that most clearly makes a conservative use of the argument of dignity, which operates mainly to justify criminalization. Both the Costa Rican judgment and the Salvadoran judgment assimilate the lives of the woman and the fetus and recognize that both have "equal" dignity. These uses amply illustrate the elasticity of the argument, and the tensions, as noted by Siegel, are deeply associated with the definition of dignity when it comes to gender.[69]

From these different approaches, we can note, first, the effort by the region's courts to incorporate dignity into the consideration of "women's" issues. These advances are not achieved, of course, without ambiguities or resistance, as reflected by the judgments of Costa Rica and El Salvador. However, it is possible to envision a redefinition of the dominant framing of the concept of dignity that has achieved more conceptual and legal richness by their applications on abortion. As we have seen, it is a concept that has been associated with physical and mental integrity, the right to freedom from torture and ill-treatment, and the principle of non-instrumentalization. Although with regards to this last point there is still a need to address all the implications of embracing a consideration of dignity as non-instrumentalization, some progress has been made. One might question to what extent and in what ways a model of restrictions fails to instrumentalize women who, without fitting the frame for abortion as currently defined, do not wish to carry their pregnancies to term. At the same time, it is also noteworthy that the references to more traditional dimensions of dignity appeal to its most negative aspects and ignore its affirmative consequences (in terms of duties to protect the comprehensive health and wellbeing of women and of state obligations to improve their life conditions).[70]

Advances achieved in the treatment of dignity contrast with the inertia observed, instead, in appeals to autonomy, or one of its formulations, privacy. The high courts, including even the most progressive courts, have been less likely to engage with this value. In fact, of the six judgments analyzed here, only the Colombian and Mexican courts made references to autonomy and privacy.

In the judgment of the Constitutional Court of Colombia, autonomy appears as reproductive autonomy in relation to motherhood and the free development of personality. The court defines individual autonomy as "the vital area composed of matters which concern only the individual" and that "takes on the character of a constitutional principle that binds public authorities, which are forbidden to interfere,"[71] thus, according to the court, making a preference for the unborn would mean denying her ethical condition, reducing her to an object.

On the other hand, the Mexican court, which had the opportunity to lay the constitutional foundations of the most liberal rule in the region, did not provide a strong argument based on autonomy. In general, the court's individual opinions that addressed the topic used the privacy argument to criticize the alternative criminalization of abortion, but not to make an affirmative point about liberalization. Some individual opinions, however, deserve attention for their consideration of this value. One of the dissenting opinions, for example, offers a broad reading of privacy that covers not only the physical space in which privacy normally operates (intimacy) but also intrusions in this area reserved for private life (privacy in the broadest sense). Although it makes no advances in the formulation of life plans, self-referential behavior, and other notions classically associated with autonomy, it is a valuable opinion because it tackles what others have eluded. In that sense, the justice looks at several privacy issues related to abortion and concludes that:

> the right to privacy of women is violated when the state forces others to denounce or expose the abortion, while also results in a state of vulnerability, as fear of an accusation leads to the avoidance of safe medical services in cases of complications or other effects resulting from an illegal abortion. The scope of the right to privacy of women also reflects acquired rights recognizing the autonomy and control of sexuality, even in cases when they have a partner.[72]

The same phenomenon that prevents the autonomy argument from prevailing probably had an impact on the conservative approach of some individual opinions with respect to the more specific right to the body in exceptional cases in which judges alluded to it. The court of El Salvador explicitly denied that there is a right to the body and sustained that such a claim was constitutionally prohibited given the recognition of the human person. In other courts, silence has been the norm, and only marginally have the courts of Colombia and Mexico taken into account women's liberty to decide over their bodies.

Unlike autonomy, which has been a more elusive value in Latin American jurisprudence, equality, in the traditional sense, and understood as equity, is a more deeply rooted ideal in the region's constitutional tradition. Perhaps this explains its incipient yet wider role in the examined judgments. Although references to equality did not receive the same attention as the right to life, in a gradual and selective sense courts that favored a certain liberalization of abortion have given equality increasing room. This framing by the courts constitutes a promising contribution as it gives the discussion on abortion greater constitutional transcendence.

The Constitutional Court of Colombia paved the way for women to achieve legal equality. For that, it relied on the 1991 constitution and new provisions on equal opportunities, affirmative action and the prohibition of discrimination against women. In fact, it is one of the few courts that referred to gender equality. However, the court did not develop the argument further; instead, it limited itself to referring to the Convention on the Elimination of All Forms of Discrimination against Women to emphasize that the laws criminalizing health interventions particularly affecting women are discriminatory and violate the obligation of states to respect internationally recognized rights.

The most original and abundant judgment addressing equality was that of the Plurinational Constitutional Court of Bolivia. The court incorporated strong references about sexism, patriarchy, and colonization that were absent in the rest of the region's jurisprudence. These ideas were also reinforced with allusions to the commitments of the 2009 constitution reform on gender equality, social justice, and quality of life. Moreover, the court devoted a special section, "State reconstruction based on paradigms of equality: gender and patriarchalization," in which sociological considerations are made of the inequality between men and women to later stress the constitutional commitments assumed to retrace those structures. Among these commitments, the court also emphasized that, with the new constitution, gender equality had become a constitutional value (Article 8 of the constitution) and therefore should guide state performance and goals (Article 9 of the constitution). It is clear, then, that although the ruling dismissed several claims of unconstitutionality, favoring abortion only as permitted under criminal law, the judgment was structured under a paradigm of gender equality incorporating the material and historical dimension of inequality.

Of course, from a more critical point of view, and considering the liberalizing power of equality-based arguments when strongly embraced, the development achieved by the constitutional discourse of the region may be considered even more limited and uneven. From this critical view, the more progressive courts still find it strikingly difficult to point conclusively to the criminalization of abortion as a form of gender-based discrimination to account for the burden of unwanted pregnancy in its physical and social dimension, and to articulate the idea of equality in difference.

Also, as with the arguments based on dignity, equality arguments have been aided by conservative claims. That was the case in Costa Rica, where the plaintiff was demanding a violation of the duty of equal treatment between the protection of unborn life and the born person. Also, the plaintiffs in Mexico claimed the right of men to participate in the decision to terminate the pregnancy.

What is also curious is the absence of arguments that combine gender with socioeconomic status, especially when one considers that the impact of unsafe abortion lies more strongly in women with fewer economic resources. Part of these argumentative inhibitions is structurally associated with the difficulties of establishing an equal right to freedom of women, in relation to pregnancy and motherhood, in a legal tradition built on the male experience.

The most interesting case to highlight the difficulties of courts in dealing with the idea of "equality in difference" is offered by the judgment from El Salvador, which denied that there had been a violation of the right to equality. The plaintiffs alleged that the failure to regulate the indications included as one of the grounds for excluding criminal responsibility constituted a violation of the equality of women because they were in an entirely different factual situation as that of any other person facing one of the grounds for excluding criminal responsibility regulated in the general regime. The court dismissed this argument very expeditiously. The justices ruled that the plaintiffs had offered no *tertium comparationis* (basis for comparison) of sufficient significance to justify an ad hoc or specific regulation. The court held that:

> a factual or purely descriptive element is insufficient, if the legal significance of the differences or similarities alleged is not demonstrated, especially in relation to the purpose and the basis for comparison, for concluding that the distinction is arbitrary or, as in this case, that the legislative equation lacks objective and reasonable grounds.[73]

In the case of Costa Rica, the plaintiff also supported the claim with conservative demands as to the right to equality. The plaintiff claimed that the difference in punishment between murder and abortion, among other rules, violated the principle of equality by differentiating between born and unborn life. This distinction, it was argued, had become unconstitutional since the judgment of the court in 2000 that recognized the legal personhood of the fetus.[74] The court did not admit this argument, but neither did it advance its reasoning on gender equality enough to reject it. The court denied directly that the 2000 judgment had changed the legal status of individuals in Costa Rica's legal system: the fetus was considered a person before that judgment, because the criminal treatment of abortion stemmed precisely from the notion that abortion violated the right to human life. Secondly, the court held that the legislature could consider circumstances other than the quality of personhood of anyone suffering the action, and thus establish different sanctions, causes of exclusion of liability, etc. Thirdly—and here the court appears to deviate from its more conservative script—the court found that the legislature was free to address criminal matters, as long as the constitutional system and human rights were respected.[75]

In the case of Mexico, two major objections, in addition to the issue of life, were made against the law of the Federal District that the Supreme Court had to resolve, which also brought up the issue of equality. The objections revolved around the participation of men in a woman's decision to have an abortion (gender equality) and the lack of specific regulation for teenagers (equality—or inequality—by reason of age). The court deemed that the case revolved around provisions in the law that the legislature had the power to define. Among other arguments, the court appealed to the differences between women and men to dismiss the claim, offering one of the few paragraphs in all the examined judgments where the equality in difference was successfully dealt with. The court said:

> The continuation of an unwanted pregnancy has distinctly permanent and profound consequences for women . . . and it is this asymmetrical involvement in the life plan that provides the basis for differentiated treatment . . . The involvement of women and men is different not simply because . . . there are consequences of the unwanted pregnancy that only fall on the woman who experiences it, but also because, although there are other burdens that could potentially be assumed by the male participants, its guarantee by the legal

> system is imperfect. In fact, the future possibility of opening a judicial process oriented at a certain person being recognized as the parent of a minor, or at contributing financially to supporting their needs is too uncertain and imperfect to cancel the original asymmetry between the position of the potential father and mother . . .[76]

Conclusion

The judgments studied here are episodes of the judicialization process and are part of a broader dispute around the regulation of abortion in Latin America. In the last decade, courts have played a typically counter-majoritarian role in a region where abortion is still a marginal and unfriendly right for the majority, or at least for most policymakers. The process of constitutionalization described in this chapter has been rudimentary. Moreover, the process shows some traits typical of the context against which the law and legal disputes operate in the region.

Like several European courts, Latin American courts have moved to accept the need to balance a set of interests and competing rights. These judgments also reveal the development of a rights-based approach, locating the classical arguments on abortion in international human rights law, the obsessions of the legal and Catholic culture for the sanctity of embryonic life, and a broader list of rights and values.

In that context, the balancing approach performed by the region's courts has begun to offer a perspective for playing down the dramatic nature of the conflict over abortion. This has created a promise of moderation, negotiation, and conciliation to positions that were formerly staged as deeply antagonistic. In addition to its potential benefits and philosophical bases, the balancing approach replaced categorical attitudes that used to restrict the opportunities for increasing the legal supply of abortions, while resulting in a good foundation for justifying judicial decisions, inspiring the search, at least, of reasonable solutions that recognize and optimize the rights and interests at stake, offering an alternative to the all-or-nothing game. Although some of these expectations seem, in some sense, to have been fulfilled in the development of judicial discourse observed in the judgments discussed in this chapter, it is also true that the balancing exercise put in place by the courts has been deficient and incomplete. Among the most significant deficiencies of the balancing approach, the most noteworthy are, first, the difficulty for judges in critically examining the suitability of criminal law. Far from identifying the persistent inefficiency of criminalization, the courts have naturalized its role in regulating abortion. In fact, constitutional debates have increased their sophistication in terms of the scope of the requirements or exceptions that justify not applying criminal punishment, but the option of abandoning punitive sanctions has not been seriously discussed by the region's courts.

A second clear deficit in the balancing approach applied by the courts resides in their inability to address and rule on how unwanted pregnancies can affect women. As illustrated in the section on rights-based arguments, even today it is extremely difficult for judges to identify and address the impact of unwanted pregnancies as a violation of women's autonomy and a breach of the duty of equal treatment by the state.

Although the studied cases are not the last word or even a "settlement" in the constitutional debate on abortion, they constitute significant contributions for the definition of public policies and for the increasing access to legal abortions. The impact of each of the judgments examined has differed according to the extent to which they confirmed or changed existing regulations on abortion at the time of the decision. In the cases of Argentina and Mexico, the decisions contributed to consolidating the liberalization process that had been opened before the introduction of new legislation embracing a trimester model or the development of a procedural shift toward the guaranteed provision of legal abortions. In other cases, the judgments clearly involved significant constitutional changes, such as in Colombia, where the created indications served to inaugurate new safe abortion policies. In the context of Bolivia, however, the contribution is more likely to have been intermediate: although the court did not introduce new grounds, it eliminated excessive requirements for accessing abortions in cases of rape. Lastly, in El Salvador and Costa Rica, the courts contributed to reinforcing restrictions while moderating the previous discourse by recognizing conflicting rights.

Questions

a What are the most emblematic characteristics of the process of constitutionalization of abortion in Latin America?

b The text makes several references to the outstanding role that international human rights law has occupied in the assessment of the criminal laws on abortion in Latin America. What transformations can be observed in the use of that source in the different judgments examined in the chapter?

c In the judgments discussed by the authors it is possible to see how Latin American judges have naturalized the role of criminal law for regulating abortion. What arguments have the courts of the Global North deployed in order to justify the repeal of criminal sanctions?

d How do arguments about dignity, autonomy and equality developed in relation to abortion compare to the same values when applied to other conflicts studied in the rest of the book?

e Identify differences in the balancing exercises deployed by the judgments of the courts studied in this chapter.

Notes

* Translated into English by Paula Arturo and revised by the authors.

1 Elisabeth Ahman and Iqbal H. Shah, *New estimates and trends regarding unsafe abortion mortality*, 115/2 International Journal of Gynecology and Obstetrics, 121–6 (2011); Unsafe abortion: global and regional estimates of the incidence of unsafe abortion and associated mortality in 2008 (2011).

2 In 2012, the Supreme Court of Brazil also issued an important judgment on abortion in a claim involving the diagnosis of anencephaly. However, in its decision, issued in 2012, the Supreme Court of Brazil avoided judging the claim as a challenge to the criminal regulation on abortion and instead ruled on the case as if it revolved around the induction of labor. Given its avoidance of the abortion debate, we have decided to exclude the Brazilian decision from this chapter. See Luis Roberto Barroso, *Bringing Abortion into the Brazilian Legal Debate*, in Abortion law in transnational perspective: cases and controversies (Rebecca Cook, Joanna N. Erdman, and Bernard M. Dickens eds, 2014).

3 Supreme Court of Argentina, case of "F.A.L.s/ Medida autosatisfactiva," March 12, 2012.

4 Constitutional Plurinational Court of Bolivia, Decision 0206/2014, February 5, 2014.

5 Constitutional Court of Colombia, Decision C-355/06, May 10, 2006.

6 Supreme Court of Costa Rica, Constitutional Chamber, Decision 02792–04, March 17, 2004.

7 Supreme Court of El Salvador, Decision 18/98, November 20, 2007.

8 Supreme Court of Mexico, Decisions 146/2007 and 147/2007, August 28, 2008.

9 Francisca Pou Giménez, *El aborto en México: el debate en la Suprema Corte sobre la normativa del Distrito Federal*, 5 Anuario de Derechos Humanos, 137–52 (2009).

10 Constitutional Court of Colombia, Decision C-133/94, March 17, 1994; Decision C-033/97, January 30, 1997; and Decision C-647/01, June 20, 2001. Luisa Cabal, Mónica Roa, and Julieta Lemaitre, Cuerpo y Derecho: legislación y jurisprudencia en América Latina (2001).

11 Rebecca Cook, Martín Hevia, Joanna N. Erdman, and Bernard M. Dickens, *Prenatal management of anencephaly*, 102/3 International Journal of Gynecology and Obstetrics, 304–8 (2008).

12 Between 2000 and 2010, several high courts' decisions addressed the constitutionality of the authorization to sell and distribute emergency contraception across Latin America. The Argentinian, Chilean, and Peruvian supreme courts are among the courts that adopted the most restrictive approach to the issue. Maria Alejandra Cardenas, *Banning Emergency Contraception in Latin America: Constitutional Courts Granting an Absolute Right to Life to the Zygote*, 6/3 HOUMBOLT AMERICAN COMPARATIVE LAW REVIEW (2009).

13 Verónica Undurraga, *Proportionality in the Constitutional Review of Abortion Law*, in ABORTION LAW IN TRANSNATIONAL PERSPECTIVE: CASES AND CONTROVERSIES (Rebecca Cook, Joanna N. Erdman, and Bernard M. Dickens eds, 2014).

14 These three shared basic aspects in the approach of the debate included: a) the need to apply a balancing or proportionality test to the assessment of the constitutionality of abortion; b) the assumption of the usefulness of criminal law; and c) the agreement about the central role of the democratic legislator in determining the scope of the use of criminal law over abortion.

15 In Colombia, grounds for abortion had been removed from the criminal code in 1979. In El Salvador, in 1997, the criminal code was reformed and the new norm and code did not contain the grounds in the previous code that dated back to 1973.

16 Paola Bergallo, *The Struggle Against Informal Rules on Abortion*, in ABORTION LAW IN TRANSNATIONAL PERSPECTIVE: CASES AND CONTROVERSIES (Rebecca Cook, Joanna N. Erdman, and Bernard M. Dickens eds, 2014).

17 Camila Gianella-Malca and Siri Gloppen, *Access denied. Abortion rights in Latin America*, 13/1 CHR. MICHELSEN INSTITUTE BRIEF (2014).

18 Supreme Court of Costa Rica, Constitutional Chamber, Decision 02792–04, March 17, 2004, point VII.

19 Supreme Court of Justice of El Salvador, Constitutional Chamber, Decision 18/98, November 20, 2007, Point II, paragraph 3.

20 Ibid., Point II, paragraph 4.

21 Ibid., Point VI, paragraph 3.

22 Ibid. Point VI, paragraph 8. See also: "That is why the legislature is free to consider the possibility of regulating, within the Salvadoran legal system, whether a clash between the rights of the mother and the unborn child is resolved prior to any action detrimental to the rights of the latter and is not subject to prosecution in criminal trial; that is, legislation that establishes that the alleged conflict can be recognized and adjudicated outside of criminal proceedings and without the action that will affect one or more rights having taken place." (Ibid., Point VI, paragraph 10).

23 Supreme Court of Salvador, Constitutional Chamber, B./ 2013. Decision 310–2013, May 28, 2013.

24 ISABEL JARAMILLO SIERRA AND TATIANA ALFONSO SIERRA, MUJERES, CORTES Y MEDIOS: LA REFORMA JUDICIAL DEL ABORTO (2008).

25 Constitutional Court of Colombia, Decision C-355/06, May 10, 2006.

26 Verónica Undurraga and Rebecca Cook, *Constitutional Incorporation of International and Comparative Human Rights Law: the Colombian Court Decision C-355/2006*, in CONSTITUTING EQUALITY: GENDER EQUALITY AND COMPARATIVE CONSTITUTIONAL RIGHTS (Susan Hoffman Williams ed., 2009).

27 Supreme Court of Argentina, case of "F.A.L. s/ medida autosatisfactiva," March 13, 2012 (F. 259. XLVI).

28 Plurinational Constitutional Court of Bolivia, Decision 0206/2014, February 5, 2014, Point I.1.1, paragraph 17.

29 Ibid., Point III.8.7, paragraph 6.

30 Ibid., Point III.8.7, paragraph 7. The court also understood that the performance of all types of abortions at any stage of the embryo's development was not constitutionally permissible and the duty to comply with the constitutional protection of the right to life of an implanted embryo was a sufficient cause for the legislative body to resort to all kinds of policies needed for their protection, policies that necessarily involve the use of criminal law in the later stages embryonic development.

31 Ibid., Point III.8.8, paragraph 10.

32 In the case of Colombia, the initial C-355/06 decision was supplemented by several other judgments where the Constitutional Court considered different barriers in the supply of legal abortions. In this regard, see Decisions T-988/07, T-209/08, T-946/08, T-388/09, T-585/10, T-636/11, and T-841/11.

33 Supreme Court of Argentina, case of "F.A.L. s/ medida autosatisfactiva," March 13, 2012 (F. 259. XLVI).

34 Ibid.

35 Ibid.

36 Argentinian Law 26,485.
37 Supreme Court of Argentina, case of "F.A.L. s/ medida autosatisfactiva," March 13, 2012 (F. 259. XLVI).
38 Constitutional Court of Colombia, Decision T-388/09, May 28, 2009.
39 Constitutional Court of Colombia, Decision C-355/06, May 10, 2006; Decision T-209/08, February 28, 2008; Decision T-388/09, May 28, 2009.
40 Constitutional Court of Colombia, Decision T-388/09.
41 Constitutional Court of Colombia, Decision C-355/06, May 10, 2006.
42 Supreme Court of Mexico, Decisions 146/2007 and 147/2007, August 28, 2008, 180.
43 Francisca Pou Giménez, *El aborto en México: el debate en la Suprema Corte sobre la normativa del Distrito Federal*, 5 Anuario de Derechos Humanos, 137–52 (2009).
44 Inter-American Commission on Human Rights, case 2141 "Baby Boy," March 6, 1981, 25/OEA/ser. L./V./II.54, available at www.wcl.american.edu/pub/humright/digest/Inter-American/english/annual/1980_81/res2381.html.
45 Inter-American Court of Human Rights, case of "Artavia Murillo et al. (In Vitro Fertilization) v. Costa Rica," November 28, 2012, CDH-12.361/177. See also Fernando Zegers-Hochschild, Bernard Dickens, and Sandra Dughman-Manzur, *Human Rights to In Vitro Fertilization*, 123/1 International Journal of Gynecology and Obstetrics, 86–9 (2013).
46 As noted, most Argentinian constitutionalism has made no appeal to the formula involving the state's interest in intrauterine life in *Roe v. Wade* and upheld in *Planned Parenthood of Southeastern Pa. v. Casey*, and *Gonzales v. Carhart*, as a basis for their decisions.
47 Supreme Court of Costa Rica, Constitutional Chamber, Decision 02792–04, March 17, 2004, Point V.
48 Supreme Court of El Salvador, Decision 18/98, November 20, 2007.
49 Ibid.
50 Constitutional Plurinational Court of Bolivia, Decision 0206/2014, February 5, 2014.
51 Ibid.
52 We must remember that most of the rulings analyzed above are prior to *Artavia Murillo v. Costa Rica*.
53 Alejandro Madrazo, *Narratives of Prenatal Personhood in Abortion Law*, in Abortion law in transnational perspective: cases and controversies (Rebecca Cook, Joanna N. Erdman, and Bernard M. Dickens eds, 2014).
54 In 1975, and then in 1992, the German Constitutional Court revised the legislation partially decriminalizing abortion, approved by the Federal Parliament. Both times, the court found that the state had a constitutional obligation to protect the fetus against the claims of the pregnant woman. It supported this on a triad: the right to intrauterine life, life as a supreme value derived from human dignity, and the duty (not just the interest) of the state to protect it. In the first judgment (1975), most German judges ruled that the state could only fulfill this obligation by using criminal punishment. Dissenting judges, on the other hand, held that criminal law was an unnecessary and inappropriate way to regulate abortion. Years later, in a second ruling, the majority adopted the view of the dissent in 1975 and concluded that the state was entitled to protect fetal life through different mechanisms, and amongst these mechanisms some were more efficient than others. One mechanism for doing so was to ensure women sufficient social support from the government.
55 Reva Siegel, *Dignity and Sexuality: Claims on Dignity in Transnational Debates Over Abortion and Same-Sex Marriage*, 10/2 *I•CON*, 355–79 (2012), available at http://ssrn.com/abstract=2137596.
56 Reva Siegel, *The Constitutionalization of Abortion*, in The Oxford Handbook of Comparative Constitutional Law (Michel Rosenfeld and Andras Sajo eds) (2012).
57 The American Declaration of the Rights and Duties of Man, the Universal Declaration of Human Rights, the American Convention on Human Rights, and the Inter-American Convention on the Prevention, Punishment and Eradication of Violence Against Women ("Convention of Belem Do Para").
58 Constitutionalism on abortion in Germany is characterized by assigning a central place to dignity, associating it to "life." This allowed the Constitutional Court first to oppose the liberalization of abortion, and then to recognize certain rights of women and to justify restrictions (namely counseling and a mandatory waiting time).
59 Reva Siegel, *Dignity and Sexuality: Claims on Dignity in Transnational Debates Over Abortion and Same-Sex Marriage*, 10/2 *I•CON*, 355–79 (2012), available at http://ssrn.com/abstract=2137596.
60 Constitutional Court of Colombia, Decision C-355/06, May 10, 2006, Point 10.1.
61 Supreme Court of Argentina, case of "F.A.L. s/ medida autosatisfactiva," Point 16.

62 United Nations Human Rights Committee, "K.N.L.H. v. Peru," Communication No. 1153/2003, UN Document CCPR/C/85/D/1153/2003, October 24, 2005.
63 Constitutional Plurinational Court of Bolivia, Decision 0206/2014, Point III.8.7, paragraph 11.
64 Constitutional Court of Colombia, Decision C-355/06, May 10, 2006, Court Considerations and Rationale (VI), paragraph 8.1.
65 Supreme Court of El Salvador, Decision 18/98, Point IV.1.A., paragraph 5.
66 Ibid., Point V.2.A., paragraph 7.
67 Ibid., Point IV.1.A., paragraph 12.
68 Salvadoran lawmakers are thus facing a mandate "to legislate and promote the content of rights established in the Constitution, both of the mother and the unborn."
69 Reva Siegel, *Dignity and Sexuality: Claims on Dignity in Transnational Debates Over Abortion and Same-Sex Marriage*, 10/2 *I•CON*, 355–79 (2012), available at http://ssrn.com/abstract=2137596.
70 Rosalind Dixon and Martha Nussbaum, *Abortion, Dignity and a Capabilities Approach*, in Feminist Constitutionalism (Beverly Baines, Daphne Barak-Erez, and Tsvi Kahana eds, 2011).
71 Constitutional Court of Colombia, Decision C-355/06, May 10, 2006, Point 8.2.
72 Supreme Court of Mexico, Decisions 146/2007 and 147/2007, Point b.6.2, paragraph 5.
73 Supreme Court of El Salvador, Decision 18/98, Point 5.3, paragraph 3.
74 Supreme Court of Costa Rica, Constitutional Chamber, Decision 2306–2000, March 15, 2000.
75 There was no clarification of those limits by the lawmakers:

> ". . . *First*, the Chamber admits that, although in both cases they are human beings, it is also true that they are in distinct stages of development, not only from the medical point of view, but also from a social perspective . . . *Second,* in the case of the unborn person in particular there is an absolute dependence on a second person . . . this entails a new differentiating circumstance . . . the fundamental rights of the mother thus need to be taken into account, which is different in the case of homicides, where that specific relationship with other people and their fundamental rights is lacking. *Third*, in favor of the validity of the differentiation in the severity of the sanction, the fact that it responds as it does, as indicated, to a particular perception, experience and sentiment not only of our society but all those that make up our cultural environment, as may be seen through the mere review of the way in which other Latin American and European countries have legislated on this, always opting for a decrease in state criminal reaction . . . it is noteworthy that, because of its relativistic nature, it could never trump other arguments nor supplant other principles that the Chamber has recognized as the foundation of our legal system and—in particular—could not prevail over the respect and consideration of human dignity, for example."

Supreme Court of Costa Rica, Decision 02792–2004.
76 Supreme Court of Mexico, Decisions 146/2007 and 147/2007, 188.

References

Ahman, Elisabeth and Iqbal H. Shah, *New estimates and trends regarding unsafe abortion mortality*, 115/2 International Journal of Gynecology and Obstetrics, 121–6 (2011).

Ahman, Elisabeth and Iqbal H. Shah, Unsafe abortion: global and regional estimates of the incidence of unsafe abortion and associated mortality in 2008 (2011).

Paola Bergallo, *The Struggle Against Informal Rules on Abortion*, in Abortion law in transnational perspective: cases and controversies (Rebecca Cook, Joanna N. Erdman, and Bernard M. Dickens eds, 2014).

Luisa Cabal, Mónica Roa, and Julieta Lemaitre, Cuerpo y Derecho: legislación y jurisprudencia en América Latina (2001).

Maria Alejandra Cardenas, *Banning Emergency Contraception in Latin America: Constitutional Courts Granting an Absolute Right to Life to the Zygote*, 6/3 Houmbolt American Comparative Law Review (2009).

Rebecca Cook, Martín Hevia, Joanna N. Erdman, and Bernard M. Dickens, *Prenatal management of anencephaly*, 102/3 International Journal of Gynecology and Obstetrics, 304–8 (2008).

Rosalind Dixon and Martha Nussbaum, *Abortion, Dignity and a Capabilities Approach* in FEMINIST CONSTITUTIONALISM (Beverly Baines, Daphne Barak-Erez, and Tsvi Kahana eds, 2011).

Camila Gianella-Malca and Siri Gloppen, *Access denied. Abortion rights in Latin America*, 13/1 CHR. MICHELSEN INSTITUTE BRIEF (2014).

Isabel Jaramillo Sierra and Tatiana Alfonso Sierra, Mujeres, cortes y medios: La reforma judicial del aborto (2008).

Alejandro Madrazo, *Narratives of Prenatal Personhood in Abortion Law*, in ABORTION LAW IN TRANSNATIONAL PERSPECTIVE: CASES AND CONTROVERSIES (Rebecca Cook, Joanna N. Erdman, and Bernard M. Dickens eds, 2014).

Francisca Pou Giménez, *El aborto en México: el debate en la Suprema Corte sobre la normativa del Distrito Federal*, 5 ANUARIO DE DERECHOS HUMANOS, 137–52 (2009).

Reva Siegel, *Dignity and Sexuality: Claims on Dignity in Transnational Debates Over Abortion and Same-Sex Marriage*, 10/2 *I•CON*, 355–79 (2012), available at http://ssrn.com/abstract=2137596.

Reva Siegel, *The Constitutionalization of Abortion*, in THE OXFORD HANDBOOK OF COMPARATIVE CONSTITUTIONAL LAW (Michel Rosenfeld and Andras Sajo eds) (2012).

Verónica Undurraga, *Proportionality in the Constitutional Review of Abortion Law*, in ABORTION LAW IN TRANSNATIONAL PERSPECTIVE: CASES AND CONTROVERSIES (Rebecca Cook, Joanna N. Erdman, and Bernard M. Dickens eds, 2014).

Verónica Undurraga and Rebecca Cook, *Constitutional Incorporation of International and Comparative Human Rights Law: the Colombian Court Decision C-355/2006*, in CONSTITUTING EQUALITY: GENDER EQUALITY AND COMPARATIVE CONSTITUTIONAL RIGHTS (Susan Hoffman Williams ed., 2009).

Fernando Zegers-Hochschild, Bernard Dickens, and Sandra Dughman-Manzur, *Human Rights to In Vitro Fertilization*, 123/1 International Journal of Gynecology and Obstetrics, 86–9 (2013).

Further reading

Luis Roberto Barroso, *Bringing Abortion into the Brazilian Legal Debate*, in ABORTION LAW IN TRANSNATIONAL PERSPECTIVE: CASES AND CONTROVERSIES (Rebecca Cook, Joanna N. Erdman, and Bernard M. Dickens eds, 2014).

Rebecca Cook, Joanna N. Erdman, and Bernard M. Dickens, ABORTION LAW IN TRANSNATIONAL PERSPECTIVE: CASES AND CONTROVERSIES (2014).

Rachel Rebouché, *Comparative Pragmatism*, 72/1 MARYLAND LAW REVIEW, 85–155 (2012).

Ruth Rubio-Marin, *Legal Transfer of Women and Fetuses: A Trip from German to Portuguese Abortion Constitutionalism*, in ORDER FROM TRANSFER: COMPARATIVE CONSTITUTIONAL DESIGN AND LEGAL CULTURE (Günter Frankenberg ed., 2013).

4 LGBTI rights

Camila Gianella and Bruce M. Wilson

Introduction

Given that Latin America is a region known for its profoundly entrenched homophobia, machismo, and patriarchy, and for the wholesale marginalization of lesbian, gay, bisexual, transsexual, and intersex (LGBTI) people, it is surprising that it is now the region that contains one-quarter of the world's countries where same-sex marriage has been legalized.[1] In spite of a well-organized conservative opposition and weak popular support, LGBTI rights have made major advances in many Latin American countries. These developments, though, have been uneven across the region, ranging from criminalization of homosexual acts in some countries to full legal equality, including same-sex marriage and adoption, in others. This chapter examines the role of courts in moving that agenda forward in some countries even where popular support remains low, and also illuminates the legal and political strategies used to hamper that expansion in others. Although it is beyond the scope of this chapter, it needs to be acknowledged that even in the countries where LGBTI people are well-served and protected by assertive courts, if they are also members of ethnic minorities, such as indigenous or Afro-Latin American populations, or other minorities, such as transsexuals, they are in practice likely to be sometimes, or even routinely, denied these same rights.[2]

Because the role of Latin American superior courts in protecting LGBTI people's rights has been so diverse across the region, we focus on three case studies—Costa Rica, Colombia, and the Inter-American Court of Human Rights—to shed some light on how courts have behaved and their impact on the lives of LGBTI people. The first two cases, Costa Rica and Colombia, are puzzling because they were among the earliest adopters of strong protections for LGBTI people but have yet to fully realize complete legal equality, including marriage equality. These cases illustrate the fissures, limits, and complexity of using easily accessible litigation arenas and strategies when popular opinion lags far behind judicial decisions.[3] This gap between rights claims and public support for those claims has allowed socially conservative, frequently religious, anti-LGBTI groups and politicians to block or hinder the writing of pro-LGBTI laws or decisions and has been used to justify legal strategies designed to impede judicial or legislative decisions advancing LGBTI rights.

Our third case study examines the increasing relevance of an international judicial body, the Inter-American Court of Human Rights, and its sister institution, the Inter-American Commission on Human Rights, to recognize, advance, and protect LGBTI rights across the region. These two human rights bodies belong to the Organization of American States and have a long history of playing a central role in the protection of human rights in the region. Until recently, the Inter-American Court of Human Rights dealt with few LGBTI cases, but it has begun to actively address LGBTI rights issues. We pay special attention to the 2012 *Atala Riffo and Daughters v. Chile* case, the Inter-American Court of Human Rights's first case dealing with LGBTI rights. Including an analysis of the Inter American Commission and Court is not fortuitous because almost every Latin American country is under the jurisdiction of the Inter-American Commission and Court, and the 2012 case has already been used in a LGBTI case in Mexico.

Costa Rica

Costa Rica, one of the oldest, most stable, and best-functioning democracies in the Americas, passed a constitutional amendment (Law 7128, passed August 18, 1989)[4] that revised Sections 10, 48, 105, and 128 of the 1949 constitution,[5] adding a new, seven-member Constitutional Chamber ("Sala Constitucional" or "Fourth Chamber") to the existing three chambers of the Supreme Court. During the congressional debate on the creation of the new chamber of the Supreme Court, it was argued that there was no demonstrated need for such a constitutional chamber.[6] The Fourth Chamber was designed to be open and easily accessible for all *amparo* and *habeas corpus* claimants and to decide all cases involving questions concerning constitutionality.[7] Any individual (including non-citizens) in Costa Rica can file a case directly with the court, 24 hours a day, seven days a week, without legal counsel or filing fees, and with few limits on standing or other legal formalities.[8]

Against all expectations, Costa Ricans use the new chamber to animate Section 27, the "freedom of petition, both collectively and individually, against any public official or official entity and the right to a speedy response,"[9] resulting in a rapid growth in its caseload from less than 1,400 cases in its first full year of operation (1990) to over 10,000 cases per year by the early 2000s and 15,000 by 2005. Its caseload appears to have peaked at approximately 17,000 cases per year in 2009 before settling between 14,000 and 15,000 per year since 2010. In its first 25 years, the Constitutional Chamber received more than 200,000 cases, of which over 90 percent have been writs of *amparo* that have forced the chamber to address nearly every part of the constitution.[10, 11, 12]

Fourth Chamber magistrate Fernando Cruz Castro argues that the creation of the Fourth Chamber transformed the Costa Rican constitution from a "document of formal reference having little consequence . . . into a living body of law with actual application to all levels of Costa Rican society."[13] The chamber quickly became an assertive accountability agent, reversing the pre-1989 Supreme Court deferential behavior of exercising "constitutional control with excessive timidity."[14] The magistrate's words are supported by the types of cases the chamber decided from its very earliest days and its willingness to rule in favor of the poorest and most marginalized members of society even against the state or powerful individuals.[15]

LGBTI rights and the courts

Before the creation of the Constitutional Chamber no LGBTI rights cases were filed with Costa Rica's superior court and the legislative assembly enacted very few pro-LGBTI laws, with the notable exception of decriminalizing homosexual behavior in 1971. The other major law affecting LGBTI people was a 1976 amendment to Law 5476, family code (*código de familia*), that explicitly prohibited same-sex marriage in Costa Rica. The scant attention given to LGBTI issues by these branches of government illustrates the lack of available political or judicial structures that these marginalized, poorly organized people could use to protect their rights. The new chamber of the Supreme Court, though, for the first time created a legal opportunity structure that allowed many marginalized, politically powerless members of society, including the weakly organized LGBTI community, to seek protection for their rights.[16]

Some selected cases illustrate the extent to which LGBTI people have sought the Fourth Chamber's power to protect their constitutional rights, which were historically routinely ignored and/or trampled on by the courts, politicians, state employees, and employers.[17] The impunity with which police regularly and routinely harassed gay people until the mid-1990s[18] was facilitated by a supreme court that had little history of protecting individual rights and a population that was distinctly hostile to gays.[19] Even once the chamber had begun to recognize and actively decide in favor of LGBTI rights claims, these cases were not always successful, and in the case of Same Sex Marriage (SSM) in 2006,[20] the litigation provoked a severe backlash from conservative religious forces in the country.

We start with two related and instructive cases concerning people living with HIV/AIDS (PLWA) seeking judicial help to access medications denied them by the state-funded and operated healthcare system, the Costa Rican Social Security Agency (CCSS: "Caja Costarricense de Seguro Social"). Although this is not strictly a case about LGBTI rights, at the time of the first HIV/AIDS case in 1992 homophobia[21] was rampant and HIV/AIDS was generally viewed as a disease that affected only gay people, which likely compounded their difficulties in accessing medications and other treatment. State-employed doctors regularly refused to treat PLWA and many families disowned any of their relatives diagnosed as HIV+; as a result, many PLWA refused to acknowledge their medical condition publicly: "given the choice of death or admitting they had AIDS, time and time again, they chose death."[22]

In 1992 a case was filed by the nascent Association Against AIDS ("Asociación de Lucha contra el SIDA") demanding that the Fourth Chamber override the CCSS's refusal to provide antiretroviral medications to PLWA. The court, though, unanimously accepted the technical, medical, and financial rationale of the CCSS, decided against the PLWA, and argued:

> The writ of *amparo* in this case was filed against the defendant's refusal to purchase the drug AZT to treat AIDS patients. However, from both oral argument and the documents attached to the case it can be gathered that a scientific report from the defendant's Pharmacotherapy Department concluded against that possibility. First, it is stated that the studies of the drug in question are inconclusive and, to date, it cannot be claimed that it leads to the patient's full recovery. Also, a number of side effects have been detected, which may even worsen the patient's health. Second, a financial element should also be taken into account: the cost of the drug would involve a huge sacrifice for the health system, which does not have a budget of its own for such an undertaking. If the system were to purchase the necessary drugs and equipment for these patients, why not do the same with other people who are gravely or terminally ill? The Chamber considers that this aspect cannot be overlooked—there are certain diseases for which there is still no budget to cope with. From this perspective, and however hard as this may seem, demanding that the social security agency disregard certain programs to assist AIDS patients is unreasonable, especially if, as this Chamber accepts, the scientific criteria that was presented to the Chamber indicates that AZT does not result in the patients' total recovery, but only in some extension of life in a deteriorated fashion. Finally, it should be noted that the right to petition is not violated if a request to the administration is not responded to positively, it is only so when the administration does not attend to the request, something which did not happen in this case. Therefore, the writ must be dismissed.[23]

In the 1992 decision the court did not consider the PLWA's right to health or the discrimination inherent in the CCSS's decision, rather it accepted the CCSS's technical argument that AZT was not a cure for HIV/AIDS and its financial argument that the drug was too expensive for the state-funded healthcare system to pay for without harming the treatment of other patients in the system.

Five years later a second, very similar, case, demanding the CCSS provide and pay for access to antiretrovirals for HIV/AIDS patients, was filed. In the intervening five years, the composition of the court had changed with the retirement of three magistrates and the addition of their replacements, but four magistrates who voted against the 1992 claim for access to state-funded antiretrovirals by PLWA remained on the bench. The court's 1997 decision, though, was a complete reversal of its position in the 1992 decision: this time, the unanimous vote was to require the CCSS to provide and fund the requested medications. What changed over the five years was a gradual development of the Fourth Chamber's health rights jurisprudence; the Fourth Chamber now recognized a very broad fundamental right to health:[24]

> In a state of law, the right to life, and in consequence the right to health, receives particular protection. Any economic criterion that pretends to annul the exercise of such rights must cede in importance . . . because without the right to life all of the other rights are useless . . . Of what use are all other rights and guarantees, the institutions and programs, the advantages and benefits of our system of liberties, if even one person cannot count on having the rights to health and life guaranteed?[25]

And the court was now less concerned with the financial implications of its decisions forcing the CCSS to pay for the medications that it claimed were too expensive:

> [I]f it is necessary to put the problem in the cold light of financial imperatives, this Chamber believes that it would be no less appropriate to ask ourselves how many millions of *colones* [local currency] are wasted because ill persons have no possibility of reintegrating themselves into the labor force and contributing, even if in a very small way, to the national wealth. If we did an accounting of these costs and all of those associated [with their care], it seems reasonable to postulate that the country loses more in direct and indirect costs due to the state of incapacity of those who are prostrated by a disease, which alternatively could be invested providing treatment that would permit them to return to a productive life.[26]

This particular decision laid the foundation for many subsequent successful health rights cases in Costa Rica including access to specific expensive medications initially denied by the CCSS, among them Gaucher type 1 disease and preventive treatment for pneumococcus for everyone over 65 years of age.[27]

The rest of the discussion of Costa Rican LGBTI rights litigation covered in this section pivots on the questions of discrimination and equal treatment of LGBTI people under the law. Many *amparos* filed at the Fourth Chamber against public or private actors' anti-LGBTI discrimination failed due to the difficulty of demonstrating that the actions were motivated by animus toward LGBTI people. Other litigation, though, was more successful, including the question of conjugal visits for gay prisoners. These cases help to illustrate both how the question of equality and non-discrimination has been handled by the court and the fluidity of the court's jurisprudence on issues affecting LGBTI people, and reveal the willingness of the

Fourth Chamber to protect the rights of one of the most marginalized vulnerable groups of people: prisoners who are gay.

An *amparo* filed in 2007 challenged the anti-LGBTI discrimination of Section 66 of the Technical Penitentiary Regulations ("Reglamento Técnico Penitenciario") that guaranteed all prisoners the right to conjugal visits, but only if the visitor is "of a sex opposite to the inmates'." The case, though, was archived when the plaintiff failed to follow up on the court's questions, which automatically left the discriminatory regulation in force.[28] The following year the public defender, Natalia Gamboa Sánchez, filed a separate case of unconstitutionality against the same regulation and received a positive, if split, decision (four to three) in 2011.[29] The court's majority sided with the Procuradora General, Ana Lorena Brenes, who argued that "there are no objective and fair reasons to discriminate against gay prisoners, using only sexual preference as the parameter.[30] In declaring the regulation unconstitutional, the court dealt with the substance of the claim and argued:

> This Chamber has long recognized that a fundamental legal principle in the country's constitution is the respect for the dignity of every human being and, consequently, the absolute prohibition of any discrimination against that dignity. But what does this principle mean? In simple words, it means giving equal treatment to equals and unequal treatment to those who are not equal, so it does not violate the constitution to recognize differences between persons or groups of people, provided that there is a reasonable and objective basis for the difference. Therefore, human dignity cannot be violated through legal norms that do not respect the inalienable right of every person to diversity, as is the case with the rules challenged in this action, which establish a ban that is contrary to human dignity without an objective justification. The ban is based on criteria regarding sexual orientation that unlawfully discriminates against those who have preferences that are different from those of the majority, whose rights or interests in no way are affected by those people's free expression of their liberties. Considering that the rule is intended to allow inmates to have contact with the outside world in order to exercise their sexual freedom, the difference in treatment is not justified, since inmates with a sexual preference for people of their same sex are in an identical factual situation as prisoners with a heterosexual orientation. This differentiation is contrary both to the right to equality and to the right of inmates to communicate with the outside world through conjugal visits. Based on the previous reasons, this Chamber believes that the language of Article 66 of the Technical Regulations of the Prison System, 'who is of a sex opposite to the inmates,' clearly violates Section 33 of the Constitution, since it restricts the right of sexual self-determination of homosexual inmates. Consequently, this Chamber grants this action, canceling the rule's phrase indicated in this judgment.[31]

A minority voted against gay prisoners' rights to the same conjugal visits as their heterosexual peers and referenced the frequently cited 1993 decision that forcibly argued that some discrimination is constitutional:

> The principle of equality contained in Section 33 of the constitution does not imply that in all cases equal treatment should be recognized regardless of potential differences of legal significance that may exist; or if it is the same, that not every inequality necessarily constitutes discrimination. Equality, as this Chamber has stated, is only violated when the inequality has no objective and reasonable justification. In addition, the justification of the act deemed as discriminatory must be assessed in relation to its purpose and effects, so

> that there should be necessarily a reasonable relationship of proportionality between the means employed and the aim itself. That is to say, equality must be understood according to the circumstances of each case in which it is invoked, so that the universal application of the law does not prohibit giving different solutions to different situations—as different treatment. All this means that equality before the law cannot be constructed as material equality or real and effective economic equality.[32]

The court returned to this judicial rationale concerning the conditions under which discrimination and unequal treatment under the law were not unconstitutional for many other cases on LGBTI rights, including two of the most contentious contemporary cases: same-sex marriage and the limits on majorities curtailing the rights of unpopular minorities in a democracy.

Same-sex marriage case and referendum on same-sex unions

The final two cases concern same-sex legal unions and both illustrate the limits of how far the Fourth Chamber is willing to go to protect the rights of unpopular minorities such as LGBTI people and reveal what the court sees as limits on its own actions in a democratic state. The first case began in 2003 when Yashin Castrillo, a lawyer, ignored the advice of gay rights organizations and filed a case challenging the constitutionality of Section 14, subsection 6, of the family code ("*código familia*"), which was amended in 1976 to explicitly prohibit same-sex marriage. Castrillo argued that the family code contravened the principles of liberty and equality contained in Articles 28 and 33 of the constitution. But after public hearings on the case and almost three years, the court delivered a five-to-two split decision. The court's majority argued that Section 14, subsection 6, of the family code, which explicitly prohibited same-sex marriage, was constitutional.[33]

The court returned to its previous decisions[34] where it had established that "equality is only violated when the inequality has no objective and reasonable justification" and explicated a long, rambling history of Western civilization's definition of marriage from Roman and Greek times to the present day. The court also appeared to cherry-pick jurisprudence from other countries' superior courts and international tribunals to bolster its decision against marriage equality for LGBTI people. Much of the recent legal development that had resulted in the legalization of same-sex marriage in Europe and the Americas was largely ignored. The court's majority quoted the frequently cited 1993 "equality" decision[35] that is cited above in the section concerning gay prisoners' conjugal visitation rights.

Another consideration for the court concerned the role of the family as delineated in the constitution. The family code was not discriminatory against lesbians and gays, the court argued, because the original intent of the constitution's writers was to give special status to the institution of the family: ". . . We believe that the family, and more precisely the family organized around the institution of marriage (an ideal within a Catholic country), is the fundamental unit of society, and must receive the special protection from the state . . ."[36] And this was reflected in Articles 51 and 52 of the constitution:

> Article 51. The family, as a natural element and foundation of society, has a right to special protection from the state. The mother, the child, the elder, and the helplessly sick will equally have a right to that protection.
> Article 52. Marriage is the essential basis of the family and rests on the equality of the rights of spouses.

The court then argued:

> Consequently, the claim that in this context the challenged rule should be declared unconstitutional is contrary to the provisions of the original constituent assembly. While this Chamber is aware that two people of the same sex have the possibility to maintain a sentimental relationship that our legal order does not ban, the term marriage as a legal, anthropological, and religious concept is exclusively reserved to monogamous heterosexual unions, and thus has been developed by all regulations regarding family relationships. This has been well recognized not only by the original constituent assembly, as explained above, but also by legislation and several instruments of international law.[37]

The court's minority accepted the historical origins of marriage, but argued that the Constituent Assembly met at a time when the Catholic Church was very powerful and that society has changed in the 50 years since it wrote the constitution. Magistrate Vargas Benavides argued:

> I believe that in this particular case the supervening unconstitutionality of the contested provision has taken place, since its meaning, originally in line with the Constitution's meaning at the time the provision was enacted, is now contrary to the evolved sense of the constitution due to social reality and progress towards a society that is both egalitarian and respectful of human dignity. Currently, gay couples not only need a sparing official recognition under the notion that sexual preferences are exercised in the most intimate sphere, which cannot be reached by the legislator. They also need the state's active intervention to remove all legal barriers that continue to exist and that prevent them from being treated equally. It is not enough that the homosexual minority is not explicitly persecuted anymore to conclude that it is no longer subject to discrimination. In addition, legal systems must evolve and respond to current needs and realities, adapting themselves to the most elementary principles that protect the human being as such. It is insufficient just to note that 'sociology,' 'most anthropologists', or 'religion' can be said to be against such marriages, not only because of the vagueness and imprecision of these sources, but also because a progressive interpretation of our constitution and of the international instruments on human rights ratified by Costa Rica does not allow to exclude the homosexual minority of the institution of marriage, as will be discussed below.[38]

Following the court's 2006 decision against same-sex marriage, a bill was submitted to Congress to create a civil unions law for same-sex couples, to afford lesbians and gays the same legal protection and property rights as married couples (without calling it "marriage"), but the two events sparked a religious conservative backlash against LGBTI rights by blocking the bill's progress and initiating a national referendum to ban same-sex unions. In 2008 the Supreme Elections Tribunal ("Tribunal Supremo de Elecciones") approved the process of collecting signatures of five percent of the electorate to authorize the referendum. By July 2010, the 135,000 signatures required to initiate the referendum were collected and certified by the Supreme Elections Tribunal, and the referendum was scheduled on December 5, 2010.

The Fourth Chamber 2010 decision on the unconstitutionality of the same-sex marriage referendum followed many of the same legal arguments raised in the 2006 same-sex marriage decision concerning liberty and equality.[39] The two justices who voted that the referendum was constitutional, Justices Castillo and Armijo Sancho, had different objections to the majority decision. Armijo Sancho's objection concerned the separation of powers rather than a consideration of individual rights. He stated:

> The mere admission of this writ has uprooted the constitutional design of the Supreme Electoral Tribunal and substantially modifies the scope of its constitutional duty to organize, manage, monitor, scrutinize and declare the results of the referendum process, which now, according to the majority, can both be challenged by a writ of *amparo* and therefore reviewed by the Constitutional Chamber. This Chamber shall then have to ultimately adjudicate conflicts related to the organization, management, monitoring, scrutinizing and declaration of the results of referenda processes which, according to the majority's new criteria, are of a legislative nature. This, I think, is a radical self-allocation of powers by the part of the Constitutional Chamber that cannot be adopted in this way.[40]

Justices Cruz and Calzada both voted with the majority against the referendum, but added separate notes amplifying their explanations; Justice Cruz, for example, agreed with the majority, but added

> The decision submitted to a referendum impacts on the development of a minority's fundamental rights, thus representing a mechanism of exclusion based on an eminently quantitative criterion.[41]

These LGBTI cases in Costa Rica reveal a maturing jurisprudence of the Fourth Chamber that is not necessarily related to the membership of the bench, but to changing realities in Costa Rica and in international jurisprudence. They also reflect the significance of the ease of access to the court even for marginalized groups to successfully enforce many of their rights, particularly in cases where the rights demanded fail to attract the attention and ire of conservative, politically organized religious groups.

Colombia

This section begins by outlining the characteristics of the legal system in which litigation takes place, and by explaining the factors that shape the litigants' opportunity structure, and then introduces the development of jurisprudence regarding LGBTI rights in Colombia. In 1991, Colombia adopted a new constitution that included major conceptual and structural innovations and contributed to the rise in judicial interventions in the field of discrimination and equality. The new constitution addressed the fundamental right to equality. Section 13 states that all persons are born free and equal before the law, and, consequently, shall be given the same protection and treatment by authorities, and enjoy the same freedoms, rights, and opportunities without any discrimination on the grounds of sex, race, national or family origin, language, religion, or political opinion. The constitution also recognizes the right to full and free personal development (Section 16).

The 1991 constitution includes a mechanism for the protection of fundamental constitutional rights, called *acción de tutela* (hereinafter *tutela*), similar in scope to Costa Rica's *recurso de amparo*. This allows any citizen to demand immediate protection of his or her constitutional rights.[42] The Constitutional Court was established "as a specialized tribunal overseeing a new 'constitutional jurisdiction,' which extended to all Colombian judges."[43]

The *tutela* was conceived as a fast and accessible tool for the enforcement of fundamental rights. According to the law, petitioners do not require a lawyer to submit a *tutela*, and unless the *tutela* is reviewed or appealed, it must be ruled on within 10 days. These characteristics have undoubtedly contributed to the popularity of the use of the *tutela*. In the first full year of operation, 8,060 *tutelas* were submitted; by 2005, the annual number reached 221,348, and 454,500 by 2013. It is estimated that currently one *tutela* is sought every minute.[44]

Even though there is no record of the exact number of *tutelas* to defend the rights of LGBTI people, the rapid growth and high total number of *tutelas* show a similar pattern to Costa Rica, where the use of litigation to protect individual constitutional rights became routine. The accessibility of the Colombian judicial system has allowed the development of jurisprudence in key issues without a strong institutional support of deep-pocketed social movements, organizations, or political allies. Some lawyers and organizations, though, have played an important role participating in many of the cases of LGBTI rights litigation. These actors, including the lawyer Germán Humberto Rincón Perfetti and institutions such as Colombia Diversa and Dejusticia, have developed an important legal expertise that has aided the litigation of Colombian LGBTI people's rights.

As in other countries, some of the first litigated LGBTI rights cases concerned issues of discrimination and the right to free development of personality, which includes sexual orientation. The significance of these cases is not a minor one. These were litigated in a context where, despite the legality of homosexuality, homosexuality (perceived or real) was still used to sanction people, discharge them from jobs, or expel them from educational institutions.

In some of its earliest decisions, the court stated that homosexuality cannot be a factor of social discrimination:[45] "[h]omosexuals cannot be discriminated against because of their status as such. The fact that their sexual behavior is not the same as that of the population does not justify unequal treatment."[46]

With this type of argument the court made it clear that being part of a minority does not provide a justification for discrimination, and that societies must respect minorities even if they do not follow the behavior of the majority. This was made apparent in decision T-101/98 against the Institute Ginebra–La Salle school, which had expelled two pupils for being homosexual. The court found that the discrimination went against the students' fundamental rights to free development of personality and education.

However, the court's stated position in these rulings left room for some legal discrimination against homosexuals. For the court, the "condition of homosexuality" can be explicit and shown in public, as long as "public behavior does not harm the interests of others or become a stumbling block, especially during childhood and adolescence."[47] This implies a moral view where homosexuality is perceived as going against social mores and thus the public expression of homosexuality could violate the rights of others. The court also distanced itself from treating homosexuals as equal to heterosexuals and referred to homosexuality as a "reprehensible behavior."[48] This view of homosexuality helped to inform the earliest rulings regarding LGBTI couples' right to adoption.

The court's understanding of homosexuality and consequently of the boundaries of discrimination changed over time, gradually becoming more progressive and wider. In Decision C-481/98, a case denouncing discrimination against school teachers based on their sexual orientation, the court stated that:

> There is not any justification to establish homosexuality as grounds for teachers' disciplinary offense. The exclusion of homosexuals from teaching is totally unjustified, since there is no evidence that these people are more prone to sexual abuse than the rest of the population, or that their presence in the classroom affects the free development of the students' personality.[49]

With this statement, the court clearly established that calling homosexuality a form of misconduct violated the rights to free development of personality and sexual orientation. In the same ruling, the court stated that homosexuality cannot be considered a disease or a pathological abnormality that has to be cured. The court also clearly established that homosexuality constitutes a legitimate sexual orientation, which is an essential and intimate part of an individual's identity and has special constitutional protection under both the constitutional right of equality and the right to free development of personality (Colombian constitution, Articles 13 and 16).[50] Although none of these cases were part of a well-planned strategy designed by LGBTI organizations, they marked the successful start of the battle for LGBTI rights recognition and protection in Colombia.

A second area of LGBTI rights litigation concerns same-sex couples' rights. Despite the developments protecting individual rights described above, the court initially refused to recognize the rights of same-sex couples. The argument used was that homosexual partnership did not match the idea of family embedded in the constitution:

> The difference in the factual circumstances of permanent [heterosexual] companions and permanent homosexual couples, and the definition and classification of the family as the subject of specific constitutional protection, prevent drawing a judicial comparison between them.[51]

Some of the arguments used by the court to deny the same rights of heterosexual couples to homosexual couples are rooted in the idea that one of the main duties of a family is reproduction, and since homosexuals cannot produce children, they cannot be considered "families." The court stated that:

> The de facto marital unions of heterosexual character, in that they constitute a family, are taken into account by the law in order to ensure their 'full protection' and, in particular, that 'women and men' have equal rights and duties (Articles 42 and 43 of the constitution), which, as the necessary object of protection, is not present in the case of homosexual couples.[52]
>
> The couple finds protection in the right to free development of personality and, as a life option, it unfolds in a private setting, constitutionally protected regardless of the heterosexual or homosexual nature of the relationship. However, heterosexual unions enjoy a higher status in the shaping of the family as the essential nucleus of society and are subject to special constitutional protection. In the context of the constitutional protection of the family, the presence of children is circumstantial and was not intended as a conditioning factor of such protection.[53]

Therefore, because heterosexual families can reproduce, they deserve integral protection, which includes property rights, access to social security, and survivor's pensions, while homosexual couples are not entitled to these rights.[54,55,56] In summary, the court protected a heteronormative definition of family; it recognized the individual right of homosexuals to be free from discrimination, but denied them the right to be considered a family or to claim the same rights as heterosexual families.

In line with this argumentation, the court's initial decisions ruled the ban on same-sex couples' adoptions to be constitutional, because it responded to public morals and defended the best interests of minors. Homosexuals have the right to decide how they want to live—this for the court is an individual and private option, and can go against public morals. However, when it comes to adoption, the state has to guarantee the best interests of the minor, and the minor has the right to receive education according to public morals, since their right overrides the right of homosexuals to become parents.[57]

In a context where the court was perceived as a hopeless venue for achieving recognition of the rights of same-sex couples, the Colombian LGBTI movement turned to the legislature.[58] In 2003, a bill was presented in the Senate to legalize same-sex marriage and recognize the rights of same-sex couples, but it was rejected in June 2007, reflecting both the lack of popular support for LGBTI rights and the political power and organization of conservative groups opposing those rights. This rejection forced LGBTI organizations to reevaluate their strategies and to use their litigation experience to return to the friendlier arena of the Constitutional Court. The court allowed more focus on legal constitutional debates and was less concerned that over 60 percent of public opinion still rejected same-sex marriage.[59]

Dealing with a sensitive issue, such as same-sex marriage, has a political cost for the court. Some actors have openly criticized the court's intervention on this issue, stating that it is the legislature and not the Constitutional Court that should decide the legality of same-sex marriage. However, politicians do not only have to face the same pressure; on such an unpopular social issue they are also likely to consider their popular support (i.e. votes), and political alliances, which might include the assertive conservative religious organizations.

Besides this, the debate of the bill in Congress did not prevent Colombians from presenting cases to the court or to international bodies. In 2007, the Human Rights Committee issued a decision that Colombia violated the Covenant on Civil and Political Rights by denying the right to a survivors' pension to a citizen who lived with his same-sex partner. The committee ordered Colombia to restore the rights of the affected individual as well as to address this type of discrimination.[60]

The constitutional court's decision concerning the central concept of family was not unanimous. Justices including Jaime Araújo Rentería stated that the Colombian legal framework did not deny different forms of family. For example, on his dissenting opinion in Decision T-349/06, Justice Araújo Rentería stated:

> It is not true that the pension system is exclusively aimed at protecting the family understood as the stable union between a man and a woman. In fact, social security in an increasingly clear way has been replacing the concept of family with that of family groups. These family groups can be integrated in various forms that are more suited to the Colombian sociological reality in which many households consist of a single mother with her children, a grandmother with some children and grandchildren, or a brother or sister with his or her sibling, to name a few of the infinite possible combinations. What is relevant is that the concept of family is, in any case, a form of union of persons that does not reflect what the concept of family groups does manage to convey—a reality of strong ties of solidarity mediated by cohabitation and the provision of assistance and help, and that are constituted by consanguinity, affinity, affiliation or the mere accidents of life.[61]

Over the years, the court's assessment of the concept of family gradually moved more in line with Judge Araújo Rentería's view and eventually became the majority position. In a 2007 decision, the court revealed the complete abandonment of its previous position on same-sex marital unions by ruling that the exclusion of same-sex couples from the economic benefits of marital union was a fundamental human rights violation. For the court, the law was unconstitutional because it imposed heterosexuality as a condition of access to those benefits.[62] However, this decision continues to address same-sex couples' rights from a discrimination perspective and the court continues to invoke the discretion of the legislative and executive branches over issues such as the definition of family.

In 2011, the court took a major step and, without denying the power of the legislative and executive branches to define "family," asked the legislature to remedy the lack of legal protection faced by same-sex couples.[63] The court instructed Congress to pass "comprehensive, systematic, and orderly legislation" by June 20, 2013 to resolve the imbalance. The court informed Congress that if it failed to pass the required legislation within the two-year window, same-sex couples could have a notary or a court recognize their partnership.

Conservative groups challenged this decision, arguing that the Constitutional Court's ruling now defined homosexual couples as families, too. According to the Colombian Inspector General's office, the decision was a break with traditional hetero-normativity embedded in the court's previous decisions and ignored Article 113 of the civil code that implies that only men and women can have families.[64] The Colombian Inspector General's office alleged that the Constitutional Court's Decision C-577/11 perpetrated a series of procedural violations and was, therefore, invalid.[65] The Inspector General's office also sought to harness the power of the courts, rather than the legislative arena, to oppose same-sex marriage recognition by filing a *tutela* against Colombia first same-sex marriage.[66] Opponents and supporters of same-sex marriage are clearly aware of the key role played by the court and the magnitude of its decisions regarding the recognition of constitutional rights.

The Inter-American Court of Human Rights

Until recently, the Inter-American Court of Human Rights was not at the forefront of legal battles for recognition and protection of LGBTI rights in the Americas, but the creation of a new unit within the Inter-American Commission on Human Rights, headed by Victor Madrigal-Borloz, demonstrates a commitment to actively addressing LGBTI rights issues. As noted, including an analysis of the Inter-American Commission and Court in this chapter is not fortuitous; almost every Latin American country has agreed to be bound by the jurisdiction of the Inter-American Commission on Human Rights, charged with investigating violations of the American Convention on Human Rights, and the Inter-American Court of Human Rights, which adjudicates violations on the recommendation of the Commission.

By early 2015, the court had issued only one decision regarding LGBTI rights, the 2012 *Atala Riffo and Daughters v. Chile* ruling that overturned a decision of the Supreme Court of Chile that removed a mother's three daughters from her care because she was a lesbian. There are different factors that could help to explain this new area of jurisprudence from the Inter-American Court of Human Rights. The first factor concerns the Inter-American Court of Human Rights' mandate, which may only decide cases brought against the member states of the Organization of American States (OAS) that have specifically accepted the Inter-American Court's contentious jurisdiction, and those cases must be first processed by the Inter-American Commission on Human Rights. Currently, the Inter-American Court may exercise its contentious jurisdiction over 20 states: Argentina, Barbados, Bolivia, Brazil, Chile, Colombia, Costa Rica, the Dominican Republic, Ecuador, El Salvador, Guatemala, Haiti, Honduras, Mexico, Nicaragua, Panama, Paraguay, Peru, Suriname, and Uruguay.

Second, only states and the Inter-American Commission on Human Rights have the power to refer contentious cases to the Inter-American Court of Human Rights, which means that individual petitions cannot be filed directly with the Inter-American Court, rather they must first go through the commission. It is the commission that receives and evaluates individual claims; if it accepts the claim, it tries to guide the claimants and the state to a friendly settlement. If this fails to materialize, the commission prepares a report containing its requirements, which it monitors for compliance; if a state fails to comply, the case will be filed with the Inter-American Court of Human Rights. Very few cases advance from the commission to the court; for example, between 2009 and 2013, approximately 15 cases per year were submitted to the court by the commission, and the average duration for a report from the commission is six years, with a further 19 months if the court has to make a decision.[67]

The third fact diminishing the role of the inter-American system is the capacity of the commission to evaluate and intervene in cases. The number of cases awaiting evaluation at the commission increases every year,[68] as does the number of petitions sent to the commission.[69] A final factor that is related to the procedure, but needs to be treated separately due to the peculiarities of the legal battles of LGBTI rights, is the system's rule of prior exhaustion of domestic remedies, which states that parties should resolve the problem first under countries' internal law. The limited participation of the Inter-American Court of Human Rights in LGBTI rights could be a consequence of the lack of cases in national courts, as well as of a good performance at local courts, i.e. in some countries, national legal systems are responding to LGBTI cases. Certainly, in Latin America, countries differ on the opportunity structure to access litigation and national courts. This could explain why in some countries, such as Colombia and Costa Rica, litigation has been used as a strategy to advance the LGBTI rights agenda, while in other countries, such as Nicaragua and Chile, it has not.

Courts across Latin America differ on their openness to deal with cases dealing with LGBTI rights. Some local courts have played a key role by recognizing rights of LGBTI people, including the rights of same-sex couples, which precludes the need for an intervention by the Inter-American Court of Human Rights. Besides this, the process in local courts is also long, especially if the petitioners have to exhaust all judicial mechanisms in their own countries before approaching the human rights bodies of the inter-American system. Moreover, it is possible that the lack of interest from the inter-American system on LGBTI rights has also prevented the presentation of LGBTI rights cases. For years, the inter-American system did not show explicit interest in LGBTI rights. This has changed in recent years, with some action being taken. The commission approved the Commission Strategic Plan, Plan of Action 4.6.i (2011–2012), which focused on the rights of lesbian, gay, transgender, bisexual, and intersex persons (LGTBI). The Inter-American Commission will establish legal standards, rule on cases, and issue reports on the situation of members of the LGBTI communities in the American states.

In November 2011, the Inter-American Commission on Human Rights created the Unit on the Rights of Lesbian, Gay, Bisexual, Trans, and Intersex Persons to build support for protecting LGBTI rights in the Americas. The commission has also organized hearings specifically on the issue of LGBTI rights,[70] and has issued precautionary measures to protect LGBTI people. However, these are measures to prevent irreparable harm to persons, and this does not necessarily show a position or development of jurisprudence in the inter-American system regarding LGBTI rights.

The case of *Atala Riffo and Daughters v. Chile* is a milestone because it went beyond the protection of people facing a situation of physical and psychological abuse and also because in its decision the Inter-American Court of Human Rights states its understanding of discrimination based on sexual orientation. The case was related to the custody process brought before the Chilean court by the father of the girls M., V., and R. against Ms Karen Atala Riffo. In his demand the father alleged that Karen Atala Riffo's sexual orientation and her cohabitation with a partner of the same sex would cause harm to the three girls. The Supreme Court of Chile agreed with the father and gave him the custody of the children.

In its ruling, the Inter-American Court of Human Rights declared the

> international responsibility of the state for the alleged discriminatory treatment and the arbitrary interference in her private and family life that Ms Atala has suffered due to her sexual orientation as part of the judicial process which resulted in the girls M., V., and R. being removed from her care and custody.[71]

Specifically, the Inter-American Court found Chile internationally responsible for having violated: a) the right to equality and non-discrimination of Ms Atala; b) the right to equality and non-discrimination of the children M., V., and R. and the obligation and guarantee of respect; c) the right to private life and family life; d) the right to the protection of honor and dignity; e) the right to be heard; and f) the guarantee of impartiality.

In its ruling, the Inter-American Court of Human Rights made clear the link between the right to equality and non-discrimination and sexual orientation. For the Inter-American Court:

> sexual orientation and gender identity are categories protected by the American Convention under the term 'other social condition' established in Article 1.1 of the Convention. Therefore, the Convention prohibits any discriminatory norm, act or practice based on a person's sexual orientation.[72]

One of the major contributions of the Inter-American Court of Human Rights' decision in the case of *Karen Atala Riffo and Daughters v. Chile* is that the court rejected the idea that it was bad for the children's development to have homosexual parents. This statement created a precedent at the regional level that could have a direct impact on domestic jurisprudence across the region regarding the right of homosexuals to raise a child. The Inter-American Court recognized the legitimacy of the principle of the best interests of the child and the assumptions of risk for the determination of best interests. However, it considered that the application of this principle,

> in cases of care and custody of minors, should be based on an evaluation of specific parental behaviors and their negative impact on the well-being and development of the child according to the case, as well as injuries and risks which are real and proven, not speculative and imaginary[,][72]

such as preconceptions regarding the attributes, behaviors, or characteristics of LGBTI or the impact these may have on children. Therefore, the child's best interests cannot be used to justify discrimination against the parents based on their sexual orientation; and, consequently, judges "cannot take this social condition into consideration as an element in a custody ruling."

Another important topic that could have a major regional impact is the definition of family, and therefore the right of LGBTI people to form a family. For the Inter-American Court of Human Rights, "the American Convention does not define a limited concept of family, nor does it only protect a 'traditional' model of the family." In that sense, the concept of family is not limited to marriage between heterosexuals; instead, the concept of family must consider other types of ties.

This type of position, from a regional court such as the Inter-American Court, could have an important impact at the domestic level. We are not arguing that jurisprudence on this kind of issues is always top-down; on the contrary, as mentioned above, the development of jurisprudence at the national and state levels is an important step in expanding equal rights for LGBTI people. However, when a regional (supranational) court issues a ruling, this ruling has an impact on the states within its jurisdiction and could create awareness among judges and civil society actors at the national level regarding the rights of LGBTI people. The ruling can and has been used as a precedent in similar cases at national courts. In December 2012 the Supreme Court of Mexico voted unanimously to overturn the ban on same-sex marriage in the state of Oaxaca. According to one of the lawyers in the case, the February 2012 decision by the Inter-American Court of Human Rights in the *Atala Riffo and Daughters v. Chile* case helped to solidify the court's jurisprudence and allow same-sex marriage in Oaxaca.[73]

Conclusions

The preceding discussion highlights the profound impact of superior courts in Latin America on strengthening the protection of LGBTI people's rights, but also illustrates some of the limitations of litigation and courts' behavior in protecting those rights in representative democracies. The chapter highlights three different courts and how the jurisprudence in the two national courts changed and developed over time, starting with a similarly negative view of LGBTI people on the part of the overwhelming majority of both countries to developing legal understandings of LGBTI people and their rights that move further and faster than public opinion. The impact of these courts' decisions has been, in many cases, profound and helped move LGBTI people out of the shadows and the margins of society and into the national polity as more equal citizens. As more and more countries independently legislate or litigate more equality for LGBTI people and require an end to state-sponsored discrimination, popular opinion on tolerance and equality for LGBTI people has improved significantly.[74] That the Costa Rican Congress has largely ignored the Fourth Chamber's 2006 suggestion that it legislate a legal equivalence to heterosexual marriage for same-sex couples is perhaps a reflection of the weak ruling from the court and the nexus of where politics and rights collide. The counterexample is the stronger decision from the Colombian court, which essentially gave the Colombian Congress two years to write a law granting same-sex couples the same legal protections and rights as married heterosexual couples; when the congress failed to write the law, same-sex marriage was available to couples who requested it from a notary or judge. In both Costa Rica and Colombia the political weakness of LGBTI groups and the relative strength of their conservative religious opponents made the legislatures unlikely and unfriendly arenas for LGBTI groups. The two cases show how jurisprudence on LGBTI rights developed over time from a more conservative position that recognised rights to protect life and individual integrity and a narrow understanding of sexuality, to positions that recognise some same sex couples rights up to and including same sex marriage and adoption. However, as the case of Costa Rica shows, this is not a natural development, but rather it suggests that if the rights claimed (as in the early cases) do not challenge the interests of vocal part of society, then courts might find it easier to rule in their favour. The limitations of the litigation strategy were made clear on the question of same sex marriage rights that generated a political backlash from anti-gay conservative, religious groups. These groups viewed the expansion of the definition of marriage as a direct and profound challenge to their traditional, religious values. The recent awakening of the Inter-American Court of Human Rights to questions of LGBTI rights has already had a direct impact on LGBTI people in Chile and an indirect impact on same sex marriage rights in Mexico. It is also possible that the Inter-American Court of Human Rights' rulings on LGBTI rights could have important effects on the jurisprudence of national courts across the Americas in the future since most states have agreed to be under that court's jurisprudence.

Questions

a Do you think that, in Resolution No. 5934–97, the Costa Rican court struck a good balance regarding the direct and indirect costs of treatment (or lack thereof) for HIV/AIDS patients?

b To what extent, if any, should courts take into account the financial burden that the satisfaction of a given right implies?

c Do you think the government had supplied, as the minority in the Costa Rican case seemed to accept, an "objective and reasonable justification" to deny gay prisoners conjugal visits?

d The Constitutional Court of Colombia argued in the 2006 decision that "heterosexual unions enjoy a higher status in the shaping of the family as the essential nucleus of society and are subject to special constitutional protection." What do you think about this proposition?

e According to the Inter-American Court of Human Rights, what do the "best interests" of the child entail?

f Consider Colombian Justice Araújo Rentería's dissenting opinion and the Inter-American Court's rationale in the *Atala* case regarding the concept of family. Do you see any common traits?

Notes

1 Freedom to Marry, www.freedomtomarry.org/landscape/entry/c/internationalILGA (2015).

2 See, for example, Juan Marsiaj, *Social Movements and Political Parties: Gays Lesbians and Travestis and the Struggle for Inclusion in Brazil*, 31/62 Canadian Journal of Latin American and Caribbean Studies, 167–96 (2006).

3 Camila Gianella and Bruce M. Wilson, *Rainbow Revolution in Latin America: The Battle for Recognition*, 14(1) CMI Brief (February 2015), available at www.cmi.no/publications/publication/?5394=rainbow-revolution-in-latin-america.

4 Ley de la Jurisdicción Constitucional (Constitutional Jurisdiction Law) (October 19, 1989), Ley No. 7,135, October 11, 1989. *La Gaceta*, No. 198, San José, Costa Rica.

5 Constitución de la República de Costa Rica (Constitution of Costa Rica), 1949. English language version available at www.costaricalaw.com/.

6 Bruce M. Wilson and Juan Carlos Rodríguez Cordero, *Legal Opportunity Structures and Social Movements: The Effects of Institutional Change on Costa Rican Politics*, 39(3) Comparative Political Studies, 325–51 (2006).

7 Ley de la Jurisdicción Constitucional.

8 Bruce M. Wilson, *Enforcing Rights and Exercising an Accountability Function: Costa Rica's Constitutional Court*, in Courts in Latin America (Gretchen Helmke and Julio Rios-Figueroa eds, 2011).

9 Section 27.

10 Supreme Court of Costa Rica, Constitutional Chamber, *Estadísticas* (2015), available at http://sitios.poder-judicial.go.cr/salaconstitucional/estadisticas.htm.

11 Bruce M. Wilson, *Changing Dynamics: The Political Impact of Costa Rica's Constitutional Court*, in The Judicialization of Politics in Latin America, at 47–66 (Rachel Sieder, Line Schjolden and Alan Angell eds, 2005).

12 Irene Vizcaíno, Confianza de los ticos sofoca a la Sala Constitucional (2004), available at www.nacion.com/ln_ee/2004/septiembre/19/pais14.html.
13 Fernando Cruz Castro, *Costa Rica's Constitutional Jurisprudence, Its Political Importance and International Human Rights*, 45(3) Duquesne Law Review, 557–76 (2006).
14 Carlos José Gutiérrez Gutiérrez, *La constitución 50 años después*, in Temas claves de la constitución política Investigaciones Jurídicas, at 49 (Carlos José Gutiérrez Gutiérrez et al. eds).
15 Bruce M. Wilson, *Claiming Individual Rights Through a Constitutional Court: The Example of Gays in Costa Rica*, 5 I•CON, International Journal of Constitutional Law, 242–57 (2007).
16 Bruce M. Wilson and Juan Carlos Rodríguez Cordero, *Legal Opportunity Structures and Social Movements: The Effects of Institutional Change on Costa Rican Politics*, 39(3) Comparative Political Studies, 325–51 (2006).
17 Anti-gay discrimination in Costa Rica has been well documented; see, for example, Jacobo Schifter, La Formación de una Contracultura: Homosexualismo y SIDA en Costa Rica (1989); or CIPAC/DDHH, Discriminación Laboral por Orientación Sexual (2006), available at www.cipacdh.org/derechos/da3.htm.
18 For a discussion of police attitudes during this period, see Jacobo Schifter, La Formación de una Contracultura: Homosexualismo y SIDA en Costa Rica (1989), and Jacobo Schifter, Public Sex in Latin Society (2000).
19 A 1999 opinion poll revealed that over 80 percent of Costa Ricans had little tolerance for gays. UNIMER, Encuesta (1999), available at www.nacion.co.cr/ln_ee/encuestas/unimer/grafico21.gif.
20 Supreme Court of Costa Rica, Constitutional Chamber, Resolution No. 2006–007262.
21 *Homosexuales y lesbianas claman por sus derechos e igualdad*, La Nación, June 27, 2004, available at http://wvw.nacion.com/ln_ee/2004/junio/27/ultima-sr2.html.
22 *Editorial*, Tico Times, September 27, 1997.
23 Supreme Court of Costa Rica, Constitutional Chamber, Resolution No. 280–92.
24 Bruce M. Wilson, *Enforcing Rights and Exercising an Accountability Function: Costa Rica's Constitutional Court*, in Courts in Latin America (Gretchen Helmke and Julio Rios-Figueroa eds, 2011).
25 Supreme Court of Costa Rica, Constitutional Chamber, Resolution No. 5934–97, translation by Alicia Yamin in *Not Just a Tragedy: Access to Medications as a Right Under International Law*, 21 Boston University International Law Journal, 116 (2004).
26 Ibid., 137.
27 Supreme Court of Costa Rica, Constitutional Chamber, Resolution No. 2009–8339. See Ole F. Norheim and Bruce M. Wilson, *Health Rights Litigation and Access to Medicines: Priority Classification of Successful Cases from Costa Rica's Constitutional Chamber of the Supreme Court*, 16(2) Health and Human Rights: An International Journal (2014).
28 Rónald Moya, *Abogada pide permitir visita conyugal a homosexuales*, La Nación, February 8, 2008, available at http://wvw.nacion.com/ln_ee/2008/febrero/08/pais1416401.html.
29 Supreme Court of Costa Rica, Constitutional Chamber, Resolution No. 2011–013800.
30 *Corte de Costa Rica permite visitas conyugales de homosexuales en prisión* zCanalRCN broadcast, 2011), available at http://portal.canalrcn.com/noticias/corte_de_costa_rica_permite_visitas_conyugales_de_homosexuales_en_prisi%C3%B3n.
31 Supreme Court of Costa Rica, Constitutional Chamber, Resolution No. 2011–013800.
32 Supreme Court of Costa Rica, Constitutional Chamber, Resolution No. 1993–00316.
33 Supreme Court of Costa Rica, Constitutional Chamber, Resolution No. 2006–007262.
34 Supreme Court of Costa Rica, Constitutional Chamber, Resolutions No. 1770–94, 1045–94 and 4883–97.
35 Supreme Court of Costa Rica, Constitutional Chamber, Resolution No. 00316–1993.
36 Act No. 17 of the National Constituent Assembly ("*Asamblea Nacional Constituyente*"), 1949.
37 Supreme Court of Costa Rica, Constitutional Chamber, Resolution No. 00316–1993.
38 Ibid., Justice's Vargas Benavides's opinion.
39 Supreme Court of Costa Rica, Constitutional Chamber, Resolution No. 2010–013313.
40 Ibid.
41 Ibid.
42 Ana Cristina González and Juanita Durán, *Impact of Court Rulings on Health Care Coverage: The Case of HIV/AIDS in Colombia*, 13(3) MEDICC Review, 54–7 (2011).
43 Alicia Ely Yamin and Oscar Parra-Vera, *Judicial Protection of the Right to Health in Colombia: From Social Demands to Individual Claims to Public Debates*, 33(2) Hastings International and Comparative Law Review, 101–27 (2010).

44 *Denuncia la Defensoría del Pueblo. Cada minuto se interpone una acción de tutela en Colombia*, El Espectador, 2014, available at www.elespectador.com/noticias/actualidad/cada-minuto-se-interpone-una-accion-de-tutela-colombia-articulo-512870.
45 See, e.g., Constitutional Court of Colombia, Decisions T-097/94 and T-539/94.
46 Constitutional Court of Colombia, Decision T-539/94.
47 Ibid.
48 Constitutional Court of Colombia, Decision T-569/94.
49 Constitutional Court of Colombia, Decisions C-098/96 and C-481/98.
50 Constitutional Court of Colombia, Decision C-481/98.
51 Constitutional Court of Colombia, Decision SU-623/01.
52 Constitutional Court of Colombia, Decision C-098/96.
53 Constitutional Court of Colombia, Decision T-349/06.
54 Constitutional Court of Colombia, Decision C-098/96.
55 Constitutional Court of Colombia, Decision T-349/06.
56 Constitutional Court of Colombia, Decision T-999/00.
57 Constitutional Court of Colombia, Decision C-814/01.
58 M. Albarracín, *Social Movements and the Constitutional Court: Legal Recognition of the Rights of Same Sex Couples in Colombia*, 8(14) Sur. International Journal, 7–31 (2011).
59 *Mayoría de colombianos se opone a matrimonio gay: encuesta. Estudio de Gallup revela que más del 60 por ciento de los consultados no apoya esta unión*, El Tiempo, 2015, available at www.eltiempo.com/politica/segun-encuesta-de-gallu-colombianos-se-oponen-a-matrimonio-gay/15340079.
60 Case X v. Colombia communication no. 1361/2005 (CCPR/C/89/D/1361/2005).
61 Constitutional Court of Colombia, Sentence T-349/06.
62 Constitutional Court of Colombia, Decision C-811/07.
63 Constitutional Court of Colombia, Decision C-577/11.
64 See, e.g., *La familia y el aborto, según el procurador*, Semana, 2011, available at www.semana.com/nacion/articulo/la-familia-aborto-segun-procurador/239746–3.
65 Procuraduría General de la Nación, Solicitud de Nulidad Sentencia C-577 (2011), available at https://jkrincon.files.wordpress.com/2013/12/solicitud-de-nulida-c-577–11-procuraduria.pdf.
66 *Anulan primer matrimonio gay en Colombia*, Semana, 2013, available at www.semana.com/nacion/articulo/anulan-matrimonio-gay-con-tutela/359664–3.
67 Ariel E. Dulitzky, *The Inter-American Human Rights System Fifty Years Later: Time For Changes*, Quebec Journal of International Law, 127–64 (2011).
68 The case docket numbers went from 1450 in 2009 to 1755 in 2013.
69 The annual number of petitions went from 1431 in 2009 to 2061 in 2013.
70 *Situation of Human Rights of Lesbian, Gay, Transexual, Bisexual and Intersex Indigenous Persons in the Americas* (147 period of sessions); and *Homicides of LGTBI Persons and Impunity in the Americas* (146 period of sessions). Participants: Colombia Diversa, Caribe Afirmativo, Santamaría Fundación, Red Lésbica Cattrachas, and Trans Siempre Amigas (TRANSSA).
71 Inter-American Court of Human Rights, case of "Atala Riffo and Daughters v. Chile," February 24, 2012.
72 Ibid.
73 Lester Feder, *Mexican Supreme Court rules for marriage equality*, Salon (2012), available at www.salon.com/2012/12/06/mexican_supreme_court_rules_for_marriage_equality/.
74 See the available LAPOP data for the Americas on these issues; Gianella and Wilson 2015 identify some of these significant changes even over a short period of time.

References

M. Albarracín, *Social Movements and the Constitutional Court: Legal Recognition of the Rights of Same Sex Couples in Colombia*, 8(14) Sur. International Journal, 7–31 (2011).

Anulan primer matrimonio gay en Colombia, Semana, 2013, available at www.semana.com/nacion/articulo/anulan-matrimonio-gay-con-tutela/359664–3.

CIPAC/DDHH, Discriminación Laboral por Orientación Sexual (2006), available at www.cipacdh.org/derechos/da3.htm.

Corte de Costa Rica permite visitas conyugales de homosexuales en prisión (CanalRCN broadcast, 2011), http://portal.canalrcn.com/noticias/corte_de_costa_rica_permite_visitas_conyugales_de_homosexuales_en_prisi%C3%B3n.

Fernando Cruz Castro, *Costa Rica's Constitutional Jurisprudence, Its Political Importance and International Human Rights*, 45(3) DUQUESNE LAW REVIEW, 557–76 (2006).

Denuncia la Defensoría del Pueblo. Cada minuto se interpone una acción de tutela en Colombia, EL ESPECTADOR, 2014, available at www.elespectador.com/noticias/actualidad/cada-minuto-se-interpone-una-accion-de-tutela-colombia-articulo-512870.

Ariel E. Dulitzky, *The Inter-American Human Rights System Fifty Years Later: Time For Changes*, QUEBEC JOURNAL OF INTERNATIONAL LAW, 127–64 (2011).

Editorial, TICO TIMES, September 27, 1997.

Lester Feder, *Mexican Supreme Court rules for marriage equality*, SALON, 2012, available at www.salon.com/2012/12/06/mexican_supreme_court_rules_for_marriage_equality/.

Freedom to Marry, www.freedomtomarry.org/landscape/entry/c/internationalILGA (2015).

Camila Gianella and Bruce M. Wilson, *Rainbow Revolution in Latin America: The Battle for Recognition*, 14(1) CMI BRIEF (February 2015), available at www.cmi.no/publications/publication/?5394=rainbow-revolution-in-latin-america.

Ana Cristina González and Juanita Durán, *Impact of Court Rulings on Health Care Coverage: The Case of HIV/AIDS in Colombia*, 13(3) MEDICC REVIEW, 54–7 (2011).

Carlos José Gutiérrez Gutiérrez, *La constitución 50 años después*, in TEMAS CLAVES DE LA CONSTITUCIÓN POLÍTICA INVESTIGACIONES JURÍDICAS, at 49 (Carlos José Gutiérrez Gutiérrez et al. eds., 1999).

Homosexuales y lesbianas claman por sus derechos e igualdad, LA NACIÓN, June 27, 2004, available at http://wvw.nacion.com/ln_ee/2004/junio/27/ultima-sr2.html.

La familia y el aborto, según el procurador, SEMANA, 2011, available at www.semana.com/nacion/articulo/la-familia-aborto-segun-procurador/239746–3.

Juan Marsiaj, *Social Movements and Political Parties: Gays Lesbians and Travestis and the Struggle for Inclusion in Brazil*, 31/62 CANADIAN JOURNAL OF LATIN AMERICAN AND CARIBBEAN STUDIES, 167–96 (2006).

Mayoría de colombianos se opone a matrimonio gay: encuesta. Estudio de Gallup revela que más del 60 por ciento de los consultados no apoya esta unión, EL TIEMPO, 2015, available at www.eltiempo.com/politica/segun-encuesta-de-gallu-colombianos-se-oponen-a-matrimonio-gay/15340079.

Rónald Moya, *Abogada pide permitir visita conyugal a homosexuals*, LA NACIÓN, 2008, available at http://wvw.nacion.com/ln_ee/2008/febrero/08/pais1416401.html.

Ole F. Norheim and Bruce M. Wilson, *Health Rights Litigation and Access to Medicines: Priority Classification of Successful Cases from Costa Rica's Constitutional Chamber of the Supreme Court*, 16(2) HEALTH AND HUMAN RIGHTS: AN INTERNATIONAL JOURNAL (2014).

JACOBO SCHIFTER, LA FORMACIÓN DE UNA CONTRACULTURA: HOMOSEXUALISMO Y SIDA EN COSTA RICA (1989).

JACOBO SCHIFTER, PUBLIC SEX IN LATIN SOCIETY (2000).

UNIMER, ENCUESTA (1999), available at www.nacion.co.cr/ln_ee/encuestas/unimer/grafico21.gif.

Irene Vizcaíno, CONFIANZA DE LOS TICOS SOFOCA A LA SALA CONSTITUCIONAL (2004), available at www.nacion.com/ln_ee/2004/septiembre/19/pais14.html.

Bruce M. Wilson, *Changing Dynamics: The Political Impact of Costa Rica's Constitutional Court*, in THE JUDICIALIZATION OF POLITICS IN LATIN AMERICA, AT 47–66 (Rachel Sieder, Line Schjolden and Alan Angell eds, 2005).

Bruce M. Wilson, *Claiming Individual Rights Through a Constitutional Court: The Example of Gays in Costa Rica*, 5 I•CON, INTERNATIONAL JOURNAL OF CONSTITUTIONAL LAW, 242–57 (2007).

Bruce M. Wilson, *Enforcing Rights and Exercising an Accountability Function: Costa Rica's Constitutional Court*, in COURTS IN LATIN AMERICA (Gretchen Helmke and Julio Rios-Figueroa eds, 2011).

Bruce M. Wilson and Juan Carlos Rodríguez Cordero, *Legal Opportunity Structures and Social Movements: The Effects of Institutional Change on Costa Rican Politics*, 39(3) COMPARATIVE POLITICAL STUDIES, 325–51 (2006).

Alicia Yamin, *Not Just a Tragedy: Access to Medications as a Right Under International Law*, 21 BOSTON UNIVERSITY INTERNATIONAL LAW JOURNAL, 116 (2004).

Alicia Ely Yamin and Oscar Parra-Vera, *Judicial Protection of the Right to Health in Colombia: From Social Demands to Individual Claims to Public Debates*, 33(2) HASTINGS INTERNATIONAL AND COMPARATIVE LAW REVIEW, 101–27 (2010).

Further reading

M. Albarracín, *Social Movements and the Constitutional Court: Legal Recognition of the Rights of Same Sex Couples in Colombia*, 8(14) SUR. INTERNATIONAL JOURNAL, 7–31 (2011).

Javier Corrales and Mario Pecheny, THE POLITICS OF SEXUALITY IN LATIN AMERICA: A READER ON LESBIAN, GAY, BISEXUAL AND TRANSGENDER RIGHTS (2011).

J. Lemaitre, *Love in the time of cholera: LGBT rights in Colombia*, 6(1) SUR. INTERNATIONAL JOURNAL ON HUMAN RIGHTS (2009).

G. Lodola and M. Corral, *Support for Same-Sex Marriage in Latin America*, AMERICAS BAROMETER INSIGHTS (2010).

5 Prisons and prisoners' rights

Juan F. Gonzalez-Bertomeu[*]

Introduction

Prison systems in Latin America are in poor shape.[1] In most countries in the region, detention conditions are deficient and inmates' rights are violated on a daily basis. This chapter attempts to survey the role of judges in addressing the crisis and defining the scope of those rights. It begins by offering some contextual information on basic trends concerning punishment and prisons in the region. It then reviews a selection of court decisions, mostly from Latin American countries' high courts, dealing with some of the main challenges posed by the condition of the prison system.[2]

Crime and punishment in Latin America

Latin American prisons seem to reflect the status of the region as being the most unequal in the world.[3] In the critical view of one commentator, the prison system in Latin America is "one of the main tools used to give answers to social problems,"[4] and "prisons are [generally] employed to control the most disadvantaged socioeconomic groups."[5] Prisoners are disproportionately poor and many or even most of them are serving time (or spending their time, as in the case of pretrial detainees[6]) for the types of relatively minor offences that are strongly prioritized in the region, such as the possession of small amounts of drugs or petty theft.[7] These problems, as some of those discussed in this chapter, are fairly widespread throughout the world, but they present themselves with particular severity in Latin America.

For most of the public, the prison system is of little priority. The fact that prisoners' political rights are heavily curtailed surely adds to this invisibility—convicted inmates typically do not vote, and the same is true of pretrial detainees in many jurisdictions. Referring to Latin America, Dammert and Zúñiga argue that "our citizenry—and therefore our policies—have focused more on punishing those who commit a crime than on rehabilitating them."[8] Thus, politicians and prison administrators can afford to run a system where the rights of prisoners are disrespected without facing serious political consequences.

Correctional facilities in Latin America are overpopulated but keep receiving a steady inflow of inmates. The region's incarceration rate—around 230 prisoners per 100,000 of national population—is above the world's average of about 160 prisoners.[9] The number of inmates in the region has been steadily growing since the 1990s.[10] Although Latin American countries differ considerably concerning the level of overcrowding, prison systems in all of them house inmates in excess of their functional capacity. Taking an average of the country's rates, by 2013, Latin American prisons operated at 189 percent of capacity,[11] with the corresponding consequences in terms of the security and well-being of inmates. This compares to a world average of 129 percent.[12]

One possible reason to account for these trends is a corresponding rise in criminality, which may have been triggered by "inequality, lack of opportunity, increased drug use, and other social problems."[13] An alternative explanation lies in what may be termed a "punitive drive"—a strong focus on punishment and security. This tendency manifests itself in the toughening up of criminal laws, both substantive and procedural, and in crime prevention strategies that have not necessarily proved successful in reducing crime but that have packed prisons.[14]

Perhaps because of the emphasis on incarceration and incapacitation, but also due to the operation of sluggish criminal processes (with inquisitorial traces and a heavy bureaucratic burden[15]), most countries in the region feature prisons that house a very large share of detainees awaiting trial.[16] While the situation of those in custody awaiting sentencing has slightly improved in the last decade,[17] the regional ratio for 2013 was still almost one pretrial detainee to one convicted inmate.[18] Forty-eight percent of prisoners in Latin America are awaiting trial, compared to a world average of 33 percent. (The former figure is over twice as much as that in either Europe or the U.S.) Furthermore, Section 8.b of the UN Standard Minimum Rules for the Treatment of Prisoners,[19] in force in many of the region's countries, establishes that pretrial prisoners and convicted ones must be separately housed. Yet in many, if not most, facilities, those convicted and those in pretrial detention are housed in the same space.[20]

Women represent a small share of the prison population. They account for a regional 7 percent of all inmates[21] (Bolivia leads the ranking with around 12 percent of female inmates[22]). However, the growth rate of this population in the last two decades has been greater than that of the male population.[23] This is related to a change in prosecution priorities, particularly in reference to the so-called "war on drugs." A large share of the female inmate population is either convicted or being prosecuted for petty theft or drug-related offenses—usually for being involved as drug "mules" in "the last link in the drug trafficking chain."[24]

Female inmates have special needs "in terms of keeping their families together and maintaining contact with their children"[25] that ought to be, though typically are not, addressed.[26] Moreover, women are the target of abuse, in some cases from fellow inmates but particularly from prison officers, many of them male.[27] In the *Miguel Castro-Castro Prison* case against Peru heard by the Inter-American Court of Human Rights,[28] the court held the country responsible for, *inter alia*, permitting that prison officers routinely carry out vaginal inspections (which were violently performed by male officers),[29] something that does not seem to be exceptional in Latin American prisons.[30] Interestingly, the prevalence of pretrial detention in the region appears to include a gender component. While women are far less prone than men to be in prison, they are, with the exception of a few countries, more likely to be in pretrial detention than men.[31]

Given these predicaments, it is not surprising that violent deaths in prison (to mention perhaps the most extreme of rights violations) are common. This chapter refers to a handful of events with a massive toll resulting from the mismanagement of crises, an inadequate reaction to fires or the violent repression of riots in overcrowded institutions. While there are other such cases, "simpler" events with fewer victims are even more routine. The lack of priority assigned to the prison system manifests itself in low budgetary allocations and inadequate infrastructure. In cases of acute crisis, such as those following violent riots and fires, a fairly usual state response, to the extent there is one, is to announce the construction of new facilities. If adequately equipped and run, these new facilities definitely help alleviate some of the problems associated with overpopulation.

Yet, the overpopulation crisis is probably as much the result of key political decisions (or the lack thereof) concerning the community's reaction towards crime as the consequence of an increase in the number of crimes. Thus, the construction of new prisons could hardly replace a serious redefinition of those political issues. Finding alternatives to massive incarceration is what may be needed the most, but those alternatives are often found politically unfeasible. For example, a proposed legal change recently discussed in Colombia to deal with overpopulation and creating a more flexible parole regime, but which would have meant the release from prison of 50,000 inmates overnight, was met with fierce criticism.[32] A level of experimentation with alternatives to full incarceration exists in the region, such as the so-called APAC (Association of Protection and Assistance to Convicted Prisoners) system in Brazil, a small-scale restorative justice program started in the 1970s.[33] But these cases are still exceptional.

The role of courts

The following sections illustrate the role played by judges in Latin America concerning the crisis in the prison system and the rights of prisoners. The intervention of courts in this realm is meant to hold prison administrators to account for the mistreatment of prisoners, to scrutinize laws and regulations that impinge on their rights, and to challenge the inertia that is the result of the low priority assigned to prisons.

Yet, asking for judges' involvement in addressing these situations can be controversial. This is especially so when such involvement potentially entails a sweeping reshaping of the institutions of the prison system in order to make up for the omissions of political authorities and prison administrators. In these "structural" cases, judges' willingness to play an active role is liable to be criticized for meddling with the political branches in issues concerning budgetary allocations, and for lacking the type of comprehensive information about the operation of the prison system that is necessary to make wise and effective decisions. For this reason, judges in these cases can (and probably should) enlist the collaboration of elected officials and other relevant stakeholders. Some have done so, however successful (or unsuccessful) they may have been in their attempt.

The status of prisoners' rights

When the state sends someone to prison, it restricts substantive rights that refer to the immediate conditions concerning the person's confinement, but, more broadly, it can also affect such civil, political, and social rights as freedom of expression, the right to vote, and the right to work. Moreover, imprisonment may curtail that person's procedural rights. The issue in the latter case is to what extent the inmate is equipped with legal tools that allow him or her to report the infringement of substantive rights and seek proper redress. In both cases, an important question is how to draw a line between rights restrictions that are legally valid and restrictions that are not.[34]

Both domestic legislation and international instruments set up rules and standards that place limits upon elected officials, criminal judges, and prison administrators as to the way a conviction should be carried out and that confer rights to inmates. They establish, *inter alia*, that the main aim of incarceration is not punishment but rehabilitation or security;[35] a duty to respect inmates' physical integrity and dignity, and not to subject them to torture or ill-treatment;[36] and a duty to separate convicted and pretrial inmates.[37]

Some courts in Latin America have embarked upon the task of infusing these rules and standards with specific meaning, thus defining the scope of the restriction of prisoners' rights. In a case involving the continuous interception of a prisoner's private correspondence, the Supreme Court of Argentina offered some preliminaries by saying that "[g]etting into prison does not deprive a man from the protection of the law, and, prominently, of the constitution."[38] Quoting a clause in the 1853 Argentinian constitution providing minimum standards for prisons and admonishing against punishment beyond what is necessary to guarantee security, the court added:

> The warning read by Dante: *lasciate ogni speranza, voi ch'entrate* [*lose all hope, you who enter here*], was written at the top of hell's door; on the contrary, at the lintel that the inmates cross, the engraving is different: 'The prisons of the nation shall be healthy and clean, for the security and not for the punishment of the prisoners confined therein; and any measure taken with the pretext of precaution which may lead to mortify them beyond the demands of security, shall render liable the judge who authorizes it.'[39]

Perhaps the best definition of this question comes from a series of decisions by the Constitutional Court of Colombia—which has had a leading role concerning prisoners' rights. In 1992, in a case involving various petitions by inmates complaining about the lack of adequate infrastructure to guarantee a humane detention, Justice Ciro Angarita wrote for the court:

> Against Kantian [or retributive] theories on the justification of punishment, which hold that punishment is a mechanism for the pursuit of absolute or metaphysical justice, nowadays it is accepted . . . that punishment is a judicial–political device designed for the protection of society through deterrence of individuals and the punishment of offenders . . . The idea of a public torment, conceived as a mechanism for spreading an example across the members of a group, has been replaced by the idea of social isolation, understood as a way for social protection and the personal rehabilitation of the offender.
>
> These two conceptions of punishment . . . conceive of the suffering of the prisoner in a radically different way. According to the former, the infliction of pain is deliberate and serves not only to achieve the restoration of justice for the social harm caused, but also as an example of good behavior and the undesirable consequences that follow social deviation. . . . For the latter, the infliction of suffering is an inevitable consequence which is not defended as an end in itself. That infliction cannot be separated from punishment, but punishment itself is not reduced to the suffering, nor does it aim for it . . . Incarceration, even though it generates distress, not only of a psychological but also of a physical nature, is not a punishment aimed directly at the body of the convict, as for example flogging and mutilation . . . and therefore should not be regarded as a physical punishment of the body.
>
> The prison is not a place outside the law. Inmates have not been removed from society. The special relationship of subjugation they have with the state does not take away from them their quality of active subjects of rights. In view of his previous antisocial behavior, the inmate has some of his rights suspended, such as freedom, other rights limited, including the right to communication or intimacy, but enjoys other rights in full, as the right to life, to physical integrity and health.[40]

Justice Angarita added:

> The suffering of the offender must be assessed from the perspective described . . . If punishment is excessive, cruel, inhuman, or degrading, it is nothing but institutional violence. Consequently, every affliction which escapes the relationship between these two elements [social protection and the offender's situation] must be considered outside the legal justification of punishment itself and must be scrutinized from a constitutional perspective in order

> to protect the person from any possible violation of fundamental rights. . . . Even though it is true that being a prisoner causes a drastic limitation on one's fundamental rights, such limitation must be the minimum necessary to achieve the intended purpose. Any additional limitation should be understood as excessive and, therefore, as a violation of such rights.[41]

That is to say, the decision to deprive someone of his liberty should only affect those rights that strictly follow from his confinement in a cell. In future cases, the court fleshed out this standard by creating a three-pronged categorization of rights: those that are unrestricted, those that are suspended, and those that can be restricted though not completely suspended. The court distinguished between:

> i) Those rights that *cannot be limited or suspended just because the right-bearer is incarcerated*. These rights are connected to human nature and, as such, it does not make any difference what the subjective conditions of the right-bearer are. The right to life, to human dignity, to personal integrity, to equality, to religious freedom, and to due process belong in this group. Precisely for this reason the state has a legal duty to respect and protect these rights in full, as well as to look for their full effectiveness . . .
>
> ii) [Those] rights which, as a result of the special status of inmates, are *temporarily suspended* or, as the case law has also described, '[are] absolutely limited since the arrest.' In these group belong personal freedom, freedom of mobility and political rights of those who have been convicted. [T]he suspension of this type of rights arises from the particular condition of the detainee and must have a close relationship with it.
>
> iii) [And those] rights which are *limited* because, even though the inmate still has them, he is *not able to exercise them completely* due to restrictions regarding his inherent status as one who is being deprived of his personal liberty. The case law has established that among these rights are those of association, assembly, work, family and personal privacy, inviolability of correspondence, and free development of the personality. Regarding these rights, the case law has been clear in that their limitation is subject to the reasonableness and proportionality of the restrictive measures . . .[42]

Other courts, including the Supreme Court of Costa Rica's Constitutional Chamber—the country's main constitutional adjudicator—have established fairly similar, if less specified, standards.[43]

Detention conditions

Inadequate detention conditions can jeopardize a bundle of rights, among them the right not to have one's physical integrity compromised, to be treated humanely, and to be assisted in the event of a medical condition. The state can violate these rights by both its action and omission.[44] The number of judicial petitions in Latin America reporting ill-treatment, abuses, and omissions in the prison system has snowballed over the last decades, most likely fueled by the worsening of conditions in prisons, the relaxation of formal strictures to bring suit, and a growing willingness of courts to assert a role in this crisis.

The unconstitutionality of Colombian prisons

In 1998, two groups of inmates filed petitions against the country's prison system, complaining about precarious detention conditions in two of the biggest prisons, in the cities of Medellín and Bogotá. The background to these petitions was the serious overcrowding of Colombian penitentiaries. Both prisons had almost tripled their capacity: they were allowed to house 1,700–1,800 inmates, but by the time of the petition they were housing 4,500–5,000. Petitioners claimed that they were forced to share their cell with many other inmates, without any separation between convicted and pretrial inmates or that reflected the seriousness of the crime perpetrated, and to sleep on the cell's floor or in a bathroom. They also reported deficient sanitary conditions—extreme cold or heat and the insufficiency of lavatories, ventilation, and fresh water—and the absence of recreational space.

The case reached the Constitutional Court, which ordered an inspection of the facilities and, relying on its findings, pronounced a very long judgment. Because of its importance, it is quoted quite at length.

The court opened with an unusually bold statement:

> Incarceration conditions in the two prisons . . . are absolutely subhuman and undignified for a human person, regardless of his personal condition. The housing conditions . . . are an embarrassment to a state that proclaims its respect for individual rights and its commitment to the marginalized.[45]

The court went on to explore the more general situation of the country's prisons, arguing that overcrowding levels were alarming (45 percent) and that 46 percent of all the inmates in the system were pretrial detainees. It said that the increase was due to the toughening up of the law, which had created new crimes and limited the release of detainees without a corresponding increase in the availability of prison cells.

The court argued that this situation was an obstacle to achieving the goal, established by law, of "rehabilitation of the offender through a reexamination of his personality, orderliness, work, study, spiritual education, culture, sports and recreation, based on a humane and caring disposition." It said:

> It is obvious that the overcrowding conditions prevent the inmates from accessing all the means designed for their rehabilitation . . . The unpredictability and disorder which have been the rule when it comes to prison infrastructure, together with overpopulation, have generated a situation in which the prisoners cannot even enjoy the minimum conditions for a dignified life in prison, such as having access to a bunk, to water and health services, and to decent conditions for family visits.[46]

Resorting to its own case law, the court insisted that while certain rights could be suspended or limited during a person's confinement, others could not. It stated:

> [This court] has already explained that the state has special duties toward the inmates so as to enable them to fully exercise those fundamental rights which have not been suspended, and, though to a limited extent, those which have been restricted. And those duties do not simply imply that the state should not interfere with the development of these rights—as would be the case of religious freedom—but also, and especially, that the state should take action to ensure the inmates the full enjoyment of such rights as dignity, health, food, and work. This conclusion follows from the special relation of subordination that prisoners have with the state, and the fact that the conditions imposed on the inmates prevents them from meeting by themselves a number of minimum requirements which must be met in order to have a decent life.
>
> . . .

> It is currently accepted that punishment does not have a single aim. Thus, the criminal code stipulates . . . that 'punishment has a retributive, preventive, protective and rehabilitating function.' However . . . the primary function of punishment must be rehabilitation. That is because the rehabilitating function is the one which best gives shape to the [constitutional definition of Colombia as a] social state under the rule of law, and to the principle of human dignity, one of the cornerstones of the constitution . . .
>
> Therefore, the scrutiny of the prison system should always revolve around the question of whether it meets its rehabilitating function . . . On this point it is important to note that rehabilitation does not consist in imposing certain values to inmates, but rather in providing the means for each of them to decide, in the exercise of his personal autonomy, his reintegration to society.[47]

The court concluded that the prison system did not rise to the occasion. After reviewing the applicable domestic and international legislation, it said:

> 48 [T]he provisions of the criminal code [and other legal provisions and precedents] seem all to be actually meaningless. Living conditions in Colombian prisons clearly violate the dignity of prisoners and threaten other rights, such as the right to life and physical integrity and the right to family. [T]he situation described above tends to confirm the cliché about prisons as schools of crime, producers of vice, violence and corruption.

The court held political authorities to blame for the situation:

> 50 . . . Although it has been known for decades that prisons' infrastructure is inadequate, that the rights of the inmates are violated, that institutions do not fulfill its primary purpose of rehabilitating, and that the country's prisons are full of people who have only been indicted and not convicted, there has not been any diligent attempt from the political branches to change this situation.
>
> The attitude of public decision makers with regard to the problem of prisons reflects the logic of the majority principle that governs in democratic regimes. Inmates are marginalized by society. [They] do not represent a pressure group which is able to make its voice heard. [T]heir demands and complaints are lost behind the countless other that overwhelm underdeveloped societies like Colombia.
>
> 51 The constitutional rationale is different from that of the majority. Fundamental rights represent a limit to the majority principle, precisely with the aim of guaranteeing the rights of minorities and individuals. The constitutional judge is required to play the role of the spokesman for neglected minorities, those groups which have hardly any access to political bodies.[48]

The court held that the prison system represented an "unconstitutional state of affairs"—namely, it was reality, in addition to a specific legal rule, that violated the constitution—and it was incumbent upon the authorities to address it. Regarding remedies, it said:

> 55 [T]he court must give notice to the president about the unconstitutional state of affairs. . . . This is done in order that, using the powers vested in him as the supreme administrative authority of the country and a key player in the legislative process,

the president performs all tasks necessary to put a quick end to this delicate situation . . . [Notice was also given to other public institutions.]

56 Prisoners must be housed in decent conditions. As it is well known, the current condition of prisons does not allow for that to be so. Therefore, it is imperative that new facilities are built. At the same time, the existing ones should be reconditioned so they can meet the minimum requirements to ensure that all inmates have a decent life.

. . . [It] is ordered [to the penitentiary administration, the ministry of justice and the department of planning] that, within the next three months, a plan of construction and restorations be developed to ensure both proper action to deal with overpopulation and that existing facilities meet the minimum requirements for housing inmates. . . . The execution of the project shall be completed within a maximum of 4 years from the notification of this judgment . . .

From a constitutional point of view, it is imperative to allocate the necessary budget so that prisons are turned into centers where fundamental rights are enforced. The investment in prisons is something that cannot be traded; nor there should arise any objections against it. The state has a constitutional obligation to offer the inmates decent living conditions. Spending on prisons . . . has a more urgent character than public social spending . . .[49]

A very large number of petitions followed suit, in which the court made reference to that ruling and issued similar structural injunctions.[50]

Compliance with the ruling has been uneven. The ruling was accompanied by an increase in investment in infrastructure, and new prisons were indeed built. This caused a decline in overpopulation figures within the short term, but a decade after the ruling, in 2010, overpopulation rates were again high—at around 141 percent of capacity,[51] a similar figure to that at the time of the ruling.[52] In 2011, in a case in which it was asked to find that its 1998 decision had not been complied with, the court merely pointed out the still-existing problems and issued a decision letting authorities know about the situation.[53] As of 2013, the official figure had jumped to 155–158 percent,[54] but, in the case of particular penitentiaries, the figure was over 250 percent.[55] Early in 2014 10 inmates died after a fire broke out in the not so aptly named "Modelo" prison in Barranquilla and most officials and commentators agreed that the prison system was in a serious crisis.[56]

The Constitutional Court itself did not escape criticism for its 1998 ruling. Some objected to the view on incarceration underlying the ruling and complained that the court fell short of providing a solution to the crisis. For those in this camp, it is no wonder that the problem of overcrowding recurred in the near future, since the court did not take issue with the bundle of legal rules that set a very low threshold for when to send someone to prison or jail. According to this perspective, with such rules, facilities will still be crammed even if new ones are built. Additionally, for this position, the court did well in acknowledging the seriousness of inmates' predicaments. Yet it showed itself to be inconsistent when it merely asked for the modernization of prisons, thus forcing the inmates to put up in the meantime with the subhuman conditions they lived in. The court arguably downplayed the need to avoid irreparable damage, which might have required redress of a more immediate nature—including the release of prisoners.[57]

In April 2015, when this book was going to print, newspapers reported about a 616-page decision adopted by a panel at the court (and still unpublished at the time), in which the panel highlighted the crisis in the prison system and gave the government an "ultimatum" to address it.[58] The panel said that, if the government did not comply within three years, it would order the shutting down of a number of overcrowded institutions.[59]

The prisons of Buenos Aires Province

In 2005 the Supreme Court of Argentina announced a decision in a case that was similar to the Colombian one. CELS, a human-rights NGO based in Buenos Aires, filed a corrective *habeas corpus* petition against Buenos Aires province, where over one-third of the country's population live. The petition was filed on behalf of all the inmates in the province housed in overcrowded police stations or penitentiaries. A particular focus was the case of pretrial detainees, who amounted to 75 percent of the total inmate population in the province. The petition claimed that, despite the fact that police stations cannot legally be used to house individuals for more than a few days, they were customarily used for longer-term detention and far in excess of their capacity. Moreover, regarding both police stations and penitentiaries, the petition painted an already familiar picture: deficient sanitary conditions, violence, and inadequate access to food and health services. It argued that the situation was even worse in the case of female and juvenile inmates. In its response, the local government recognized the existence of the crisis, though it said that it lacked the resources necessary to successfully tackle it.

After a public hearing, the court sided with the petitioner. In particular, it held that the UN Standard Minimum Rules for the Treatment of Prisoners (partly recognized in a federal statute) would become the main guidelines that any detention should follow. Moreover, it ordered local judges and authorities to abstain from aggravating detention conditions through cruel and inhuman treatment, and that, within 60 days, they stop using police stations to house juveniles and sick people. Finally, it ordered the provincial executive to submit a report every two months detailing the measures adopted to alleviate the crisis, and encouraged both the local executive and legislature to weaken the tough legislation in force concerning pretrial detention, in order to put it in line with what was required by both the constitution and international documents.

Given the complexity of the case, the court mainly held back from devising "command-and-control" remedies to deal with other structural aspects of the case. Instead, it set up a process for the petitioner, local government, and other NGOs to come up with a negotiated solution. In the court's view,

> it is wise to implement a performance criterion that, with the right balance and participation of civil society, takes into account the interests at stake . . . with the purpose of achieving an improvement of detention conditions in Buenos Aires Province. Therefore, this court deems it appropriate to entrust the province . . . to set up a roundtable to which the plaintiff and other organizations that filed *amici curiae* briefs in the case should be invited [the court left open the door to welcome other sectors of civil society] . . . An environment of facilitated discussion can help participants reach solutions that have a degree of consensus and are sustainable.[60]

As in the case of Colombia, the effect of this ruling has been relatively modest. The local government did take some steps to alleviate the crisis, but they were probably not decisive. In 2010 the UN Human Rights Committee (which monitors implementation of the International Covenant on Civil and Political Rights) issued a report on the matter.[61] The report concluded that the number of detainees in prolonged pretrial detention was still large, and that local legislation still did not meet international standards.[62] The court, however, has shown itself hesitant to take up the case again.

A new problem in Costa Rica

The overcrowding of prisons in Costa Rica is below regional levels, although it has been growing. Until recently the prison system had not exceeded its general capacity, though some particular prisons had. By 2009, however, prisons were operating at 109 percent of capacity, and by 2013 the figure was already 139 percent.[63] The number of inmates per 100,000 inhabitants tripled in the 1992–2012 period, from 107 to 314.[64] Each month, around 650 new inmates walk into a prison in Costa Rica, a small country of around 5 million people.[65]

As in the case of Colombia, Costa Rica's main constitutional adjudicator has been issuing countless decisions concerning detention conditions, particularly since the late 2000s. Many of them discuss the situation at the La Reforma prison, located in the city of San Rafael de Alajuela, but they also refer to penitentiaries in the cities of Liberia, Pococí, Pérez Zeledón, and San Sebastián. Apart from the obvious deterioration of detention conditions, a reason explaining the profusion of decisions (both in Costa Rica and Colombia) is the well-known flexibility of legal tools in both countries relative to others in the region. This has motivated a strong judicialization of prison matters.

In an early case from 1991, the Constitutional Chamber issued a decision concerning detention for misdemeanors. A person who had been detained for a few hours for drunkenness complained about the inadequate conditions of the center to which he had been sent, without any sanitation or a place to rest. The chamber agreed:

> This Chamber considers that the problem of building and maintaining prisons has been relegated by many societies because of a misconception . . . based on the idea that investing in such buildings is not a priority. As the Minister has admitted, the problem exists and it is serious, but it should not continue.
>
> . . .
>
> On the other hand, [the Chamber] recognizes that solving the problem requires a gradual and sustained action, which cannot be achieved within days or even months; and therefore it is necessary . . . to grant the Ministry of Interior and Police a reasonable but mandatory term to put all the penitentiaries employed for administrative detention in appropriate conditions so that they do not offend the dignity of the detainees.[66]

As in the other cases discussed, the chamber claimed that the Standard Minimum Rules for the Treatment of Prisoners had to be treated as the relevant guidelines. As a matter of fact, the chamber internalized or constitutionalized said guidelines—it said that they had the same status as the domestic constitution.[67]

In 2000, the chamber heard another petition by an inmate complaining about structural deficiencies in the capital city's Centro de Atención Institucional de San José. It found that the penitentiary's population exceeded its capacity. The chamber gave the government one year to follow the guidelines, and issued an injunction banning it from sending new inmates to the penitentiary and ordering the gradual reduction of the number of inmates down to its institutional capacity.[68] Many of the chamber's subsequent decisions about overpopulation and deficient detention conditions follow the main tenets of that previous decision. Typically, the chamber found those conditions to be unconstitutional and issued a "command-and-control" type of decision in which it ordered the government to deal with the situation. Depending on the complexity of the problem, the scope of the remedy, and the urgency of the situation, the chamber often gave the government a concrete deadline to comply with the judgment—ranging from one month to one year[69]—though in some cases it demanded an immediate solution.[70] Like in the 2000 decision, in some cases the chamber curbed the government's power to send new prisoners to overcrowded penitentiaries.[71]

As a response to the crisis and the chamber's decisions, the government has invested in the prison system to renew and expand the existing infrastructure.[72] However, as in the case of Colombia, the growing problem of overpopulation seems to be the result not only of insufficient infrastructure but also of criminal regulations meant to go hard on crime—by toughening up punishment, making detention the default option for those awaiting trial, and restricting parole decisions. Through its decisions, the chamber did not necessarily put these regulations into question.

Honduras and Peru

The prison system in Honduras is seriously collapsed.[73] The number of inmates in the country more than doubled in the period from 1990 to 2005.[74] By 2004, 79 percent of all the inmates were awaiting trial,[75] and, though it had decreased by 2014, the level remained quite high at 54 percent.[76] Early in 2012 a fire broke at one of the most overcrowded penitentiaries—Comayagua—killing around 360 people.[77]

One case decided by the country's supreme court in 2007 stands out. A special prosecutor filed a corrective habeas corpus petition on behalf of seven people housed in one cell of the San Pedro Sula prison, complaining about the cruel, inhuman, and degrading treatment due to the harsh detention conditions they faced—among them, the lack of access to sanitation and of mattresses.[78] The Supreme Court of Honduras upheld a lower decision ordering the "transfer of some of the prisoners to other centers nearer their place of residence, and the transfer of others to a place that meets basic conditions of sanitation."[79] As in other jurisdictions, the causes of the crisis seem to be the low priority the prison system has in the public agenda and the lack of legal regulations that expedite both trials and the release of prisoners on parole.[80]

Similarly, in Peru, the number of inmates grew by 129 percentage points in the period between 1992 and 2007.[81] By 2008, the system was operating at 186 percent of capacity,[82] a figure that skyrocketed to 227 percent in 2014,[83] one of the worst levels in the region. In 2002 the country's constitutional court issued a decision in a corrective *habeas corpus* petition on behalf of 34 inmates who had been transferred from a prison in Lima, the capital city, to the Challapalca maximum security prison, and who asked to be sent back to the former institutions.[84] The petition complained about deficiencies similar to those in the cases previously discussed, but the case had two additional elements. One was that the prison was located far away from the country's main cities—in the southeastern part of the country, near the border with Bolivia—which made visitation very difficult. The other element was that the prison had been built at about 15,000 feet (4,600 meters) above sea level, which made it particularly hazardous for the inmates' health.[85] In 2000, the Inter-American Commission on Human Rights had recommended that the center be shut down.[86]

The court granted the petition, finding that the inmates were subject to cruel and inhuman treatment and that their right to health was being violated. It ruled:

> That the National Penitentiary Institute transfer, to any other prison in the state, all those inmates whose poor health conditions . . . do not allow them to remain housed in the prison of Challapalca . . . All the remaining prisoners should be provided adequate medical care and the National Penitentiary Institute should facilitate the transport of their families, at least fortnightly.[87]

As of 2015, the Challapalca prison was still running, though the country had declared an emergency in the prison system.[88]

The Inter-American System

Both the Inter-American Commission and Court have played a very important role in the region with regard to prison conditions.[89] The former has received many petitions reporting country violations of the American Convention on Human Rights in matters related to such conditions—against Argentina, Uruguay, Brazil, and Venezuela, among other countries. In instances that it deemed urgent, the commission has asked the court to adopt provisional measures, in order to force the state into action even before the court has made a recommendation or judgment.[90] In other cases the commission has publicly voiced its concern about the violation of human rights in the prison systems of the region.[91]

The commission has decided to submit some cases to the Inter-American Court due to the states' lack of headway concerning its recommendations. The court has pronounced final decisions in a few cases—*inter alia*, against Paraguay,[92] Venezuela,[93] Peru,[94] and Ecuador[95]—declaring that states have incurred international responsibility for violating the convention. Apart from issuing recommendations and decisions in particular cases, the inter-American adjudicatory bodies have provided guidance to domestic courts as to the interpretation of the American Convention.

Due process and the right to vote

The two last topics covered in this chapter are due process rights and political rights. Starting with the former, as noted, a key issue regarding prisoners' rights is whether there exists access to adequate legal recourse for complaints about alleged aggravations of detention conditions. The scope of this issue is broad and includes the availability of a straightforward action defined by law to challenge those conditions (which is absent in most Latin American countries), a mechanism to ensure that there is no retaliation against complaining inmates, the granting of standing to NGOs and public officials to file on behalf of prisoners, and the expansion of the effects of judicial decisions taken in particular cases.

A concrete and obvious way in which due process can be affected pertains to decisions taken behind prison walls by corrections officers, who are typically immune from scrutiny. The Supreme Court of Argentina tackled some of these questions in a 2005 judgment. In the case, a convicted inmate challenged a decision by the prison administrators ordering him to spend two weeks in solitary confinement for bad behavior. The decision had been adopted without any hearing or opportunity for the inmate to present his view or to offer and contrast evidence. For the first time, the court recognized that such procedural rights existed:

> One of the principles that acquire particular significance regarding prisons is that of legality. The way in which prison authorities give concrete content to the execution of a criminal sentence and the subsequent alterations of it can generate a substantial change of the sentence and, therefore, can affect the principle of legality.[96]

The Supreme Court of Costa Rica's Constitutional Chamber decided several cases concerning due process rights. In one of them, from 1990, a convicted person complained that prison administrators had changed the open prison regime which he was enjoying for a higher security regime. The authorities claimed that the inmate had violated the conditions for the former, but the chamber sided with petitioner. It argued that the change had been unilateral, without giving petitioner the chance to defend himself or offer evidence. The chamber offered a standard for when due process rights could be suspended, which had not been met:

> [D]ue process and inmates' rights . . . do not prevent the relevant authorities of the prison system from taking necessary measures in urgent cases to ensure security and order within the system. But this can be allowed only insofar as a procedure is initiated in order to establish whether, in light of the facts, an inmate may lose the rights that he has acquired (because of having reached a particular stage of his sentence).[97]

The last subject treated in this chapter is the right to vote. Most inmates in Latin America are not allowed to exercise this right. In many countries, this is the case of both convicted individuals and pretrial detainees. Costa Rica, where any inmate is able to vote unless a decision to convict has expressly deprived the person of his political rights, is the exception.[98] The American Convention on Human Rights, which is binding upon all Latin American states, establishes that signatory states may "regulate" the right but only in the case of convicted individuals.[99] While a discussion may exist as to whether it is legitimate for the state to suspend the right even in the case of these individuals, and, if so, for how long, it seems natural that pretrial detainees be allowed to vote, since they are innocent for all legal purposes.

Countries in the region are increasingly facing legal actions aimed at removing the existing obstacles to pretrial detainees' vote. In 2002, in the *Mignone* decision, the Supreme Court of Argentina upheld a decision striking down a federal regulation preventing pretrial detainees in federal facilities from casting their ballot. The court relied heavily on the aforementioned clause in the American Convention. In one of the decision's concurring opinions, Justices Fayt and Petracchi argued:

> 18 [F]rom what has been said, it follows that universal suffrage is a fundamental value pertaining to the entire constitutional order. Pretrial detention, in turn, is not a type of anticipatory punishment and its implementation must be consistent with the purposes for which it stands. It is true that, by necessity, some rights are restricted under detention but, also by necessity, a bundle of rights should remain unchanged inside the prison . . . Depriving a citizen—who is incarcerated but has not yet been convicted—of his right to vote constitutes an impermissible restriction of a fundamental right that bears no relation to the purpose of the detention or the needs of the prison system.[100]

In order to abide by the ruling, the Argentinian Congress passed a federal statute in 2003.[101] To be sure, declaring that a right exists is very important, but it is often not sufficient to ensure it is widely respected. Only years after *Mignone* would registered pretrial detainees in the country be able to vote in federal elections.[102] The mismatch between the legal recognition of a right and the conditions for its enjoyment clearly arises in a decision announced by the Constitutional Court of Colombia. In 1993 Colombia passed a statute making it possible for pretrial detainees to vote.[103] Three detainees, however, filed a petition arguing that a polling place had not been set up in the penitentiary where they were housed. The court sided with the petitioners, emphasizing the state's duty to act in order to guarantee that the right is satisfied.

The court's rapporteur, Justice Cifuentes, wrote:

> Political participation in the form of the right to vote includes not only the subjective activity that is necessary to exercise the right, but also state action aimed at creating the conditions for such exercise to take place. The latter is a prerequisite of the former . . . The core of the right to vote [should include] the possibility of accessing the logistic and informative means that are necessary to participate effectively in the selection of rulers. [T]he exercise and fulfillment [of the right to vote] are dependent on the existence of an adequate . . . and efficient electoral organization that facilitates their realization.[104]

Chile's constitution—enacted under the Pinochet regime—establishes that the right to vote is suspended when a person is accused of a serious crime.[105] In 2011, in an advisory opinion on a draft law on elections, the country's supreme court said that the constitutional clause violated the presumption of innocence of the accused before conviction. It added that it considered as central that the political branches ensured that the right to vote by non-convicted individuals could be exercised. The court argued:

> It is necessary to make available those mechanisms that ensure that the people who are deprived of their liberty but not convicted are able to exercise their right to vote. The country's constitution's Article 1 guarantees citizens' right to participate in the political arena with equal opportunities. In order to comply with this constitutional mandate, it is necessary that a structural regulatory policy is implemented that allows the equal exercise of voting in penitentiaries and establishes the conditions under which prisoners can vote.

The court concluded:

> Allowing prisoners to vote is a measure aimed at inclusion and the strengthening of democracy that aspires to greater equality in political participation of all citizens and to a more intense promotion of their human rights.[106]

Courts in some jurisdictions have started to hear claims for the right to vote to be extended to those convicted of a crime. In 2013 the High Court of Buenos Aires City, in the capital city of Argentina, struck down a city statute clause banning those convicted of crimes and misdemeanors from voting. According to this court, the restriction was disproportionate and did not have any link with the crime committed. Profusely citing a number of human rights treaties which in Argentina have the same standing as the constitution, the court added that the restriction was discriminatory, illegitimate, and arbitrary.[107] In the view of Justice Ana María Conde,

[It] is nowadays inadmissible, under the criteria imposed by the human rights treaties . . . to suggest that punishment entails the social uprooting of the convicted person . . . to the point of destroying his right to express himself politically . . . Far from being prohibited, [the person's right to express his ideas] should be promoted, since it represents a way both to rehabilitate into society and to include the person into democratic life and, duly managed, it cannot but benefit the treatment of the convicted. This is so because, by getting informed and debating, the person may acquire knowledge of the law, of his own rights and of other people's rights, and may learn to respect different forms of expression.[108]

Conclusion

As is apparent from the preceding discussion, Latin American high courts have been taking some steps to strengthen the protection of prisoners' rights. They have drawn attention to the existence of a crisis in the prison system and in some cases provided redress—often in quite innovative ways—regarding key aspects of it. The impact of the courts' rulings seems to have been moderate, though by no means negligible. Now, the magnitude of the crisis is such that it may not be surprising that judicial involvement provides only partial solutions. Ultimate responsibility seems largely to lie in the political branches. An adequate response to the crisis may demand a change of priorities, pushing the situation of the prison system to the forefront of the public agenda and perhaps also redefining criminal policies even to the point of calling into question the very notion of incarceration. Courts appear to have been helpful in the former respect, but not much in the latter. As in other subject matters and issues, the main question is to what extent courts in unequal or unjust societies can change reality. A fair answer may be that courts can effect *some* degree of change. Whether this is interpreted as a half-empty or half-full glass is incumbent upon the reader.

Questions

a In many of the decisions reviewed in this chapter, a situation of overcrowding was reported, and different courts (or the same court in different decisions) chose different ways to deal with the problem. Some ordered the adoption of "command-and-control" types of measures and some opted instead to engage the parties and other relevant stakeholders in the joint definition of a remedy. Which of these options is preferable, and in which circumstances?

b In the decisions discussing detention conditions and overcrowding, should courts have adopted a more sweeping measure such as the immediate release of (at least some of the) prisoners? What would be the advantages and disadvantages of such a measure?

c Should pretrial detainees be allowed to vote? What about convicted prisoners?

d The chapter argues that the short-term, concrete impact of some judicial decisions concerning the prison system has been moderate. Is this a good way to measure the success of courts' intervention or other indicators should be employed? Is the intervention of courts in any way still useful in cases where their decisions are weakly complied with? To the extent that courts have leeway to select their own docket, should they take part in cases—and, if so, in what way—when they know beforehand that their decision will likely remain under-enforced?

Notes

* The author wishes to thank Mariana Acevedo Nuevo, Johanna Hardwick, Cecilia Hopp, Rafael Colombo, Theo Baizabal Lagunes, and Miriam Itzel Hernández for research and editing assistance, and Libardo Ariza, Paola Bergallo, Domingo Lovera Parmo, and Miguel Sarre for their insightful comments on an earlier version of this chapter.

1 See, e.g., Inter-American Commission on Human Rights, Rapporteurship on the Rights of Persons Deprived of Liberty, REPORT ON THE HUMAN RIGHTS OF PERSONS DEPRIVED OF LIBERTY IN THE AMERICAS, OEA/Ser.L/V/II. Doc. 64 (December 2011); LUCÍA DAMMERT AND LIZA ZÚÑIGA, PRISONS: PROBLEMS AND CHALLENGES FOR THE AMERICAS 149 (2008); Randal Archibold, *Inmate's Lament: "Rather Be Dead Than Here,"* THE NEW YORK TIMES, March 13, 2012.

2 A single chapter can touch upon only so many judicial decisions from a few countries. The criterion that guided the selection of decisions was the novelty, and promise, of the courts' approaches and interventions. Also, the chapter does not address the ever-pressing questions of whether and under

what conditions punishment in the form of imprisonment is legitimate and what alternatives exist, all questions that ought to be expanded upon and debated.

3 Heraldo Munoz, *Lessons from the World's Most Unequal Region*, speech by UN Assistant Secretary General and Director Regional Bureau for Latin America and the Caribbean, www.undp.org/content/rblac/en/home/presscenter/speeches/2013/07/10/lessons-from-the-world-s-most-unequal-region.html.

4 Libardo J. Ariza, *Reformando el infierno: los tribunales y la transformación del campo penitenciario en América Latina*, in Los muros de la infamia: prisiones en Colombia y en América Latina, at 26 (Manuel Iturralde and Libardo J. Ariza eds, 2011) (author's own translation).

5 Ibid., 28.

6 As this chapter will show, in Latin America, the legally mandated separation between institutions for convicted prisoners and for pretrial detainees is largely ignored in practice.

7 See Nidia Marin, *Saturan cárceles sentenciados por delitos menores*, El Sol de México, March 4, 2012, available at www.oem.com.mx/laprensa/notas/n2453707.htm.

8 Lucía Dammert and Liza Zúñiga, Prisons: Problems and Challenges for the Americas 149 (2008).

9 Own estimation, based on data published by the International Center for Prison Studies, available at www.prisonstudies.org/.

10 See Inter-American Commission on Human Rights. Rapporteurship on the Rights of Persons Deprived of Liberty, Report on the Use of Pretrial Detention in the Americas, OEA/Ser.L/V/II. Doc. 46/13 (December 30, 2013); Lucía Dammert and Liza Zúñiga, Prisons: Problems and Challenges for the Americas 41–50 (2008).

11 Own estimation, based on data published by the International Center for Prison Studies, available at www.prisonstudies.org/.

12 Ibid. Some public officials, judges, and scholars have proposed (partial) solutions to the overpopulation crisis, including the implementation of a policy under which a judge would need to make sure that adequate facilities can house a person in humane conditions before sending him or her to prison. In Argentina, the federal prison administration has drafted a proposal in this regard, available at www.ppn.gov.ar/?q=node/1924. The topic is being discussed in other countries, like Uruguay: Quieren fijar "cupos" para internación en cárceles, El País, Uruguay, August 12, 2010, available at http://historico.elpais.com.uy/100812/pnacio-507850/nacional/Quieren-fijar-cupos-para-internacion-en-carceles/. See also Juan F. Gonzalez-Bertomeu and María Paula Saffon, Ni un preso más sin cupo, SinPermiso, December 6, 2010, available at sinpermiso.info.

13 Lucía Dammert and Liza Zúñiga, Prisons: Problems and Challenges for the Americas 149 (2008).

14 The Colombian court acknowledged this situation in a case discussed in the text below.

15 Máximo Langer, *Revolution in Latin American Criminal Procedure: Diffusion of Legal Ideas from the Periphery*, 55 American Journal of Comparative Law, 617–76 (2007).

16 See Inter-American Commission on Human Rights. Rapporteurship on the Rights of Persons Deprived of Liberty, Report on the Use of Pretrial Detention in the Americas, OEA/Ser.L/V/II. Doc. 46/13 (December 30, 2013). See also Richard M. Aborn and Ashley D. Cannon, *Prisons: in Jail, but not Sentenced*, 7/1 Americas Quarterly (2013).

17 Lucía Dammert and Liza Zúñiga, Prisons: Problems and Challenges for the Americas 70 (2008).

18 The ratio varies from country to country, in some cases significantly. In Bolivia, 83 percent of all prisoners are under preventive detention; this figure is 73 percent in Paraguay and between 62 and 67 percent in Uruguay, Venezuela, and Panama. International Center for Prison Studies, available at www.prisonstudies.org/ *(data published in 2013)*.

19 Approved in 1957.

20 A recent development that accompanies this trend and that is worth mentioning is the phenomenon of the privatization of the state's punitive response. A number of Latin American countries—Brazil, Colombia, Chile, Mexico, and Uruguay among them—have begun to experiment with different schemes involving the privatization of prison facilities. See Verónica Smink, *Brasil tendrá las primeras cárceles privadas de América Latina*, BBC Mundo, June 6, 2011, available at www.bbc.co.uk/mundo/noticias/2011/06/110616_brasil_carcel_privada_vs.shtml; Camilo E. Bernal Sarmiento, *Hacinamiento y privatización de las cárceles: lecciones de la experiencia chilena*, Semana, December 4, 2012, available at www.semana.com/opinion/hacinamiento-privatizacion-carceles-lecciones-experiencia-chilena/165928–3.aspx; *Cárceles privadas en México*, El Universal, October 2, 2013, available at www.eluniversal.com.mx/nacion-mexico/2013/impreso/carceles-privadas-en-mexico-209636.html; *Tres empresas privadas construirán la primera cárcel privada*, Espectador,

May 26, 2014, available at www.espectador.com/sociedad/291820/tres-empresas-construiran-la-primera-carcel-privada.

21 Own estimation, based on data published by the International Center for Prison Studies, available at www.prisonstudies.org/.

22 Ibid. In Bolivia, all female prisoners are housed in only three correctional facilities. See *Estudio: Solo existen tres cárceles para mujeres en Bolivia*, Opinión.com.bo, March 15, 2013, available at www.opinion.com.bo/opinion/articulos/2013/0315/noticias.php?id=89068.

23 See Centro de Estudios Legales y Sociales, Mujeres en prisión: los alcances del castigo 10–11 (2011). See also Lucía Dammert and Liza Zúñiga, Prisons: Problems and Challenges for the Americas 83–84 (2008).

24 See Jenny Pontón Cevallos, *The Forgotten Women in Ecuador's Prisons*, in Prisons: Problems and Challenges for the Americas, at 92 (Lucía Dammert and Liza Zúñiga, 2008).

25 Lucía Dammert and Liza Zúñiga, Prisons: Problems and Challenges for the Americas 12 (2008).

26 Ibid., 85–6.

27 Centro de Estudios Legales y Sociales, Mujeres en prisión: los alcances del castigo 109–20 (2011).

28 Inter-American Court of Human Rights, case of "Miguel Castro-Castro Prison v. Peru," November 25, 2006.

29 The court held that vaginal examinations "constituted sexual rape that due to its effects constituted torture" under Section 2 of the Inter-American Convention to Prevent and Punish Torture.

30 Centro de Estudios Legales y Sociales, Mujeres en prisión: los alcances del castigo 127 (2011).

31 Lucía Dammert and Liza Zúñiga, Prisons: Problems and Challenges for the Americas 68–9 (2008).

32 See *Reforma al Código Penitenciario dejaría libres a 48 mil presos*, El Espectador, April 3, 2013, available at www.elespectador.com/noticias/politica/reforma-al-codigo-penitenciario-dejaria-libres-48-mil-p-articulo-413945. A more moderate version of the bill was passed and adopted in 2014. See *Reforma al Código Penitenciario aún no refleja la descongestión en cárceles*, El Universal, January 30, 2014, available at www.eluniversal.com.co/colombia/reforma-al-codigo-penitenciario-aun-no-refleja-la-descongestion-en-carceles-150072.

33 Lyla Bugara, *Unique Brazilian Prison Alternative Celebrates 40-Year Anniversary*, Prison Legal News, March 15, 2014, available at www.prisonlegalnews.org/news/2013/mar/15/unique-brazilian-prison-alternative-celebrates-40-year-anniversary/.

34 To the extent that pretrial detention is deemed legitimate for a limited set of cases, this question also applies, although the restriction of the person's rights should naturally be less intrusive than in the case of convicted inmates.

35 See International Covenant on Civil and Political Rights, United Nations General Assembly Resolution 2200A (XXI), entered into force March 23, 1976, Section 10.3; American Convention on Human Rights, Sections 5 and 6; Constitución de la Nación Argentina (Constitution of Argentina), August 22, 1994, Section 18.

36 See International Covenant on Civil and Political Rights, Sections 7 and 10.1; American Convention on Human Rights, Sections 5.1 and 5.2; Constitución Política de los Estados Unidos Mexicanos (Political Constitution of Mexico), February 5, 1917, Section 19; Constituiçao da República Federativa do Brasil (Constitution of Brazil), October 5, 1988, Section 5.III.

37 See International Covenant on Civil and Political Rights, Section 10.2; American Convention on Human Rights, Section 5.4. There are other documents, like the UN Standard Minimum Rules for the Treatment of Prisoners (approved in 1957), that provide an even more comprehensive set of rules, though they are not necessarily binding upon states.

38 Supreme Court of Argentina, case of "Dessy s/habeas corpus," October 19, 1995 (D. 346:XXIV).

39 Ibid.

40 Constitutional Court of Colombia, Decision T-596/92, December 10, 1992.

41 Ibid.

42 Constitutional Court of Colombia, Decision T-896A/06, November 2, 2006 [emphasis added].

43 Supreme Court of Costa Rica, Constitutional Chamber, Decision 1175–98, December 3, 1998. See also Luis Paulino Mora Mora, *Sobrepoblación penitenciaria y derechos humanos: la experiencia constitucional*, in Justicia penal y sobrepoblación penitenciaria, at 70 (Elías Carranza ed., 2001).

44 In some cases, the distinction between these two categories will be blurry. When someone is forced to share a cell with many others, the violation is as much the result of the state's omission as it is of its direct action.

45 Constitutional Court of Colombia, Decision T-153/98, April 28, 1998.

46 Ibid.

47 Ibid.
48 Ibid.
49 Ibid.
50 According to official data, between 2002 and 2008 the number of *tutela* petitions complaining about lack of access to healthcare grew by 1,500 percentage points. Juzgado 56 Penal del Circuito de Bogotá, Acción de tutela 2012–0158, January 30, 2013.
51 Own estimation, based on data published by the International Center for Prison Studies, available at www.prisonstudies.org/.
52 Constitutional Court of Colombia, Auto 41/2011, December 9, 2011.
53 Ibid. See also Daniella Sánchez Russo, *Orden a las prisiones*, El Espectador, May 20, 2011, available at www.elespectador.com/impreso/judicial/articulo-271233-orden-prisiones.
54 The International Center for Prison Studies (www.prisonstudies.org/) reports 58 percent, while the Colombian prison administration reports 55 percent for the beginning of 2013; INPEC, *Informe Estadístico Mayo 2013*, www.inpec.gov.co.
55 The most extreme of these cases was the Riohacha prison. By the end of 2013 it was operating at 389 percent of capacity. See *La 'bomba' carcelaria explotó*, Revista Semana, February 1, 2014, available at www.semana.com/nacion/articulo/crisis-carcelaria-una-bomba-de-tiempo-que-exploto/375789–3.
56 Ibid. As mentioned above, a new statute was passed in 2014 to deal with the crisis.
57 See Libardo J. Ariza, *Reformando el infierno: los tribunales y la transformación del campo penitenciario en América Latina*, in Los muros de la infamia: prisiones en Colombia y en América Latina at 56–8 (Manuel Iturralde and Libardo J. Ariza eds, 2011).
58 See *Ultimátum de Corte Constitucional al Gobierno por crisis carcelaria*, El Tiempo, April 20, 2015.
59 Ibid.
60 Supreme Court of Argentina, case of "Verbitsky s/habeas corpus," May 3, 2005 (V. 856. XXXVIII). See also Centro de Estudios Legales y Sociales, Informe Anual 2007, chapter 7.
61 United Nations, Human Rights Committee, Consideration of reports submitted by States parties under article 40 of the Covenant, 98th session, New York, March 8–26, 2010, paragraphs 16–18.
62 That same year, a group of law professors filed an amicus brief in the Supreme Court detailing the lack of compliance with the decision's standards. Available at www.cels.org.ar.
63 Own estimation, based on data published by the International Center for Prison Studies, available at www.prisonstudies.org/. On the 2012 rate, see *Costa Rica registra una sobrepoblación carcelaria del 28,1 por ciento*, SDP noticias, March 7, 2012, available at www.sdpnoticias.com/notas/2012/03/07/costa-rica-registra-una-sobrepoblacion-carcelaria-del-28-1-por-ciento.
64 Figures from 1992–2007 come from Lucía Dammert and Liza Zúñiga, Prisons: Problems and Challenges for the Americas 59 (2008) and José María Rico, *Reflexiones sobre el sistema penitenciario*, La Nación, January 28, 2011, available at www.nacion.com/archivo/Reflexiones-sistema-penitenciario_0_1174082597.html. The figure from 2012 comes from Roy Walmsley, World Prison Population List, 3 (International Center for Prison Studies, 2013), available at www.prisonstudies.org/.
65 David Delgado, *650 nuevos reos al mes agravan hacinamiento en cárceles ticas*, La Nación, December 12, 2010, available at http://wfnode01.nacion.com/2010–12–12/Sucesos/NotaPrincipal/Sucesos2602956.aspx.
66 Supreme Court of Costa Rica, Constitutional Chamber, Decision 709–91, October 4, 1991. Other decisions from the 1990s reporting bad detention conditions include Decisions 1032–96, 2835–96, 4896–96, 4576–96, 5091–96, 49–97, 1774–97, and 1801–98.
67 Luis Paulino Mora Mora, *Sobrepoblación penitenciaria y derechos humanos: la experiencia constitucional*, in Justicia penal y sobrepoblación penitenciaria, at 73 (Elías Carranza ed., 2001). This was possible because, since 1989, the country's constitution established that the *amparo*, a special writ for the protection of rights, could be used when fundamental rights conferred by international human rights instruments applicable to Costa Rica were in jeopardy. Constitución Política de Costa Rica, (Constitution of Costa Rica), November 7, 1949, Section 48. See also Mora Mora, id., at 70.
68 Supreme Court of Costa Rica, Constitutional Chamber, Decision 7484–00, August 25, 2000.
69 See, e.g., Supreme Court of Costa Rica, Constitutional Chamber, Decision 17942–10, October 29, 2010. See also Decisions 19767–10, 3742–11, 4815–11, 5644–11, 5878–11, 7361–11, 7988–11, 8906–11, 10803–11, 11108–11, 12316–11, and 14245–11. See also Luis Paulino Mora Mora, *Sobrepoblación penitenciaria y derechos humanos: la experiencia constitucional*, in Justicia penal y sobrepoblación penitenciaria (Elías Carranza ed., 2001).
70 See, e.g., Supreme Court of Costa Rica, Constitutional Chamber, Decision 8383–04, July 30, 2004. See also Decisions 7745–05, 2983–06, 11762–06, 1332–09, 2785–09, 16783–09, 1872–10, 5424–10,

8384–10, 14059–10, 14807–10, 16283–10, 17176–10, 659–11, 222–11, 2118–11, 2630–11, 5711–11, 7110–11, 8465–11, 11685–11, 13160–11, 13912–11, 14066–11, 14311–11, and 14650–11.

71 See, e.g., Supreme Court of Costa Rica, Constitutional Chamber, Decision 7980–05, June 22, 2005.

72 See David Delgado, *650 nuevos reos al mes agravan hacinamiento en cárceles ticas*, La Nación, December 12, 2010, available at http://wfnode01.nacion.com/2010–12–12/Sucesos/NotaPrincipal/Sucesos2602956.aspx.

73 *Afirman que el sistema carcelario está colapsado*, El Heraldo, February 16, 2012, available at www.elheraldo.hn/Secciones-Principales/Al-Frente/Afirman-que-sistema-carcelario-esta-colapsado.

74 Lucía Dammert and Liza Zúñiga, Prisons: Problems and Challenges for the Americas 45 (2008).

75 Diego Cevallos, *Rights: Latin America's Prisons—Hell on Earth*, IPS, September 14, 2004, available at www.ipsnews.net/2004/09/rights-latin-americas-prisons-hell-on-earth/.

76 International Center for Prison Studies (www.prisonstudies.org/).

77 Ibid. See also *Autoridades corrigen la cifra de muertos por incendio en prisión hondureña*, CNN México, February 19, 2012, available at http://mexico.cnn.com/mundo/2012/02/19/autoridades-corrigen-la-cifra-de-muertos-por-incendio-en-prision-hondurena.

78 Three years before the Supreme Court's decision in the case, 107 inmates had died in the prison in yet another fire. *Honduras admite responsabilidad en tragedia de cárcel en 2004*, El Heraldo, February 28, 2012, available at www.elheraldo.hn/Secciones-Principales/Pais/Honduras-admite-responsabilidad-en-tragedia-de-carcel-en-2004. In 2012 the Inter-American Court of Human Rights held the state responsible for the violation of the American Convention with regard to this event. Inter-American Court of Human Rights, case of "Pacheco Teruel et al. v. Honduras," April 27, 2012.

79 Supreme Court of Honduras, SJCSJ-RH0159, Decision of March 7, 2007. See also Libardo J. Ariza, *Reformando el infierno: los tribunales y la transformación del campo penitenciario en América Latina*, in Los muros de la infamia: prisiones en Colombia y en América Latina, at 45 (Manuel Iturralde and Libardo J. Ariza eds, 2011).

80 Robert Marín García, *Nada en centros penales funciona*, El Heraldo, February 20, 2012, available at www.elheraldo.hn/Secciones-Principales/Al-Frente/Nada-en-centros-penales-funciona.

81 Lucía Dammert and Liza Zúñiga, Prisons: Problems and Challenges for the Americas 52 (2008).

82 Ibid., 52.

83 International Center for Prison Studies (www.prisonstudies.org/).

84 Luis Alberto Huerta Guerrero, *Hábeas Corpus y Condiciones de Reclusión*, Comisión Andina de Juristas, 6, available at http://perso.unifr.ch/derechopenal/assets/files/obrasportales/op._20080612_38.pdf.

85 Ibid.

86 Inter-American Commission on Human Rights, Second Report on the Situation of Human Rights in Peru, Chapter IX. Prison Conditions, paragraph 24, recommendation 12, June 2000 (recommending that "the prisons at Challapalca and Yanamayo be deemed unfit to serve that purpose, and that the personnel detained at those prisons be transferred to other prisons").

87 Constitutional Court of Peru, File No. 1429–2002, November 19, 2002. The Inter-American Commission issued another report in 2003, insisting on its recommendation: Special Report on the Human Rights Situation at the Challapalca Prison, Department of Tacna, Peru, October 2003.

88 See Yuvisa Martínez *and* Manuel Rodríguez, *Trasladan a 29 cabecillas de las más peligrosas bandas a prisión de Challapalca*, La Republica, April 26, 2015, available at http://larepublica.pe/26-04-2015/trasladan-a-29-cabecillas-de-las-mas-peligrosas-bandas-a-prision-de-challapalca; *Peru Declares Emergency in Prison System*, Peruvian Times, February 23, 2012, available at www.peruviantimes.com/23/peru-declares-emergency-in-prison-system/15117/.

89 On the role of the Inter-American Commission and Court, see Chapter 13.

90 Recent provisional measures include PM 351/11–Ananias Laparra Martinez (Mexico, 2011); PM 425/11–X (Argentina, 2011); PM 199/11–People Deprived of Their Freedom at Professor Aníbal Bruno Prison (Brazil, 2011); PM 219/11, Relatives of Inmates at the Rodeo I and Rodeo II Prisons (Venezuela, 2011); PM 393/10–Luis Alvarez Renta (Dominican Republic, 2010); Matter of Urso Branco Prison (Brazil, 2009); PM 304/08–Diomedes Carvajalino Meneses (Colombia, 2008); Adolescents in the Public Prison of Guarujá (Brazil, 2007); Center for the Defense of Children's and Adolescents' Rights of the Federal District (Brazil, 2006); Matter of the Mendoza Prisons (Argentina, 2004).

91 See, e.g., Inter-American Commission on Human Rights, Rapporteurship on the Rights of Persons Deprived of Liberty, Report on the Human Rights of Persons Deprived of Liberty in the Americas, OEA/Ser.L/V/II. Doc. 64 (December 2011); see also *La CIDH exige medidas urgentes para evitar la violencia en las cárceles*, CNN Mexico, July 29, 2011, available at http://mexico.cnn.com/

nacional/2011/07/29/la-cidh-exige-medidas-urgentes-para-evitar-la-violencia-en-las-carceles; *CIDH preocupada por superpoblación en cárceles de Uruguay*, La Prensa Gráfica, July 25, 2011, available at www.laprensagrafica.com/Movil/el-salvador/lodeldia/207464-cidh-preocupada-por-superpoblacion-en-carceles-de-uruguay; Inter-American Commission on Human Rights, La Comisión Interamericana deplora muertes violentas en cárcel de Venezuela (January 6, 2012), available at www.oas.org/es/cidh/prensa/comunicados/2012/001.asp; Inter-American Commission on Human Rights, CIDH reitera necesidad de prevenir actos de violencia en cárcel de Venezuela (February 22, 2011), available at www.oas.org/es/cidh/prensa/comunicados/2011/014.asp.

92 Inter-American Court of Human Rights, case of "Juvenile Reeducation Institute v. Paraguay," September 2, 2004.

93 Inter-American Court of Human Rights, case of "Montero-Aranguren et al. (Detention Center of Catia) v. Venezuela," July 5, 2006.

94 Inter-American Court of Human Rights, case of "Neira-Alegría et al. v. Peru," January 19, 1995.

95 Inter-American Court of Human Rights, case of "Tibi v. Ecuador," September 7, 2004.

96 Supreme Court of Argentina, case of "Romero Cacharane, H.A. s/ejecución penal," March 9, 2005 (R. 230. XXXIV).

97 Supreme Court of Costa Rica, Constitutional Chamber, Decision 239–90, 1990.

98 See Luis Antonio Sobrado González, *Experiencia costarricense del voto de personas privadas de libertad*, 3 Revista de Derecho Electoral, Tribunal Supremo de Elecciones (First Semester, 2007).

99 American Convention on Human Rights, Section 23.

100 Supreme Court of Argentina, case of "Mignone, Emilio H. s/habeas corpus," April 9, 2002 (M. 1486. XXXVI. / M. 1491. XXXVI).

101 Law 25,858, December 29, 2003. See also Decree 1,291, June 30, 2006.

102 Voting in Argentina is compulsory, but an official identity document is necessary to do so. Pretrial inmates who lack such document are thus prevented from voting. *El voto de los presos*, Página 12, April 27, 2015, available at www.pagina12.com.ar/diario/elpais/1–271472–2015–04–27.html; Presos sin condena también votaron, Argentina Elecciones, October 23, 2013, www.argentinaelecciones.com/noticia-voto-presos-sin-condena-1241.html.

103 Law 65, August 20, 1993, Section 57.

104 Constitutional Court of Colombia, Decision T-324/94, July 14, 1994.

105 Constitución Política de Chile (Constitution of Chile), October 10, 1980, Section 16.2.

106 Supreme Court of Chile, Oficio 21–2011, Informe Proyecto de ley 54–2010, January 25, 2011.

107 *Condenados con derecho a voto*, Página 12, September 12, 2013, available at www.pagina12.com.ar/diario/elpais/1–228833-2013-09-12.html.

108 High Court of Buenos Aires City, case of "Asociación por los Derechos Civiles c/ GCBA s/ acción declarativa de inconstitucionalidad," September 6, 2013.

References

Richard M. Aborn and Ashley D. Cannon, *Prisons: in Jail, but not Sentenced*, 7/1 Americas Quarterly (2013).

Afirman que el sistema carcelario está colapsado, El Heraldo, February 16, 2012, available at www.elheraldo.hn/Secciones-Principales/Al-Frente/Afirman-que-sistema-carcelario-esta-colapsado.

Randal Archibold, *Inmate's Lament: "Rather Be Dead Than Here,"* The New York Times, March 13, 2012.

Libardo J. Ariza, *Reformando el infierno: los tribunales y la transformación del campo penitenciario en América Latina*, in Los muros de la infamia: prisiones en Colombia y en América Latina, at 26 (Manuel Iturralde and Libardo J. Ariza eds, 2011).

Autoridades corrigen la cifra de muertos por incendio en prisión hondureña, CNN México, February 19, 2012, available at http://mexico.cnn.com/mundo/2012/02/19/autoridades-corrigen-la-cifra-de-muertos-por-incendio-en-prision-hondurena.

Lyla Bugara, *Unique Brazilian Prison Alternative Celebrates 40-Year Anniversary*, Prison Legal News, March 15, 2014, available at www.prisonlegalnews.org/news/2013/mar/15/unique-brazilian-prison-alternative-celebrates-40-year-anniversary/.

Cárceles privadas en México, El Universal, October 2, 2013, available at www.eluniversal.com.mx/nacion-mexico/2013/impreso/carceles-privadas-en-mexico-209636.html.

Elías Carranza (ed.), Justicia penal y sobrepoblación penitenciaria (2001).

Centro de Estudios Legales y Sociales, Informe Anual 2007.

Centro de Estudios Legales y Sociales, Mujeres en prisión: los alcances del castigo (2011).

Diego Cevallos, *Rights: Latin America's Prisons—Hell on Earth*, IPS, September 14, 2004, available at www.ipsnews.net/2004/09/rights-latin-americas-prisons-hell-on-earth/.

CIDH preocupada por superpoblación en cárceles de Uruguay, La Prensa Gráfica, July 25, 2011, available at www.laprensagrafica.com/Movil/el-salvador/lodeldia/207464-cidh-preocupada-por-superpoblacion-en-carceles-de-uruguay.

Condenados con derecho a voto, Página 12, September 12, 2013, available at www.pagina12.com.ar/diario/elpais/1–228833–2013–09–12.html.

Costa Rica registra una sobrepoblación carcelaria del 28,1 por ciento, SDP noticias, March 7, 2012, available at www.sdpnoticias.com/notas/2012/03/07/costa-rica-registra-una-sobrepoblacion-carcelaria-del-28–1-por-ciento.

Lucía Dammert and Liza Zúñiga, Prisons: Problems and Challenges for the Americas (2008).

David Delgado, *650 nuevos reos al mes agravan hacinamiento en cárceles ticas*, La Nación, December 12, 2010, available at http://wfnode01.nacion.com/2010–12–12/Sucesos/NotaPrincipal/Sucesos2602956.aspx.

El voto de los presos, Página 12, April 27, 2015, available at www.pagina12.com.ar/diario/elpais/1–271472–2015–04–27.html;

Estudio: Solo existen tres cárceles para mujeres en Bolivia, Opinión.com.bo, March 15, 2013, available at www.opinion.com.bo/opinion/articulos/2013/0315/noticias.php?id=89068.

Robert Marín García, *Nada en centros penales funciona*, El Heraldo, February 20, 2012, available at www.elheraldo.hn/Secciones-Principales/Al-Frente/Nada-en-centros-penales-funciona.

Juan F. Gonzalez-Bertomeu and María Paula Saffon, *Ni un preso más sin cupo*, Sin Permiso, December 6, 2010.

Luis Antonio Sobrado González, *Experiencia costarricense del voto de personas privadas de libertad*, 3 Revista de Derecho Electoral, Tribunal Supremo de Elecciones (First Semester, 2007).

Luis Alberto Huerta Guerrero, *Hábeas Corpus y Condiciones de Reclusión*, *Comisión Andina de Juristas*, 6, available at http://perso.unifr.ch/derechopenal/assets/files/obrasportales/op._20080612_38.pdf.

Alvaro Herrero and Leonardo Filippini, *Los condenados también tienen derecho a votar*, Diario Clarín, October 6, 2011, available at www.clarin.com/opinion/condenados-derecho-votar_0_567543332.html

Honduras admite responsabilidad en tragedia de cárcel en 2004, El Heraldo, February 28, 2012, available at www.elheraldo.hn/Secciones-Principales/Pais/Honduras-admite-responsabilidad-en-tragedia-de-carcel-en-2004.

INPEC, *Informe Estadístico Mayo 2013*, www.inpec.gov.co.

Inter-American Commission on Human Rights, *CIDH reitera necesidad de prevenir actos de violencia en cárcel de Venezuela* (February 22 2011), available at www.oas.org/es/cidh/prensa/comunicados/2011/014.asp.

Inter-American Commission on Human Rights, *La Comisión Interamericana deplora muertes violentas en cárcel de Venezuela* (January 6, 2012), available at www.oas.org/es/cidh/prensa/comunicados/2012/001.asp.

Inter-American Commission on Human Rights, Second Report on the Situation of Human Rights in Peru, Chapter IX. Prison Conditions (June 2000).

Inter-American Commission on Human Rights, Special Report on the Human Rights Situation at the Challapalca Prison, Department of Tacna, Peru (October 2003).

Inter-American Commission on Human Rights, Rapporteurship on the Rights of Persons Deprived of Liberty, Report on the Human Rights of Persons Deprived of Liberty in the Americas, OEA/Ser.L/V/II. Doc. 64 (December 2011).

Inter-American Commission on Human Rights. Rapporteurship on the Rights of Persons Deprived of Liberty, Report on the Use of Pretrial Detention in the Americas, OEA/Ser.L/V/II. Doc. 46/13 (December 30, 2013).

La 'bomba' carcelaria explotó, Revista Semana, February 1, 2014, available at www.semana.com/nacion/articulo/crisis-carcelaria-una-bomba-de-tiempo-que-exploto/375789–3.

La CIDH exige medidas urgentes para evitar la violencia en las cárceles, CNN Mexico, July 29, 2011, available at http://mexico.cnn.com/nacional/2011/07/29/la-cidh-exige-medidas-urgentes-para-evitar-la-violencia-en-las-carceles.
Máximo Langer, *Revolution in Latin American Criminal Procedure: Diffusion of Legal Ideas from the Periphery*, 55 American Journal of Comparative Law, 617–76 (2007).
Nidia Marin, *Saturan cárceles sentenciados por delitos menores*, El Sol de México, March 4, 2012, available at www.oem.com.mx/laprensa/notas/n2453707.htm.
Yuvisa Martínez and Manuel Rodríguez, *Trasladan a 29 cabecillas de las más peligrosas bandas a prisión de Challapalca, La Republica, April 26, 2015, available at* http://larepublica.pe/26–04–2015/trasladan-a-29-cabecillas-de-las-mas-peligrosas-bandas-a-prision-de-challapalca.
Luis Paulino Mora Mora, *Sobrepoblación penitenciaria y derechos humanos: la experiencia constitucional*, in Justicia penal y sobrepoblación penitenciaria, at 70 (Elías Carranza ed., 2001).
Heraldo Munoz, *Lessons from the World's Most Unequal Region*, speech by UN Assistant Secretary General and Director Regional Bureau for Latin America and the Caribbean, www.undp.org/content/rblac/en/home/presscenter/speeches/2013/07/10/lessons-from-the-world-s-most-unequal-region.html.
Peru Declares Emergency in Prison System, Peruvian Times, February 23, 2012, available at www.peruviantimes.com/23/peru-declares-emergency-in-prison-system/15117/.
Jenny Pontón Cevallos, *The Forgotten Women in Ecuador's Prisons*, in Prisons: Problems and Challenges for the Americas, at 92 (Lucía Dammert and Liza Zúñiga, 2008).
Presos sin condena también votaron, Argentina Elecciones, October 23, 2013.
Quieren fijar "cupos" para internación en cárceles, El País, Uruguay, August 12, 2010.
Reforma al Código Penitenciario dejaría libres a 48 mil presos, El Espectador, April 3, 2013, available at www.elespectador.com/noticias/politica/reforma-al-codigo-penitenciario-dejaria-libres-48-mil-p-articulo-413945.
José María Rico, *Reflexiones sobre el sistema penitenciario*, La Nación, January 28, 2011, available at www.nacion.com/archivo/Reflexiones-sistema-penitenciario_0_1174082597.html.
Daniella Sánchez Russo, *Orden a las prisiones*, El Espectador, May 20, 2011, available at www.elespectador.com/impreso/judicial/articulo-271233-orden-prisiones.
Camilo E. Bernal Sarmiento, *Hacinamiento y privatización de las cárceles: lecciones de la experiencia chilena*, Semana, December 4, 2012, available at www.semana.com/opinion/hacinamiento-privatizacion-carceles-lecciones-experiencia-chilena/165928–3.aspx.
Verónica Smink, *Brasil tendrá las primeras cárceles privadas de América Latina*, BBC Mundo, June 6, 2011, available at www.bbc.co.uk/mundo/noticias/2011/06/110616_brasil_carcel_privada_vs.shtml.
Tres empresas privadas construirán la primera cárcel privada, Espectador, May 26, 2014.
Ultimátum de Corte Constitucional al Gobierno por crisis carcelaria, El Tiempo, April 20, 2015.
United Nations, Human Rights Committee, Consideration of reports submitted by States parties under article 40 of the Covenant, 98th session, New York, March 8–26, 2010.
Roy Walmsley, World Prison Population List (International Center for Prison Studies, 2013), available at www.prisonstudies.org/.

Further reading

Victor Abramovich, *Presentación y agradecimientos*, in Colapso del sistema carcelario (2005).
Elías Carranza (ed.), Cárcel y justicia penal en América Latina y El Caribe. Cómo implementar el modelo de derechos y obligaciones de las Naciones Unidas (2009).
Elías Carranza, Mario Houed, Nicholas Liverpool, Luis P. Mora, and Luis Rodríguez Manzanera, Sistemas penitenciarios y alternativas a la prisión en América Latina y el Caribe (1992).
Due Process of Law Foundation, Independencia judicial insuficiente, prisión preventiva deformada (2013).
Leonardo Filippini, *El derecho al voto de los condenados*, La Ley Suplemento Constitucional, February 13, 2012.

David Garland (ed.), MASS IMPRISONMENT (2001).

David Garland and R.A. Duff (eds), A READER ON PUNISHMENT (1995).

DAVID GARLAND, PUNISHMENT AND MODERN SOCIETY (1993).

Andrea Pochak, *Condiciones de detención. Prólogo*, Asociación por los Derechos Civiles, available at www.adc-sidh.org/index.php?idsec=15.

Mark Ungar, *Prisons and Politics in Contemporary Latin America*, 25/4 HUMAN RIGHTS QUARTERLY, 909–34 (2003).

6 Freedom of expression and social protest

Roberto Gargarella and Ramiro Alvarez Ugarte[*]

Introduction

Social protest is not new in Latin America; the continent is known for its high levels of mass mobilization and political activism. However, there is a novelty to the type of social protest that has arisen in the region over the last few decades, particularly in the late 1990s. Over that time, many (previously non-existent) factors were combined to give way to very peculiar forms of social conflict.

By then, a vast process of deep reforms (known, perhaps misleadingly, as neoliberal reforms) that had changed the structure of the state as it had been for almost an entire century was about to be concluded. The central characteristic of this structure had been the strong presence of the state in the economy; the reforms of the 1990s should be understood as intended to end with the Keynesian–interventionist state. According to Ocampo, they constituted "an array of reforms oriented towards the expansion of the role of market forces."[1] Among the measures taken, one can note budget discipline, fiscal reform, the liberalization of commerce—particularly international commerce—the open reception of foreign capital, the privatization of parts of the economy previously under state control, and the deregulation policies advanced in several parts of the economy.[2] These economic changes brought along a sudden increase in the unemployment index and similar increases in the poverty and inequality indexes.[3] At the same time (and in good measure, for the same reasons), unions—which had carried a lot of weight in the previous period—saw their number of affiliations strongly diminished. As a consequence, they lost negotiating power in dealing with corporations and the state, as well as a good share of their ability to manage social conflict. Moreover, and inconsistently, this period of increasing social difficulties was accompanied by a rebirth of a socially oriented practice of the law—a rebirth that included new constitutions openly committed to social justice, as well as the renewed importance of international human rights law. The context surrounding these processes was also very particular: in most countries, democracy was still extremely young and fragile after long years of military dictatorship or authoritarian government.

All of these elements—drastic economic reforms, substantial increases in unemployment, weakened power of state intervention, less relevant unions, and a more socially oriented practice of the law—combined to give rise to new forms of social protest. In many cases, these protests adopted rather extreme forms, partly because of the situation affecting the capacity of the state and the unions to frame and limit social conflict. These protests were conducted by the unemployed, the socially excluded, or indigenous groups, encouraged and welcomed by an inclusive and generous legal order. They also involved the use of paralegal resources that directly challenged the legal order in force, which deeply contrasted with a tradition of labor activism conducted through the channels provided by formal collective bargaining. Road blocks, boycotts of mining companies, and restrictions to the provision of basic commodities were some of the many means that the protesters resorted to in order to advance their demands.

There is another distinctive characteristic of the new protests: in order to see their demands satisfied, usually in relation to the violation of basic constitutional rights, many groups resorted to a kind of protest aimed, more than anything, at attracting a level of media attention they would not get by other means. This particularity reminds us, insistently, of a crucial point: the crisis affecting the political system and its institutions, particularly their power to represent the electorate's demands, and the people's chances of equal access to the system and to take part in public debate.

The legal response to these social changes was, at first, as predictable as it was disappointing. That being said, attention should be paid to what has been happening from a legal point of view ever since. In spite of a rough start and a series of theoretically misinformed decisions and opinions, the region showed some, if limited, progress. In many cases, we can point to improvements in the debate that cannot be found in other regions equally marred by problems of inequality, lack of social justice, institutional deficit and civil discontent. We will see the way in which judges and scholars gradually started to give more sophisticated and sensible arguments, increasingly put into question the answers to social protest traditionally offered by criminal law dogma, and finally showed a surprising and healthy openness to constitutional arguments when dealing with questions belonging, in principle, to the criminal law field. Thus, in a Dworkinian fashion, some jurists in the region inaugurated a road to theoretical ascent, taking notice of the public gravity of the issues at stake that forced them to look outside of "local" law.[4] Lawyers in the region dared to question the limits to freedom of expression (for example, could these new kinds of protest be taken as "expression"? Did the new protests involve violations to regulations of "time, place, and manner" that can be applied to freedom of expression?), which implied a translation of social protest into the language of freedom of expression. This allowed, in some cases, a more honest approach to the question of social rights. In the best scenario, this new kind of reflection proposed a theoretical revision of the academic debate on democratic theory, or the questioning of traditional visions of the theory of political authority.

The context

As stated in the previous section, these new types of protest were born in the specific context of the "neoliberal reforms" that took place in the 1990s. It is appropriate, then, to summarize some of the most important social conflicts in the decade in which the phenomenon we are studying came about.

One of the first manifestations of these new kinds of protest can be found in the so-called *piquetero* movement, which originated in Argentina during the 1990s. At this time, the government promoted reforms that included, among other measures, the sale of state-owned companies, among which was the national oil corporation, Yacimientos Petrolíferos Fiscales (Fiscal Oilfields) (YPF). The sale of YPF to foreign investors initiated a process of internal restructuring that ended up with the closure of many plants located in towns in the northern and southern regions of the country, towns that had grown and developed around the plants and strongly depended on them. According to Svampa and Pereyra, "the privatization of YPF oilfields, plants and distilleries . . . involved the layoff of about

90 percent of their employees, through the forced retirement of 2,400 to 3,500 people . . . In 1997, the unemployment index in [some of the affected regions] reached 50 percent."[5] Far away from the geographical center of power, with no response from the authorities, and desperate because of the disappearance of their jobs and social framework, the recently unemployed workers of YPF gathered together in diverse organizations and started blocking national roads as a way to attract the attention of the authorities, Buenos Aires's (the political capital) media, and the general public. Protests arose in Jujuy and Salta, two northern provinces, and Neuquén, a province in the Argentinian Patagonia region.[6] Their demands were met with repression and criminalization by the authorities. Yet soon their methods would expand and reach workers' organizations in the main urban centers and their surroundings.

At the beginning of the new century, in Bolivia, a set of conflicts emerged that articulated diverse social movements "around certain goals that had in common the rejection of the neo-liberal movement."[7] These processes focused mainly on the control of natural resources and were advanced by a diverse group of organizations that acquired relevance after the decline of the Central Obrera Boliviana.[8]

The so-called Guerra del Agua (Water War), for example, started after the Bolivian Congress approved the privatization of drinking water provision, which provoked strong opposition from many sectors.[9] In September 1999 the government signed the privatization contracts, ignoring the demonstrations against that deal.[10] The opposition movement was led by the Water Coordination, a coalition of social and professional organizations that led many direct measures of protest. As some negotiations initiated by the authorities were interrupted by the protests and the difficulties they were causing, on April 6 the government gave the order to arrest all the Coordination negotiators. This measure provoked an authentic popular revolt by virtue of which the government lost control of the city of Cochabamba to the protesters. The social chaos grew to such a proportion that the government was forced to give in to the Coordination's demands.

The Guerra del Gas (Gas War) was another protest based on a dispute for the control and ownership of natural resources. This time, the idea was to question the measures taken by the Sánchez de Lozada administration aimed at exporting gas to the US: under the terms of the agreement, for every dollar cashed by the Bolivian government in taxes and profits, the private companies would get 24.[11] The conflict started in the city of El Alto, where 82 percent of the population perceived themselves as Native Americans.[12] These protests also adopted forms of direct disruptive action, involving the occupation of avenues, squares, and neighborhoods in order to stop the normal functioning of the city of La Paz, paralyzing commerce, banks, and transportation.[13] As a consequence of the blockade of important roads, certain basic goods became scarce in La Paz. The Sánchez de Lozada administration responded with repression, provoking the spread of the protest to other cities. Eventually, the situation deteriorated and resulted in the resignation of President Sánchez de Lozada. In nine days, 76 people were killed and more than 400 wounded.[14]

These two cases are just some of the many social conflicts that ended in heterodox forms of protest.[15] In the context of these two examples, it is worth asking why these methods spread so rapidly and over so many countries in the region. Would it have something to do with the social indicators we mentioned before? Could it be that state institutions were incapable or unwilling to give answers to popular demands? President Banzer claimed to be "used" to the sound of protest, as if it were background music to government decision making and not a relevant sign that it was time to pay attention to the demands. There is the question, moreover, of whether these contexts are relevant to the judges intervening in these conflicts. Is the judiciary capable of analyzing the extremely complex political, economic, and cultural factors that lie behind the inequalities that are the cause of these manifestations? What should the state response be?

Generally, Latin American politicians have taken more or less direct measures to discourage social protest. On many occasions, those measures included curtailing the protesters' rights. A very well-documented case is that of Ecuador, where hundreds of criminal prosecutions against aboriginal communities, civil society organizations, and communitarian groups are brought only to be suspended. The goal of these prosecutions does not seem to be to gain a conviction, but simply to produce a chilling effect on expressions that question, among other things, the extractivist policies regarding natural resources that have been expanding in Latin America in the last years. As Daniela Salazar Marin wrote,

> In the very few cases that have passed pre-trial stages and been analyzed by a judge, one sees the same lack of an analysis that takes into account the different rights at stake. The fact that penal sanctions in protest situations should be applied in only exceptional situations (where there is sufficient proof that the rights to life and personal integrity are being violated) is completely overlooked. Since this sort of cases has not been analyzed by superior courts and judges, there's no jurisprudence in Ecuador that analyzes whether the application of penal sanctions is justified under the standards of the Inter American Court, which establishes the need to prove that the criminalization of protest satisfies a public interest imperative and necessary for the correct functioning of a democratic society.[16]

Something similar seems to be occurring in Colombia, where prosecutions are initiated against human rights activists that do not move forward but still have the effect of threatening the subjects of those prosecutions. A report by Human Rights First points that "there is a clear pattern of fake penal investigations against human rights activists."[17] According to this report, it is very common that human rights activists are prosecuted and judged without proof, accused of the crime of rebellion or belonging to a terrorist organization. Also, the judge intervening at the last stage frequently acquits the accused.[18]

At first glance, the situation in Argentina is different. After many deaths occurred in the context of diverse social protests, Nestor Kirchner's government (2003–2007, followed by his wife's) initiated a policy that proclaimed itself against the repression of social conflicts.[19] According to Svampa and Pereyra, Kirchner's policy "consisted in enacting, simultaneously, a variety of available strategies to integrate, coopt, discipline, and/or insulate the piquetero movement, discriminating the different currents and organizations."[20] According to Lodola, the strategy "consisted in politically coopting the most numerous groups (some of them related to Peronism) and ignoring the most radical of them (usually associated with small left wing parties)."[21] Normative judgements notwithstanding, it is praiseworthy that, at least in discourse, the highest state authorities recognized the legitimacy of social demands and their form of expression. However, in October 2010, a regrettable event occurred that complicated the government's position on this issue. While demanding the permanent hiring of railway workers, the Partido Obrero activist Mariano Ferreyra was killed by thugs connected with the railway union. The Partido Obrero denounced a sort of "outsourcing" of repression to violent groups belonging to unions that are allies of the government.[22] This significant fact, together with the prosecution and silent jailing of social activists for diverse crimes, places Argentina in a very similar situation to other countries in Latin America.

The initial legal reactions

The first reactions to the protests shown by the legal establishment were extremely hostile. Neither judges nor scholars seemed comfortable within the new landscape, which had brought repeated and massive disturbances of social peace, in the context of recently recovered democracies. In this respect, a scholar said that:

> . . . the law has not been particularly sensitive to the interests of the majority of the disadvantaged groups that take part in this kind of confrontations. The Argentinian case is a clear example. In Argentina, for many years, the government has failed to guarantee the social rights mandated in the constitution. At the same time, the judicial branch has not known how (or has not wanted) to make the government fulfill its constitutional obligations. What is even more important for our subject matter, the judicial branch acted against the activists involved in direct actions (typically, *piqueteros* blocking national roads), assuming these were simply criminal actions that they, as judges, were obliged to stop.[23]

Rather than pay attention to the significance of the protests, in the context of societies marked by poverty and inequality, both courts and legal doctrine seemed prepared to justify its suppression. As the Chilean jurist Jaime Guzmán said, during the constitutional debates in his country: "If it were said tomorrow that massive concentrations are not allowed in squares and streets in the city, I actually think no fundamental right would be violated, since there are places farther located where this kind of meetings could take place."[24]

The Argentinian case is paradigmatic, because of both the level reached by social mobilization after the reforms of the 1990s and the multiple judicial responses that emerged since. In fact, these responses would go on to be historically relevant, at least in the south of the continent, as a symbol of the economic crisis and the social reactions to it. The legal response at that juncture did not seem to assimilate what was at stake. What the law offered was a traditional answer, marked by a certain dogmatism and an unsophisticated interpretation of criminal law. In one early case, which took place in Salta, at the extreme north of the country, protesters were investigated by the federal judge Abel Cornejo, who, in a very brief and scarcely argued decision, found some of the defendants guilty of the extremely serious charge of sedition. The law would show a very similar response shortly after, in the extreme south of the country (in Comodoro Rivadavia) in the context of virtually identical circumstances.[25]

Meanwhile, local doctrine seemed to support these views emphatically, at least at the beginning. For example, the scholar Gregorio Badeni argued then that "the specific right to petition, as any liberty, is not absolute, since its exercise should conform to rules dictated in the spirit of reasonableness . . . and respecting the limit instituted by the constitution itself in Article 22 to avoid incurring in the crime of sedition."[26] Other renowned jurists demonstrated very similar positions. María Angélica Gelli considered the political leadership's indulgence towards "the blocking of roads and streets" seditious,[27] and Juan Carlos Cassagne criticized some of the protesters, arguing, among other things, that "it might be more fair that citizens channel their protests through the Congress, in a well ordered and peaceful manner, considering that it constitutes the natural environment of a representative democracy in which the people do not deliberate or rule but through its representatives."[28] Neither one of them seemed to notice that protesters were not turning to extra-institutional means by choice, but rather because of a desperate conviction that institutional channels were bluntly immune to their requests (in many cases, these convictions were the product of a persistent failure of appeals to institutional channels).

Social protests and penal law

Reaching out to criminal law was the first and immediate response of judges and scholars to the incipient protests. Time and again, judges just pointed out the existent tensions between the accused's behavior and the penal codes. With the idea of censoring the conduct of those accused, judges also commonly turned to much more serious crimes such as sedition (in Argentina and Uruguay), *asonada* (in Colombia), or even the very crime of "terrorism," used by the Chilean judiciary when dealing with conflicts with the Mapuche population. Actually, the Ley Antiterrorista No. 18,431 (Antiterrorist Law) was used in Chile to prosecute Mapuche leaders for protesting, for example, for rights of land ownership.[29] This law was questioned by, among others, the Human Rights Committee of the United Nations, whose members considered it to be written in an extremely vague way, recommending that the state adopt

> a narrower definition of crimes of terrorism, so as to ensure that it is not applied to individuals for political, religious or ideological reasons. Such a definition should be limited to offences which can justifiably be equated with terrorism and its serious consequences, and must ensure that the procedural guarantees established in the [International Covenant on Civil and Political Rights] are upheld.[30]

Minor offenses, however, can also restrict freedom of expression: according to the Carabineros de Chile annual report for 2008, a total of 17,673 people were charged with committing the crime of "public disorder."[31]

Going against these trends, some renowned criminal lawyers in the region sought to show that criminal law was well-equipped to resist the temptation of criminalizing such conduct. The responses can be divided into two types. On the one hand, they tried to show that many of the conducts that were being scrutinized by the judiciary did not constitute a crime because the conduct was not described in the law with the necessary degree of precision. On the other, there was an attempt to preserve a minimalist profile for criminal law, reserving the use of state coercion for extreme situations. A good example of this type of strategy can be found in the work of Raul Zaffaroni, a famous Justice of the Supreme Court of Argentina, who has used both forms of argument.[32] He has tried to prove that actions such as stopping or hindering a train journey, or preventing the normal functioning of traffic, without creating situations of danger, do not typically qualify as actions capable of seriously affecting the legally protected value in question. On the other hand, Zaffaroni has said that the best contribution criminal law can make in relation to social protest is to reduce and contain the punitive reaction to situations of intolerable violence, and to those people who seize the opportunity to commit crimes.[33] It is unreasonable, in his opinion, to claim the contrary—to expand the use of criminal norms to encompass more and more types of behavior.[34]

Following these criteria, on a few occasions, regional justice systems have managed to put an end to public calls to use the most extreme criminal charges to repress social protest. For example, Judge María Cristina Nazar, in Argentina, in the context of an occupation of public space by poor groups demanding their right to shelter be recognized, insisted on the need to keep criminal law confined to a narrow frame. She said then that "we find ourselves facing a social issue that should not be criminalized and that has to be solved in an administrative way." She added: "This issue exceeds criminal law's framework and pertains to a social problem that has to be studied and solved, as it happens, through the institutions set up by the local constitution."[35]

Similarly, the Supreme Court of Justice of Colombia dealt with a criminal case filed against a member of the Vichada Municipality Council who had supposedly been involved in a crime called *asonada.* In this regard, the law states that "those who in a tumultuous and violent way demand from the authority the execution or disregard of any act proper to its functions will receive sixteen (16) to thirty-six (36) months of prison." In that case, the council official had led a demonstration at the gates of the Municipality Council. Through a restrictive interpretation of the crime's definition, the Supreme Court understood that not every gathering could be characterized as "tumultuous" or as meeting the structural element required by the *asonada* crime's description. The court deemed essential for this crime that there be a "concrete and specific requirement to the public authority . . . carried out through violent means, that is, through the use of force."[36]

Regarding this case, the court pointed out that the demand made to the authority was not "concrete and specific." Nevertheless, the decision leaves many questions unanswered. For example, the jurist Rodrigo Uprimny Yepes discussed that the court's decision made no attempt to analyze the "shady areas" around the concept of *asonada.*[37] In other words, what does it mean to be, in fact, in a situation of violence? Are insults and slurring chants addressing public officials violent? What about paintings on public property infringing the regulations in force? The burning of tires? Throwing paint on public buildings? These are concrete examples of protests that usually involve the aforementioned circumstances.

In Peru, for example, a group of 300 indigenous people belonging to the Kichwa and Achuar communities demanded that Pluspetrol Norte SAC raise the wages of indigenous employees. According to the facts of the case, the demonstrators took the local airfield, entered the offices, and took vehicles which they used to call more people to join the demonstration. The intervening court made some important distinctions and supported the indigenous people's rights to demonstrate even after they had taken the airdrome.[38]

In this sense, it is worth mentioning the Supreme Court of Mexico's decision related to the so-called "Atenco Massacre," the name given to a series of confrontations between the Preventive Federal Police and activists from the Frente de Pueblos en Defensa de la Tierra (Front of Towns in Defense of the Land) organization and other adherents to the La Otra Campaña of the Ejército Zapatista de Liberación Nacional (The Other Campaign of the National Liberation Zapatista Army) (EZLN). The conflict arose when these social organizations stood up for some flower vendors who had been evicted from a park in Texcoco. As part of the protest, the demonstrators had blocked a road. The state responded with the repression and legal prosecution of some of the leaders of the Frente de Pueblos en Defensa de la Tierra. Some of them were sentenced to up to 67 years in prison. The Supreme Court granted the *amparo* against these rulings and ordered the release of the convicted people. The court's majority based its decision on the existence of an unfair trial; however, Justice Juan Silva Meza affirmed that the real objective of the disproportionately high sentences was the criminalization of social protest.

> The unlawfulness of the appealed sentence is even more notorious, from my perspective, when the authority emphasizes the claimants' responsibility derived from their relation with social organizations such as Frente de Pueblos en Defensa de la Tierra, starting from a totalitarian ideology, where the exercise of the rights to freedom of expression and assembly themselves generate a presumption of dangerousness and of the deployment of behaviors—seen as crimes—by members of the organization, disregarding whether they are properly proven, in breach of the system of protection of fundamental rights of our entire Mexican state, embodied in different legal orders. The expression of ideas

> and social demands are not synonymous with crime per se. To think otherwise and use that as grounds to issue a conviction is to act against our justice system. It is to dishonor the most basic rights and freedoms of citizens . . . [For these reasons, my opinion is] to grant the *amparo* and consequently to order . . . the immediate and absolute release of the person . . .[39]

Some Mexican scholars celebrated this decision from the highest Mexican court, understanding that:

> social discontent must have space in any robust democracy. It is not about allowing it to reach certain extremes such as to kidnap people or threaten public officials, but neither is it about 'manufacturing' court records to silence dissent, even if it appears radical or disruptive to many. Organized dissidence is part of modern democracies and the authority must learn to live with it, attempting to minimize the damage it might inflict to other people's fundamental rights through its manifestation, but always respecting these rights.[40]

In line with decisions such as the one quoted above, it would be useful to analyze the links between social protest and the right to express oneself freely, as they have developed slowly over time.

Freedom of expression

One of the most interesting new features in the discussion of social protest, from a rights perspective, came about when judges and scholars took a step back from criminal law and started analyzing the constitutional implications of these cases. Without a doubt one of the most fertile and productive areas of this discussion has been the one associated with the constitutional right to freedom of expression. Indeed, slowly, scholars and specialists started to point out that, in legal discussions about social protest, it could not be overlooked that these conflicts demanded not only the revision of the criminal laws involved but also of other components, typically of an expressive nature.

It was clear that, in a great number of cases, what motivated protestors was not a propensity to defy the law but rather the desire to claim the recognition of rights that the state had systematically violated. In this respect, the Special Rapporteur for Freedom of Expression of the Organization of American States declared:

> The most impoverished sectors of our hemisphere face discriminatory policies and actions; their access to information on the planning and implementation of measures that affect their daily lives is incipient and, generally, the traditional channels to air their complaints are frequently inaccessible. Given this scenario, in many countries of the hemisphere, protest and social mobilization have become tools for petitioning the public authority and channels for public complaints regarding human rights violations.[41]

A report from the Center for Legal and Social Studies (CELS) published in Argentina in 2001 sheds light on the issue:

> According to the *piqueteros* themselves, one should not attend a protest with inflexible requirements but rather to establish a dialogue with the state. They vindicate the arguments

> with which they are disqualified by the powerful. They are accused of being organized, of having political overtones in what they do and of encouraging neighbors. They claim that 'there is indeed a long history of organization, that among the poor relationships are brewing of a certain type that may have a deep effect on culture.' The political purpose that they recognize as their own is 'to discuss poverty, exclusion and unemployment in Argentina.' And therefore they encourage their neighbors not to feel violated by this social situation determined by the markets.[42]

As we see, freedom of expression is at the very core of the protest: given their lack of access to more traditional means of communication, they resort to disruptive methods that allow them to appeal to the state and to be heard. Although no one can be required to listen to another person, the state has very special obligations towards its citizens, especially when those citizens are victims of gross violations of their most basic human rights. Not taking into account the illocutionary aspects of actions such as cutting off a street or blocking the entrance to courts came to be seen as a problem. And this consideration enriched the ongoing legal discussions in different ways.

Firstly, the complex bundle of rights that social conflict situations usually involve became apparent. It became legally incorrect to define these cases exclusively as violations of one right or another, namely drivers' right to free transit, lawyers' right to enter a court building, or the right of a mining company directors to exploit an oil field.

Secondly, and as a consequence of that recognition, it became possible to make a distinction between the type of rights that protesters could claim in their favor—rights that had constitutional hierarchy, including the right to submit claims before the authority, the right to express criticism, or the right to hold political meetings.

Thirdly, this recognition has brought with it another one: that rights such as those mentioned above had a privileged status when balancing different rights in conflict. The importance of preserving and taking into account the expressive component of fundamentally non-verbal acts could hardly be denied (even when courts put up some resistance to arriving at such conclusions).

Fourthly, this last argument required not only that the special value of expression within the constitutional rights system be taken into account, but also that the special value of *political* and *critical* expression in a democratic society be considered. The right to political criticism deserves a special place in the "bill of rights" because, in a sense, it gives support to all other rights: if the right to political criticism is not guaranteed, the whole structure of rights and the very idea of democratic self-government is at risk.

Such a position was shared by the Constitutional Court of Peru, which identified a right to protest that derived from freedom of expression and the right to assemble and which pointed out, in particular, to the privileged space that this right should occupy within the constitution's bill of rights. Indeed, Justice Eto Cruz remarked:

> According to the constitutional content of the fundamental right to protest, citizens have a right to show, individually or as a group, their discontent with the authorities' actions or omissions at the state, regional or local level, or with actions or omissions of private entities that provide public services or constitute centers of power in relation to citizens; to publicly state or proclaim legitimate purposes, or to express their opposition, disapproval or criticism towards public polices considered to be contrary to their constitutional rights. Its recognition is permanently linked to such high values as human dignity, the democratic rule of law, the principle of popular sovereignty or the republican form of government

> . . . While it cannot be held that the fundamental right to protest is the most important of all rights, it can be said that this right is essential to ensure many other basic rights (freedom of speech, of opinion, of expression, of assembly, etc.).[43]

All of this was reinforced by another indisputable fact: in fundamentally unequal and unjust societies, few things should be more important to ensure accountability than the preservation of the critical voices of the disadvantaged groups of society. That judges repeatedly adopted the opposite position—for example, condemning those they should have protected—could not but ratify the difficulties the law was facing when approaching these cases.

This last argument is relevant, for it allows us to recognize the difference between the criminal approach and the constitutional approach to protests. The more critical views of criminal law were satisfied with finding ways (sometimes excuses) not to criminalize protest. The critical views of constitutional law, on the other hand, sought to recognize the weight of the expressive component present in demonstrations. And, in the case of a conflict between rights, these views urged us to act contrary to what we were used to: instead of removing all rights related to expression straightaway (so as to prosecute demonstrators, for example), it was suggested that we pay attention to the expressive content of those acts and that we preserve that content as much as possible.

Regulating the protest

Once the right to protest is placed within the realm of freedom of expression, it obviously acquires greater legal strength. Jurists, judges, and scholars all identify a special value in expression and a strong negative presumption of any attempt to restrain its content. At the same time, however, when understanding protest as expression, there arises the possibility of designing regulations on the modalities of protest such as those the law has conceived for hundreds of years around the manner in which the expression is carried out. Herein lies an important issue, for the same right that has been strengthened is left at serious risk of suffering restrictions through the regulation of its form.

Regarding the modalities of the right to freedom of expression, scholars and judges have typically insisted on the need to give special protection to political demonstrations in public spaces usually destined for them (the public forum doctrine[44]); but they have also designed and accepted regulations of time, place, and manner as a means to articulate the rights of those who protest with everyone else's rights to not be affected by the protest and to be able to carry on with their lives normally.[45] An example of such restrictions would be, for instance, the reasonableness of requiring loud protesters to avoid protesting near a school or at four o'clock in the morning. However, these regulations should not be understood as a way of authorizing restrictions on expression through the back door that were not allowed through the front door. There is a need to be conscious of the ways in which these regulations of time, manner and place can be used as an excuse to impair freedom of expression. As was held some time ago, those regulations may be acceptable only to the extent that they are effectively "neutral as to their content, are designed as narrowly as possible, come to satisfy fundamental government interests, and at the same allow ample alternative channels of communication."[46]

Interesting case law regarding the possibility of regulating the right to protest was developed in Puerto Rico. In the case of *Juan Mari Bras y otros c. Juan F. Castañas*, the Supreme Court of Puerto Rico ruled on various regulations that, among other things, prohibited the use of loudspeakers on election day. The court found that:

> . . . the use of loudspeakers for the dissemination of ideas and concepts is protected by the constitutional right that guarantees free speech. In fact, it is just the utterance of words, mechanically expanded. Not only do technological advances require that the protection is not limited to the usual and proverbial forms of expression, but economic needs do so as well, considering the control exercised by a limited group over other mass media and that this is a means available to those who cannot effectively use the press, radio and television because of their costs. On the other hand, the right to free speech entails being heard and the use of amplification means only ensures that the message will reach a greater number of people.[47]

Notably, the court made similar considerations regarding the nature of streets as public forums and the possibility of putting up posters in some public spaces.

It is important to strictly scrutinize regulations on expression, for in Latin America, too, there seems to be a willingness of the authorities to resort to regulations on forms of expression as a *de facto* limit on the content of the expression. Consider, for instance, the requirement of prior permission or an authorization request to the authorities to carry out certain public demonstrations. In Chile, for instance, in order to carry out a demonstration, an authorization request has to be filed two days in advance. The applicant has to fill out a form in which it is necessary to record the entity organizing the event. In addition, the organization's representative must be individualized, with his or her full name, profession, address, municipality, identity card, and phone number, and he or she must specify the purpose of the act, the starting place, route, place of dissolution, and number of attendees.

In Colombia, an objection was raised to such requirements through a writ for protection ("*acción de tutela*") against the decision of a mayor who denied permission to march. In that case, the Constitutional Court of Colombia held:

> It is important to note that the purpose of the notice, in light of the 1991 constitution, cannot be to create a basis for prohibiting the assembly or demonstration. It aims to inform the authorities for them to take the necessary measures to facilitate the exercise of the right without significantly hindering the normal development of community activities. . . . Generally, limitations on the exercise of the right of assembly and demonstration are linked to the maintenance of public order. Criteria to determine the factual situations in which dissolving an assembly or stopping it from being carried out are justified have been established to avoid possible bias. In general terms, these criteria must be oriented exclusively at avoiding grave and imminent threats. An eventual or generic threat, or a mere suspicion or fear are usually insufficient. The nature of the right of assembly, itself polemical, cannot be the justifying cause of any rules limiting it. The right of public assembly should not be considered synonymous with public disorder so as to apply restrictions to it.[48]

The case seems interesting as it establishes a thorough criterion to allow the prohibition of public meetings. It mentions "grave and imminent threats," which appears to suggest a strict proportionality analysis that brings to mind the clear and present danger test elaborated by the US Supreme Court.[49] Nevertheless, what does the statement that the constitution guarantees the public and peaceful exercise of the right to assembly mean? What does it mean to say that the constitution guarantees to the "peaceful public" the right of assembly? Does participating in demonstrations with faces covered affect the public character of the event? This circumstance was taken into account by Argentinian judges when disapproving of demonstrations that disrupt the public order, such as blocking roads or streets. Indeed, a judge said that demonstrators who hide their face "do it with the obvious purpose of avoiding the subsequent consequences of their behavior."[50]

On the other hand, in the aforementioned case, the court did not examine whether the requirement to request prior permission could have inhibitory effects in relation to the exercise of the right. In effect, these legal problems must be considered within the context of unequal and unjust societies in Latin America: to the extent that protesters choose to hide their face because they know that the state's response will most likely be criminal prosecution, could requiring prior authorization be—by itself—a deterrent? What happens when it involves radical or minority groups that have reasonable grounds to fear the state?

Another interesting case, in this sense, was decided in Peru, where a municipal decree had restricted the right to assemble in the Historical Center of Lima, as a measure to conserve "archaeological and historical monuments." It is important to note that the Historical Center was declared a World Heritage Site by UNESCO. The country's constitutional court, when analyzing a legal action challenging the rule, held that the right of assembly is intrinsically linked to freedom of expression, and considered it an individual right that "can only be exercised collectively."

The constitutional court considered that the rule did not pass the proportionality test. It stated:

> Even when it pursues a constitutionally valid purpose (protecting the Historical Center as cultural heritage) and uses a suitable method for this (banning meetings in the area), by banning any gathering at the Historical Centre of Lima (with the exception of traditional events) it results in an absolutely unnecessary measure, since the same objective could be achieved by evaluating, case by case, the objective, sufficient and grounded reasons that might justify such measures restricting the exercise of the right of assembly, a prohibition being the *last resort* for the administrative authority to apply.[51]

However, beyond the decision in the case, the ruling leaves the door open for certain repressive measures to be taken against public demonstrations in the Historical Center of Lima. Indeed, the justices noted that it would be possible to prohibit public meetings if there were objective evidence and not a mere suspicion of a "violent tendency of the people or leaders of the organizing party;"[52] if there were another meeting scheduled in a place nearby on the same date; if other meetings were called repeatedly in the same place, compromising, objectively, its preservation and its ornamentation; or if the number of people attending would, for certain, exceed the site's capacity, or that of the routes proposed as its itinerary, among other circumstances. Also, the justices considered of vital importance that the demonstrators gave prior notice to the authority.

In any event, it is interesting to consider the restrictions on the regulations of "time, place, and manner" that the case law has been recognizing in countries where legal discussion of this topic is more developed. These regulations have been considered acceptable insofar as it is ensured that they "are justified without reference to the content of the regulated speech, to the extent that they serve a significant government interest, and as long as they leave open wide alternative channels for transmitting information."[53] From this point of view, it must be asked what a group with a "violent tendency" means. Is it possible to predict in all circumstances the number of people who will attend a public meeting? On the other hand, it should be borne in mind that the Government Palace, the seat of the executive branch, and the Municipality of Lima, among other agencies of government, are located in the Historical Center of Lima. Public demonstrations calling for recognition of violated rights tend to address public officials working in these buildings. Should this circumstance affect the way we analyze this type of regulation? On the other hand, is it possible to put the protection of cultural heritage on an equal footing with the exercise of the right to freedom of expression?

Social rights

Without a doubt, it proved to be very important that judges and scholars in the region began, slowly, to recognize the close links between the right to protest and freedom of expression. Even so, that recognition, able to provide greater protection to social protests, was seemingly accompanied by other, less attractive consequences. Paradoxically, the strengthening of the expressive argument tended to entail the undervaluation of the social rights argument. Or, to put it more clearly, after a while, the legal debate began to turn, repeatedly, upon the expressive rights of the plaintiffs, but this seemed to happen at the expense of the visibility of their affected social rights—precisely those social rights that gave reason and meaning to the protest. Judges and scholars, conservative or progressive, began to focus their disputes on the scope of the protesters' expressive rights, as if the real or main purpose of protests were to "express" instead of to demand recognition of what are often deeply affected social rights (e.g., lack of social security, housing, or education). The truth is that no proper discussion regarding protest should focus on the expression of the complaint and its forms, rather than the content of the complaint and its reasons. In the cases that concern us here (not all of those that can be included under the heading of the right to protest), what is usually at stake is that the state does not comply with certain fundamental obligations it is committed to by the very words of the constitution.

In any case, it should be noted that, although with limitations, the law has again come to recognize the seriousness of certain violations of the social rights of protesters, and the special responsibility of the state in their generation and persistence. We can recall, for instance, what happened in the abovementioned Peruvian case when the Achuar and Kichwa communities protested against Pluspetrol Norte SAC, demanding wage increases and better working conditions for indigenous employees. In this case, the court first highlighted the poor conditions in which the indigenous groups leading the protest lived. Secondly, the court underscored "the serious responsibility of the state and governments who ignored the rights of indigenous peoples and communities."[54] Quoting a report by the Catholic Church, the court emphasized that:

> by ignoring the use and occupation of the land for generations, the government leaves the plight of indigenous and riverside populations who want integral development without answer. In practice, the right of Amazonian peoples to be heard, enshrined in both the Political Constitution of the State and International Treaties on Human Rights, has not been taken into account . . .[55]

The court also considered:

> The state's lack of capacity to provide a satisfactory solution to the claims formulated by various sectors and social groups, usually of low or no economic resources that are

> excluded from society is confirmed daily . . . The answer that the state has been giving to growing social demands and protests is the judicialization or criminalization of them, pursuing social activists instead of providing solution to the demands, and involving the judiciary in matters not within its jurisdiction to resolve since they are social conflicts. To this end, the court endorses the statement made by the President of the Judiciary, Dr Javier Villa Stein, in that we do not accept to become an instrument of persecution and that we are subject only to the legal system in force . . . The court considers it necessary to note that social conflict situations require of us the utmost care to avoid criminalization of poverty and protest of indigenous communities and their members. It behooves us to be extremely careful to avoid undermining the very rights that need maximum protection. The court shares the statements by the president of the judiciary, Dr Javier Villa Stein, in the central ceremony of Judges' Day this year (2009), in the sense of not being 'bubble judges' but committed judges, not because of an ideology, but because of the sensitivity to know the impact a decision has on victims, the accused and society, before making it. To observe the actual circumstances of the facts before us, it is important to consider some essential concepts common to the collective action of all social movements. It should be borne in mind that a social movement takes on meaning by making an unfair and unacceptable situation visible, pointing out those responsible for this state of affairs and proposing solutions. In concrete terms, this task is carried out through collective action, through a repertoire of protest actions. To mobilize people, collective action relies on mobilization structures, which are permanent organizations where people build their relationships with others . . . The protest by Andoas community members and others is framed within the constitutional right of petition, so that the fact of having participated in the occupation of the runway of the Andoas airfield and in an act of force does not constitute a crime because the claim in situations of actual poverty and lack of reasonable state responses becomes a justifying state of necessity referred to in paragraph 4 of Article 20 of the penal code.[56]

As we can see, the court assessed a) the exclusion of those who carried out the demand, b) the lack of response from the authorities, and c) the criminalization of social protest as an unacceptable response by the state. In addition, the justices analyzed the place that public demonstrations and social protest occupy in the exercise of the right to freedom of expression of these communities. These circumstances enabled them to see that there was a justification for the actions of indigenous communities. In the specific analysis of each of the allegations raised by the prosecution ("violence and resisting authority," "riots," "aggravated theft," "grave injuries," and "murder"), the justices found that the prosecution's charges were poorly made, that certain statements had been distorted, and that, in short, either there was no criminality in those actions ("violence and resisting authority" or "riots"), or there was a lack of sufficient evidence ("aggravated robbery," "serious injury," or "murder"). The justices analyzed the facts of the case in light of the context of social conflict that existed in Peru in relation to indigenous peoples who resist mining development on their ancestral lands.

Democratic theory

Theoretical reflection of scholars and courts on the right to protest had one of its highest and most interesting peaks in the emerging and renewed discussion that followed, thereafter, on questions of democratic theory. And this is because, in order to reflect on the protest, and its limits and scope, it becomes necessary, ultimately, to reflect on the kind of democratic system in which we live and the type of democratic system which the constitution appears committed to uphold. For those who are serious about this reflection, questions are inescapable. Do we undermine democracy or, conversely, do we strengthen it when we protest for our rights? What kind of civic activism does our constitutional democracy tolerate and/or require, and why? Of course, many of the protagonists of this story would deny that, through their writings, they continually engage in reflections on democratic theory. Nonetheless, there is no decision on the matter that does not involve, in one way or another, taking sides on a certain conception of democracy.

One of the most explicit—and most unattractive—manifestations that regional case law has offered on the matter is defended in the *Schifrin* ruling, decided by the highest criminal court in Argentina, in connection with a protest carried out by a group of teachers who were complaining about their working conditions. On that occasion, the court relied in part on the constitutional scholarship in the country to hold that:

> The claim contained in Article 22 of the constitution is that the *only legitimate and verifiable way of sovereign expression of the people is voting*. Through it, the people reject or accept the alternative that the political class proposes. This Article rejects the anarchy of populism and authoritarianism of right and left, as well as any attempt to breach the constitutional system and political institutions. Other types of alleged expression of the popular will, different from suffrage (such as large gatherings in public places, surveys, strikes, lock-outs, or other means of direct action, whether or not they are accompanied by weapons do not truly reflect the majority opinion of the people, but at most that of a seditious group.[57]

It other words, the court committed itself to an extremely restrictive conception of democracy, according to which the term "democracy" was associated, in a necessary and sufficient way, with voting periodically. Anything that transcends the periodic vote, said the chamber, should be understood, in principle, as an affront to democracy, nothing less than a seditious act. It should be noted that starting from this narrow view of democracy was a necessary and crucial step to explain the final content of the judgment, upholding the conviction of one of the protesters.

From more demanding views of democracy—such as the one the Argentine Constitution ultimately and explicitly embraces—activities such as those described as affronts to democracy by the ruling could have been described, rather, as citizens' tribute to the democratic system in which they lived, that is, as ways to stand up in defense of constitutional rights, despite the insults the authority reserved for them.

Another significant example of the link between the positions assumed regarding protest and certain theories of democracy can be seen in the Annual Report on Human Rights in Chile in 2009, prepared by the Human Rights Center at Diego Portales University. There, a very interesting parallel between democratic dialogue and public demonstrations is made. Chilean public officials, in the context of a conflict between school authorities and the student body in Santiago de Chile, had indicated that students were "violent" and ignored "dialogue":

> This way of understanding dialogue in a democracy has two effects: it narrows the concept of freedom of expression and explains the appearance and reiteration of social protest. It narrows the concept of freedom of expression because it invests with an aura of

> illegitimacy some forms of intervention in matters of public interest, such as demonstrations, when the constitution guarantees all people '[f]reedom to express opinion . . . without prior censorship, in any form and by any medium' (Article 19, subsection 12). . . . And it explains the reasons for the protests because those conversations to which civil society, in this case students, are invited, operate on the basis of decisions that have already been adopted; the invitations seek to legitimize a process of consultation that is ultimately irrelevant to the decisions taken . . .[58]

From this point of view, it is useful to ask what role judges should play within the framework of democratic institutions that—at best—operate with serious structural flaws that result, among other problems, in the social exclusion of broad sectors of society from the traditional mechanisms of political participation and democratic debate. Under these circumstances, it is possible to argue that the work of judges must be to protect the voices of the most disadvantaged and ensure that they can access the political debate and the decision-making process, even if such access is achieved by non-traditional mechanisms like the ones we have studied in this chapter. One can hold this position even from the standpoint of very modest views of democracy, such as those that are anchored, and limited, to the traditional concept of representation, which presuppose a limited participation by the people. As we saw in this chapter, some judges have followed that path and have taken into account the particular contexts, the local institutions, and their specific limitations in solving these complex social conflicts, so that even when exceeding—in causes as well as effects—the scope of the judiciary, they do not completely exclude it from positively intervening in their solution.

Conclusion

In a social context of unemployment, inequality, and the disappearance of social institutions which used to mediate on social conflicts, new forms of political engagement appeared. These were, as we saw, led by the worst-off members of society, those who were on the losing end of the social distribution of resources. And these resources were not only economic, but also cultural, social, and political. The rise of disruptive public demonstrations was first received by the legal world with scorn: legal scholars argued for necessary limits to freedom of expression and prosecutors began to frame these conducts as serious crimes which violated public order. Some within the legal establishment, however, chose to bring a different perspective into the analysis. They argued that these conducts were not crimes, and that criminal law should not be the way to respond to the grievances of public demonstrators. From a constitutional perspective, arguments were made that put their political exclusion at the center of the stage: if these people had no adequate access to the political process, and if redress mechanisms that used to channel their demands no longer existed or were no longer available (e.g., the unemployed are not represented by unions) then their claims should be received as petitions made by citizens looking for reparations of gross human rights violations. Freedom of expression arguments widened the breathing space for these kinds of protests. As we saw, these arguments, in the hands of judges willing to make them, kept many demonstrators outside of prison and arguably allowed these kinds of protests to keep taking place. But were these arguments enough to include those who were protesting in the political process? An answer to this question would go far beyond the scope of this chapter, but the question is interesting nevertheless, especially for the scholar concerned with how constitutional law and constitutional rights arguments play out in practice. Freedom of expression standards include the legitimate grounds of restriction case law. And, as we saw, those restrictions have the potential to actually render the voice of protestors hardly audible. Overall, we think that these concerns are worthy of attention, especially if we look at future developments on a region which seems to have adopted, and not rejected, these repertoires of action, as we saw in the mostly middle-class road blockings in Argentina in 2008, through which farmers protested against an increase in taxes, and as we saw in the protests by opposition sectors in Venezuela in 2014.

In the last couple of decades, Latin American judges and scholars have built strong protections for public demonstrations that are messy, noisy, and disruptive. It is, probably, the region of the world where the right to protest is more thoroughly protected from a legal point of view. However, Latin America remains the most unequal region in the world. This suggests two possible conclusions. On the one hand, the limited breathing space created by the law curbed the level of repressive responses by the state, a development which favors the exercise of this right. On the other, the pervasiveness of these protests should not make us forget that they have a goal: to redress human rights violations. The law should not be content with letting people make noise every now and then. The goal of the law should be to foster meaningful citizen participation in the political process. And that requires more than just letting citizens express themselves: it also demands that public officials listen.

Questions

a The process of neoliberal reforms that took place in Latin America during the 1990s raised the levels of unemployment and inequality and the traditionally strong unions of the region lost, as a result, their place as mediator of social conflict. Is this context relevant from a legal point of view to understand the development of the right to protest in this particular Latin American context? When answering your question, think about the citizenship status of those claiming rights and the different mechanisms established by the state to receive petitions and listen to citizens' grievances. Are those mechanisms available to all on an equal basis?

b Think about Bolivian president Hugo Banzer's remarks on how he considered the sound of public demonstrations outside the presidential palace as "background music" he was used to. What does this remark say in terms of his attitude towards citizens' opinions? How should elected public officials react towards petitions or demonstrations issued by citizens?

c Many of the recent Latin American protest movements seem bizarre from the point of view of recent constitutional law practices in developed countries such as the United States. But think about the popular uprising in Massachusetts during 1786 and 1787 led by Daniel Shays, or about the tax protests in 1791, during the presidency of George Washington, known as the Whiskey Rebellion. Larry Kramer has famously argued that these forms of crowd action were somehow common in the early stages of the American constitutional experience.[59] Could you think of any reason why those practices disappeared in the United States but seem to remain in Latin America?

d The legal academy reacted to the increased level of social unrest by signaling that rights are "not absolute" and could be subject to reasonable restrictions. Should the judgment on the rationality of restrictions be informed by the social context that sparked public demonstrations?

e Demonstrators were accused of extremely serious crimes, such as terrorism and sedition. It is interesting that the crime of sedition has a relevant place in American constitutional history: in 1798, a Federalist Congress passed the Alien and Sedition Acts, which were signed into law by President John Adams. The Federalists were famous for showing a certain degree of contempt towards the political energy of ordinary citizens, while the Democratic-Republicans led by Thomas Jefferson and James Madison were more confident and less concerned about the participation of citizens in the daily life of the Republic.[60] Jefferson campaigned against the Sedition Act and won the presidency in the election of 1800. Do you find any parallel between the Sedition Act of 1798 and the use of the sedition crime we described in Latin America?

f When judges and scholars began to look at public demonstrations from a freedom of expression perspective, they were forced to look at the "legitimate grounds" for restricting this right. And, traditionally, these grounds included restrictions in terms of manner, place, or time. Public demonstrations seem particularly vulnerable to such restrictions. In the context of the United States, for instance, protestors must abide by a series of requirements in order to be able to protest without risking being arrested. When do you think these kinds of restrictions move from being legitimate to being an indirect way of restricting freedom of expression? Think about Section 13.3 of the Inter-American Convention of Human Rights, which states that "[t]he right of expression may not be restricted by indirect methods or means . . . or by any other means tending to impede the communication and circulation of ideas and opinions." How do you judge restrictions in the United States according to said standard?

g When framing public demonstrations as issues involving citizens' freedom of expression, the protective international standards become available. In particular, the inter-American system of human rights has a strong case law which protects freedom of expression, in cases usually involving journalists. But is it not the case that these demonstrations are more closely linked with the right to petition authorities than with the expression of opinions? If that is the case, should the treatment of these cases be different? Think about a common practice in the United States: writing to your congressperson. This is not common in Latin America: in fact, when NGOs in Argentina in 2013 organized a campaign to gather signatures asking 14 members of the House to vote against a judiciary reform bill, they were reproached by a majority vote in the Senate. Is there any difference between the act of writing letters to representatives and public demonstrations? If so, what are they?

h Think about the Peruvian case in the section "Regulation the Protest". There the judges mentioned the social exclusion suffered by protesters and the lack of response to their petitions by relevant authorities and said that the criminalization of social protest was an unacceptable answer to their grievances. However, they seem to have decided the case on narrower terms, questioning the work of the prosecution on technical grounds. Do you think the case could have been decided on the former, more substantial grounds? Why do you think the judges made reference to both a) the substantive arguments based on the situation of protestors and the response offered by the state and b) the technical shortcomings of the prosecutors' case?

i Compare the arguments provided in the *Schifrin* case (section "Democratic Theory") with the following paragraph by Christopher G. Fritz in AMERICAN SOVEREIGNS, analyzing the different constitutional positions in the early stages of the American Republic:

> For other Americans, once the people created a government, it became the conduit and the enforcer of that sovereign's will. If the people placed procedures in their constitution, they effectively exercised their unlimited power to limit themselves by those

> procedures. The people could not ignore the procedures they imposed upon themselves. This view of constitutionalism asserted that the people's unbounded power included the ability to bind themselves by their constitution and to bind future generations.[60]

Do you see a connection between the arguments in *Schifrin* and the need to submit to existing institutions suggested by the quoted paragraph?

Notes

* Translated into English by Brian Burton and Tamara Tenenbaum and revised by the authors. The authors wish to thank Johanna Hardwick for her editing assistance.

1 José Antonio Ocampo, Más allá del Consenso de Washington: una agenda de desarrollo para América Latina 8 (2005).

2 Ramón Casilda Béjar, *América Latina y el Consenso de Washington*, 2803 Boletín Económico del ICE, 19–38 (2004).

3 In relation to Argentina, Maristella Svampa and Sebastian Pereyra explain that there were two important developments in economic and social matters: "First, the gap between rich and poor is the largest one in the last 30 years. Data from December 2003 indicate that throughout the country, the richest 10% hold on to 38% of the wealth produced, and earn 31 times more than the poorest 10%. Second, the change in economic model brought about a novel situation of the coexistence of economic growth and an increase in unemployment" (Maristella Svampa and Sebastian Pereyra, Entre la ruta y el barrio: la experiencia de las organizaciones piqueteras (2003)).

4 Ronald Dworkin, Justice in Robes (2006).

5 Maristella Svampa, *Los movimientos sociales en la Argentina de hoy. Piquetes y Asambleas. Tres Estudios de Casos*, 27 (2007), available at http://maristellasvampa.net/archivos/ensayo07.pdf.

6 Maristella Svampa and Sebastian Pereyra, Entre la ruta y el barrio: la experiencia de las organizaciones piqueteras (2003).

7 Pablo Stefanoni, *Siete preguntas y siete respuestas sobre la Bolivia de Evo Morales*, 209/3 Nueva Sociedad, 47–65, 54 (2007).

8 Thomas Kruse, *La "Guerra del Agua" en Cochabamba, Bolivia: terrenos complejos, convergencias nuevas*, in Sindicatos y Nuevos Movimientos Sociales en América Latina, at 122 (Enrique de la Garza ed., 2005). ("Structural adjustments from 1985 onwards, combined with privatizations from 1993 onwards have produced profound changes in the realm of work, quantitatively and qualitatively undermining the foundations of trade unionism, and provoking what has been called by many the 'death of the COB.'")

9 Thomas Kruse, *La "Guerra del Agua" en Cochabamba, Bolivia: terrenos complejos, convergencias nuevas*, in Sindicatos y Nuevos Movimientos Sociales en América Latina, at 143–5 (Enrique de la Garza ed., 2005) (where the author argues that these new contracts implied a considerable increase in gas rates in urban centers and put the future of self-managed systems in doubt, principally in rural areas). See also D. Hall and E. Lobina, *La privatización del agua en América Latina* (Report before the Water Conference of the Americas, San José, Costa Rica, July 2002) ("It was calculated that the average water bill was equivalent to 22% of the monthly income of a self-employed man, and to 27% of that of a woman.").

10 The contracts were signed even whilst a large manifestation against them was taking place. At the time, President Hugo Banzer remarked: "I'm used to that background music." (Thomas Kruse, *La "Guerra del Agua" en Cochabamba, Bolivia: terrenos complejos, convergencias nuevas*, in Sindicatos y Nuevos Movimientos Sociales en América Latina, at 146 (Enrique de la Garza ed., 2005)).

11 Raúl Ornelas, *La guerra del gas: cuarenta y cinco días de resistencia y un triunfo popular*, 16 Revista Chiapas, available at www.revistachiapas.org/No16/ch16ornelas.html.

12 Jeffrey R. Webber, *Indigenous Struggle in Latin America: The Perilous Invisibility of Capital and Class*, 49/3 Latin American Politics and Society, 203 (2007).

13 Ibid.

14 Mamani Ramírez, Microgobiernos barriales: levantamiento de la ciudad de El Alto (octubre 2003) 23 (2005).

15 Similar conflicts took place in other countries in the region. In Peru, for example, towards the middle of 2009, members of the Awjun indigenous community blocked highways in protest against

the "indiscriminate exploitation" of the Amazon jungle. The government ordered reprisals, and 10 members of the indigenous community and 24 police officers died. According to a parliamentary investigation, the motive for the repression was to "teach the indigenous people a lesson" (see Raúl Zibecchi, *Un año de la masacre de Bagua*, La Jornada, June 4, 2010; and Raúl Zibecchi, *Un año de la masacre de Bagua, nuevos actores frente a un Estado en crisis*, June 11, 2010, available at www.cipamericas.org/es/archives/2523). In Ecuador, where the extraction-based model also clashed with indigenous communities, various similar incidents came about in the south of the country in response to the passing of the Mining Law at the beginning of 2009. See, for example, Gloria Chicaiza, *The mining enclave of the "Cordillera del Cóndor"*, March 2010, available at www.ceecec.net/wp-content/uploads/2008/10/CORDILLERA_CONDOR_ECUADOR_V2.pdf.

16 It could be said that part of the problem in question is related to the periodical concession of amnesties, which put an end to open investigations only to make space for the opening of new criminal cases based on new events. This strategy has the curious effect of impeding cases from reaching, by way of appeal, the higher tribunals that could put a stop to the criminal persecution. In Ecuador the situation reached such severe levels that it was debated in the 2008 Constituent Assembly. It was then argued: "Within this setting of protest and opposition by the communities to the hydroelectric extraction projects, the companies (with the support of state representatives) have used a series of mechanisms to delegitimize and silence the communities and opponents, unleashing or deepening instability and social conflict . . . Their demands have been neglected . . . and have been considered criminal acts that must be repressed with the full force of the law . . . in order to eliminate or neutralize resistance; in many cases, a series of tactical or concrete actions have been designed and carried out, [such as] the criminalization of protest by way of presenting complaints or legal actions against the protest leaders and inhabitants . . . Harassment through administrative demands and criminal complaints aims to immediately imprison the leaders or inhabitants who present the greatest resistance, have leadership and are well respected in the community, or environmental activists, using the figure of flagrant offence, of the institution of the judicial order, of pretrial detention and of the perverse identification of the political acts of resistance with the crimes typified in the Penal Code. Complaints have been received which point to the persecution and harassment of defenders through the successive initiation of judicial cases that are dismissed a couple of months later with the people being processed being found not responsible for the events investigated. Despite said dismissals, new investigations—in most cases with different evidence but related to similar accusations—are opened and, as a consequence, new detentions or judicial restrictions are ordered. The Commission has received complaints about various cases of opening and dismissal of criminal accusations against just one person, as well as the opening and dismissal of investigations regarding various leaders from the same organization or group . . . What they are, then, are complaints and accusations presented in order to arbitrarily detain and either provisionally or definitively deprive of their liberty those people who exercise their right to protest and try to protect the environment and public heritage." (Asamblea Constituyente. Mesa de Legislación y Fiscalización. Informe favorable para conceder amnistía a las personas acusadas de varios delitos vinculados con la protesta y movilización. Montecristi, (Constituent Assembly, Legislative and Fiscal Table of Negotiations. Favorable report to grant amnesty to the persons accused of several felonies related to protest and mobilization) March 11, 2008).

17 Human Rights First, Los defensores y defensoras de derechos humanos acusados sin fundamento. Presos y señalados en Colombia 8 (2009).

18 Ibid.

19 In part, the decision was a product of the murder of two activists in the *piquetero* movement at the hands of the Buenos Aires Province Police in June 2002.

20 Maristella Svampa and Sebastian Pereyra, Entre la ruta y el barrio: la experiencia de las organizaciones piqueteras 103 (2003).

21 Germán Lodola, Cultura política de la democracia en Argentina, 2010. Consolidación democrática en las Américas en tiempos difíciles (forthcoming) (manuscript at 229) (on file with authors).

22 There is nothing new about the outsourcing of the repression of protest activities. In this regard, in the cases of *Ríos* and *Perozo*, both against Venezuela, the Inter-American Court of Human Rights recognized that various "countermarches" which culminated in violence against opponents of the government had been initiated by the ruling party's sympathizers. IACHR, "Ríos and others vs. Venezuela". Decision of January 28, 2009; IACHR, "Perozo and others vs. Venezuela". Decision of January 28, 2009.

23 Roberto Gargarella, *Un diálogo sobre la ley y la protesta social*, 61 Revista de la Facultad de Derecho de la Pontificia Universidad Católica del Perú, 19–50, 20 (2009).
24 Francisco Cox, *Criminalización de la protesta social: "No tiene derecho a reunirse donde le plazca,"* in ¿Es Legítima la Criminalización de la Protesta Social? Derecho Penal y Libertad de Expresión en América Latina, at 77 (Eduardo Bertoni comp., 2010).
25 See, for example, Roberto Gargarella, El derecho a la protesta, el primer derecho (2005).
26 Gregorio Badeni, Derecho Constitucional. Libertades y garantías 272 (1999). See also Gregorio Badeni, La convivencia democrática 1286 (2001).
27 María A. Gelli, Constitución de la Nación Argentina (2001).
28 Juan Carlos Cassagne, Reflexiones sobre los "cacerolazos" 1398 (2002).
29 Víctor Toledo Llancaque, *Cronología de los principales hechos en relación a la represión de la protesta social mapuche, Chile 2000–2007*, VIII/22 Observatorio Social de América latina—CLACSO (2007).
30 UN Human Rights Committee, "Concluding observations of the Human Rights Committee, Chile", CCPR/C/CHL/CO/5, April 17, 2007, paragraph 7.
31 Francisco Cox, *Criminalización de la protesta social: "No tiene derecho a reunirse donde le plazca,"* in ¿Es Legítima la Criminalización de la Protesta Social? Derecho Penal y Libertad de Expresión en América Latina (Eduardo Bertoni comp., 2010).
32 Raúl Zaffaroni, *El derecho penal y la criminalización de la protesta social*, Bulletin 13 November, IV/7 Jurisprudencia Argentina (2002).
33 To that effect, see, for example, Raúl G. Ferreyra, La Constitución vulnerable (2003), María Piqué and Marina Soberano, *El derecho penal y la protesta social*, in Teoría y Crítica del Derecho Constitucional (Roberto Gargarella comp., vol. 2, 2008).
34 *Zaffaroni se pronunció en contra de criminalizar las protestas sociales*, Clarín, August 24, 2005, available at http://edant.clarin.com/diario/2005/08/24/elpais/p-01001.htm.
35 Juzgado en lo Penal, Contravencional y de Faltas No. 26 de la Ciudad de Buenos Aires, Decision by the judge María Cristina Nazar, March 1, 2011.
36 Rodrigo Uprimny Yepes and Sánchez Duque, *Derecho Penal y Protesta Social*, in ¿Es Legítima la Criminalización de la Protesta Social? Derecho Penal y Libertad de Expresión en América Latina, at 54 (Eduardo Bertoni comp., 2010). Supreme Court of Colombia, Case No. 12,486 (April 21, 1998).
37 Rodrigo Uprimny Yepes and Sánchez Duque, *Derecho Penal y Protesta Social*, in ¿Es Legítima la Criminalización de la Protesta Social? Derecho Penal y Libertad de Expresión en América Latina, at 55 (Eduardo Bertoni comp., 2010).
38 In effect, it indicated that the protest was "framed within the constitutional law of petition. Therefore, the fact of having participated in the occupation of the Andoas airstrip runway and some act of force does not constitute a crime since the demand when faced with situations of real poverty and the lack of reasonable responses from the State constitutes a justifying state of necessity, contemplated in paragraph 4.a of Article 20 of the Penal Code" (Second Circuit of the Criminal Superior Court of Justice of Loreto, judgment of December 10, 2009). A more exhaustive review will be conducted in the following section.
39 Supreme Court of Justice of Mexico, First Chamber, Public Session, Minute number 23, June 23, 2010.
40 Miguel Carbonell, *La Corte sube el listón*, Reforma, August 1, 2010.
41 Relatoría Especial para la Libertad de Expresión de la CIDH, Informe Anual 2005 de la Relatoría Especial para la Libertad de Expresión de la CIDH (2005 Annual Report by the Special Rapporteurs on Freedom of Expression in the CIDH), Chapter V, paragraph 1.
42 Centro de Estudios Legales y Sociales, 2001 Annual Report, Chapter IV, section 2.1.
43 Constitutional Court of Peru, File No. 00012–2008-PI/TC, "Cinco Mil Trescientos Noventaitres [*sic*] Ciudadanos," July 14, 2010, vote by Justice Eto Cruz, point 5.
44 Supreme Court of the United States, case of "Hague v. Committee of Industrial Organization," June 5, 1939.
45 Supreme Court of the United States, case of "Linmark Associates, Inc. v. Township of Willingboro," May 2, 1977.
46 Supreme Court of the United States, case of "Perry Education Association v. Perry Local Educators' Association et. al.", February 23, 1983.
47 Supreme Court of Puerto Rico, case of "Juan Mari Bras y otros c. Juan F. Castañas," May 10, 1968.
48 Constitutional Court of Colombia, Decision T-456/92, July 14, 1992.

49 According to Justice Holmes, "The question in every case is whether the words used are used in such circumstances and are of such a nature as to create a clear and present danger that they will bring about the substantive evils that Congress has a right to prevent." (Supreme Court of the United States of America, case of "Schenck v. United States," March 3, 1919).
50 National Court of Cassation in Criminal Matters of Argentina, case of "Alais, Julio alberto y otros s/ recurso de casación," April 23, 2004, opinion of Justice Riggi.
51 Constitutional Court of Peru, File Number 4677–2004-PA/TC, December 5, 2005.
52 Ibid.
53 Heffron v. Internac. Society, 452 US 640 (1981).
54 Constitutional Court of Peru, 00012–2008-PI/TC, case of "Cinco Mil Trescientos Noventaitres [*sic*] Ciudadanos," July 14, 2010.
55 Ibid.
56 Ibid.
57 National Court of Cassation in Criminal Matters of Argentina, Chamber One, "Schifrin, Marina", Decision of July 3, 2002. Article 22 reads: "The people neither deliberate nor govern except through their representatives and authorities established by this Constitution. Any armed force or meeting of persons assuming the rights of the people and petitioning in their name, commits the crime of sedition."
58 Human Rights Center, Diego Portales University. Annual Report on Human Rights in Chile, 2009, p. 46–47.
59 Larry Kramer, The People Themselves, 27 (2004).
60 On this point, see Christian G. Fritz, American Sovereigns: The People and America's Constitutional Tradition Before the Civil War, 41–2 (2008).
61 Christian G. Fritz, American Sovereigns: The People and America's Constitutional Tradition Before the Civil War, 4 (2008).

References

Gregorio Badeni, Derecho Constitucional. Libertades y garantías (1999).

Gregorio Badeni, La convivencia democrática (2001).

Miguel Carbonell, *La Corte sube el listón*, Reforma, August 1, 2010.

Ramón Casilda Béjar, *América Latina y el Consenso de Washington*, 2803 Boletín Económico del ICE, 19–38 (2004).

Juan Carlos Cassagne, Reflexiones sobre los "cacerolazos" (2002).

Centro de Estudios Legales y Sociales, 2001 Annual Report.

Gloria Chicaiza, *The mining enclave of the "Cordillera del Cóndor*," March 2010, available at www.ceecec.net/wp-content/uploads/2008/10/CORDILLERA_CONDOR_ECUADOR_V2.pdf.

Francisco Cox, *Criminalización de la protesta social: "No tiene derecho a reunirse donde le plazca,"* in ¿Es Legítima la Criminalización de la Protesta Social? Derecho Penal y Libertad de Expresión en América Latina (Eduardo Bertoni comp., 2010).

Ronald Dworkin, Justice in Robes (2006).

Raúl G. Ferreyra, La Constitución vulnerable (2003).

Christian G. Fritz, American Sovereigns: The People and America's Constitutional Tradition Before the Civil War (2008).

Roberto Gargarella, *Un diálogo sobre la ley y la protesta social*, 61 Revista de la Facultad de Derecho de la Pontificia Universidad Católica del Perú (2009).

Roberto Gargarella, El derecho a la protesta, el primer derecho (2005).

María A. Gelli, Constitución de la Nación Argentina (2001).

D. Hall and E. Lobina, *La privatización del agua en América Latina* (Report before the Water Conference of the Americas, San José, Costa Rica, July 2002).

Human Rights First, Los defensores y defensoras de derechos humanos acusados sin fundamento. Presos y señalados en Colombia (2009).

Larry Kramer, The People Themselves (2004).

Thomas Kruse, *La "Guerra del Agua" en Cochabamba, Bolivia: terrenos complejos, convergencias nuevas*, in Sindicatos y Nuevos Movimientos Sociales en América Latina (Enrique de la Garza ed., 2005).

Germán Lodola, Cultura política de la democracia en Argentina, 2010. Consolidación democrática en las Américas en tiempos difíciles (forthcoming) (on file with authors).

Mamani Ramírez, Microgobiernos barriales: levantamiento de la ciudad de El Alto (octubre 2003) (2005).

José Antonio Ocampo, Más allá del Consenso de Washington: una agenda de desarrollo para América Latina (2005).

Raúl Ornelas, *La guerra del gas: cuarenta y cinco días de resistencia y un triunfo popular*, 16 Revista Chiapas, available at www.revistachiapas.org/No16/ch16ornelas.html.

María Piqué and Marina Soberano, *El derecho penal y la protesta social*, in Teoría y Crítica del Derecho Constitucional (Roberto Gargarella comp., vol. 2, 2008).

Relatoría Especial para la Libertad de Expresión de la CIDH, Informe Anual 2005 de la Relatoría Especial para la Libertad de Expresión de la CIDH.

Pablo Stefanoni, *Siete preguntas y siete respuestas sobre la Bolivia de Evo Morales*, 209/3 Nueva Sociedad (2007).

Maristella Svampa and Sebastian Pereyra, Entre la ruta y el barrio: la experiencia de las organizaciones piqueteras (2003).

Maristella Svampa, *Los movimientos sociales en la Argentina de hoy. Piquetes y Asambleas. Tres Estudios de Casos*, 27 (2007), available at http://maristellasvampa.net/archivos/ensayo07.pdf.

Víctor Toledo Llancaque, *Cronología de los principales hechos en relación a la represión de la protesta social mapuche, Chile 2000–2007*, VIII/22 Observatorio Social de América latina—CLACSO (2007).

UN Human Rights Committee, "Concluding observations of the Human Rights Committee, Chile", CCPR/C/CHL/CO/5, April 17, 2007, paragraph 7.

Rodrigo Uprimny Yepes and Sánchez Duque, *Derecho Penal y Protesta Social,* in ¿Es Legítima la Criminalización de la Protesta Social? Derecho Penal y Libertad de Expresión en América Latina? (Eduardo Bertoni comp, 2010).

Jeffrey R. Webber, *Indigenous Struggle in Latin America: The Perilous Invisibility of Capital and Class*, 49/3 Latin American Politics and Society, 203 (2007).

Raúl Zaffaroni, *El derecho penal y la criminalización de la protesta social*, Bulletin 13 November, IV/7 Jurisprudencia Argentina (2002).

Zaffaroni se pronunció en contra de criminalizar las protestas sociales, Clarín, August 24, 2005, available at http://edant.clarin.com/diario/2005/08/24/elpais/p-01001.htm.

Raúl Zibecchi, *Un año de la masacre de Bagua, nuevos actores frente a un Estado en crisis*, June 11, 2010, available at www.cipamericas.org/es/archives/2523.

Raúl Zibecchi, *Un año de la masacre de Bagua*, La Jornada, June 4, 2010.

Further reading

Archon Fung, *Deliberation before the Revolution*, 33/2 Political Theory, 379–419 (June 2005).

Eduardo Bertoni (ed.), Es legítima la criminalización de la protesta social? (2010), available at www.palermo.edu/cele/pdf/Protesta-social.pdf.

Olivier Fillieule and Danièle Tatakowsky, La Manifestation (2013).

Roberto Gargarella, *Law and Social Protests*, 6 Criminal Law and Philosophy, 15–27 (2012).

Dieter Rucht, Ruud Koopmans et al., Acts of Dissent. New developments in the study of protest (1999).

7 Transitional justice

Leonardo Filippini and Agustín Cavana[*]

Introduction

Following a serious conflict or extended period of violence, while political transitions are undertaken or acknowledged, communities face the harsh legacy of human rights violations. These scenarios constitute the battlefield of transitional justice, the purpose of which is, in simple terms, to further justice despite contextual challenges and to take advantage of opportunities for change, to define a new context in which respect for human rights is an achievable and daily promise.[1]

In 1997, under the direction of the new UN subcommittee, expert Louis Joinet drew on these practices and identified three fundamental rights of victims and obligations of states in such cases: the right to truth, the right to justice, and the right to reparation, to which was later added the need of non-repetition guarantees.[2] Since then, this view of the issue has expanded and the international community has been developing the key aspects of these aspirations.

However, we must not lose sight of the fact that transitional justice processes are influenced and conditioned by the political juncture, which may limit the possibilities of rendering them operational. Still, it is worth highlighting that they are, in turn, identified with a normative human rights framework that functions as a driver of political action and an insurmountable limit for government action by establishing crucial baselines for any state action and functioning as benchmarks for evaluating contextual limitations.[3]

Although there is a certain consensus regarding key elements, each transitional process requires special consideration, given that there is no such thing as uniform and universally valid procedures. On the contrary, sometimes novel methods are needed for achieving some measure of justice.[4] Thus, the purpose of this chapter is to report some of the developments occurring in the region and, in particular, to highlight the questions that the inter-American system and local courts have asked throughout this process.

To this end, we will briefly describe the discussion in four key points: criminal justice, truth, reparation, and vetting, while attempting to describe answers to questions like the following: What is the value of amnesty laws enacted by democratic and/or *de facto* governments? In these cases, to what extent should we acknowledge the principles of *res judicata* and *ne bis in idem*? What is the point of prosecuting individuals who are no longer in power? What are the implications of the right to truth? How does it relate to the right to justice? Who has a right to reparation? What should reparation consist of?

Criminal justice

For a large part of the Latin American experience, criminal justice seems to express a relevant manifestation of the aspiration of justice for a violent past. Criminal prosecution is, perhaps, the most direct, problematic, and debated tool in a transitional context. This is because it replicates the problem of punishment on the one hand, while presenting new and unique risks on the other; these include the possibility of destabilizing an incipient democracy as no other institution can.[5] The decision to move forward with criminal prosecutions against perpetrators of grave human rights violations is, therefore, never simple.

This is why the outcome of such prosecutions has proven controversial and, in several cases, has also involved the dilemma of reopening criminal cases that had previously been closed through amnesties or pardons, such as is the case in Argentina, Uruguay, Chile, Peru, Guatemala, or Brazil. Delayed justice generates doubt about the situation of the accused, who may be hoping for no criminal prosecution at all. Many perpetrators have even been subject to prosecution or convicted before they could benefit from impunity norms, but the amount of time that elapsed may still favor oblivion or the need to close the door of the past and concentrate on the future.

A large number of ongoing prosecutions in the Southern Cone, for example, focuses on elderly individuals who have generally been stripped of the power to resist prosecution. However, despite that, many countries chose to put their trust in the virtue of justice while investigating and punishing crimes against humanity, regardless of the time that has elapsed since their commission. And, in such countries, criminal trials seem to have created a turning point, renovating trust in institutions and contributing to the restoration of the dignity of victims in a way that would not otherwise have been possible.

Meanwhile, inter-American bodies and local courts have responded to numerous controversial questions and shed some light on the role of criminal justice in such processes: what is the value of amnesty laws sanctioned by *de facto* governments? And those sanctioned by democratic governments? In these cases, to what extent should we acknowledge the principle of *res judicata* and *ne bis in idem*? Was there retroactive enforcement of criminal law? What is the ultimate end of prosecuting individuals who no longer hold positions of power?

In the case of *Barrios Altos v. Perú,*[6] for example, the Inter-American Court of Human Rights summarized one of the most important and influential views in the region. This case investigated a massacre carried out by the Peruvian army. The case reached the Inter-American Commission of Human Rights as a result of a series of laws aimed at closing an already-problematic ongoing prosecution. Law No. 26,479, which was enacted without any parliamentary debate or public announcement, exonerated military and police personnel—as well as civilians—from responsibility for any human rights violations occurring between 1980 and 1995 and put an end to a large number of the ongoing prosecutions. However, the measure failed after being declared unconstitutional by the intervening judge.

This led to the enactment of Law No. 26,492, which declared that the amnesty was mandatory and not reviewable in court, while expanding the scope of Law No. 26,479 to unreported cases. Months later, the 11th Criminal Chamber of the Superior Court of Lima revoked the decision of the first-instance judge and put a definitive end to the process. This set forth the intervention of the Inter-American Commission, which recommended, in Report 28/00[7], that the Peruvian state revoke its amnesty laws and conduct a serious, unbiased, and effective investigation of the case. However, the lack of response led to the intervention of the Inter-American Court, which then ordered the investigation of the events to identify and sanction its perpetrators.

This decision later became a source of reference for many transitional processes and, to some extent, synthesized what is perhaps a dominant option in how Latin American countries face questions about criminal law today. Through this decision, which was subsequently upheld in similar cases, the Inter-American Court indicated that amnesty, statutes of limitations, and any other rule aimed at hindering investigations and sanctions against perpetrators of grave human rights violations can lead to victim helplessness and the perpetuation of impunity, thus violating the American Convention on Human Rights:

> The court considers that amnesty laws adopted by the Peruvian state kept the victims and their families from being heard by a judge, as stated in Section 8.1 of the American Convention on Human Rights, therefore violating their right to judicial protection, established in Section 25. They prevented the investigation, prosecution, capture, indictment and punishment of those responsible for the events in Barrios Altos, in violation of Section 1.1 of the Convention and obstructed clarification of the facts of the case. Finally, by adopting self-amnesty laws incompatible with the Convention, the Peruvian state failed to fulfill its obligation to adapt domestic law to the Convention, an obligation enshrined in Section 2.[8]

This notion was later upheld in the case of *Almonacid Arellano v. Chile*,[9] where the Inter-American Court found that the self-amnesty law[10] of the Chilean armed forces violated Section 2 of the American Convention, and stated that the demand of justice and rights of victims, as well as the letter and spirit of the convention, can trump the *ne bis in idem* principle, which is particularly inapplicable when there is no will to subject perpetrators to the justice system, and when such perpetrators are acquitted and released from criminal action or responsibility by means that lack independence or impartiality. Judgments in such cases are fraudulent and, therefore, investigations can be reopened if new evidence should arise.[11]

> The state may not invoke any domestic law provisions to set aside the order of the court to investigate and punish those responsible for the death of Mr Almonacid Arellano. Chile may not reapply Decree 2191, due to the considerations presented in this judgment, especially those contained in paragraph 145. In addition, the state cannot argue prescription, non-retroactivity of criminal law, or the *ne bis in idem* principle in order to avoid its duty to investigate and punish those responsible for the act.[12]

Later, in the case of *Gelman v. Uruguay*,[13] the Inter-American Court ratified its position while paying no regard to the impunity option that had been subject to referendums, sustaining not only that amnesties constituted grave human rights violations because they were inconsistent with the convention, but also because of how they had been enacted and the authority that had carried out the enactment; thus, in the view of the court, grave violations to international law cannot remain unpunished. This is because the incompatibility of such dispositions with the American Convention in these cases does not derive from a mere formality—such as questions of origin—but from material aspects that constitute the violation of rights enshrined in Sections 8 and 25.

> Amnesties for serious violations of human rights are inconsistent with the Convention, and this is not restricted to so-called 'self-amnesties,' not only because of the process of their adoption and the authority who issued them, but rather because of its *ratio legis*: letting serious violations of international law go unpunished. The incompatibility of the amnesty laws with the American Convention in cases of gross violations of human rights is not a matter of formality, as it would be their origin, but a matter of principle, in terms of the violation of the rights embodied in Section 8 and 25, in relation to Sections 1.1 and 2 of the Convention.[14]

Many of these discussions helped guide the debate in different local scenarios. Such was the case in Argentina where, immediately after the return of democracy, the National Congress annulled the self-amnesty law[15] enacted by the military government, and then President Raúl Alfonsín created a truth commission and ordered the prosecution of the members of the military junta that had ruled the country between 1976 and 1983. The Juntas Trial ("Juicio de las Juntas") took place between April and December 1985 and concluded with the conviction of the former presidents Jorge Videla and Roberto Viola, Admirals Emilio E. Massera and Armando Lambruschini, and General Orlando R. Agosti.

After the Juntas Trial, the courts began to investigate hundreds of other officials involved in the commission of atrocious crimes, while the armed forces began to exert strong pressure over the executive branch in order to stop the criminal proceedings. As a result of this maneuver, in 1986, the National Congress enacted Law No. 23,492, known as the Full Stop Law ("Ley de Punto Final"), which mandated the termination of criminal proceedings against members of military forces or terrorist groups who had not been summoned for deposition, or who were not summoned within 60 days of the enactment of the law. The Full Stop Law, however, did not work as intended by the government, as it provoked an avalanche of complaints and intense judicial activity.

In this context, in 1987, the National Congress enacted Law No. 23,521, known as the Due Obedience Law ("Ley de Obediencia Debida"), which established that those who were working as commanding officers, junior officers, and enlisted personnel of the military forces, security forces, police, and prisons, were not punishable for crimes committed between March 24, 1976 and September 26, 1983, for having acted under superior orders. That same year, the law was validated by the Supreme Court of Argentina, which rejected a constitutional challenge against it and foreclosed any possibility of criminal prosecution against those responsible of gross human rights violations.[16]

Finally, in 1989, President Carlos Menem pardoned all of those who had been convicted, including the members of the juntas, and ordered the discontinuance of any proceedings against persons indicted for human rights violations.[17] Since then, human rights organizations, victims, and relatives have pressed to retake the judgments, but it was only in March 2001, when these laws were first declared unconstitutional in the case of *Poblete/Simón*,[18] that a second cycle of criminal prosecutions commenced. This decision was later confirmed by the Federal Chamber of Appeals, which also returned previously-closed cases to their acting judges for their possible reopening.

In 2003, the National Congress enacted Law No. 25,779, declaring that the Due Obedience and Full Stop laws were null and void; and in 2005, the Supreme Court of Argentina decided the case of *Poblete/Simón*[19] and, by a majority of its members, revoked the doctrine established in the case of *Camps*[20] and *Riveros*[21] confirming the constitutionality of Law No. 25,779. In that case, based on Report No. 28/92[22] of the Inter-American Commission on Human Rights, Justice Petracchi held that *Barrios Altos v. Perú* cleared away all doubt regarding the extent of the Argentinian state's obligations concerning the Full Stop and Due Obedience laws, and that their democratic origin was irrelevant for determining their compatibility with the American Convention.[23]

Thus, the Supreme Court of Argentina transferred the conclusions of the Inter-American Court to its own case, as a corollary of the duty to interpret the decisions of such courts in good faith and as jurisprudential guidelines.

> Applying the resolution reached by the Inter-American Court in the 'Barrios Altos' case to the Argentinian case is imperative, if the international court's decisions are to be interpreted in good faith as jurisprudential guidelines. Certainly it is possible to find many arguments to distinguish the two cases, but such distinctions would be purely anecdotic . . . The decisive matter is . . . that the Full Stop and Due Obedience laws have the same

> flaws that led the court to reject the Peruvian law of 'amnesty.' Both are *ad hoc* laws, whose purpose is to prevent the prosecution of severe human rights violations.[24]

The court had anticipated this solution in 2004 when deciding in the case of *Arancibia Clavel*.[25] In this judgment, the Supreme Court of Argentina referenced for the first time the decision of the Inter-American Court in *Barrios Altos v. Perú*, and declared the imprescriptibility[26] of the criminal prosecution of Enrique Arancibia Clavel—a former intelligence agent of Chile's *de facto* government—for crimes against political opponents in Argentina.

> The ground for imprescriptibility lies in the fact that crimes against humanity are generally committed by the same punitive agencies that operate outside the control of criminal law. It is not reasonable to try to legitimize genocidal power by limiting the state's punitive reaction, which purportedly has preventive effects. Therefore, it cannot reasonably be argued that it is necessary to ensure the extinction of criminal action by the passage of time in crimes of this nature . . . the Convention on the Non-Applicability of Statutory Limitations to War Crimes and Crimes Against Humanity . . . only declares the imprescriptibility of those crimes, which implies the recognition of a standard already in force (*jus cogens*) in customary public international law . . . At the time they were executed, the events under investigation were already considered crimes against humanity under the international law of human rights which was binding for the Argentinian state. Therefore, the inevitability of their prosecution trial and the subsequent imprescriptibility follow as a logical consequence.[27]

The court's doctrine was completed in the case of *Mazzeo*,[28] where it invalidated President Menem's pardon of the military junta while sustaining, on the basis of inter-American jurisprudence, that international instruments impose the obligation to identify and prosecute individuals responsible for crimes against humanity, regardless of the amount of time elapsed, existing amnesties, or similar measures, thus rendering the *ne bis in idem* principle inoperable.

> In international humanitarian law, axiological principles acquire full prominence guiding interpretation, both in defining the *ne bis in idem* doctrine and the *res judicata* doctrine. This is so to the extent that both statutes of international criminal tribunals and the principles underlying universal jurisdiction tend to ensure that no abhorrent acts go unpunished . . . [Quoting a justice's opinion in a previous case, it added:] '[S]ince the Inter-American Court of Human Rights' decision in the 'Barrios Altos' case . . . strong restrictions have been established on the possibility of invoking the defense of res judicata to hinder the prosecution of conducts as [those here investigated]' . . . Therefore, the principles that within domestic law are commonly employed to justify the *res judicata* and the *ne bis in idem* doctrines are not applicable regarding such crimes against humanity because 'the international legal instruments that establish this category of offenses and the consequent state duty to identify and prosecute those responsible do not provide, and therefore do not allow, this obligation to cease by the passage of time, amnesties or other measures to dissolve the possibility of criminal prosecution' . . .[29]

In Peru, *Barrios Altos* led to similar decisions when motivating the Constitutional Court to order the reopening of the case, rejecting an appeal by one of the perpetrators who had been acquitted by the Supreme Council of Military Justice. According to the Constitutional Court, the state's obligation to investigate the events and sanction those responsible for the violation of human rights, as per the judgment of the Inter-American Court of Human Rights, led to the annulment not only of trials that had applied amnesty laws after it had been declared that such laws lacked judicial effect, but also of any practice aimed at hindering the investigation or sanctioning violations of the right to life or personal integrity.[30]

> The state's obligation to investigate the facts and punish those responsible for the violation of human rights declared in the judgment of the Inter-American Court of Human Rights not only included the invalidity of those processes where amnesty laws had been applied after declaring that such laws have no legal effect, but also any practice intended to prevent the investigation and punishment for the violation of the rights to life and personal integrity.[31]

In Honduras, the supreme court found Amnesty Decrees No. 199/87 and 87/91 to be unconstitutional and deemed that the power of government officials in Congress to grant amnesty for ordinary and extraordinary political crimes as stipulated in the Constitution of Honduras did not extend to crimes aimed at "attempting against the existence and inner security of the State, the system of government and the rights of citizens."[32] In El Salvador, the Constitutional Chamber of the Supreme Court of Justice held that the General Amnesty Law for the Consolidation of Peace was not applicable to cases of serious human rights violations.[33]

In Uruguay, the Supreme Court declared the unconstitutionality of the Statute of Limitations Law[34] and held that similar norms had been invalidated by the international community and states that had undergone analogous processes, and that both this similarity and the relevance of said decisions could not be ignored when examining the local reality.[35] This decision, which expressly authorized the early resolution of similar cases, was prior to the Inter-American Court of Human Rights' decision in the case of *Gelman* and, although it was taken into account in the latter and deemed to constitute an adequate measure, it proved insufficient for preventing the state's responsibility for non-compliance with the duty to investigate grave human rights violations and to adapt local legislation to the American Convention.[36]

> [T]he unlawfulness of an amnesty law enacted to benefit military and police officials who committed [serious violations of human rights], and who enjoyed impunity during de facto regimes, has been stated by courts from both the international community and the states who went through similar processes . . . Such statements could not be ignored in considering the constitutionality of Act No. 15,848 and have been taken into account . . . in this ruling.[37]

In an opposite sense, the Supreme Court of Brazil upheld an amnesty act,[38] in the case of *the Breach of Fundamental Obligation No. 153*,[39] holding that it was up to the legislative branch to repeal it.[40] However, in their dissenting opinions, Justices Lewandowski and Ayres Brito said that the amnesty was unconstitutional and contrary to international law, and that the fact that it included "both sides" did not imply that it was not a self-amnesty law enacted by the regime.[41] The debate remained open in Brazil, and the Inter-American Court of Human Rights's recent decision in the case of *Gomes Lund*,[42] criticizing the decision of the Supreme Court of Brazil, could help to change the direction that seems to be dominant in the region today.

Truth

The right to truth was originally conceived as stemming from the obligation of states to provide victims of human rights violations and their families with a quick and simple legal recourse for their protection, which included the right to know the fate of their loved ones.[43] However, probably as a result of the amnesties and pardons issued across the region, its content evolved until it was collectively conceived as the search for a common account of an abusive past.[44] The truth must be fully exposed, and this does not mean some sort of subsidiary vindication that depends on the success of the criminal process, but a phenomenon that transcends the punitive scope and requires autonomous protection.[45]

The state has a duty to prove its commitment to the defense and protection of human rights. This involves, among other things, investigating and revealing what was hidden about illegal repression and ensuring access to the truth for each of the victims.[46] The full knowledge of these circumstances is deemed as a kind of moral reparation for society in general and victims' families in particular, who often value truth beyond pecuniary compensation.[47] Sometimes, the mere revelation of the truth can help repair the stigma and guilt that haunts those who have suffered grave human rights violations.

This social dimension of the law and its importance as a form of reparation was acknowledged on several occasions by the Inter-American Court, which held that the state has a duty to carry out any necessary efforts for revealing the fate of victims and the whereabouts of their remains to their families and society in general, as well as to adopt measures to prevent repetition of these grave violations. It also highlighted that preventive and non-repetition measures begin with the revelation and acknowledgement of the atrocities of the past, given that society has the right to know the truth about these events in order to develop the capacity to prevent similar events in the future.[49]

> The possibility of the victim's relatives to know what happened to her, and, in case she was murdered, where her remains are, constitutes a means of redress and therefore an expectation that the state must satisfy to the victim's family and to society as a whole . . . It is the state's duty . . . to ensure that these grave violations are not repeated. Accordingly, it should make all necessary efforts to achieve this end. Preventive and non-repetition measures start with the revelation and recognition of past atrocities . . . Society has the right to know the truth regarding such crimes, so it has the ability to prevent them in the future.[49]

Recently, in the same vein, the court reaffirmed that knowing the truth is a fair expectation that must be met by the state through investigation and publication of its results. It also held that this means determining patterns of joint action and identifying individuals who participated in the violations, as well as their role, and that, in compliance with this duty, states may establish truth committees that contribute to the construction and preservation of historical memory, the revelation of the facts and the determination of institutional, social, and political responsibility within a historical period.[50]

In fact, these commissions are the most common institution for ensuring this right, even when the Inter-American Court of Human Rights has stated that their reports do not waive the state duty to establish the truth through judicial processes.[51] That was the case in Argentina, with the National Commission on the Disappearance of Persons (CONADEP); in Chile, with the National Commission on Truth and Reconciliation and the National Reparation and Reconciliation Commission and its successor; in El Salvador, with the Commission on the Truth for El Salvador; in Uruguay, with the Commission for Peace; in Guatemala, with the Commission for Historical Clarification; in Paraguay; in Honduras; in Colombia; and, more recently, in Brazil, with the Truth Commission, among others.

The relationship between commissions and other transitional institutions varies with different experiences. In some cases, such as that of El Salvador, the commission has been conceived as an exclusive alternative to justice, while in other countries, such as Argentina and Peru, it has functioned as a necessary supplement. Independence of mandates and powers between the criminal justice system and truth committees can prevent potential conflicts; however, the separation of activities is not logically possible, nor have experiences in places in which both actions were carried out simultaneously proven to justify this option.[52]

The characteristics of these commissions differ on a case-by-case basis, but they have at least some things in common. In general, they each have an official status that stems from their recognition at the state or international level, while they operate within a limited timeframe and are subject to mandates that justify their operation and powers.[53] These bodies usually consist of independent expert groups dedicated to investigating cases and patterns of systematic human rights violations during a specific period in a country's history or during a particular conflict, while later reporting their findings. Their aim is to determine the events that took place, to create awareness of what happened, and to contribute to repairing the damage suffered by victims.

The Commission for Truth and Reconciliation of Peru (CVR), for example, was created in 2001 with the mission of analyzing the causes of violence, proposing measures for Peruvian society to overcome the situation, and contributing to the justice system in the identification of responsibility for grave human rights violations. Its work was accompanied by victims, human rights organizations, and various sectors of civil society, and culminated with the presentation of a final report in 2003 that paved the way for the prosecution of those responsible and influenced the work of the courts, such as the decision of the Constitutional Court of Peru (CCP) that ordered the investigation of the disappearance of Genaro Villegas Namuche.[54]

At that time, the CCP held that society had the right to know the truth about the facts or about any unjust and painful events caused by multiple forms of state and non-state violence. This was an inalienable and collective legal right, through which knowledge of the circumstances of time, manner, and place in which events occurred can be demanded, as well as the reasons that prompted the perpetrators. And thus it established that, despite the time elapsed, those affected are entitled to be informed of the identity of the perpetrators, as well as the date, location, details, reasons for the perpetrators' actions, and location of the remains of the dead, among other things.

In Argentina, then President Alfonsín created CONADEP to investigate the fate of the disappeared. After analyzing and documenting thousands of cases and compiling research from around the country and statements from victims, families, and perpetrators, CONADEP published an official report in 1984 summarizing its work and making recommendations for initiating legal actions against perpetrators and a partial list of disappeared persons, thus not only providing the courts with evidence at that time, but also constituting a key tool in the current proceedings.

Another example is the Truth Commission of El Salvador, created in 1992 for the purpose of promoting national reconciliation and investigating the most serious and egregious acts of violence since 1980. In its final report, the commission recommended sanctioning those responsible, transforming the judicial system, and providing material and moral reparations to victims. Their findings, nevertheless, were discarded by the General Amnesty Law for the Consolidation of Peace of 1993. Years later, however, one of the documented cases was submitted to the Inter-American Commission on Human Rights which, in report 1/99, recommended that El Salvador nullify the law, investigate what happened, and repair the damage suffered by the victims.[55]

The commissions were the most common but not the only development linked to the search for truth. The right to grief of the families of the disappeared, for example, made it possible to promote investigations as to their fate without the limitations of criminal investigations.[56] Similarly, genetic identification techniques enabled the identification of abducted persons—for example, babies born to captive mothers—and have continued to serve this purpose many years later. The case of *Lapacó*[57] in Argentina, which occurred while the impunity laws were effective and involved public statements made by a marine officer regarding the unlawful repression that took place during the dictatorship, is an interesting example of this.

In May 1995, Carmen Aguiar de Lapacó, a Plaza de Mayo Mother and member of the Board of Directors of the Center for Legal and Social Studies (CELS), requested before the National Federal Court in Criminal and Correctional Matters, the investigation of what happened to her daughter Alejandra, who had disappeared in 1977, claiming her right to know the truth and that continuing the investigation was feasible even if there was no possibility of a criminal sanction against the alleged perpetrator. In her claim, she also requested that the Ministry of Defense provide all pertinent information about the fate of detainees and disappeared persons in the hands of the army and security and intelligence forces.

Her claim was admitted by the court, which acknowledged her right to truth and grief, and stated that even though amnesty laws and decrees made it impossible to impose criminal sanctions, they did not put an end to proceedings. However, the General Secretary of the Army replied that no such data were available, thus motivating an additional claim that was rejected by the court, deeming that the conflict exceeded its purview and had to be resolved by the executive. This decision was confirmed by the Supreme Court, which argued that once the purpose of the criminal investigation had been exhausted—i.e. once the existence of an actual offense is verified—continuing with the investigation is no longer admissible.[58] The issue concluded with an agreement before the Inter-American Commission[59] and a state commitment to do everything within its power to determine the facts.

Another example is that of Colombia, where the enactment of Law No. 975 of 2005 constituted an attempt to reconstruct the truth through transactional mechanisms that reduced the penalties for paramilitary groups in exchange for their accounts of the crimes in which they were involved and their compliance with reparation measures, such as public acknowledgement of their responsibility or effective collaboration for locating kidnapped, disappeared, or murdered persons. This policy was considered superior to peace processes carried out in the past, which had basically consisted of forgiving and forgetting the crimes that had been committed,[60] but it has also been heavily criticized, because those testifying are not obliged to tell the truth or subject to adequate sanctions if they lie or omit relevant information.[61]

Many further developments were also influenced by the need for a common past. Human rights education, museums, and other forms of collective remembrance are tools for society as a whole to face the past with a forward-looking perspective.[62] In 2007, for example, the Brazilian government published the book *The Right to Memory and Truth*[63] ("Direito à verdade e à memória"), the first official text recognizing the state's responsibility in the crimes of the dictatorship, telling the story of over 400 political militants that fell victim to the dictatorship. Later, it published *Stories of Boys and Girls Marked by the Dictatorship*[64] ("Direito à Memória e à Verdade: histórias de meninas e meninos marcados pela ditadura") and *Memoirs of Femininity*[65] ("Direito à memória e à verdade: Luta, substantivo feminino"); the government also created the portal Memories Revealed[66] ("Memórias Reveladas"), which is a database of documents held by the dictatorship between 1964 and 1985.

Reparations

Transitional justice also recognizes the rights of victims of systematic human rights violations and the right to effective and adequate reparations. Reparations help to prevent the recurrence of violations and can be aimed both at individuals as well as communities or groups of people.

In addition, on a material level, they may consist of the payment of money or the provision of service, as well as collectively or alternatively covering medical or administrative expenses, such as lost work days for political reasons, while, on a symbolic level, they may consist of a state-issued apology, the construction of memorials, or the establishment of commemorative dates.

According to the Inter-American Commission on Human Rights, reparations tend to erase the effects of past violations, which is why their nature and amount should depend on the material and immaterial damage caused.[67] However, in addition to repairing and, imperfectly, acknowledging the suffering of victims and their loved ones, reparation policies are aimed at restoring confidence in the state, reestablishing ties based on social solidarity, and supplementing other elements that are necessary in a transition.[68] Truth policies, for example, can seem like an empty gesture in the absence of adequate reparations, while reparations without truth can be perceived as an attempt to silence the victims.[69]

Inter-American jurisprudence also recognizes the right to adequate compensation as a duty of the state that cannot rest solely on the initiative of victims or their families,[70] and establishes that the reparation of damages resulting from the breach of an international obligation requires full restitution or restoration to the previous situation. When that is not possible, then measures must be taken to ensure the rights that were previously violated, repair the consequences of violations, and provide monetary compensation for damages.[71]

> The reparation of damages caused by the infringement of an international obligation requires, whenever possible, full redress (restitution *in integrum*), which consists in reestablishing the previous situation. If this is not possible . . . a set of measures should be announced to guarantee the rights infringed, redress the consequences of the violations and establish payment of a compensation for the damages caused.[72]

In this vein, the Inter-American Court of Human Rights has ordered various remedial measures in order to acknowledge the suffering of victims and preserve their collective memory. Thus, Guatemala had to create a scholarship and name a square or traveled street "Myrna Mack Chang," and place a plaque in her memory.[73] Suriname had to reopen a school and institute a foundation to assist the victims of murder and torture committed by the military.[74] Bolivia had to name an educational establishment in the city of Santa Cruz "José Carlos Trujillo Oroza," in a public ceremony attended by his family, to preserve this victim's memory and raise awareness of the need to prevent the repetition of harmful acts.[75] And Peru had to finance the university studies of Luis Cantoral Benavídes or restore his life project.[76]

We look now at some experiences. In Argentina, it all began in 1984 with Laws No. 23,053 and 23,117, which were succeeded by Laws No. 23,238, 23,523, and 23,278 in 1985. The first three reincorporated officials and state employees into office and acknowledged their time of inactivity for labor and social security purposes, while the others addressed bank employees and those forced into exile, laid off, or forced to resign for political or union-related reasons.[77] By 1986, Law No. 23,466 had already granted pensions to the spouses and children of disappeared persons. Many victims of illegal repression, however, took legal action to obtain compensation for the damages and losses suffered.

Most claims were found inadmissible as per the statute of limitations, but some were granted on the basis of judicial decisions that took into account the difficulty in filing claims during the dictatorship. However, those that had been rejected resorted to the Inter-American Court of Human Rights, giving rise to a series of hearings that culminated in a friendly settlement and the issuance of Decree No. 70/91, later validated by Law No. 24,043, authorizing the payment of compensation to those who proved that they had been detained by the executive during the dictatorship and who filed their claim before December 10, 1985.

This norm was succeeded by Law No. 24,411 of 2003, which granted economic compensation to victims of forced disappearance and to successors of people killed by security forces or paramilitary groups. One year later, Law No. 25,914 included those born during the imprisonment of their mothers, minors who were detained as a result of the arrest or disappearance of their parents for political reasons, and victims of identity substitution, thus completing the Argentinian government's policy on economic repairs.

The multiplicity of norms, however, did not close the discussion that in some cases, such as those of exiles, continued in the courts. This ended in the judgment of the case of *Yofre de Vaca Narvaja,*[78] where the scope of these provisions was extended by the court. These measures were also supplemented by other symbolic measures, such as the creation of the Space for the Memory, Promotion and Defense of Human Rights ("Espacio para la Memoria y para la Promoción y Defensa de los Derechos Humanos") on the campus of the School of Naval Mechanics, which had once operated as a clandestine detention center, and the issuance of Law No. 26,085, which turned March 24 (the day of the military coup) into the National Day of Memory, Truth and Justice ("Día Nacional de la Memoria por la Verdad y la Justicia").

Unlike the case of Argentina, in Brazil, the reparation process was conceived during the military dictatorship with the amnesty law (Law No. 6,683 of 1979) which, in attempting to obey both a social demand and the aspirations of impunity of the regime, contemplated measures such as the restoration of political rights to the persecuted and the right to be reinstated in their jobs for civilian and military public servants who had been arbitrarily dismissed.[79] In addition, agencies were created to carry out this policy, such as the Special Committee on Political Deaths and Disappearances, recognizing the state's responsibility for the death and disappearance of individuals (Law No. 9,140/1995), and the Amnesty Commission, intended to redress acts of emergency (Law No. 10,559/02).

The Brazilian program, which was later extended by attributing constitutional status to the right to reparation, and by amply granting reparations both in the public and private sector, did not limit itself merely to the economic dimension either, and provided rights such as recognition of the status of political refugee, the computation of time away from work because of persecution for retirement purposes, and guaranteed reinstatement into public schools and the localization of the remains of disappeared persons.[80] These were all complemented by symbolic measures, such as the construction of the Amnesty Memorial, a research and archive center, and amnesty caravans ("*caravanas da anistia*"), in which the Minister of Justice visits the places where crimes were committed, heads there an official act, and apologizes on behalf of the Brazilian state.

In Uruguay, one of the first measures of the transitional government was sanctioning Law No. 15,737, which pardoned perpetrators of serious human rights violations and political prisoners and created the National Commission for Repatriation, which allowed thousands of Uruguayan exiles to return home.[81] This norm was succeeded by Laws No. 15,783, 16,561, and 16,194, which reincorporated public servants and private sector employees who had been dismissed for political reasons, Law No. 17,449, which enabled the computation of time in detention and exile for retirement purposes, Law No. 17,949, which, together with other norms, benefited military members who had been removed for political or ideological reasons and provided financial compensation for unfair dismissal during the *de facto* period, and Law No. 18,033, which granted a reparation pension to individuals who had been tried by civil or military courts, and deprived of their liberty, during the dictatorship.[82]

Colombia also implemented a reparations policy that began with Laws No. 104 of 1993, aimed at providing care to victims of "narcoterrorism;" 397 of 1997, which created the National System of General Attention to the Population Displaced by Violence; and 418 of 1997, dedicated to the civilian population affected by terrorist actions in the context of the internal armed conflict,[83] and regulated by Decree No. 128 of 2003, which launched the program for reintegration into society and socioeconomic benefits for members of armed organizations who decided to abandon them and surrender. These laws preceded the Justice and Peace Law ("Ley de Justicia y Paz"), enacted in 2005 with the intention of setting the foundations for reconciliation and peaceful coexistence through truth, justice, and comprehensive reparation of victims, and a transitional justice policy on the prosecution of criminal behavior.[84]

This law created the Fund for the Reparation of Victims and the National Commission for Reparation and Reconciliation (NCRR) and acknowledged the right to reparation; however, the precariousness of its implementation mechanisms was questioned, as was the fact that it only recognized as victims those affected by illegal organizations.[85] Its critics also pointed out that it focused on symbolic reparations in detriment of material reparations and conditioned the duty to repair of offenders on their having ill-gotten assets and on an explicit claim to that effect.[86] Other critics, however, point to the budgetary limitations prescribed for the payment of compensation in court and the excessive governmental component of the NCRR and its lack of real power.

The Constitutional Court of Colombia corrected some of these shortcomings and, in an action of unconstitutionality, eliminated the budgetary restraint, authorized the issuance of precautionary measures against the assets of demobilized combatants, and stipulated that they had to surrender all their assets as a necessary condition for guaranteeing the rights of victims and for fighting impunity.[87] According to the court, the state must only afford subsidiary payment when the perpetrator's resources are insufficient or where its agents have had some degree of participation; however, by no means should they be exempted from responsibility for their crimes.[88]

Decree No. 1,290/08 supplemented this law through a program that granted compensation, guarantees of non-repetition, and restitution and rehabilitation measures for victims of illegal armed groups. But this scenario was recently changed with the enactment of the Victims and Land Restitution Act (1448/11) that incorporated the victims of state agents and attempted to adjust deficiently operating mechanisms.[89] This norm also created a legal–administrative system to expeditiously meet the claims of those stripped of their land as a result of forced displacement by the conflict and to provide them with some benefits, such as the flexibilization of evidentiary burdens and the creation of presumptions of dispossession.[90]

Disqualification of officers

It is often necessary to account for what happened during periods of violence and to transform the public framework that was part of the authoritarian regime into a guarantor of the rule of law and a barrier against future abuse.[91] Therefore, the reform of public institutions is another central concern in the transitional process, where disqualification or vetting is a fundamental tool used as a sort of "administrative justice" that can generate, for example, conditions for the effective functioning of key sectors, such as the judiciary and security forces, for the prosecution of perpetrators.

The terms "vetting" or "disqualification" are employed to describe procedures used to assess the integrity of a person (understood as an adherence to relevant standards on human rights and professional conduct) and to determine their suitability for public office.[92] As isolated measures, they are mechanisms that can be used to exclude people who are tied to grave human rights violations from public service; however, they can also be part of a broader reform process that includes reviewing the administrative and organizational structure of an institution.[93]

This kind of procedure does not generally reach the entire public sector; instead, it focuses on some state institutions, on certain positions of one organization in particular or several organizations in general, on available resources, or on political conditions or records of existing human rights violations. In general, efforts have focused on the armed and security forces and the judiciary because of the important role they play both during periods of abuse and during transitions; their effectiveness largely depends on the availability, reliability, and measurability of the information and evidence available.

The criteria used to screen candidates and officials, as well as sanctions applied to candidates not certified, procedures, and timeframes vary depending on the case. Regarding the first point, it is safe to say that, as a general rule, involvement in grave human rights violations is always a cause for disqualification.[94] The difficulty lies, of course, in defining what constitutes a grave human rights violation and how to prove involvement (conviction or declaration of criminal liability, truth commission report, etc.) in a way that addresses the political and operational difficulties in its implementation.

Enforcement agencies, on the other hand, have a direct and symbolic impact on individuals and on the overall transition. In some cases, disqualification has constituted an alternative to criminal law responses, and criminal sanctions have taken different forms, such as denying promotion, suspension, transfer, retirement, forced retirement, and disqualification from holding public office. Procedures are also diverse. In some cases, there were specialized official bodies and, in other cases, victims, families, and human rights organizations had to resort to the justice system, rely on mechanisms that were originally created for other purposes, or simply put pressure on applicable authorities.

In El Salvador, for example, an ad hoc committee was created that focused on the higher ranks of the armed forces, and was responsible for verifying whether applicants to public service and staff had been involved in human rights violations and whether they were capable of adapting to the new context.[95] It also had the power to abolish a particular institution, or part thereof, and to dismiss its staff by total veto,[96] evaluate an institution's staff to determine if someone should be removed from their position by direct veto, or establish future disqualification mechanisms for a given organization through indirect veto.[97] For legal and political reasons, however, the commission could only recommend disqualification to hold public office. In addition, it was also subject to accusations of bias because of its failure to investigate crimes committed by guerrilla organizations.[98]

In Argentina, however, there was no general review process, but the constitutional reform of 1994 that disqualified participants of the coup from holding public office caused families and organizations to channel their claims through existing mechanisms[99] (such as the procedure for the appointment of senior military commanders, requiring the approval of a legislative committee) and was used to exert pressure, culminating in a reform in 2002 that favored the dissemination of the statements submitted by the executive, while creating the possibility of monitoring candidates to military and judiciary positions.[100]

Another interesting point of the transition was the challenge against candidates for electoral positions. In 1999, the House of Representatives of Argentina refused, by majority of its members, the inauguration of elected national congressman and former repressor Antonio Bussi, based on the opposition of several lawmakers who questioned his moral suitability. Bussi filed a writ of *amparo* against this decision, which was rendered moot since its processing exceeded his term. However, the Supreme Court of Argentina ruled on the case for the sole purpose of interpreting the scope of Section 64 of the constitution, which gives the House the power to judge the validity of the qualifications of its members, on the grounds of institutional interest.

The majority of the court condemned the House's proceedings on the grounds that the prohibition can only result from a conviction for an offense and not just from participation in a particular historical event, since the contrary would involve appealing to moral qualities in violation of the presumption of innocence and republican ethics.[101] However, Justices Petracchi and Highton issued a dissenting opinion in which they embraced the recommendation of the Attorney General, who claimed that having held a powerful position during the *de facto* government already denoted unethical behavior that is incompatible with public office.[102] The same discussion arose again in 2005 with the case of *Luis Patti*, but the outcome was quite different because, in the latter case, the court, based on the doctrine established in *Bussi*, unanimously invalidated the House's decision.[103]

> There is no legal disability for people who have acted in certain ways in the past, since the impediment only stems from a judicial conviction for the commission of a crime. The consequences of the state of innocence cannot be ignored by abandoning the requirement of a criminal conviction through an appeal to the moral qualities of the person . . . To avoid applying these rights by arguing that there is a power to reject any person who violates 'the Republican ethics' can have extremely serious consequences for the very system the authorities are allegedly intent on protecting.[104]

A third noteworthy experience is that of Guatemala, where former *de facto* president Ríos Montt attempted legal action to circumvent the prohibition for military coup leaders to hold presidential office, established in the Guatemalan constitution of 1986. The request was denied by the Constitutional Court, which held that it was a categorical and permanent prohibition.[105] Montt filed a claim before the Inter-American Commission, which led it to decide on the compatibility of this restriction with the text of the American Convention. The commission said that regulations of this type should be considered in context and fall within the conditions that every constitutional legal system establishes for ensuring its effective functioning and defending the integrity of the rights of its citizens.[106]

> Defending the effectiveness of the political rights and the transparency of elections has led to various forms of regulation for choosing a country's president . . . The cause of ineligibility emerges from an act of the Constitutional Assembly, chosen by democratic vote, in which the Guatemalan people decided through their representatives to the Convention that it was necessary to maintain this cause of ineligibility that already existed in Guatemala's constitutional history . . . and that it was necessary to make it a permanent cause . . . These are among the conditions that every legal system needs to uphold in order to function in an effective way, and to be able to defend the integrity of citizens' rights.[107]

Conclusion

We saw that, in the region, there have been significant events for defining the content and scope of the rights to justice, truth, and reparation. Developments in the field have been strongly influenced by the characteristics of each transition, the need to ensure peace and to consolidate democracy, available material resources, and social demands. In several cases, however, there were significant developments that helped shape a new context and allowed a more or less shared narrative about what happened.

The Inter-American Court has played a significant role in this process by setting the parameters from which to examine state practices in the field and by driving progress in different countries of the region through decisions that, in some cases, have had a positive impact on other ongoing transitions. As explained above, the court has issued judgments to establish minimal content and insurmountable barriers that clash with the possibilities offered by the relevant context and political calculations.

Moreover, in other cases, governments and local courts have taken these duties seriously and implemented relevant measures for achieving justice. In Argentina and Peru, for instance, human rights violators were prosecuted. Several countries established truth commissions and took steps to disseminate their findings, identify perpetrators, keep the memory of the victims alive, and honor the dead. Several remedial laws have also been enacted and courts have awarded reparations to individuals. And, finally, some countries have revised and instituted new practices for access to employment and public service in particularly vulnerable institutions.

Still, there are many pending issues. In several cases, the roles of civilian accomplices of *de facto* governments have not been clarified, and such persons have not been penalized or required to compensate victims. Sexual violence, often exercised in secret detention centers, has not received its deserved attention. Many actors and participants in unlawful violence continue to occupy important positions, and face no obstacles in accessing such positions. Likewise, many forgotten victims continue to demand compensation for damages before national and international bodies.

In short, all this reveals that the task has not been—and still is not—simple. And despite the dilemmas posed by the belated realization of these rights, progress has been made in the path of justice, while time has contributed to the creation of a framework for deeper understanding and the progressive strengthening of victims, who were once persecuted by the state, in their capacity to once again trust institutions and have the ability to publicly voice their needs.[108] Their once-silenced voices are now being heard as they lead the decision to reject all forms of impunity and oblivion as a collective escape to the past.

Questions

a Which are the purposes and tools of transitional justice? Are there uniform and universally valid procedures to achieve its goals?

b What are the advantages and risks of the use of criminal prosecution in transitions? Which goals are pursued by criminal prosecutions against perpetrators of grave human rights violations? Why would you say it is important to convict them (if it is)? Which are the most common obstacles faced by criminal prosecutions against the perpetrators of grave human rights violations?

c According to the above mentioned Inter-American Court precedents, what is the value of amnesty laws enacted by *de facto* governments? Are those sanctioned by democratic governments any different? Which arguments could be made to defend the opposite conclusion?

d To what extent should the principle of *res judicata* and *ne bis in idem* be acknowledged in these cases?

e What are the implications of the right to truth? How does it relate to the right to justice? Which institutions or tools have been used to ensure this right to victims?

f How do truth commissions relate to criminal proceedings? What are their distinctive features?
g Who has a right to reparation? What should reparation consist of? Which government offices are usually responsible for assuring this right?
h How do reparations relate to the rights to truth and justice? Is reparation a valid substitute for other forms of justice that are unavailable or not possible?
i Which factors should be taken into account to establish fair monetary compensation? Should perpetrators and accomplices also be held liable for the damages they caused directly or indirectly?
j Which institutions are commonly subjected to reform during a transition? Why? Describe the procedures commonly known as vetting or disqualification.
k What kind of problems may arise when defining vetting or disqualification criteria? How do these procedures relate to other tools of transitional justice?

Notes

* This chapter was translated into English by Paula Arturo.
1 Leonardo Filippini and Lisa Margarell, *Instituciones de la Justicia de Transición y Contexto Político*, in ENTRE EL PERDÓN Y EL PAREDÓN. PREGUNTAS Y DILEMAS DE LA JUSTICIA TRANSICIONAL, at 144 (Angelika Rettberg ed., 2005).
2 LOUIS JOINET, QUESTION OF THE IMPUNITY OF PERPETRATORS OF VIOLATIONS OF HUMAN RIGHTS (CIVIL AND POLITICAL RIGHTS): FINAL REPORT (UN, E/CN.4/Sub.2/1996/18, June 20, 1996).
3 Leonardo Filippini and Lisa Margarell, *Instituciones de la Justicia de Transición y Contexto Político*, in ENTRE EL PERDÓN Y EL PAREDÓN. PREGUNTAS Y DILEMAS DE LA JUSTICIA TRANSICIONAL, at 144–5 (Angelika Rettberg ed., 2005).
4 Ibid., 146.
5 Leonardo Filippini, *La persecución penal en la búsqueda de justicia*, in HACER JUSTICIA. NUEVOS DEBATES SOBRE EL JUZGAMIENTO DE CRÍMENES DE LESA HUMANIDAD IN ARGENTINA, at 19 (Centro de Estudios Legales y Sociales (Argentina) and International Center for Transitional Justice, 2011).
6 Inter-American Court of Human Rights, case of "Barrios Altos (Chumbipuma Aguirre et al.) v. Perú," March 14, 2001.
7 Inter-American Commission of Human Rights, Report 28/00, case 11,528, "Barrios Altos v. Peru", March 7, 2000.
8 Ibid., paragraph 42.
9 Inter-American Court of Human Rights, case of "Almonacid Arellano v. Chile," September 26, 2006 (Preliminary Objections, Merits, Reparations and Costs).
10 Law-Decree No. 2,191.
11 Inter-American Court of Human Rights, case of "Almonacid Arellano v. Chile," September 26, 2006 (Preliminary Objections, Merits, Reparations and Costs), paragraph 154.
12 Ibid., paragraph 151.
13 Inter-American Court of Human Rights, case of "Gelman v. Uruguay," February 24, 2011 (Merits and Reparations).
14 Ibid., paragraph 229.
15 Law No. 22,924.
16 Supreme Court of Argentina, case of "Camps, Ramón Juan Alberto y otros," June 22, 1987 (Decisions 310:1162).
17 See Decrees No. 1002/89, 1003/89, 1004/89, 1005/89, 2741/90, 2742/90, 2743/90, 2744/90, 2745/90, and 2746/90.
18 National Federal Court in Criminal and Correctional matters No. 4 of Argentina, case No. 8686/2000 "Simón, Julio, Del Cerro, Juan Antonio s/sustracción de menores de 10 años," March 6, 2001, available at http://bit.ly/1rlYiUa.
19 Supreme Court of Argentina, case of "Simón, Héctor Julio y otros s/ privación ilegítima de la libertad, etc." June 14, 2005 (Decisions 328:2056).

20 Supreme Court of Argentina, case of "Camps, Ramón Juan Alberto y otros," June 22, 1987 (Decisions 310:1162).
21 Supreme Court of Argentina, case of "Riveros, Santiago Omar y otros," May 22, 1988 (Decisions 311:734). In this case the Supreme Court of Argentina ruled in favor of the constitutionality of the Due Obedience Law.
22 Inter-American Court of Human Rights, Report 28/92, Cases 10,147, 10,181, 10,240, 10,262, 10,309 and 10,311, Argentina, October 2, 1992.
23 Supreme Court of Argentina, case of "Simón, Héctor Julio y otros s/ privación ilegítima de la libertad, etc." June 14, 2005 (Decisions 328:2056), opinion of Justice Petracchi, paragraphs 20 and 23.
24 Ibid., paragraph 24.
25 Supreme Court of Argentina, case of "Arancibia Clavel, Enrique Lautaro s/ homicidio calificado y asociación ilícita y otros," August 24, 2004 (Decisions 327:3312), paragraph 23 of the majority vote.
26 The term "imprescriptibility" ("*imprescriptibilidad*" in Spanish), refers to the absence of statutory limitations for some crimes, like those qualified as "crimes against humanity."
27 Supreme Court of Argentina, case of "Arancibia Clavel, Enrique Lautaro s/ homicidio calificado y asociación ilícita y otros," August 28, 2004 (Decisions 327:3312), paragraph 23 of the majority vote.
28 Supreme Court of Argentina, case of "Mazzeo, Julio Lilo y otros s/rec. de casación e inconstitucionalidad," June 13, 2007 (Decisions 330:3248).
29 Ibid., paragraph 35 of the majority vote.
30 Constitutional Court of Peru, case of "Santiago Martín Rivas," Extraordinary Appeal, File No. 4587–2004-AA/TC, November 29, 2005, paragraph 63.
31 Ibid., paragraph 63.
32 Supreme Court of Honduras, Decision "RI20–99—Unconstitutionality of Decree No. 199–87 and Decree No. 87–91," June 27, 2000.
33 Constitutional Chamber of the Supreme Court of Justice of El Salvador, Decision 24–97/21–98, September 26, 2000.
34 Law No. 15,848.
35 Supreme Court of Justice of Uruguay, case of "Sabalsagaray Curutchet Blanca Stela—Denuncia de Excepción de Inconstitucionalidad," Decision No. 365, October 19, 2009, paragraphs III.8 and 15.
36 "Gelman v. Uruguay," paragraphs 142, Section c, and 239.
37 "Sabalsagaray Curutchet Blanca Stela,", paragraphs III.8 and 15.
38 See Law No. 6,683 of 1979 of the Federative Republic of Brazil. Text in Portuguese, translated into Spanish by the authors of this chapter.
39 Supreme Court of Brazil, ADPF 153, April 29, 2010, opinion of Justice Eros Grau, paragraph 56.
40 Ibid., paragraph 50.
41 Ibid., paragraphs 99–130 and 134–46.
42 Inter-American Court of Human Rights, case of "Gomes Lund et al. (Guerrilha do Araguia) v. Brazil," November 24, 2010 (Preliminary Objections, Merits, Reparations and Costs).
43 Inter-American Commission on Human Rights, El derecho a la verdad, available at http://bit.ly/16d6DTE (last accessed 16/04/2014).
44 Gustavo Maurino, *A la búsqueda de un pasado en la Democracia Argentina*, Revista del INECIP (October 2003).
45 Leonardo Filippini and Lisa Margarell, *Instituciones de la Justicia de Transición y Contexto Político*, in Entre el Perdón y el Paredón. Preguntas y Dilemas de la Justicia Transicional, at 145 (Angelika Rettberg ed., 2005).
46 Leonardo Filippini and Lisa Margarell, *La justicia penal y la verdad en la transición democrática*, in El Legado de la Verdad. La justicia penal en la transición Peruana, at 21 (Leonardo Filippini and Lisa Margarell eds, 2006).
47 Emilio F. Mignone, *The Experience of Argentina*, at Seminar on the Right to Restitution, Compensation and Rehabilitation for Victims of Grave Violations of Human Rights and Fundamental Freedoms, 125–9, Maastricht, the Netherlands, March 1992.
48 Inter-American Court of Human Rights, case of "Bámaca Velásquez et al. v. Guatemala," February 22, 2001, paragraph 76–7.
49 Ibid.
50 Inter-American Court of Human Rights, case of "Anzualdo Castro v. Peru," September 22, 2009 (Preliminary Objection, Merits, Reparations, and Costs), paragraph 119.

51 Inter-American Court of Human Rights, case of "Radilla Pacheco v. United States of Mexico," November 23, 2009 (Preliminary Objections, Merits, Reparations, and Costa), paragraph 179.
52 Ibid.
53 Rolando Ames Cobián and Félix Reátegui, *Toward Systemic Social Transformation: Truth Commissions and Development*, in TRANSITIONAL JUSTICE AND DEVELOPMENT. MAKING CONNECTIONS, at 150 (Pablo De Greiff and Roger Duthie eds, 2009).
54 Constitutional Court of Peru, File. No. 2488–2002-HC/TC, March 18, 2004.
55 Inter-American Commission on Human Rights, Report 1/99, Case 10,480, January 27, 1999.
56 Martín Abregú, *La tutela judicial del derecho a la verdad en Argentina*, 24 REVISTA IDH, 20.
57 Supreme Court of Argentina, case of "Suárez Mason, Carlos Guillermo s/ homicidio, privación ilegal de la libertad," August 13, 1998 (Decisions 321:2031).
58 Ibid.
59 Inter-American Commission on Human Rights, Report 21/00, case No. 12,059, "Carmen Aguiar de Lapacó," Argentina, February 29, 2000.
60 Rodrigo Uprimny Yepes and María Paula Saffon Sanin, *Derecho a la verdad: alcances y límites de la verdad judicial*, in ¿JUSTICIA TRANSICIONAL SIN TRANSICIÓN? VERDAD, JUSTICIA Y REPARACIÓN PARA COLOMBIA, at 160 (Rodrigo Uprimi Yepes ed., 2006).
61 Ibid., 161.
62 Leonardo Filippini and Lisa Margarell, *Instituciones de la Justicia de Transición y Contexto Político*, in ENTRE EL PERDÓN Y EL PAREDÓN. PREGUNTAS Y DILEMAS DE LA JUSTICIA TRANSICIONAL, at 146 (Angelika Rettberg ed., 2005).
63 BRASIL, SECRETARIA ESPECIAL DOS DIREITOS HUMANOS, DIREITO Á MEMORIA E Á VERDADE. COMISSÃO ESPECIAL SOBRE MORTOS E DESAPARECIDOS POLÍTICOS (2007), available at http://bit.ly/1IlaDWg.
64 PRESIDÊNCIA DA REPÚBLICA DE BRASIL, SECRETARIA ESPECIAL DOS DIREITOS HUMANOS, DIREITO À MEMÓRIA E À VERDADE: HISTÓRIAS DE MENINAS E MENINOS MARCADOS PELA DITADURA (2009), available at http://bit.ly/1xqQJUQ.
65 Tatiana Merlino and Igor Ojeda (eds), DIREITO À MEMÓRIA E A VERDADE, LUTA, SUBSTANTIVO FEMININO, MULHERES TORTURADAS, DESAPARECIDAS E MORTAS NA RESISTÊNCIA À DITADURA, (2010), available at http://bit.ly/1uq9xyN.
66 Available at www.memoriasreveladas.gov.br/.
67 INTER-AMERICAN COMMISSION ON HUMAN RIGHTS, MAIN GUIDELINES FOR A COMPREHENSIVE REPARATIONS POLICY, OAS/Ser/L/V/II.131, Doc. 1, February 19, 2008, item 1.
68 Pablo De Greiff, *Justice and Reparations*, in THE HANDBOOK OF REPARATIONS, at 464 (Pablo De Greiff ed., 2006).
69 Ibid., 461.
70 INTER-AMERICAN COMMISSION ON HUMAN RIGHTS, REPORT ON THE IMPLEMENTATION OF THE JUSTICE AND PEACE LAW: INITIAL STAGES IN THE DEMOBILIZATION OF THE AUC AND FIRST JUDICIAL PROCEEDINGS, OAS/Ser. L/V/II 129 Doc. 6, October 2, 2007, paragraph 97.
71 Inter-American Court of Human Rights, case of "Myrna Mack Chang v. Guatemala," November 25, 2003 (Merits, Reparations and Costs), paragraphs 235–6.
72 Ibid.
73 Ibid., paragraphs 285–6.
74 Inter-American Court of Human Rights, case of "Aloeboetoe v. Suriname," September 10, 1993 (Reparations and Costs), operative paragraph 5.
75 Inter-American Court of Human Rights, case of "Trujillo Oroza v. Bolivia," February 27, 2002 (Reparations and Costs), paragraph 122.
76 Inter-American Court of Human Rights, case of "Cantoral Benavídez v. Peru," December 3, 2001 (Reparations and Costs), operative paragraph 80.
77 MARÍA JOSÉ GUEMBE, LA EXPERIENCIA ARGENTINA DE REPARACIÓN ECONÓMICA DE GRAVES VIOLACIONES A LOS DERECHOS HUMANOS (2004).
78 Supreme Court of Argentina, case of "Yofre de Vaca Narvaja, Susana c/ M° del Interior," October 14, 2004 (Decisions 327:4241).
79 Paul Abrão and Marcelo Torelly, *Las razones de la eficacia de la ley de amnistía en Brasil y las alternativas para la verdad y la justicia en relación a las graves violaciones de derechos humanos ocurridas durante la dictadura militar (1964–1985)*, 8 REVISTA DO INSTITUTO DE HERMENÊUTICA JURÍDICA, 183–219 (2010).
80 Ibid.

81 Jorge Errandonea, *Justicia Transicional in Uruguay*, 47 Revista IDH, 48.
82 Ibid., 49.
83 Rodrigo Uprimny Yepes and Luis Manuel Lasso, *Verdad, Reparación y justicia para Colombia: algunas reflexiones y recomendaciones*, in Conflicto y seguridad democrática en Colombia. Temas críticos y propuestas (José Ernesto Borda Medina ed., 2004).
84 Constitutional Court of Colombia, Decision C-914/10: Unconstitutionality claim of Section 15 of Law No. 418 of 1997, amended by Section 6 of Law No. 782 of 2002, and Section 49 of Law No. 418 of 1997, November 16, 2010, paragraph 44.
85 Rodrigo Uprimny Yepes and María Paula Saffon Sanin, *La ley de 'justicia y paz': ¿una garantía de justicia y paz y de no repetición de las atrocidades?*, in ¿Justicia transicional sin transición?, at 180 (Rodrigo Uprimny Yepes ed., 2006).
86 Ibid.
87 See Constitutional Court of Colombia, Decision C-370/06, May 18, 2006.
88 Ibid.
89 Rodrigo Uprimny Yepes and Camilo Sánchez, Ley de Víctimas: avances, limitaciones y retos, available at http://bit.ly/1iY5jGW (last accessed August 7, 2014).
90 Ibid.
91 Diego Morales, *Limitaciones al acceso a cargos públicos para implicados en crímenes de lesa humanidad*, in Hacer Justicia. Nuevos Debates sobre el juzgamiento de crímenes de lesa humanidad in Argentina, at 81 (Centro de Estudios Legales y Sociales (Argentina) and International Center for Transitional Justice, 2011).
92 Roger Duthie, *Introduction*, in Justice as prevention. Vetting public employees in Transitional societies, at 17 (Alexander Mayer-Rieckh and Pablo De Greiff eds, 2007).
93 Alexander Mayer-Rieckh, *Vetting to Prevent Future Abuses. Reforming the Police, Court's and Prosecutor's Office in Bosnia and Herzegovina*, in Justice as prevention. Vetting public employees in Transitional societies, at 206 (Alexander Mayer-Rieckh and Pablo De Greiff eds, 2007).
94 ICTJ-UNDP, *Vetting Public Employees in Post-Conflict Settings: Operational Guidelines*, in Justice as prevention. Vetting public employees in Transitional societies, at 559 (Alexander Mayer-Rieckh and Pablo De Greiff eds, 2007).
95 Rubén Zamora and David Holiday, *The Struggle for Lasting Reform: Vetting Processes in El Salvador*, in Justice as prevention. Vetting public employees in Transitional societies, at 87 (Alexander Mayer-Rieckh and Pablo De Greiff eds, 2007).
96 As was the case, for example, with the combat forces of the "Farabundo Martí" National Liberation Front. See Ibid.
97 Ibid.
98 Ibid., 104.
99 Roger Duthie, *Introduction*, in Justice as prevention. Vetting public employees in Transitional societies, at 26 (Alexander Mayer-Rieckh and Pablo De Greiff eds, 2007).
100 Valeria Barbuto, *Strengthening Democracy: Impugnacion Procedures in Argentina*, in in Justice as prevention. Vetting public employees in Transitional societies, at 49 (Alexander Mayer-Rieckh and Pablo De Greiff eds, 2007).
101 Supreme Court of Argentina, case of "Bussi, Antonio Domingo c/Estado Nacional (Congreso de la Nación—Cámara de Diputados) s/incorporación a la Cámara de Diputados," July 13, 2007 (Decisions 330:3160), paragraphs 9 and 10.
102 Procuracion General de la Nacion, "Antonio D. Bussi c. Estado Nacional", B. 903. XL, May 31, 2005, items. XIII and XIV.
103 Supreme Court of Argentina, case of "Patti, Luis Abelardo s/promueve acción de amparo c/ Cámara de Diputados de la Nación," April 8, 2008 (Decisions 331:548).
104 Ibid., paragraphs 9 and 10 of the majority vote.
105 Inter-American Commission on Human Rights, Report No. 30/93, case 10,804, October 12, 1993, paragraph 8.
106 Ibid., paragraphs 30 and 37.
107 Ibid.
108 Leonardo Filippini, *La persecución penal en la búsqueda de justicia*, in Hacer Justicia. Nuevos Debates sobre el juzgamiento de crímenes de lesa humanidad in Argentina, at 44 (Centro de Estudios Legales y Sociales (Argentina) and International Center for Transitional Justice, 2011).

References

Paul Abrão and Marcelo Torelly, *Las razones de la eficacia de la ley de amnistía en Brasil y las alternativas para la verdad y la justicia en relación a las graves violaciones de derechos humanos ocurridas durante la dictadura militar (1964–1985)*, 8 Revista do Instituto de Hermenêutica Jurídica, 183–219 (2010).

Martín Abregú, *La tutela judicial del derecho a la verdad en Argentina*, 24 Revista IDH, 20.

Valeria Barbuto, *Strengthening Democracy: Impugnacion Procedures in Argentina*, in in Justice as prevention. Vetting public employees in Transitional societies (Alexander Mayer-Rieckh and Pablo De Greiff eds, 2007).

Brasil, Secretaria Especial dos Direitos Humanos, Direito á Memoria e á Verdade. Comissão Especial sobre Mortos e Desaparecidos Políticos (2007), available at http://bit.ly/1lIaDWg.

Rolando Ames Cobián and Félix Reátegui, *Toward Systemic Social Transformation: Truth Commissions and Development*, in Transitional Justice and Development. Making Connections (Pablo De Greiff and Roger Duthie eds, 2009).

Pablo De Greiff, *Justice and Reparations*, in The Handbook of Reparations at 464 (Pablo De Greiff ed., 2006).

Roger Duthie, *Introduction*, in Justice as prevention. Vetting public employees in Transitional societies, at 17 (Alexander Mayer-Rieckh and Pablo De Greiff eds, 2007).

Jorge Errandonea, *Justicia Transicional in Uruguay*, 47 *Revista IDH*, 48.

Leonardo Filippini and Lisa Margarell, *La justicia penal y la verdad en la transición democrática*, in El Legado de la Verdad. La justicia penal en la transición Peruana (Leonardo Filippini and Lisa Margarell eds, 2006).

Leonardo Filippini and Lisa Margarell, *Instituciones de la Justicia de Transición y Contexto Político*, in Entre el Perdón y el Paredón. Preguntas y Dilemas de la Justicia Transicional (Angelika Rettberg ed., 2005).

Leonardo Filippini, *La persecución penal en la búsqueda de justicia*, in Hacer Justicia. Nuevos Debates sobre el juzgamiento de crímenes de lesa humanidad in Argentina (Centro de Estudios Legales y Sociales (Argentina) and International Center for Transitional Justice, 2011).

María José Guembe, *La Experiencia Argentina de Reparación Económica de Graves Violaciones a los Derechos Humanos* (2004).

ICTJ-UNDP, *Vetting Public Employees in Post-Conflict Settings: Operational Guidelines*, in Justice as prevention. Vetting public employees in Transitional societies (Alexander Mayer-Rieckh and Pablo De Greiff eds, 2007).

Inter-American Commission on Human Rights, El derecho a la verdad, available at http://bit.ly/16d6DTE (last accessed 16/04/2014).

Inter-American Commission on Human Rights, Main guidelines for a comprehensive reparations policy, OAS/Ser/L/V/II.131, Doc. 1, February 19, 2008.

Inter-American Commission on Human Rights, Report on the Implementation of the Justice and Peace Law: Initial Stages in the Demobilization of the AUC and First Judicial Proceedings, OAS/Ser. L/V/II 129 Doc. 6, October 2, 2007.

Gustavo Maurino, *A la búsqueda de un pasado en la Democracia Argentin*, Revista del INECIP (October 2003).

Alexander Mayer-Rieckh, *Vetting to Prevent Future Abuses. Reforming the Police, Court's and Prosecutor's Office in Bosnia and Herzegovina*, in Justice as prevention. Vetting public employees in Transitional societies, at 206 (Alexander Mayer-Rieckh and Pablo De Greiff eds, 2007).

Tatiana Merlino and Igor Ojeda (eds), Direito à Memória e à Verdade, Luta, Substantivo Feminino, Mulheres torturadas, desaparecidas e mortas na resistência à ditadura, (2010), available at http://bit.ly/1uq9xyN.

Emilio F. Mignone, "The Experience of Argentina", at Seminar on the Right to Restitution, Compensation and Rehabilitation for Victims of Grave Violations of Human Rights and Fundamental Freedoms, 125–9, Maastricht, the Netherlands, March 1992.

Diego Morales, *Limitaciones al acceso a cargos públicos para implicados en crímenes de lesa humanidad* in HACER JUSTICIA. NUEVOS DEBATES SOBRE EL JUZGAMIENTO DE CRÍMENES DE LESA HUMANIDAD IN ARGENTINA (Centro de Estudios Legales y Sociales (Argentina) and International Center for Transitional Justice, 2011).

Presidência da República de Brasil, Secretaria Especial dos Direitos Humanos, Direito à Memória e à Verdade: histórias de meninas e meninos marcados pela ditadura (2009), available at http://bit.ly/1xqQJUQ.

Rodrigo Uprimny Yepes and María Paula Saffon Sanin, *Derecho a la verdad: alcances y límites de la verdad judicial*, in ¿JUSTICIA TRANSICIONAL SIN TRANSICIÓN? VERDAD, JUSTICIA Y REPARACIÓN PARA COLOMBIA, (Rodrigo Uprimi Yepes ed., 2006).

Rodrigo Uprimny Yepes and Camilo Sánchez, Ley de Víctimas: avances, limitaciones y retos, available at http://bit.ly/1iY5jGW (last accessed August 7, 2014).

Rodrigo Uprimny Yepes and Luis Manuel Lasso, *Verdad, Reparación y justicia para Colombia: algunas reflexiones y recomendaciones*, in CONFLICTO Y SEGURIDAD DEMOCRÁTICA EN COLOMBIA. TEMAS CRÍTICOS Y PROPUESTAS (José Ernesto Borda Medina ed., 2004).

Rubén Zamora and David Holiday, *The Struggle for Lasting Reform: Vetting Processes in El Salvador*, in JUSTICE AS PREVENTION. VETTING PUBLIC EMPLOYEES IN TRANSITIONAL SOCIETIES (Alexander Mayer-Rieckh and Pablo De Greiff eds, 2007).

Further reading

M.C. Bassiouni, UN Commission on Human Rights, 56th Session, *The right to restitution, compensation and rehabilitation for victims of grave violations of human rights and fundamental freedoms, Final Report of the Special Rapporteur, M. Cherif Bassiouni, submitted pursuant to Commission resolution 1999/93*, Doc. E/CN.4/2000/62, 2000.

PRISCILLA HAYNER, UNSPEAKABLE TRUTHS: CONFRONTING STATE TERROR AND ATROCITY (2002).

Louis Joinet, *Question of the impunity of perpetrators of violations of human rights (civil and political rights): final report* (UN, E/CN.4/Sub.2/1996/18, June 20, 1996).

SUSANNE JONAS, OF CENTAURS AND DOVES: GUATEMALA'S PEACE PROCESS (2000).

N. Kritz (ed.), TRANSITIONAL JUSTICE: HOW EMERGING DEMOCRACIES RECKON WITH FORMER REGIMES, vol. I (1995).

MARTHA MINOW, BETWEEN VENGEANCE AND FORGIVENESS (1997).

STEVEN R RATNER AND J.S. ABRAMS, ACCOUNTABILITY FOR HUMAN RIGHTS ATROCITIES IN INTERNATIONAL LAW: BEYOND THE NUREMBERG LEGACY (1997).

R Rotberg and D. Thompson (eds), TRUTH V. JUSTICE (2000).

RUTI G. TEITEL, TRANSITIONAL JUSTICE (2000).

UN, *The rule of law and transitional justice in societies experiencing or emerging from conflict*, Report of the Secretary General, UN Doc. S/ 2004/616, 2004.

8 The protection of social rights

*Oscar Parra-Vera**

Introduction

Despite poverty, exclusion, and inequality levels in Latin America, the jurisprudence of certain high courts on the enforcement of economic and social rights has gained recognition at a comparative level as an example of the complex relationship between the judiciary and the distribution of limited resources in the Global South.[1] In fact, some courts in the region have tried to face the deep gap between constitutional provisions and the difficult reality of Latin America.

Within the framework of the discussion of economic, social, and cultural rights (ESCR), the difficulties facing Latin America are directly tied to the impact of such phenomena as neoliberalism and neoextractivism. Examples of this are the free markets for which neoliberalism advocated, as well as its rejection of state intervention, attacks on freedom of association, and several labor flexibility strategies and the cutting off of social benefits. Neoliberalism has sought to hinder solidarity.[2]

This neoliberal process occurred in parallel with other constitutional reform processes in the region. Some constitutions have broadly acknowledged social rights and the institutional design of some states facilitates the judicial protection of those rights. However, in other countries, it was court interpretations that facilitated relevant jurisprudential development in terms of social rights. Protection of these rights has been generally associated with constitutional reforms or trends that, unlike more 'traditional' constitutionalism, actively promote the safeguard of substantive aspects of the constitution. Thus, many courts tend to protect the normative strength of provisions on social rights, instead of just reviewing the proceedings through which social policies are designed or regulated.[3]

These two processes—arbitrary neoliberalism and neoconstitutionalism—have caused Latin American judges to permanently face the tension between the vigorous integration of social rights in constitutions and laws and the dismantling of many benefits and the weakening of such rights as a result of structural adjustment programs.[4]

On the other hand, contextual, institutional, and economic conditions greatly restrict the chances of success of many creative judicially conceived initiatives. Hence, the negative, unwanted, or unforeseen impact of certain judicial interventions is under increasing discussion. All of this takes place in a context of constant criticism against the high economic impact of any failures and challenges that inherently arise when these kinds of protection are extended to the most vulnerable sectors on a case-by-case basis.

In light of the above context, in this chapter I will present an assessment of some of the region's contributions to the global discussion of social rights. In this map, which is far from comprehensive, my intention is to illustrate the following: a) narratives that specify the scope of social rights as justiciable rights; b) criticism of the inequitable effects of certain judicial interventions; and c) certain trends that respond to these concerns about equality. In this last section, I particularly highlight the trends that have been anchored in deliberative and dialogic activism, which seek to enhance both the structural scope of the judicial review of social policies, as well as public and democratic deliberation.

Standards for judicial protection of social rights

Several Latin American courts have developed arguments of various kinds for establishing social rights as enforceable rights. Certain courts, in particular, have used different cases to specify the contents of social rights and determine the specific actions that the state is obligated to take, while rejecting the notion that certain issues must be deemed technical or political in nature and, thus, are non-enforceable. In addition, they have broadly interpreted procedural norms that restrict these types of lawsuits, particularly those involving collective goods or collective suits.[5] International law pertaining to social rights has played a significant role in these arguments. Below are some landmark examples of the development of these criteria.

Social rights as fundamental rights and control of discretion and arbitrariness in the management of social policies

One of the main concepts used by the Constitutional Court of Colombia to build its jurisprudence on "fundamental social rights" is that of a "minimum standard of living." The court has noted that the state has an obligation to adopt all necessary positive measures to prevent individuals from being denied the basic conditions for a decent existence. The minimum subsistence income ("*mínimo vital*") has involved central topics such as extreme poverty and due payment of an already recognized salary or pension, so that citizens' only source of living is secured.[6] The court also addressed the issue of the right to housing:

> the administration violates the right to adequate housing, in terms of standard of living and minimum subsistence, when it fails to take appropriate and necessary measures for timely completion of a process for relocating families who are living in precarious conditions that may lead to the loss of their homes from either physical or legal reasons.[7]

In Colombia, the "right to a basic level of subsistence" allows for legal protection through a writ of *tutela*, even when there are pending judgments or other legal proceedings in ordinary jurisdictions different from that of the Constitutional Court.

However, in addition to protection strategies focused on minimum essential levels, decisions have been made in the region that extend beyond this modicum toward accountability for gradual progress in the realization of the rights and enforceability of their positive dimensions ("*dimensiones prestacionales*"). In other words, what is judicially reviewed is the impact in specific cases of the proper management of available resources.

In this regard, a ruling by the Constitutional Court of Colombia made a major conceptual clarification to overcome views arguing that judicial protection of political and civil rights has no economic impact, unlike the justiciability of social rights. The court held that all rights have both a negative and a positive dimension (they impose both positive and negative duties). This approach rejects the classic distinction where first-generation rights only impose negative duties of respect, while second-generation rights impose only positive duties of satisfaction.

> . . . Since its inception, constitutional case law has indicated that while the positive [*prestacional*] character of constitutional rights is 'closely' related to economic, social, and cultural rights, we are not facing two identical categories, just two categories that coincide.
>
> 3.3.6. Some of the obligations that arise from a fundamental right and that have a positive [*prestacional*] character are carried out *immediately*, either because they demand simple action from the state, which does not require additional resources (e.g., the obligation to provide information of their rights to patients before undergoing medical treatment), or because, despite the need to mobilize resources required for the work at hand, the severity and urgency of the case demands immediate state action (e.g., the obligation to take appropriate steps to ensure health care for every baby during his or her first year of life—art. 50, PC—). Other obligations of positive [*prestacional*] character derived from a fundamental right are carried out *progressively*, because of the complexity of the actions and resources required to guarantee the effective enjoyment of these protective aspects of the right . . .[8]

In addition, the court noted that: "the fact that a positive duty [*prestación*] that is protected by a right may be programmatic in nature does not mean that it is not enforceable or that it can be permanently violated." In that respect, the court indicated that:

> 3.3.14. In conclusion, the positive [*prestacional*] and progressive aspect of a constitutional right allows its holder to legally demand at least (1) the existence of a public policy, (2) aimed at ensuring the effective enjoyment of the right, and (3) that includes mechanisms for stakeholder participation.[9]

Another tendency worth highlighting is the court's rejection of the doctrine of "non-justiciable political questions." It was long believed that courts could not review decisions made by governments in socioeconomic matters, particularly in times of crisis. However, courts in Latin America have achieved prominence in the control of administrative discretion. An example of this is a case in which the Supreme Court of Argentina analyzed how retirees who were receiving pensions above the minimum levels were being affected by the fact that their pensions had not been properly updated. The court noted that:

> . . . the policy of granting increases only for the lowest pensions results in the flattening of the range of benefits, and leads to those who have proportionally contributed the most to the system on the basis of their income to receive the lowest benefits, putting them on equal terms with those who made different contributions and denying them the right to receive a pension that is consistent with their contributory efforts.
>
> . . . as a result, the lack of increases in the plaintiff's pension does not seem to stem from a valid distribution system, given that the aim of the constitutional guarantee at hand is to support pensions throughout time and strengthen them as their value compared to active salaries decreases.[10]

The court ordered Congress to enact a law for enforcing the constitutional right to salary increases. As pointed out by Abramovich, the court rejected the idea that these increases should depend solely on the availability of government funds, because that had led to "transforming the right to a mere expectation subject to discretion and the possibility of government revenue."[11] The court left margins of discretion for Congress to regulate this matter on the basis of "the complexity of public expenditure management and multiple needs" that the state "is designed to meet." However, the court set some minimum criteria that should be considered by Congress, for example, for the increases to be reasonably proportional to the income of active workers, given that retirement pensions replace salaries.

Congress then used the national budget of 2007 to enact a standard for retirement pension increases. The court found this standard inadequate for remedying Mr. Badaro's (the plaintiff in this specific case) situation; thus, the court deemed itself authorized to substitute the law and amend its unconstitutionality. As a result, it ordered a procedure for calculating and applying increases to Mr. Badaro, based on price indexes, and once again urged the state to adopt a general regime to increase pensions. The court stated that:

> 23) In terms of the projection of this decision on the large number of lawsuits in which similar controversies are discussed, it is recalled that the considerations in this decision *in terms of the plaintiff's increases during the period in question are limited only to this specific case* . . . This is so because the judiciary does not have the authority to . . . issue a general ruling that could override all the provisions in question, as that is the role of Congress . . .[12]

In 2008, Congress passed a retirement pension statute that sparked several debates as the decision in the case of *Badaro* has not been generally applied to other cases.[13] Regardless of this limitation in terms of impact, *Badaro* is a relevant regional example of control over state discretion in the management of retirement pensions. It is also a detailed example of judicial intervention when other public authorities do not take necessary measures to safeguard constitutional principles.

The role of international human rights law in promoting the enforceability of social rights

As noted by Rossi and Filippini,[14] in Latin America, invoking the obligations assumed under international law has been useful for taking certain social claims to court which were traditionally understood to be outside the scope of judicial review. International law has also allowed courts to legitimately engage other political powers that are accountable against these international obligations. In addition, international law—in particular through a broad concept of effective remedy—has favored the definition not only of substantive standards, but also of procedural standards for driving the justiciability of social rights in the domestic sphere.[15]

Decision C-376/10 of the Constitutional Court of Colombia provides an example of the role of international law in this regard. In that judgment, human rights treaties were used to clarify the obligation of free basic education. The case involved a claim of unconstitutionality against the General Education Act of Colombia for allowing the imposition of school fees for primary education.

Article 67 of the constitution had been interpreted as enshrining free education without prejudice to people's capacity to pay; therefore, whoever had the capacity to pay had the obligation to do so. This was contrary to international treaties according to which free primary education is an immediate state obligation. In addition, the ombudsman had documented the existing relationship between tuition fees and school drop-out rates, the discriminatory stratification of students, and other barriers to access and retention in the education system. If the court found that the constitution prevailed over treaties, it was possible to uphold the requirement to pay. However, the most favorable interpretation of human rights required integrating the treaties and the constitution, recognizing that both types of rules have the same rank. The court integrated them as follows:

> In short, according to the standards set out in international human rights treaties regarding guarantees that comprise the right to education, the 'academic fees' stipulated in article 67 of the constitution cannot be applied in formal educational institutions at primary level, where access to public education must be free, regardless of socio-economic status. The scope of these fees shall apply solely to educational levels where fees are progressively allowed: high school, higher education, and preschool . . .
>
> The law in question, to the extent that it allows the application of academic fees at the level of basic primary education, which constitute barriers that obstruct free of charge and compulsory, accessibility, violates international standards that clearly and unequivocally establish that primary education must be compulsory and available for free to all . . . as per the constitutional bloc. In that respect, the law violates Article 13 of the ICESCR, Article 28 of the International Convention on the Rights of the Child, Article 13.3 a.) of the San Salvador Protocol and Article 67 of the constitution, interpreted in harmony with these international instruments.[16]

This judgment is relevant if we consider the debate in Colombia around free education. The discussion was between positions that believed income-based subsidies for education were more equitable than those advocating for free universal education as a strategy that, among other things, would create fewer barriers to access and prevent distortions both in information and incentives that could arise with income-based strategies.[17] In analyzing the impact of this case, Red-DESC argued that, according to the World Bank, before the above judgment, Colombia was the only country in the region that lacked free primary education, thus shedding light on the special relevance of clarifying that the state has an international obligation to guarantee free primary education.[18] Moreover, the court established that the obligation is due on demand, without the possibility of justifying any delay in implementation on the basis of scarcity of resources. As far as implementation of the judgment is concerned, some local authorities have based themselves on this decision, not only for implementing free primary education, but also for breaking down barriers to access to education that manifest through indirect costs such as books and uniforms. Furthermore, taking into account the court's decision, the government issued a decree to specifically regulate free primary and secondary education and to establish limits for the collection of fees for complementary services in state-owned institutions.[19]

"Connectedness" and "interdependence" between civil and political rights and social rights

Another valuable trend in the region is the use of the criteria of connectedness and interdependence to circumvent rules that do not allow for the direct protection of social rights (Colombia and Costa Rica). A paradigmatic case is that of the decision of the Fourth Chamber of the Supreme Court of Costa Rica (the so-called Constitutional Chamber) to protect the rights to health and life of an 11-year-old girl with Type 1 Gaucher's Disease, who was denied treatment drugs by the Costa Rican Office of Social Security on the basis of the high cost of treatment and the budgetary deficit such treatment would entail. The girl suffered serious ailments in her legs and a swollen spleen. She urgently needed a drug called Cerezyme (Imiglucerase) which was the only treatment for this disease and was highly expensive. The Costa Rican Office of Social Security claimed that bearing the cost of the requested medication meant not being able to treat other patients, and that financial constraints prevented the government from providing care to this group of patients without neglecting other vulnerable populations, thus creating an ethical dilemma in the need to establish priorities for the provision of these services. In this regard, the Constitutional Court stated that:

> . . . if the right to life is especially protected in all modern legal states and, therefore, so is the right to health, any economic criteria that negatively affects the exercise of such rights must be put aside because . . . without the right to life all other rights are useless.[20]

The court acknowledged the Costa Rican Office of Social Security's budgetary limitations due to the central government's debt to social security. However, the court stressed that the Office had a duty to "optimize its management of available resources, decreasing administrative costs, so that the resources of the social security system may be efficiently used."[21] Given the severity of the girl's disease and her parent's incapacity to pay for treatment, the claim was found admissible and the court ordered the provision of treatment.

This judgment reveals the regional trend towards the protection of the social rights of the most vulnerable groups, regardless of the economic impact of such decisions. In the case at hand, the cost of treatment represented a significant percentage of the country's health budget. The case also involved a multinational pharmaceutical company that benefits from the high cost of treatment. The multinational company was not a party to the suit but, according to media reports, the case was supported by the company which used its local connections to take the case to the ombudsman in order to litigate at the Fourth Chamber of the Constitutional Court.[22]

Some of the examples mentioned above alluded to some kind of negative or unintended consequences of social rights litigation. This explains a series of criticisms of the role of courts in these areas, which will be described in the following sections.

Criticisms concerning the economic impact of judicial protection of social rights

Some decisions of high courts in the region began to achieve significant public notoriety, considering their high institutional and economic impact, their strong financial implications or criticism by various actors alleging "legal uncertainty" that hinders investment programs in some countries. Some decisions were based on arguments of "connectedness" and "interdependence" to elude internal regulations that in cases involving, for example, the right to health, left out certain medical procedures or drugs, or included services that were not stipulated in basic plans. Such decisions have been criticized for being unfair and, in some cases, unreasonable, *inter alia*, for the following reasons:[23]

a Lawsuits are mostly used by those who are included in the specific public policy to the detriment of those who have not yet been included and who are, therefore, more vulnerable. Similarly, those who have access to such benefits also have sufficient capacity to pay, which generates privileges that are not necessarily based on need and justice. Thus, litigation excludes from these privileges the poorest population, whose access to justice is minimal.[24]

b There is debate about the legitimacy of courts to solve difficult cases where granting a benefit in a given case could involve denying that same benefit in other cases, for example when high-cost health treatments are involved. Imposed judicial decisions weaken universality, since it is not feasible for all judicially ordered benefits to be provided universally to everyone who requires them. Thus, the benefit is only granted to those who resorted to the courts.[25]

c Similarly, it is noted that granting benefits not covered by a specific public policy associated with a social right could lead the system designed to implement this right to imbalance or default. Thus, there is tension between what derives from the normative protection of social rights and what the state can really do given its budgetary restrictions.

d This inequality is further deepened by the meddling of courts in the spheres of congressional and executive decisions, where officials have more political responsibility and accountability.

e Courts do not have the big picture, mainly because they lack the necessary tools, technical elements and macro-vision; thus, they arbitrarily allot resources. An example of this can be found in the criticisms against the Constitutional Court of Chile declaring unconstitutional an article that allowed the Superintendency of Health and Health Insurance Institutions (ISAPRE) to unilaterally change the prices of health plans according to criteria such as the age and gender of their affiliates.[26]

While the Chilean court's judgment was part of an effort by courts to curb abuses by private sectors in the provision of public services governed by the laws of the market, some critics highlighted that it was hard to understand

> how was it possible for an adult's inability to afford her ISAPRE [private health plan] and depend on [the public system] FONASA to be a constitutional issue, when the reality is that this public health system provides service to the greater majority of Chileans, who have never had any other alternative?[27]

In that sense, it was alleged that this judgment could have inequitable effects because it improved access to privileged individuals who could afford ISAPRE while creating setbacks and difficulties for the public system, which benefits the poorest and is comprised of those who cannot choose an insurance provider.[28]

f Given the lack of resources for ensuring the social rights of all, decisions—which are sometimes tragic—limiting the guarantee of certain rights have to be made throughout the democratic process by elected authorities, thus judicial decisions ultimately elude necessary democratic debate.

These criticisms of judicial intervention in the protection of social rights have generated various types of reactions, particularly regarding the type of orders issued by courts. It is these orders and remedies that may have financial impacts and generate institutional imbalances.

Below are three issues that reveal the trend in some Latin American courts toward structural assessments of the financial impact of certain decisions, the protection of vulnerable groups, and the need to seek judicial protection based on equality. The first is access to healthcare for people with HIV and particularly how judicial decisions revealed the discriminatory lack of protection of these vulnerable groups and activated public policy reforms. The second issue is the so-called "prohibition of retrogression" (non-regression principle) in debates surrounding retirement pension reforms in the past. Finally, there is the trend toward using "macro-judgments" with multiple and open remedies in response to procedural insufficiencies in the case-by-case assessment of structural situations associated with the systematic violation of social rights.

Promoting equity through judicial protection

The way that some courts in the region have tried to conceive of this criticism and offer approaches that take into account the impact of judicial decisions and their possible inequitable effects may be reflected in these words from the opinion of Justice Rodrigo Uprimny Yepes:

> 11 . . . a constitutional rationale that articulates the protection of social rights with the realization of equality could also represent an important step toward overcoming opposition between a purely deontological and a purely consequential reasoning in this field. . . . Judges can only take social rights seriously if they also take budget constraints and resource constraints that affect the realization of these rights seriously.
>
> 12 The above conclusion does not mean that I am advocating for reducing the legal discussion on social rights to an economic logic . . . as that implies viewing efficiency, understood as wealth maximization, as the only worthy goal of the law . . . This view does not seem acceptable, as it leaves out two essential dimensions of any form of constitutional reasoning. On the one hand, equity issues and resource allocation are ignored, because the search for efficiency is carried out from a given initial distribution of wealth. On the other hand, the role of individual rights is minimized, as a right becomes simply an interest or preference to be integrated into the overall calculation of utility that will determine the efficient way to maximize the wealth of a society. But clearly, as authors such as Rawls, Dworkin, or Sen have vigorously insisted, a right is not to be confused with an interest or a preference . . .
>
> However, the opposite point of view, according to which all ethical and legal reasoning must be purely deontological and rights must be defended regardless of the consequences, is also unsatisfactory, not only because the absolute defense of a right can result in the impairment of other rights, but also because it is reasonable to assume that greater economic development allows for better satisfaction of social rights . . .
>
> 13 Similarly, we have noted the importance of articulating, whenever possible, the defense of rights with the promotion of democratic deliberation . . .[29]

The examples discussed below reveal efforts to achieve this type of equal and dialogic judicial protection with special emphasis on adequate protection of disadvantaged groups and the search for a more equitable impact on the population.

Protecting access to healthcare for people with HIV

In this line, one of the most important topics is that of litigation concerning access to healthcare for people with HIV/AIDS. Some of these court disputes have highlighted narratives that can drive greater recognition and inclusion for groups requiring special protection. Also, some of these cases have had an important impact on public policies. As an example of regional relevance, in Argentina, Costa Rica, and Colombia, some forms of judicial intervention have led to the inclusion of various services for basic care programs. Similarly, there have been tensions in Brazil between judicial interventions focused on individual cases and government efforts to address this problem globally.[30]

As noted by Paola Bergallo, in Argentina the case of *Asociación Benghalensis*[31] is particularly relevant for assessing the impact of judicial interventions in breaking the "political and ideological blockade" that prevented the proper implementation of domestic rules relating to the protection of persons with HIV,[32] as well as for contributing to the transformation of the political agenda after granting higher priority to HIV and AIDS treatment, which had been previously nonexistent, and for redefining the National Program for the Fight against AIDS and its articulation with provincial authorities.

In Colombia, the jurisprudence of the Constitutional Court has had a strong impact on access—through a writ of *tutela*—to antiretroviral drugs, which were not being provided under the mandatory health plan that stipulates minimal benefits. In addition, the court's case law contributed to the inclusion of viral load testing in the plan.[33] The Constitutional Chamber of the Supreme Court of Costa Rica has also ordered the provision of antiretroviral drugs.[34]

Determining the scope of the progressivity and non-regression principles

Two recurring themes in Latin America are, first, the necessary level of judicial review of progressivity towards the realization of social rights and, in parallel, efforts to reduce or eliminate certain social benefits when facing economic crises. Some Latin American courts have faced these situations by prohibiting the use of regressive measures affecting social rights. These judicial narratives attempt to prevent unjustified or disproportionate setbacks and, in some instances, base their arguments on empirical studies regarding the proposed justifications for the specific policies. An important characteristic of certain rationales is to conceive of the prohibition of retrogression not as an absolute rule that is broken with each regression, but rather as a principle that must be weighed against all other underlying interests and principles in each case. The relevant case law constitutes one of the possible answers to the previously analyzed criticisms regarding the potential unfairness of case-by-case judicial protection.

In this regard, the Constitutional Court of Guatemala formulated requirements for progressive advancements in a case that involved the suspension of certain hospital services between 2005 and 2006 stemming from a debt worth millions owed by the Ministry of Health and Social Assistance to medical service providers. The Guatemalan court defined the role of the progressivity principle in these terms:

> there is no excuse for regressing or falling back from a minimally satisfactory service to an absolutely unsatisfactory one—or worse. On the contrary . . . the state must preserve the attained standard, with the obligation to progressively improve minimal healthcare standards, as per its pressing duty to provide positive benefits for the satisfaction of this right

> . . . because the discontinuation of such benefits violates the principle of non-regression or non-social decline . . . The principle of non-retrogression is a constitutional limitation on the regulation of fundamental rights forbidding public authorities from adopting measures or allowing situations that reduce the level attained by such social rights and the benefits granted to the public, especially in situations of extreme precariousness and poverty.[35]

A paradigmatic discussion in that regard is that of efforts to dismantle pension schemes or other social guarantees when these schemes are anchored in other unfair or arbitrary privileges. The conflict arises with respect to expectations or acquired rights that need to be removed for greater equity and financial sustainability. The debate is between positions that believe any regression violates social rights and those that believe regressions are acceptable when the objective is to achieve greater equity and protection for the most vulnerable and to include structural considerations on the financial and economic sustainability of the systems in which social rights are realized.

For example, the Constitutional Court of Peru had to analyze a constitutional and legislative reform amending a pension scheme and, thus, the rights acquired by those who, under that scheme, already had access to pensions. The reform was motivated by the system's financial sustainability problems and by the inequity generated by the pension scheme, given the enormous difference between the highest and lowest pensions. The court stressed that:

> although the pension scheme reform reduces the benefits of its beneficiaries, this regression is not unconstitutional because, according to criteria of reasonableness and proportionality, it does not violate the essence of the right to a pension, and because, far from transgressing it, the reform seeks to realize the principles of solidarity and progressivity as legitimate state actions with purposes of equity and social justice for all workers.[36]

The reform was intended to reduce a number of benefits to reinvest savings as budget increases for lower pensions. Certain kinds of automatic pension increases were prohibited to that effect. Similarly, pension ceilings were introduced. The court emphasized that the principle of solidarity requires state intervention when the socioeconomic reality directly contravenes social welfare. In this sense, it is not justifiable:

> in order to cover high pensionable amounts of a number of objectively unrepresented people in the community . . . to make a significant and continuing disbursement of budgetary resources that should be aimed at readjusting the pensions of those most disadvantaged, and thus preventing inequities for the future of the pension system.[37]

Regarding the principle of equality, the court noted that the constitutional analysis did not have to be determined on the basis of the specific impact of the reform on those already sheltered by the regime, but on the overall impact on the working population that aspires to qualify for a pension. A valuable contribution of this decision is its view of the principle of solidarity. According to the court, this principle creates the obligation of redistributing the benefits contributed by citizens and requires a global assessment of their circumstances:

> If the objective and proportional reduction of the pensions of the minority is planned by equally weighing the right to a pension against the right to human dignity of the majority, then the principle of progressivity is not affected . . . Therefore, the principle is not

> violated when seeking justice and equality among pensioners pursuant to a democratic ideal of common justice. A minority group of pensioners cannot be benefited in detriment of the majority of pensioners.[38]

Regarding the right to a pension as a fundamental right, the court stated that its minimum core, which is not subject to limitation by the legislature, is constituted by the right of access to a pension, the right not to be arbitrarily deprived of one, and the right to a minimum living pension. Within the non-essential content of that right are pension ceilings and pension increases. The Peruvian court acknowledged that some acquired rights not related to the minimum core—such as increases—can be restricted if principles of proportionality and reasonableness are respected. The court deemed that the principle of progressiveness was not violated because progressive developments were being achieved for the global population and not only for a specific group, such as the system's beneficiaries.

For its part, the Constitutional Court of Colombia has defended an intermediate view[39] between positions that disregard the prohibition of regression and those that sustain it as an absolute right that contemplates no exceptions and hence that all regressions are always to be deemed unconstitutional. Some of the court's judgments have used this approach to avoid the potential rigidity of a view that bans any adjustment to social policies.[40]

The above intermediate argument contemplates the prohibition of regression as a principle and not as a rule. When this principle comes into conflict with other interests and rights, then the principles of legal certainty, legitimate expectations, and non-arbitrariness need to be weighed. In addition, the petrification of laws and absolute irreversibility of a given policy need to be prevented, taking into account the socioeconomic dynamics of the state. This view enables democratic organs to analyze the proportionality, reasonableness, and necessity of retrogressive measures considering the country's reality, without failing to protect those who have legitimate expectations of not experiencing arbitrary changes to their situation. The need for a regression must be justified under important and even compelling constitutional purposes, with special attention to avoiding the deterioration of the condition of vulnerable groups. Additionally, there is a criterion of temporality,[41] according to which the law can only be restricted when there are conditions justifying said restriction.

Moreover, the court works with a presumption of unconstitutionality, based on which the burden of proof is transferred to the authorities, thus requiring thorough and strict justification which, when failing, would entail the unconstitutionality of the measure.

The practical application of these criteria has sparked serious debates. An example of this is Decision C-754/04, which analyzed the constitutionality of a norm (modifying a transitional regime) that made more stringent the requirements for workers who wished to receive pension benefits. To resolve this dispute, the court recognized the distinction between acquired rights (the meeting of conditions allowing the enforceability of the right) and mere expectations (when conditions have not been fulfilled but will be met in the future). The court noted that expectations can usually be modified or lowered by the legislature, but added that people whose age was near the required age did have a right to a pension. Thus, since these people had not only an expectation but a constitutionally protected and acquired right, the legislature did not have the freedom to undermine it by issuing a new law changing its conditions and benefits.

Three of the judges wrote a dissenting opinion to this judgment.[42] They argued that the court made a conceptual error when assimilating the legitimate expectations of those workers who were in the transitional pension regime to the existence of a vested right. According to the minority's dissent, only when legal requirements for a pension are met is the individual entitled to that pension; in addition, those who were close to meeting such legal conditions had a reasonable expectation to receive said pension that could not be changed with future laws except when there were compelling reasons that met the criteria of proportionality and reasonableness. Thus, the dissenting judges criticized the fact that the majority had not employed a test for measuring the reasonability or proportionality of the norm under question:

> the above does not mean that the special measures of protection adopted by the legislator at one point become intangible, so as to give rise to an 'acquired right to a specific legal regime,' as . . . it remains at the level of expectations, with a special degree of protection, but not at the level of an acquired right.[43]

On the other hand, the dissenting judges said that the majority ignored the importance of the country's socioeconomic situation when performing judicial review based on notions of proportionality and reasonableness, particularly because benefits were being granted to people who had higher incomes than the average population while the majority of older adults had no pension or other benefits. They noted that the majority, when concluding that the transitional regime could not be altered, prevented Congress from maintaining the sustainability of the pension system and reducing inequities, given that low-income workers end up subsidizing higher income pensioners.

Dialogic activism and structural judicial intervention[44]

Some decisions reveal the importance of breaking down certain procedural barriers that prevent a more global view of social rights cases. An example of this is revealed by the inter-party or exclusive effects on the case at hand, impeding judicial intervention on the structural problems that motivate the recurrent use of the judiciary on a given subject. In addition, some courts have had to face an increase in the number of lawsuits regarding certain social rights or the lower courts' failure to follow established standards in previous case law. When dealing with these situations, there is a tendency toward "dialogic activism" in which judicial intervention prompts the general review of a public policy that has an impact on the massive violation of rights. Some courts have resorted to notions such as that of an "unconstitutional state of affairs" while others have issued general orders aimed at competent authorities to review the main problems of a specific public policy.

Unlike traditional litigation, these "structural remedies" are not meant to determine the remedies for a violation of an individual right by looking to the past. Instead, based on an assessment of the potential consequences of a judicial decision, these orders seek to adjust the future behavior of the parties and, particularly, of relevant stakeholders and actors involved in a specific public policy. In other words, they do not seek to solve the specific case, but rather to generally contemplate that case and many others. This public-interest litigation thus relates to cases involving multiple issues, subjects, and agencies within the government, agencies in charge of oversight, and legislative authorities. As a result, these decisions did not pinpoint a specific stakeholder, but instead established general criteria applicable to all relevant actors in the implementation of the policy at hand. In addition, the decision did not put an end to the case, as plaintiffs could request continued judicial review of compliance with decisions. The above could bring down barriers and institutional bureaucracies impeding access to certain rights through an "institutional experimentation" that, in principle, is aimed at strengthening democracy and the judiciary's legitimacy.[45]

Examples of macro-judgments on social rights issued by the Constitutional Court of Colombia are analyzed below, relating to forced displacement and the crisis in healthcare access. The dialogic role of the Supreme Court of Argentina in the case of *Riachuelo* and certain dialogic orders issued by the Fourth Chamber of the Supreme Court of Costa Rica are also analyzed.

Decision T-025/04 and social rights of victims of forced displacement

One of the most terrible consequences of the armed conflict in Colombia during the last 50 years is related to the more than 4 million people displaced by political violence. For over a decade the Constitutional Court of Colombia received thousands of individual claims related to problems faced by internally displaced persons (IDPs), particularly regarding access to certain social rights. In 2004, the court decided to confront the structural problems behind these individual claims. The main focus of the court was "(i) the precariousness of the institutional capacity to implement [the public policy on the issue], and (ii) the insufficient appropriation of funds."[46] The court believed that a case-by-case intervention was insufficient given the extent of the problem. It noted that:

> The distribution of functions and responsibilities between the different entities is vague . . . These deficiencies hamper the coordination of the different entities' actions, preclude an adequate follow-up of the conduct of affairs, and undermine the establishment of priorities . . .
>
> . . . (a) no deadlines are set for achieving the stated objectives, (b) there is no indication of the level of budgetary appropriations required to comply with these stated goals, (c) there is no concrete provision of the human resources needed to implement the policies, and (d) the appropriate administrative resources required for executing the policies are not assigned either.
>
> . . . The requirements and conditions to have access to housing loans do not match the economic necessities of displaced households. The requirements of savings periods, personal and commercial references, and other conditions, are in many cases impossible to meet by the displaced population. Such demands are discriminatory, and constitute entry barriers for access to this type of aid . . .[47]

The court, therefore, declared an "unconstitutional state of affairs" given:

> (i) massive and widespread violations of various constitutional rights that affect a significant number of individuals; (ii) prolonged failure of the authorities in fulfilling their obligations to ensure rights; (iii) the adoption of unconstitutional practices, such as the requirement of the filing of a writ of *tutela* as part of the proceeding to receive state protection for a right violation, (iv) the failure to issue necessary legislative, administrative or budgetary measures to prevent the violation of rights; (v) the existence of a social problem whose solution compromises the intervention of several entities, requires the adoption of complex and coordinated actions and a level of resources that demands significant additional budgetary efforts; (vi) if all

> the people affected by the same problem filed a writ of *tutela* to ensure their rights, there would be still greater judicial congestion.[48]

Consequently, although some urgent benefits were awarded, the court ordered the executive to clearly determine the necessary public policy for resolving the "unconstitutional state of affairs." The court required the executive to specify the policy's timing and strategies, without imposing a particular criterion, except that of minimum human rights to be respected. In this regard, the court ordered:

> (i) the development and regular updating of a diagnosis of the situation in which these rights are exercised and enjoyed by the population;
> (ii) the design of public policies aimed at progressively achieving the full realization of such rights, including specific goals to measure progress within the time limits;
> (iii) regular dissemination of the results achieved and corrective or complementary measures taken so that stakeholders and social actors—including non-governmental organizations—participate in the monitoring of the relevant public policies and the identification of failures, difficulties or circumstances that inhibit the full realization of these rights, for the purpose of reviewing these policies or developing more appropriate ones.[49]

The Constitutional Court established a specific chamber for monitoring compliance with the judgment. It has issued several follow-up orders over the last 11 years, held public hearings, and received several technical reports from stakeholders. Some of those public hearings included participation from ministers, senior officials, control agencies, and civil society organizations. This exercise was an important stage of accountability. Hearings have also been used for topics of special complexity, with the aim of promoting citizen control over issues that were often reduced to a minority group of technical experts. I am referring, in particular, to the adoption of indicators to verify compliance with the ruling. In 2007, the court adopted "results indicators," "indicators of effective enjoyment of rights," "complementary indicators," and "associated indicators," some of them confined specifically to certain social rights.[50] Using indicators to encourage better implementation of the judgment was a unique experience in the region and allowed to reach consensus, based on technical criteria, even between people with different professional backgrounds. Therefore, as a technical tool, indicators have helped to build a political will that was not clearly present before the judgment.[51]

Similarly, when analyzing the impact of this ruling, César Rodríguez and Diana Rodríguez[52] have associated this decision with dialogic activism, in which judicial intervention creates democratic spaces of deliberation with stakeholders, and the issuance of detailed orders that hinder the debate on the implementation of public policies for solving social problems is avoided. These authors said that the judgment had material and instrumental effects—both direct and indirect—as well as direct and indirect symbolic effects.

In fact, they documented an "unlocking effect" of the prior institutional blockade illustrated by the lack of state actions for improving the situation of IDPs. By shaking the state machinery, the political discussion surrounding displacement was rephrased in more democratic terms and a door was opened for new procedures that were previously unheard of. For instance, the state and NGOs jointly constructed indicators for measuring the enjoyment of rights on behalf of the displaced population. In addition, the state machinery was invigorated after interagency coordination was strengthened and emergency programs were issued. In terms of budget, at the beginning, the court ordered that state entities calculate the amount of investment within a month. The government requested that the deadline be extended to two years, but the court denied this request; otherwise, the government would have been allowed to remain passive. However, the court later established new goals and deadlines that gave the government more room to maneuver.

The judgment also had a deliberative effect because it created and drove participation and discussion procedures between a wide range of social actors involved in monitoring compliance. In public hearings, in particular, there was ample participation from organizations representing the displaced people, human rights NGOs, state entities, and international organizations, such as the UNHCR. This dialogic activism is also characterized by the issuance of more open orders, in which details pertaining to the construction of public policies are not described in depth. These details are in the hands of the respective authorities. However, Rodríguez and Rodríguez noted that the court was strict in its enforcement of deadlines, thus forcing the government to take action to solve the issue of displacement. These authors believe that the deliberative effects of the judgment have had instrumental consequences by driving specific public policies; but they also believe it has had symbolic effects by changing the way in which the issues are comprehended by society as a whole.

On another note, the authors also stressed that Decision T-025/04 has had effects on the development, implementation, and monitoring of public policies on displacement and related budgetary increases. In addition, it has also had a coordinating and articulating effect, particularly through the reactivation of the National Council for Comprehensive Assistance to the Displaced Population. This entity is now responsible for monitoring compliance with T-025/04 and for developing public policies to that effect. Lastly, it has changed the situation of displaced persons, although problems in information systems make it difficult to estimate the impact of these changes on this vulnerable group.

Structural judicial response to the crisis in the health system of Colombia: Decision T-760/08

Another example of structural judicial intervention, relating to issues of health, is that of Decision T-760/08, issued by the Constitutional Court of Colombia.[53] Between 1999 and 2008, over 400,000 protection writs ("*acción de tutela*" or "*tutela*") had been filed in reference to the right to health. This occurred in the context of a health system designed in the light of the market-based allocation of health care and neoliberal principles. The health system faced countless problems because of the nearly absolute absence of supervision, monitoring, and public control, which explained the fact that the filing of writs for the protection of rights replaced administrative regulations. The structural orders contained in T-760/08 follow the court's assessment of the state of affairs and the unfortunate consequences of dealing with the problems in the health system through individual writs.

Decision T-760/08 includes 22 claims for protection that were selected by the Constitutional Court to illustrate the systemic problems in the supervision and regulation of the health system which had led to the overuse of these writs. In its judgment, the court stated that a structural view of the system's problem was necessary because:

> . . . responsible bodies of what might loosely be called the regulation of the health system have failed to adopt decisions that guarantee people their right to health without having to resort to *tutela* claims.[54]

The court issued 16 general orders in which it analyzed how failures in regulation involved a violation of the obligation to respect, protect and ensure the right to health. The four major regulatory failures were related to: a) accuracy, updating, unification, and access to a basket of health services, considering that defining the content of the benefit plans is essential for clarifying the scope of financing; b) financial sustainability and adequate flow of resources within the health system; c) determination of rights and duties of patients; and d) universal coverage. The orders involved, among other things: a) clearly defining the baskets of the mandatory health plan (POS); b) conducting institutional audits in order to inform users of the performance of the different service providers and insurers, and other measures to strengthen supervision over such undertakings; c) facilitating compliance with *tutela* claims; d) developing a contingency plan to ensure appropriate and timely refunds in cases with associated costs of care that are not covered by the mandatory health plans; and e) a comprehensive review of capitation rates, which had not been thoroughly revised for many years. The court required a process that included the "direct and effective involvement of the medical community and users of the health system,"[55] particularly of those who would be affected the most by possible changes in policies.

In 1993 the legislature established two different mandatory health plans for those with payment capacity (the contributory scheme) and those without such capacity (the subsidized regime). The aim was to unify these plans in 2001, in order to eliminate the difference based on financial capacity. In Decision T-760/08 the court found insufficient efforts to reach that goal after 15 years. It ordered the Commission on Health Regulation (CRES) to unify both baskets of health services, initially for children and, progressively, for adults, taking into account not only the financial sustainability but also the epidemiological profile of the population. In addition, the planning process for unification had to be participatory, transparent, and include indicators and relevant comparison parameters. Further, the ruling ordered the government to take deliberate measures to progressively achieve universal coverage and set the deadline to do so for 2010. According to the court:

> The right to health is not absolute but limited. However, limitations on the right must be reasonable and proportionate. In other words . . . although the benefit plan does not contain an infinite selection of services, any restrictions on health services must respect the principles of reasonableness and proportionality in a context of resource allocations that are consistent with health priorities. It is therefore essential to carefully justify each deletion as a measure that better allows for addressing new priorities in health, and not as a reduction in the scope of the right.[56]

The court did not claim to be the most knowledgeable body in terms of what treatments or medicines should be included in the baskets associated to the mandatory health plans, nor did it wish to establish the ethical criteria for such choices. Instead, it urged the CRES to comply with its legal duties. The court's approach is consistent with the proposals of ethicist Norman Daniels regarding "accountability for reasonableness."[57] Daniels argues that we need not have fully defined principles telling us precisely how to equitably resolve health needs—criteria to determine what priority to give to those who are worse off—when it is not possible to meet all these needs. This author believes that what is needed is a fair process, namely one that is: a) transparent, in the sense that the reasoning behind the decisions is public; b) based on relevant grounds (for example, proper care for patients), rather than on racial or gender stereotypes; c) reviewable by some sort of appeals procedure, as there will always be new elements that need to be considered, in addition to those that involve atypical cases; and d) enforceable.

Decision T-760/08 requires this kind of deliberative and transparent process to help to update and unify benefit plans.

In seven years, the Monitoring Chamber has issued more than 40 generic orders and dozens of other orders related to the 16 main orders in the judgment. The ruling has had a significant impact on resource flow in the health system, on the adoption of anti-corruption measures in resource management, and on drug price fixing.

The court has convened two public hearings on resource flow and the unification of mandatory health plans. Regarding system resource flow, the court emphasized that what caused the system's financial imbalance was "improper allocation of resources, embezzlement, and lack of greater diligence on the part of certain inspection, monitoring and control agencies."[58] The court noted the existence of cost overruns due to the intermediation of insurers, which caused drugs in Colombia to have a much higher price compared to other countries.[59]

An important instrumental effect of the judgment was that, over these years, certain control agencies have been empowered[60] on the basis of the orders issued by the court. Decision T-760/08 generated spaces for accountability that have been harnessed by certain control agencies to boost their inspection and surveillance.

Several economists have argued that the universalization and unification ordered in Decision T-760/08 was unsustainable because the number of citizens in the contributory regime was much lower than in the subsidized regime. Despite these objections coming from some sectors, for four years the government took action to unify and update the POS. These measures were been analyzed in more than 15 specific resolutions issued by the court. In 2012 the court issued a critical opinion on the upgrading and unifying processes, pointing out that there was no evidence of measures aimed at streamlining access to health services by users, that no incentives had been placed to increase enrollment of those with economic capacity, and that, in the process of unifying plans, the active participation of users and the medical community had not been established.[61]

Finally, the judgment has had a major impact on health system reform in general and a statutory bill adopted in 2015 in particular. However, some critics have accused the court of having put too much faith in the existence of a deliberative process and of ignoring the asymmetrical power relations between different population groups. In particular, Colombia offers complex challenges to dialogic judicial activism, since there are many conditions that make the process difficult. Profound social and power inequalities, violence, and its direct consequences over social mobilization, as well as other structural problems for the rule of law, make real democratic dialogue extremely difficult. The sociopolitical reasons that led to greater judicialization of social rights also limit the chances of achieving transformative social change in the field of health through judicial intervention in Colombia.[62]

The case of Mendoza and the promotion of procedures for environmental protection

The Supreme Court of Argentina has engaged in dialogic judicial activism in its decisions over the last decade. One of the most relevant cases is that of 17 residents in the Matanza–Riachuelo basin who filed a complaint before the Supreme Court against the national state, the Province of Buenos Aires, the Autonomous City of Buenos Aires, and 44 companies, for compensation of damages suffered as a result of pollution in the basin, cessation of pollution, and environmental restructuring. In 2006 the Supreme Court issued a preliminary order including, among other things, the creation of a public fund involving the resumption of a government plan aimed at tackling the problem. In that decision, the court highlighted the need to deal with both the collective scope of the rights involved and compensation regarding irreversible damage.

The court orders prompted a dialogue between different affected sectors, as well as public hearings and meetings between stakeholders and state agencies. Finally, in July 2008, the court delivered its judgment, in which it ordered defendants to engage in actions aimed at improving the quality of life of residents, recasting the environment and the prevention of future damage, and establishing an intervention program requiring the Matanza–Riachuelo Basin Authority (ACUMAR) to follow a timetable for action. The court delegated the enforcement of the judgment to a first-instance court and created a collegiate body, consisting of the Ombudsman's Office and NGOs, to encourage public participation in the implementation of the judgment and in overseeing compliance. The court said:

> . . . [H]earings have been held and reports from defendants have been received that show deficiencies that this court must bear in mind . . . [T]here are significant differences between versions of these reports and, in many respects, there is no updated elaboration; instead, previously existing documents are reused that date back several years. There have also been difficulties for obtaining objective, public, and measurable data on different existing situations, which has been compounded by the dispersion of the sources of information and the lack of consistent terminology.
>
> Furthermore, implementation efficiency requires a program that defines the mandated behavior with technical accuracy, identifies the persons who are obliged to comply and the existence of objective indicators that allow regular monitoring of results, and ensures broad participation in control mechanisms.[63]

The Basin Authority was obliged to organize, within 30 working days, a digital public information system for the general public. Other issues for which a timetable was set out included: a) industrial pollution; b) the sanitation of landfills; c) the cleaning up of river margins; d) the expansion of drinking water networks; e) storm sewers; f) sewage sanitation; and g) a health emergency plan. Likewise, the court highlighted the importance of strengthening citizen participation in monitoring compliance with the program described, and ordered the intervention of the Ombudsman's Office.[64]

By late 2010, the collegiate body recognized several advances but noted a breach of court orders and requested that the responsible public officials be fined. Nonetheless, the intervention of an entity comprising different jurisdictions helped to correct the issues of dispersion and overlapping of applicable authorities and norms, and to improve the exercise of administrative power over polluting activities. The judgment opened instances of social participation in the design and monitoring of policies.[65]

The Constitutional Chamber of the Supreme Court of Costa Rica and the order to overcome structural problems with waiting lists[66]

In a recent case, the Constitutional Chamber of the Supreme Court of Costa Rica addressed the issue of waiting lists in the provision of health services and it took measures to ensure an impact beyond this particular case. Waiting lists have been a structural problem in Costa Rica.[67] The facts that led to the judgment involved a patient who was on a waiting list with 200 other people for knee surgery. Because of the delay in providing service to the complainant, his quality of life was affected, so he requested that the Constitutional Chamber order medical authorities to perform the procedure he needed. The defendants argued saturation and insufficient resources.

The Fourth Chamber noted that the bodies responsible for rendering such services had an overriding and urgent obligation to adapt to the particular needs of their patients, especially when they required immediate and urgent medical attention, "without the lack of human and material resources becoming a legally valid argument to fail to meet such obligations."[68] Since it was a generalized situation, the chamber made a decision that went beyond the specific case and indicated that the health institution could not transfer the consequences of its inefficiency and inexperience onto its patients, especially when it came to fundamental rights such as the right to health.

The chamber requested technical studies that would make it possible to develop a plan within 12 months of the notification of the judgment. The plan had to define reasonable waiting times per pathology or level of urgency, and objective criteria for inclusion and location of patients on waiting lists. Similarly, the chamber indicated that a timetable had to be set for administrative and technical measures to meet the goals of the plan. Thus, within a maximum of 12 months following the plan's approval, existing waiting lists could only involve reasonable waiting periods that were consistent with the medical specialty and diagnosis. The chamber requested semiannual compliance reports. The Costa Rican Department of Social Security [Caja Costarricense de Seguro Social] launched a "Service Guide to Waiting Lists," among other measures to implement the orders issued by the Fourth Chamber.

Conclusions

In this chapter I have outlined some very general trends in Latin American jurisprudence on social rights. While at first the discussions focused on whether these rights were justiciable or fundamental, over time the debate moved toward the proper kind of legal remedy offered by judges in order to address the structural conditions that explain the patterns and contexts involving violations of many social rights. In particular, jurisprudence has shown growing concern over the impact of judicial decisions and has sought structural changes beyond the specific cases submitted to the courts.

These trends are part of a process that has been very dynamic, but not without paradoxes, contradictions, and complexity. The difficult situation in Latin America has demanded from various high courts particular creativity and technical accuracy to try to make social rights a reality in a region marked by poverty and inequality. Moreover, the remedies associated with macro-judgments and dialogic judicial activism have focused on strict judicial review of the structural transformation of public policies. This has allowed various responses to critics of the intervention of the courts in these matters. But it has also created new dilemmas, due to the long wait for the proper implementation of remedies aimed at promoting better governance and greater democratic deliberation. That long delay accentuates the justified skepticism in the region from popular sectors regarding the possibility of major social transformations through institutional channels.

However, Latin American courts continue to move towards greater harmonization of strict judicial review of constraints assessments—creative in the substantive protection of social rights and in ensuring its equitable impact—and the significant promotion of public discussion and democratic deliberation. The high hopes that this inspires also represent a challenge for the future, considering that participation and actual possibilities of democratic deliberation depend on the sociopolitical context. And that social context in Latin America continues to involve severe social exclusion, inequality, sociopolitical violence, and poverty, with significant asymmetries between the actors who are discussing the implementation of judgments, and with important gaps in the institutions in charge of realizing social rights. Therefore, courts must continue to play a key role in the restructuring of power asymmetries, preventing the exclusion of certain voices in the public debate, ensuring fairness of procedures, encouraging the widest possible public deliberation and the recognition of groups deserving special protection, and ensuring wealth redistribution.

Questions

a What are the advantages and disadvantages of judicial protection based on the notions of need and urgency to ensure a minimum living subsistence level? What about legal protection based on the connectedness of social rights with the rights to life and personal integrity?
b What criteria have been provided by courts for assessing the best equitable judicial protection of social rights? What kind of judicial intervention has problematic and inequitable effects?
c What are the main characteristics of dialogic judicial activism? What are their strengths and limitations?
d Should the prohibition of regression on social rights be understood as a rule or a principle? What are the advantages and disadvantages of taking one position over another?
e How far should judicial review extend over the realization of social rights?

Notes

* This chapter was translated into English by Paula Arturo and revised by the author. The author would like to thank the research assistance of Karina Carpintero and Jorge Parra.
1 See Alicia Ely Yamin and Siri Gloppen (eds), LITIGATING HEALTH RIGHTS: CAN COURTS BRING MORE JUSTICE TO HEALTH? (2011); SIRI GLOPPEN, BRUCE M. WILSON, ROBERTO GARGARELLA, ELIN SKAAR, AND MORTEN KINANDER, COURTS AND POWER IN LATIN AMERICA AND AFRICA (2006).
2 See, among many others, Rodrigo Gutiérrez, *El neoliberalismo contra los derechos económicos, sociales, culturales y ambientales*, in EL MITO DEL DESARROLLO Y LAS TRANSICIONES A LA DEMOCRACIA. TERCERAS JORNADAS SOBRE GLOBALIZACIÓN Y DERECHOS HUMANOS (Luis T. Díaz Müller, coord., 2006).
3 Rodrigo Uprimny Yepes and César Rodríguez Garavito, *Constitución, Modelo Económico y Políticas Públicas: Una Propuesta de Integración a propósito del Debate sobre el Derecho a la Educación en Colombia*, in DERECHOS SOCIALES: JUSTICIA, POLÍTICA Y ECONOMÍA EN AMÉRICA LATINA (Pilar Arcidiácono, Nicolás Espejo Yaksic, and César Rodríguez Garavito eds, 2010).
4 Víctor Abramovich, *El rol de la justicia en la articulación de políticas y derechos sociales*, in LA REVISIÓN JUDICIAL DE LAS POLÍTICAS SOCIALES. ESTUDIO DE CASOS, at 7 (Victor Abramovich and Laura Pautassi eds, 2009).
5 Christian Courtis, *Judicial Enforcement of Social Rights: Perspectives from Latin America*, in COURTS AND SOCIAL TRANSFORMATION IN NEW DEMOCRACIES. AN INSTITUTIONAL VOICE FOR THE POOR? (Roberto Gargarella, Pilar Domingo, and Theunis Roux eds, 2006).
6 RODOLFO ARANGO, EL CONCEPTO DE DERECHOS SOCIALES FUNDAMENTALES (2005).
7 Constitutional Court of Colombia, Decision T-544/09, August 6, 2009.
8 Constitutional Court of Colombia, Decision T-760/08, July 31, 2008.
9 Constitutional Court of Colombia, Decision T-595/02, August 1, 2002.
10 Supreme Court of Argentina, case of "Badaro, Adolfo Valentín c/ ANSES s/ reajustes varios," August 8, 2006 (Badaro I).
11 Víctor Abramovich, *El rol de la justicia en la articulación de políticas y derechos sociales*, in LA REVISIÓN JUDICIAL DE LAS POLÍTICAS SOCIALES. ESTUDIO DE CASOS, at 20–21 (Victor Abramovich and Laura Pautassi eds, 2009).
12 Supreme Court of Argentina, case of "Badaro, Adolfo Valentín c/ ANSeS s/reajustes varios," November 26, 2007 (V. 856. XXXVIII, Badaro II).
13 The National Administration of Social Security and the Attorney General's Office held that extending the decision in the case of *Badaro* to all other retirees could threaten the financial sustainability of the pension system. *Jubilaciones en delicado equilibrio*, PÁGINA 12, August 22, 2013, available at www.pagina12.com.ar/imprimir/diario/economia/2-227325-2013-08-22.html.

14 Leonardo Filippini and Julieta Rossi, *El Derecho Internacional en la Justiciabilidad de los Derechos Sociales en Latinoamérica*, in Derechos Sociales: Justicia, Política y Economía en América Latina (Pilar Arcidiácono, Nicolás Espejo Yaksic, and César Rodríguez Garavito eds, 2010).

15 Inter-American Commission on Human Rights, El Acceso A La Justicia Como Garantía De Los Derechos Económicos, Sociales Y Culturales. Estudio De Los Estándares Fijados Por El Sistema Interamericano De Derechos Humanos, September 7, 2007, available at www.cidh.oas.org/countryrep/AccesoDESC07sp/Accesodescindice.sp.htm (last accessed September 5, 2014).

16 Constitutional Court of Colombia, Decision C-376/10, May 19, 2010.

17 This debate is explained in depth in Rodrigo Uprimny Yepes and César Rodríguez Garavito, *Constitución, Modelo Económico y Políticas Públicas: Una Propuesta de Integración a propósito del Debate sobre el Derecho a la Educación en Colombia*, in Derechos Sociales: Justicia, Política y Economía en América Latina (Pilar Arcidiácono, Nicolás Espejo Yaksic, and César Rodríguez Garavito eds., 2010).

18 Red-DESC, "Decision C-376/10 of the Colombian Constitutional Court", available at www.escr-net.org/es/docs/i/1407210 (last Access October 28th 2015).

19 Decree No. 4807/2011. See Esteban Hoyos-Ceballos and Camilo Castillo-Sanchez, *Toward Recognition of the Right to Free Education in Colombia*, 17 Interights Bulletin, 64–5 (2013).

20 Supreme Court of Costa Rica, Constitutional Chamber, Decision 8377–03, 2003.

21 Supreme Court of Costa Rica, Constitutional Chamber, Decision 8377–03, 2003.

22 Stephen Heuser, *One girl's hope, a nation's dilemma*, Boston Globe, June 14, 2009, available at www.boston.com/news/world/latinamerica/articles/2009/06/14/one_girls_hope_a_nations_dilemma/. Heuser mentioned that: "in countries from Colombia to Taiwan to Libya, the Cambridge firm [Genzyme] has compiled an extraordinary track record of searching out patients like Tania, providing desperately needed treatment, and then successfully pressing their governments, even poor ones, to pay full price for the most expensive drugs in the world." See also Mindy Jane Roseman and Siri Gloppen, *Litigating the Right to Health: Are Transnational Actors Backseat Driving?*, in Litigating Health Rights: Can Courts Bring More Justice to Health? (Alicia Ely Yamin and Siri Gloppen eds, 2011).

23 Rodrigo Uprimny Yepes and Juanita Durán, Equidad y protección judicial del derecho a la salud en Colombia (2014) and Alicia Ely Yamin, Oscar Parra-Vera, and Camila Gianella, *Colombia: Judicial protection of the right to health: An elusive promise?*, in Litigating Health Rights: Can Courts Bring More Justice to Health? (Alicia Ely Yamin and Siri Gloppen eds, 2011).

24 Carlos Portugal Gouvêa, *Derechos sociales en contra de los pobres*, in Seminario en Latinoamérica de Teoría Constitucional y Política, El Constitucionalismo en Transición (2011) and Octavio Luiz Motta Ferraz, *Harming the Poor Through Social Rights Litigation: Lessons from Brazil*, 89 Texas Law Review, 1643–68 (2011).

25 Octavio Luiz Motta Ferraz, *Harming the Poor Through Social Rights Litigation: Lessons from Brazil*, 89 Texas Law Review, 1643–68 (2011).

26 Constitutional Court of Chile, Decision 1710/10, August 6, 2010.

27 Santiago Montt and José Luis Cárdenas, *La Declaración de Inconstitucionalidad del artículo 38 ter de La Ley de Isapres: Mitos y Realidades de un Fallo Histórico*, in Anuario de Derecho Público 2011, at 45–6 (2011).

28 Luis Cordero Vega, *Comentario a la sentencia de inconstitucionalidad de la tabla de factores de ISAPRES: un aparente triunfo de los derechos sociales*, in Anuario de Derechos Humanos 2011, at 158–9 (2011).

29 Constitutional Court of Colombia, Decision T-654/04, concurring opinion of Justice Rodrigo Uprimny Yepes, July 8, 2004.

30 On the contrary, as Angel and Lovera have explained, HIV litigation in Chile is an example of the fact that, in Chile, socioeconomic rights have been far more a matter of politics than litigation. Natalia Angel-Cabo and Domingo Lovera Parmo, *Latin American Social Constitutionalism: Courts and Popular Participation*, in Social and Economic Rights in Theory and Practice: Critical Inquiries (H. Alviar, K. Klare, and L. Williams eds, 2014).

31 Supreme Court of Argentina, case of "Asociación Benghalensis y otros c/ Ministerio de Salud y Acción Social—Estado Nacional s/ amparo ley 16.986," June 1, 2000 (A. 186. XXXIV).

32 Paola Bergallo, *Courts and Social Change: Lessons from the Struggle to Universalize Access to HIV/AIDS Treatment in Argentina*, 89 Texas Law Review, 1611–41 (2011).

33 Ana Cristina Gonzalez and Juanita Duran, *Impact of Court Rulings on Health Care Coverage: The Case of HIV/AIDS in Colombia*, 13/3 MEDICC Review, 54–7 (July 3, 2011).

34 Supreme Court of Costa Rica, Constitutional Chamber, Decision 5934–97, 1997.
35 Constitutional Court of Guatemala, File 2643–2008, August 16, 2010.
36 Constitutional Court of Peru, Process of Unconstitutionality, Judgment of June 3, 2005.
37 Constitutional Court of Peru, Process of Unconstitutionality, Judgment of June 3, 2005.
38 Ibid.
39 Rodrigo Upriminy Yepes and Diana Guarnizo, *¿Es posible una dogmática adecuada sobre la prohibición de regresividad? Un enfoque desde la jurisprudencia constitucional colombiana*, in La ciencia del derecho procesal constitucional. Estudios en homenaje a Héctor Fix-Zamudio en sus cincuenta años como investigador del derecho, T. IV Derechos Fundamentales y tutela constitucional (Eduardo Ferrer Mac-Gregor and Arturo Zaldívar Lelo de Larrea coords, 2008).
40 See Constitutional Court of Colombia, Decisions C-038/04, January 27, 2004, on the constitutionality of the labor reform that diminished labor benefits to drive greater employment, and C-931/04 of 2004, regarding standards on salary indexing.
41 See, among others, Constitutional Court of Colombia, Decision C-1017/03, October 30, 2003.
42 The justices were Rodrigo Uprimny Yepes, Manuel José Cepeda, and Rodrigo Escobar Gil.
43 Constitutional Court of Colombia, Decision C-754/04, August 10, 2004.
44 For more on this, see Roberto Gargarella, *"We the People" Outside of the Constitution: The Dialogic Model of Constitutionalism and the System of Checks and Balances*, 67 Current Legal Problems, 1–47 (2014). and Cesar Rodríguez-Garavito, *Beyond the Courtroom: The Impact of Judicial Activism on Socioeconomic Rights in Latin America*, 89/7 Texas Law Review, 1669–98 (2011).
45 Similarly, Charles Sabel and William Simon (*Destabilization of Right: How public law litigation succeeds,* 117 Harvard Law Review, 1016 (2004)) have defended a "new remedial paradigm" associated with the "experimental litigation" model.
46 Constitutional Court of Colombia, Decision T-025/04, January 22, 2004.
47 Ibid.
48 Ibid.
49 Ibid.
50 Constitutional Court of Colombia, Auto 109/07, May 4, 2007.
51 Rodrigo Uprimny Yepes and Nelson Camilo Sánchez, *Juzgar y medir. El uso de indicadores de derechos humanos por la Corte Constitucional colombiana*, in La medición de derechos en las políticas sociales (Víctor Abramovich and Laura Pautassi eds, 2010).
52 Cesar Rodríguez-Garavito and Diana Rodríguez-Franco, Cortes y Cambio Social 137–269 (2010).
53 For a more thorough analysis of this judgment, see Alicia Ely Yamin and Oscar Parra Vera, *Judicial Protection of the Right to Health in Colombia: From Social Demands to Individual Claims to Public Debates*, in 33/2 Hastings International & Comparative Law Review, 431–59 (2010) and Alicia Ely Yamin, Oscar Parra-Vera, and Camila Gianella, *Colombia: Judicial protection of the right to health: An elusive promise?*, in Litigating Health Rights: Can Courts Bring More Justice to Health? (Alicia Ely Yamin and Siri Gloppen eds, 2011).
54 Constitutional Court of Colombia, Decision T-760/08, July 31, 2008.
55 Constitutional Court of Colombia, Decision T-760/08, July 31, 2008.
56 Constitutional Court of Colombia, Decision T-760/08, July 31, 2008.
57 Norman Daniels, *Accountability for reasonableness*, 321 BMJ, 1300–01 (2000) and Norman Daniels, Just health: Meeting health needs fairly (2008).
58 Constitutional Court of Colombia, Decision T-760/08, July 31, 2008.
59 Decree No 263, November 16, 2012, legal basis 4.2.10.
60 Particularly the Comptroller General's Office of the Republic, the Superintendents of Health and of Industry and Trade, and disciplinary processes driven by the Attorney General's Office.
61 Constitutional Court of Colombia, Order 261 of November 16, 2012.
62 Alicia Ely Yamin and Oscar Parra Vera, *Judicial Protection of the Right to Health in Colombia: From Social Demands to Individual Claims to Public Debates*, in 33/2 Hastings International & Comparative Law Review, 431–59 (2010).
63 Supreme Court of Argentina, case of "Mendoza, Beatriz y otros c. Estado Nacional," June 20, 2006.
64 Supreme Court of Argentina, case of "Mendoza, Beatriz y otros c. Estado Nacional," June 20, 2006.
65 Regarding this case, see Carolina Fairstein and Diego Morales, *En busca de soluciones judiciales para mejorar la calidad de vida de los habitantes de la cuenca Matanza-Riachuelo*, in CELS, Informe Anual (2009).
66 Supreme Court of Costa Rica, Constitutional Chamber, Decision 4621–13, April 13, 2013.

67 Fernando Castillo Víquez, *Derecho a la salud,* available at http://sitios.poder-judicial.go.cr/sala constitucional/cefcca/Documentos/Derechoalasalud/CONFERENCIADERECHOALASALUD.pdf. According to the 2012 annual report issued by the Costa Rican Social Security Institute, there are over 650,000 people on waiting lists.

68 Supreme Court of Costa Rica, Constitutional Chamber, Decision 4621–13, April 13, 2013.

References

Víctor Abramovich, *El rol de la justicia en la articulación de políticas y derechos sociales*, in La Revisión Judicial de las Políticas Sociales. Estudio de casos, at 7 (Victor Abramovich and Laura Pautassi eds, 2009).

Natalia Angel-Cabo and Domingo Lovera Parmo, *Latin American Social Constitutionalism: Courts and Popular Participation*, in Social and Economic Rights in Theory and Practice: Critical Inquiries (H. Alviar, K. Klare and L. Williams eds, 2014).

Paola Bergallo, *Courts and Social Change: Lessons from the Struggle to Universalize Access to HIV/AIDS Treatment in Argentina*, 89 Texas Law Review, 1611–41 (2011).

Luis Cordero Vega, *Comentario a la sentencia de inconstitucionalidad de la tabla de factores de ISAPRES: un aparente triunfo de los derechos sociales*, in Anuario de Derechos Humanos 2011 at 158–9 (2011).

Christian Courtis, *Judicial Enforcement of Social Rights: Perspectives from Latin America*, in Courts and Social Transformation in New Democracies. An Institutional Voice for the Poor? (Roberto Gargarella, Pilar Domingo and Theunis Roux eds, 2006).

Norman Daniels, *Accountability for reasonableness*, 321 BMJ, 1300–01 (2000).

Norman Daniels, Just Health: Meeting Health Needs Fairly (2008).

Carolina Fairstein and Diego Morales, *En busca de soluciones judiciales para mejorar la calidad de vida de los habitantes de la cuenca Matanza-Riachuelo*, in CELS, Informe Anual (2009).

Roberto Gargarella, *"We the People" Outside of the Constitution: The Dialogic Model of Constitutionalism and the System of Checks and Balances*, 67 Current Legal Problems, 1–47 (2014).

Siri Gloppen, Bruce M. Wilson, Roberto Gargarella, Elin Skaar, and Morten Kinander, Courts and Power in Latin America and Africa (2006).

Carlos Portugal Gouvêa, *Derechos sociales en contra de los pobres*, in Seminario en Latinoamérica de Teoría Constitucional y Política, El Constitucionalismo en Transición (2011).

Rodrigo Gutiérrez, *El neoliberalismo contra los derechos económicos, sociales, culturales y ambientales*, in El mito del desarrollo y las transiciones a la democracia. Terceras Jornadas sobre Globalización y Derechos Humanos (Luis T. Díaz Müller, coord., 2006).

Octavio Luiz Motta Ferraz, *Harming the Poor Through Social Rights Litigation: Lessons from Brazil*, 89 Texas Law Review, 1643–68 (2011).

Ana Cristina Gonzalez and Juanita Duran, *Impact of Court Rulings on Health Care Coverage: The Case of HIV/AIDS in Colombia*, 13/3 MEDICC Review, 54–7 (July 3, 2011).

Esteban Hoyos-Ceballos and Camilo Castillo-Sanchez, *Toward Recognition of the Right to Free Education in Colombia*, 17 Interights Bulletin, 64–5 (2013).

Inter-American Commission on Human Rights, El Acceso A La Justicia Como Garantía De Los Derechos Económicos, Sociales Y Culturales. Estudio De Los Estándares Fijados Por El Sistema Interamericano De Derechos Humanos, September 7, 2007, available at www.cidh.oas.org/countryrep/Acceso DESC07sp/Accesodescindice.sp.htm (last accessed September 5, 2014).

Jubilaciones en delicado equilibrio, Página 12, August 22, 2013, available at www.pagina12.com.ar/imprimir/diario/economia/2–227325–2013–08–22.html.

Santiago Montt and José Luis Cárdenas, *La Declaración de Inconstitucionalidad del artículo 38 ter de La Ley de Isapres: Mitos y Realidades de un Fallo Histórico*, in Anuario de Derecho Público 2011, at 45–6 (2011).

Cesar Rodríguez-Garavito, *Beyond the Courtroom: The Impact of Judicial Activism on Socioeconomic Rights in Latin America*, 89/7 Texas Law Review, 1669–98 (2011).

Cesar Rodríguez-Garavito and Diana Rodríguez-Franco, Cortes y Cambio Social (2010).

Mindy Jane Roseman and Siri Gloppen, *Litigating the Right to Health: Are Transnational Actors Back-seat Driving?*, in Litigating Health Rights: Can Courts Bring More Justice to Health? (Alicia Ely Yamin and Siri Gloppen eds, 2011).

Charles Sabel and William Simon, *Destabilization of Right: How public law litigation succeeds,* 117 Harvard Law Review, 1016 (2004).

Rodrigo Uprimny Yepes and Juanita Durán, Equidad y protección judicial del derecho a la salud en Colombia (2014).

Rodrigo Uprimny Yepes and Nelson Camilo Sánchez, *Juzgar y medir. El uso de indicadores de derechos humanos por la Corte Constitucional colombiana*, in La medición de derechos en las políticas sociales (Víctor Abramovich and Laura Pautassi eds, 2010).

Rodrigo Upriminy Yepes and Diana Guarnizo, *¿Es posible una dogmática adecuada sobre la prohibición de regresividad? Un enfoque desde la jurisprudencia constitucional colombiana*, in La ciencia del derecho procesal constitucional. Estudios en homenaje a Héctor Fix-Zamudio en sus cincuenta años como investigador del derecho, T. IV Derechos Fundamentales y tutela constitucional (Eduardo Ferrer Mac-Gregor and Arturo Zaldívar Lelo de Larrea coords, 2008).

Rodrigo Uprimny Yepes and César Rodríguez Garavito, *Constitución, Modelo Económico y Políticas Públicas: Una Propuesta de Integración a propósito del Debate sobre el Derecho a la Educación en Colombia*, in Derechos Sociales: Justicia, Política y Economía en América Latina (Pilar Arcidiácono, Nicolás Espejo Yaksic and César Rodríguez Garavito eds, 2010).

Alicia Ely Yamin and Siri Gloppen (eds), Litigating Health Rights: Can Courts Bring More Justice to Health? (2011).

Alicia Ely Yamin and Oscar Parra Vera, *Judicial Protection of the Right to Health in Colombia: From Social Demands to Individual Claims to Public Debates*, in 33/2 Hastings International & Comparative Law Review, 431–59 (2010).

Alicia Ely Yamin, Oscar Parra-Vera, and Camila Gianella, *Colombia: Judicial protection of the right to health: An elusive promise?*, in Litigating Health Rights: Can Courts Bring More Justice to Health? (Alicia Ely Yamin and Siri Gloppen eds, 2011).

Further reading

Rodolfo Arango, *Basic Social Rights, Constitutional Justice and Democracy*, 16/2 Ratio Juris, 141–54 (2003).

Rodolfo Arango, El Concepto de Derechos Sociales Fundamentales (2005).

Libardo Ariza, *Economic and social rights, prisons, and the Colombian constitutional court*, in Constitutionalism on the Global South: The Activist Tribunals of India, South Africa, and Colombia (Daniel Bonilla Maldonado ed., 2013).

Daniel M. Brinks and William Forbath, *The Role of Courts and Constitutions in the New Politics of Welfare in Latin America*, in Law and Development of Middle Income Countries (Randall Peerenboom and Tom Ginsburg eds, 2014).

Christian Courtis, *Argentina*; Flavia Piovesan, *Brasil*; and Enrique González, *Venezuela*, in Social Rights Jurisprudence: Emerging Trends in Comparative and International Law (Malcolm Langford ed., 2008).

Courtis, Christian, "Socio-economic rights before the courts in Argentina," in Fons Coomans (ed.), Justiciability of Economic and Social rights: Experiences from Domestic Systems (Antwerpen: Intersentia, 2006).

Gloppen, Siri, Bruce M. Wilson, Roberto Gargarella, Elin Skaar, and Morten Kinander. "Explaining the Rise of Accountability Functions of Costa Rica's Constitutional Court" and "The Accountability Functions of Latin American Courts," in Siri Gloppen, Bruce M Wilson, Roberto Gargarella, Elin Skaar, and Morten Kinander, Courts and Power in Latin America and Africa (New York: Palgrave Macmillan, 2006).

Lucas Grosman, Escasez e Igualdad. Los derechos sociales en la Constitución (2008).

Hoffmann, Florian F and Fernando R N M Bentes. "Accountability for Social and Economic Rights in Brazil," in Varun Gauri and Daniel M. Brinks (eds), Courting Social Justice. Judicial Enforcement of Social and Economic Rights in the Developing World (New York: Cambridge University Press / World Bank, 2008).

Everaldo Lamprea Montealegre, *Colombia's Right-to-Health Litigation in a Context of Health Care Reform*, in The Right to Health at the Public/Private Divide. A Global Comparative Study (M. Coleen Flood and Aeyal Gross eds, 2014).

David Landau and Julián Daniel López-Murcia, *Political Institutions and Judicial Role: An approach in context, the case of the Colombian Constitutional Court*, Universitas, 55–92 (2009).

Claudio Nash Rojas, *Los Derechos Económicos, Sociales y Culturales y la Justicia Constitucional Latinoamericana: Tendencias Jurisprudenciales*, 9/1 Estudios Constitucionales, 65–118 (2011).

Uprimny Yepes, Rodrigo, "The Enforcement of Social Rights by the Colombian Constitutional Court: Cases and Debates," in Roberto Gargarella, Pilar Domingo and Theunis Roux (eds), Courts and Social Transformation in New Democracies. An Institutional Voice for the Poor? (Aldershort: Ashgate, 2006).

Katharine Young and Julieta Lemaitre, *The Comparative Fortunes of the Right to Health: Two Tales of Justiciability in Colombia and South Africa*, 26 Harvard Human Rights Journal (2013).

9 The protection of the environment

*María Florencia Saulino and Luis José Torres Asencio**

Introduction

Regulatory and jurisprudential developments in environmental rights represent one of Latin America's main contributions to human rights law, particularly with regard to the scope and enforceability of these rights in constitutional democracies. To a large degree, the region has overcome debates on the constitutional recognition of these rights, and its courts have generated a wealth of case law endowing them with strength and enforceability. Perhaps that is why, 20 years ago, Fabra Aguilar claimed that, "[a]rguably, no other region in the world has witnessed the promotion and protection of environmental rights with the enthusiasm and progressiveness as Latin America," alluding to the rapid development of constitutional environmental law in the region.[1]

As a result of democratic transitions and the strengthening of various movements or social groups throughout the region, several states enacted new constitutions or substantially amended existing ones. In most cases, reforms included clauses with a broad recognition of economic, social, and cultural rights, which prominently featured environmental rights.[2] Thus, today, the constitutions of Argentina,[3] Bolivia,[4] Brazil,[5] Chile,[6] Colombia,[7] Costa Rica,[8] Cuba,[9] Ecuador,[10] El Salvador,[11] Guatemala,[12] Haiti,[13] Honduras,[14] Mexico,[15] Nicaragua,[16] Panama,[17] Paraguay,[18] Peru,[19] Puerto Rico,[20] the Dominican Republic,[21] Uruguay,[22] and Venezuela,[23] among others, have at least one clause relating to issues of environmental protection and natural resource conservation. In fact, the vast majority of these constitutions explicitly recognize some form of constitutional right to an adequate environment.[24]

Most of the courts in these countries have accompanied the constitutionalization of environmental law by implementing and enforcing both the provisions and the comprehensive legislation that strengthen the constitutional texts. While the role of the judiciary in handling legal environmental disputes is still under discussion in other regions, Latin American courts have developed jurisprudence that is rich in content and ambitious in scope. By doing so, these courts have overcome concerns about the alleged vagueness or over-broadness of these rights, the boundaries of the judiciary's role in their implementation, and claims pertaining to the antidemocratic nature of judicial decisions concerning environmental rights.[25] Their decisions are, therefore, fundamental contributions to the debates on the justiciability of constitutional environmental rights, as well as their scope, their boundaries, and their relationship to other rights with which they may conflict.

This chapter presents some of the jurisprudential contributions of the region to constitutional environmental law. It examines cases that define or clarify the scope of the constitutional right to an adequate environment, decisions on *locus standi*, and access to environmental justice, judgments that explore the relationship between environmental protection and the rights of indigenous peoples, as well as case law on access to environmental information.

The scope of rights protecting the environment

While most of the constitutions of the region have explicitly recognized environmental rights, the scope of these rights varies considerably.[26] In the most heavily anthropocentric constitutions, this recognition is closely linked to the protection of the health of citizens, whose right to a "healthy" or "adequate" environment is recognized.[27] The main criticism against this approach is that it excludes from the sphere of constitutional protection any damage to the environment that does not directly harm human beings.[28]

An intermediate category consists of what Bruckerhoff calls "weak anthropocentrism provisions." In these cases, environmental rights recognized by the constitution include, in addition to the right to a healthy environment, expansive language that also covers the balance of ecosystems, sustainable development, and concern for the impact of present decisions on future generations.[29] For example, in Brazil, environmental rights were not recognized until relatively recently, with the reform of the federal constitution in 1988. Even though, prior to this reform, the absence of environmental rights was not an impediment for the adoption of environmental regulations, these regulations found support in the protection of human health—under the notion that human health could not be secured in a degraded environment—or in the articles related to production and consumption.[30] Antonio Benjamin notes that "environmental degradation is [under this conception] synonymous with sanitary degradation, or worse, a mere appendage of the larger universe of production and consumption. That is, a fangled and strictly anthropocentric argument, of an economistic and utilitarian nature that is impossible to conceal."[31] For this author, by devoting a chapter and various scattered provisions to the environment, the federal constitution of 1988 meant a shift in the strictly anthropocentric view. Indeed, the new provisions recognized the right to an ecologically balanced environment and charged public authorities and the community alike with the duty to defend and preserve the environment for present and future generations.[32]

Likewise, the constitution of Argentina expressly refers to the connection between the protection of the environment and that of future generations. Article 41 of the constitution recognizes the right of all inhabitants "to a healthy and balanced environment, fit for human development and for productive activities to meet present needs without compromising those of future generations."[33] This last sentence, which includes the concept of sustainable development, has led the court to assess the impact on present and future generations when addressing land-clearing permissions granted by a provincial government. According to the court:

> There was . . . a clear danger of serious damage because the whole climate in the region could have been substantially changed, affecting not only present inhabitants, but future generations as well. Had this damage occurred, it would have been irreversible, because returning things to their previous state would be rendered impossible.[34]

As a result, the court ordered local authorities to suspend authorizations for logging and land clearing until a cumulative environmental impact assessment was conducted, including, among other variables, potential benefits to both the parties involved and future generations.[35]

Unlike other constitutions in the region, the constitution of Ecuador adopted a strongly eco-centric view, under which nature is a subject of the law, while maintaining the right to a healthy environment for its inhabitants. In fact, the constitutional reform of 2008 was the first to recognize the rights of nature, or *pachamama*, including the right "to its existence, maintenance, and regeneration of its vital cycles, structure, functions, and evolutionary processes," (Article 71) and "the right to full restoration" in case of damages (Article 72). As far as the reform is concerned, the president of the National Constituent Assembly of Ecuador noted:

> Nature must be viewed as a subject of rights. This includes rights of Nature that must be recognized from the perspective of human beings who deem themselves as part of Nature. And from this broad and inclusive perspective, the new constitutional legal framework of our country will, therefore, have to recognize that Nature is not just a set of objects that can be owned by someone, but also a proper subject with legal rights and legal standing.[36]

The following cases seek to illustrate the different approaches adopted by the constitutions of the region concerning the constitutional right to a healthy environment and its interpretation by the courts. In the first case, *Monroy Céspedes*, the Constitutional Court of Colombia addressed the close connection between environmental protection and public health.

> Dr Simón Rodriguez Rodriguez delivered the opinion of the court:
> . . . This writ of protection was submitted by Antonio Mauricio Céspedes, who notes that the construction of a landfill for the city of Villavicenio . . . poses a serious threat to the health and integrity of the environment; he, therefore, requests that construction be immediately ceased, under the grounds that it could cause irreparable harm to the community . . . [A]s observed in the Stockholm Declaration and the International Covenant on Economic, Social and Cultural Rights, there is a direct relationship between the environment and the right to life and personal integrity, as well as to well-being and physical and mental health; no one can enjoy perfect health if exogenous contaminating factors are invading the environment and rendering nature hostile to humans . . . The above considerations have led this court to conclude that the right to the environment cannot be separated from the right to human life and health. In fact, environmentally disruptive factors can cause irreparable damage to human beings and, inasmuch as it does, then the environment is a fundamental right for the existence of humanity . . . The social responsibility of protecting natural resources and preserving a healthy environment are merely a logical result of the state's responsibilities to seek to ensure human sustainability . . .[37]

In the second, *Richard Frederick Wheeler*, the Provincial Court of Loja, Ecuador, admitted, for the very first time, protective proceedings in defense of the rights of nature.

> Mr Richard Frederick Wheeler and Ms Eleanor Geer Haddle appear before the court, and . . . submit a writ for the constitutional protection of Nature, particularly in favor of Vilcamba River and against the Provincial Government of Loja . . . The plaintiffs claim that, approximately three years ago, the Provincial Government of Loja, with no prior environmental impact assessment, deposited in Vilcabamba River . . . rocks and excavation supplies that had been extracted from the road that is being built between Vilcabamba and Quinara, severely harming Nature. The rocks and other materials deposited in River Vilcabamba caused serious damage during the rainy season in March and April 2009, when the flow of River Vilcabamba rose . . . FIFTH: Given the indisputable, elemental and overriding importance of Nature, and taking into account the known or obvious fact of its degradation, a writ of protection is the only suitable and effective action to put an immediate end to the situation and obtain remedy for a localized environmental damage. This

> Chamber believes that, until it is objectively proven that there is no probable or imminent danger of pollution or environmental damage resulting from the work that is being carried out in a specific area, constitutional judges have a duty to immediately order or enforce the legal protection of the rights of Nature . . . SEVENTH: Our Constitution recognizes the right of Nature as a subject of law, which is unprecedented in human history . . . The importance of Nature is so obvious and indisputable that any argument to the contrary is irrelevant and dismissible; thus, damages to nature are 'generational damages,' which consist of harms 'whose magnitude is such that the repercussions will be felt not only by the current generation, but also by future generations who will be impacted by its lingering effects.' . . . TENTH: The plaintiffs need not prove the damage, instead the Provincial Government of Loja must provide compelling evidence that the construction of a new road does not affect, and will not, affect the environment . . . TWELFTH: In regards to the allegation of the Provincial Government that the populations of Quimara, Vilcabamba, Malacatos, etc., need roads: . . . the interest of these populations in the construction of a road is trumped by their interest in a healthy environment that affects a larger number of people . . . Even though there is a clash between two collective interests, the environment is of greater importance. No more arguments are needed to conclude that the need for roads does not empower the Provincial Government of Loja to open or broaden roads without environmental impact assessments, as was the case.[38]

Access to justice and environmental protection

The recognition of environmental rights in national constitutions becomes a mere statement of good intentions if it is not accompanied by mechanisms for accessing justice to enforce these rights. In most Latin American countries, there are legal remedies that enable litigation in defense of recognized environmental rights, although the characteristics of these instruments vary considerably between jurisdictions.

For example, the constitution of Brazil recognizes two procedural tools for the protection of environmental rights in court: the so-called popular action ("*ação popular*") and the public civil action ("*ação civil pública*"). Through the former, any citizen can challenge in court the validity of acts that harm either the environment or historic and cultural heritage. For its part, the public civil action allows citizens to take legal action in defense of diffuse and collective interests.

In addition to these instruments of protection, Article 129, III, paragraph 1, of the constitution establishes the duty of the public prosecutor to carry out investigations and civil proceedings to protect the environment. In that vein, the National Environmental Policy Act ("Lei da Política Nacional do Meio Ambiente") recognizes the standing of the Public Prosecutor to initiate civil and criminal proceedings in cases involving environmental damage. Lesly McAllister argues that the work conducted by members of the public prosecutor in Brazil significantly improved access to justice in environmental matters, thus increasing the effectiveness of the rights recognized in the constitution of 1988:

> By using extrajudicial instruments, particularly investigations and conduct adjustment agreements, the Ministério Público came to serve as a forum of dispute resolution itself. Moreover . . . the Brazilian Ministério Público has filed thousands of environmental public civil actions, many on the basis of a complaint by a concerned citizen or an environmental group. While environmental public civil actions may be filed by a variety of other nongovernmental and governmental actors, about 97 percent of environmental public civil actions

> have been filed by the Ministério Público. The Ministério Público has thus served as the primary vehicle through which environmental interests have received access to the courts, lending significant judicial force to environmental protection laws.[39]

On the other hand, there are countries such as Mexico, where, until 2011, access to *amparo* proceedings for the protection of the right to an adequate environment was not possible.[40] Similarly, in Paraguay, access to the courts for proceedings filed in defense of the constitutional right to a healthy environment is much discussed and currently seems impossible.[41] Sheila Abed argues that:

> the juridical configuration of the Paraguayan environmental judicial system is dysfunctional with regards to the objective of guaranteeing the right to live in a healthy and ecologically balanced environment. This is because the process lacks two of the ideal tools mostly used to deal with environmental matters, namely, [public] participation and environmental justice . . .[42]

With respect to legal standing for initiating proceedings in defense of the environment, Latin American law is not consistent.[43] Argentina, for example, recognizes the standing of affected individuals, environmental organizations, and the Ombudsman, while Colombia, El Salvador, Nicaragua, and Panama recognize standing to the general public.[44] In Costa Rica, anyone can submit a writ of *amparo* for the protection of a constitutional right, even without legal counsel or paying court fees.[45] In fact, in the case of *Carlos Roberto Mejía Chacón*, the Constitutional Chamber admitted a writ of *amparo* submitted by Carlos Mejía Chacón, who was a minor.

> VI) —STANDING: . . . In environmental law, the procedural prerequisite of standing tends to extend and develop in such a dimension that it necessarily leads to the abandonment of the traditional concept; thus, it must be understood that in general terms, any person can file for proceedings and that right does not flow from property rights, or other rights . . . instead, their procedural standing stems from what modern scholars call a diffuse right, by which the original standing of an interested party . . . is diffused among all members of a certain category of persons that are equally affected by the unlawful actions in question . . . [D]iffuse interests have a dual nature, as they are at the same time collective—because they are common to the general population—and individual, and therefore can be individually claimed. That is precisely what happened in this case, where the appellant, evidently, has an individual interest because he is affected by the pollution in his community, but is also representing a collective interest, because the community is being harmed as a whole. Therefore, since it is a case of environmental law, human beings have standing in their capacity as such, because the harm to this fundamental right affects both the community as a whole and the individual in particular . . . [T]he Chamber believes that not only standing, but also necessary conditions to have standing in a legal procedure—either as plaintiff or defendant—. . . are and must be as broad as it is possible and prudent to recognize, and also that this broadness should imply that . . . even a minor and elementary school student may have standing, as well as any other person that has the capacity to clearly articulate his or her claim and interest.[46]

Indigenous peoples, democracy and environmental protection

Latin American case law on the rights of indigenous peoples and their relationship to state jurisdiction deserves an analysis that exceeds the scope of this chapter.[47] The same can be said of the complex relationship between indigenous peoples and the environment, and the way in which that relationship is affected by the national, international, or indigenous law. We shall focus here on an issue that has sparked considerable debate in case law involving indigenous peoples: the right to "prior consultation."

The right to prior consultation is an integral part of the right of indigenous peoples to actively participate in the decision-making processes within their territories, as well as of their right to their own culture and cultural identity.[48] It is, therefore, a right that closely relates to the constitutional guarantees of several states towards democratic multiculturalism,[49] in that it "balances the difference in political and economic power between cultural minorities, on the one hand, and states and cultural majorities, on the other."[50]

The right applies in two contexts. On the one hand, it arises in controversies related to projects that involve the exploitation of natural resources within indigenous territory.[51] Several courts have issued opinions on this matter, recognizing the fundamental nature of the right to prior consultation and analyzing its connection to the right of indigenous peoples to communal property.[52] In these cases, prior consultation is required before the state makes its decision regarding the project and demands, among other things, that the process be inclusive in terms of participation, made in good faith, and carried out with utmost respect for the deliberative processes of indigenous peoples, who must also be provided with all necessary means for making an informed decision.[53]

Prior consultation is also required when states consider legislation and/or regulations that directly affect indigenous societies. Although this type of prior consultation is required by Article 6 of ILO Convention 169, as well as by the constitutional provisions of several Latin American countries, it was not until recently that higher courts from three jurisdictions in the region had the opportunity to issue opinions on this matter.[54] These decisions, which recognize the importance of the prior consultation requirement when enacting legislation that directly impact indigenous peoples, enrich the debates on the rights of cultural minorities within constitutional democracies.

Decision C-030/08 of the Constitutional Court of Colombia, in 2008, examined a claim challenging the constitutionality of Law No. 1021 of 2006, known as the General Forestry Act. The decision emphasized the distinction between the right of consultation before the enactment of legislation that directly affects indigenous peoples, and the participation of indigenous peoples in the formal legislative enactment process in Congress. The applicants claimed that, even though several groups and organizations of indigenous peoples had participated in the enactment process of the General Forestry Act, and had achieved certain amendments, the Act still violated the constitution of Colombia and ILO Convention 169 because it did not meet the prior consultation requirement before the bill was submitted to Congress.

> 4.2.2.2.1 . . . [T]he duty of prior consultation is not applicable to every single piece of legislation that could potentially affect indigenous communities, but only to those that could affect them directly, in which case . . . the consultation stipulated in article 6 of ILO Convention 169 must be interpreted in the terms contained in the constitution and the law . . . There is no doubt that laws, in general, affect their recipients. In this regard, while a law that applies to the general Colombian population also affects those members of indigenous and tribal communities that are Colombian nationals, that does not mean that under Article 6 of

ILO Convention 169 prior consultation of those communities is an imperative condition for the valid enactment of that bill. Holding the contrary would be equal to affirming that a very significant part of all legislation should be submitted to a specific prior consultation process with indigenous and tribal communities . . . which exceeds the scope of Convention 169 . . . Initially, due to their general and abstract nature, laws do not directly affect their recipients, who are only affected when the law is enforced. However, they are indeed directly affected when the law alters their status as persons or as a community, either through restrictions or taxes or, conversely, the granting of benefits.

Therefore, consultation is warranted when a law contains provisions that could directly affect its recipients, regardless of whether its effect is positive or negative; this, in turn, is precisely what should be the object of the consultation.

On the other hand, it is clear that the consultation should revolve around those measures that affect the indigenous community in its capacity as such, and not around provisions that are uniformly aimed at the general Colombian population . . . 4.2.2.2.2. As far as the conditions of time, manner and place in which the consultation must take place, in light of the fact that Convention 169 does not establish procedural rules and, provided that said rules have not been stipulated by law, they must be interpreted with the flexibility accorded by the convention and without losing sight of the fact that, in accordance with the convention, the consultation must be carried out in consistency with the principle of good faith. This means, on the one hand, that it is for the states to establish the conditions for carrying out the consultation and, on the other, that to ensure its consistency with the constitution, the consultation must be effective and conducive, but with no peremptory or inescapable terms and conditions. This is aimed at promoting the creation of timely spaces for participation that enable useful interventions by sufficiently representative spokespersons focusing on the measure at hand. Thus, for example, when the object of a regulation is state intervention in the exploitation of natural resources in a specific territory in which a particular indigenous community lives, a consultation process must clearly be carried out with the legitimately constituted authorities of that community. However, if the object of a regulation is, for example, how consultation processes with indigenous and tribal communities are to be carried out, since there is no authority that can represent all of these communities and it would be impossible to consult each and every authority of indigenous or tribal peoples, the government must, in good faith, resort to consultation processes that seem most appropriate . . .

In Judgment C-891 of 2002, the court established guidelines for carrying out consultations in regards to government initiatives and stressed, first, that '[w]hen a government entity autonomously drafts a bill on any subject within its powers, there is no violation of the constitution, even if that subject involves indigenous rights, because that is the natural exercise of its functions.' . . . However, 'in such cases, before the bill is submitted to Congress, communities must have the opportunity not only to know the specifics of the project, but also—more importantly—to actively participate in their modification, if necessary.'

The court stated that this consultation process can be deemed fulfilled when there is evidence that before the bill was submitted to Congress its text was distributed to the interested communities and that said communities were informed of its scope and provided with adequate discussion forums.

In that case, the court stressed, on the one hand, that the scenario prior to the presentation of the bill was not the only space for deliberation in which indigenous peoples could participate during the process for discussing norms that could affect them. This is due to the fact that, in Congress, the participative process is not suspended but, rather, indigenous peoples are provided there with a space for discussion and participation in the framework of a democratic state, under which they can channel their proposals through elected representatives. On the other hand, 'prior consultation before the enactment of a law is to be carried out in addition to the participation of indigenous peoples from the moment of entry into force, that is, after the law is enacted, including the special care that must be observed by authorities that are responsible for the administrative development of the law, particularly with regards to the adoption of administrative measures that may directly affect the interests of such peoples.'...

5.1. As noted, in this case, the constitutional issue that was submitted to the court leads to the question of whether Law No. 1021 of 2006, or the General Forestry Act, should have been subjected to a process of consultation with indigenous and tribal communities prior to its enactment.

[The court summarizes the process by which the law was enacted, highlighting some of the criticisms levied against the bill and its amendments, which were the result of the contribution of several groups, including representative bodies of indigenous peoples.]

... [T]his court believes that neither the changes that were made to the bill throughout ordinary sessions nor the changes that were made as a result of presidential objections suffice to overcome the deficiencies in the consultation process ...

According to this court ... even though the above mentioned provisions limit the impact of the law on indigenous and tribal communities and their territories, they are not enough for overcoming the need to previously consult these communities. There are two main reasons for this:

On the one hand, the general and comprehensive nature of the law makes it impossible to exclude indigenous and tribal communities from its scope ...

On the other hand, and in close connection with the above, this law, which is comprehensive and applicable throughout the entire country, deals with the exploitation of forests, an aspect that is intimately connected to the identity of indigenous and Afro-Colombian communities and their chances of survival.

In this context, this court observes that the provisions of the Forestry Act could have a significant impact in areas of the territory that, while not having been formally designated as indigenous territories nor assigned as common property of black communities, are still part of the natural habitat of these communities, so that their impairment could significantly alter their way of life. These communities establish a close relationship with their environment, even beyond the formal boundaries of their territories, and the Forestry Act could have a considerable impact on issues such as the conservation of biodiversity, pressure over the land, water resource management, etc. ...

5.2. From the history of the law on file, it can be easily concluded that there was no prior consultation of indigenous and tribal peoples before enacting Law 1021 of 2006 in terms of ILO Convention 169. There was a broad process of socialization that did not satisfy, however, the criteria established by the Constitutional Court because it was not specific, and there is no evidence that the communities were duly informed and notified of the impacts that the project could have on them. No spaces were created for consultation.

While it is true that, as noted, there is some flexibility around the way in which consultations are to be conducted ... the fact remains that a bill of this dimension, complexity and implications, seeking to regulate forestry issues in a comprehensive

> manner demanded that, as a precondition for its submission to Congress, the government had brought forth a specific consultation process with indigenous and tribal communities, enabling the fulfillment of their right of participation. Said process would have made it possible to identify problems, establish relevant differences in approaches, look for alternatives, and, in any case, enrich the debates in Congress through the inclusion of . . . positions that, regardless of not requiring consensus, could neatly reveal issues considered problematic from the perspective of these communities . . .
>
> In order for the consultation requirement to have been considered satisfied, communities should have been made aware of the bill through the notification of sufficiently representative entities; they should have been informed about its scope and the way in which they could be affected by it; and they should have been given effective opportunities to voice their opinions. This process was not followed; therefore, this court concludes that, because the law deals with a matter that is profoundly related to both the worldview of these communities as well as their relationship to their lands and that, either through actions or omission, it can directly and specifically affect them, there is no choice but to rule that the law is unconstitutional.[55]

In Decision No. 001–10-SIN-CC, March 18, 2010, the Constitutional Court of Ecuador for the Period of Transition adopted a different interpretation regarding compliance with the prior consultation requirement. In this case, the court decided on an action of unconstitutionality that challenged the Mining Act of Ecuador, claiming that it had been enacted without prior consultation. The applicants also averred that the law authorized the displacement of indigenous communities and enabled mining exploration and exploitation within their territories, in violation of ILO Convention 169 and the constitution of Ecuador.

> In the opinion of this court, although pre-legislative consultation is part of the elements that make up the process for enacting laws, it is not a mere formality or procedure. In fact, in the opinion of this court, and in accordance with Article 57, paragraph 17 of the Constitution of the Republic, the pre-legislative consultation is a constitutional right of a collective nature . . .
>
> [U]nder regular and/or ordinary institutional conditions, the pre-legislative consultation is a *sine qua non* prerequisite that conditions the constitutionality of any measure of a legislative nature that could affect any of the collective rights of municipalities, communities, peoples and nationalities of Ecuador . . .
>
> [I]t is important to remember that the direct effect of the entry into force of the present constitution was the transformation of the Ecuadorian legal system, which resulted in a substantial change of circumstances. As a result of this substantial change, Ecuador is undergoing a transition that involves, among other things, a necessary adaptation of the country's institutional structure to the guidelines listed in the current constitution. In this context, the adoption of decisions, particularly in regards to a series of laws enacted by the former Commission on Legislation and Oversight, as well as the current National Assembly, have been subjected to the terms provided in the transitional provisions set out in the constitution.
>
> Under these circumstances, as a result of those terms, the Commission on Legislation and Oversight had to expedite the law-enactment process and debates to meet these objectives and constitutional obligations. In regards to the case at hand, there is an evident *absence* of prior infra-constitutional regulation on how to implement the pre-legislative

consultation process stipulated and guaranteed in Article 6 of ILO Convention 169, and Article 57, paragraph 17 of the Constitution . . .

[The court examines a letter sent by the Minister of Mining and Energy to the President of the Confederation of Indigenous Nationalities of Ecuador attaching a draft of the act.]

[T]here is no doubt that, to some extent, requesting the participation of a sector of indigenous communities, peoples and nationalities also denotes a direct application of Article 57, paragraph 17 of the constitution.

[The court examines a letter addressed to the Committee on Economic Production and Development, in which several organizations that represented indigenous peoples argued that the act suffered from constitutional flaws, requested that it be tabled, and proposed 'the generation of a real opportunity for dialogue among all sectors' interested in the matter.]

At this point, it should be noted that it was the representatives of a number of indigenous communities, peoples and nations themselves who decided to participate and present their arguments to show the Committee on Economic Production and Development the alleged unconstitutionality of the draft Mining Law. Therefore, their actions are a clear example of a process of information and participation of several representatives of the indigenous communities, peoples and nationalities, an aspect that, once again, presents a case of direct application of the constitutional provision that regulates and ensures the right to prior pre-legislative consultation as a collective right . . .

Based on the analyzed arguments and documents, this court insists, as part of its decision, that the process of development and enactment of the Mining Act was framed in an exceptional context that is part of the substantial change in circumstances arising out of the constitutional transition, which is known in international law as the principle of *rebus sic stantibus*: *a substantial change of circumstances*; and this exceptional situation must be taken into consideration in this case.

Aware of the historical context and the circumstances under which the process for enacting the Mining Act was carried out, and in the absence of a prior infra-constitutional regulation that establishes the procedure for pre-legislative consultation, this court finds that in the enactment of the law, mechanisms for compiling information, ensuring participation, and receiving suggestions from a segment of existing indigenous districts, communities, peoples, and nations . . . were implemented. This confirms that a direct application of the constitution took place; while these mechanisms do not fully equate to a pre-legislative consultation processes, this court declares that they contain substantial elements of that process.[56]

Democracy and access to information

Access to environmental information, access to environmental justice and public participation in environmental decision-making processes are considered the three pillars of environmental democracy.[57] The right of access to information is crucial for individuals and environmental associations to be able to actively participate in the formulation of environmental policies and bring actions to protect the environment. In this sense, Principle 10 of the Rio Declaration of 1992 emphasizes that:

> Environmental issues are best handled with participation of all concerned citizens, at the relevant level. At the national level, each individual shall have appropriate access to information concerning the environment that is held by public authorities, including

> information on hazardous materials and activities in their communities, and the opportunity to participate in decision-making processes. States shall facilitate and encourage public awareness and participation by making information widely available. Effective access to judicial and administrative proceedings, including redress and remedy, shall be provided.[58]

The right has also been explicitly recognized in several constitutions in the region[59] and, in some cases, it has been incorporated as a constitutional right through an extensive reading of the right to freedom of expression.[60] Access to information has also been linked to the most basic conceptions of democracy, which—even under a limited representative conception—requires an informed and active citizenship that participates in the discussion of public issues.[61]

In *Claude Reyes y otros v. Chile*, a group of people and NGOs filed a complaint against the Chilean government concerning its refusal to provide all requested information from the Foreign Investment Committee in relation to a deforestation project that could "be prejudicial to the environment and to the sustainable development of Chile."[62] The government claimed that the information was confidential and that its disclosure could infringe the privacy of its owners, thus endangering the activities of investors in the country. The Inter-American Court of Human Rights said:

> 86 The State's actions should be governed by the principles of disclosure and transparency in public administration that enable all persons subject to its jurisdiction to exercise the democratic control of those actions, and so that they can question, investigate and consider whether public functions are being performed adequately. Access to State-held information of public interest can permit participation in public administration through the social control that can be exercised through such access.
>
> 87 Democratic control by society, through public opinion, fosters transparency in State activities and promotes the accountability of State officials in relation to their public activities. . . . Hence, for the individual to be able to exercise democratic control, the State must guarantee access to the information of public interest that it holds . . .
>
> B) The restrictions to the exercise of the right of access to State-held information imposed in this case
>
> 88 The right of access to State-held information admits restrictions . . .
>
> 89 In relation to the requirements with which a restriction in this regard should comply, first, they must have been established by law to ensure that they are not at the discretion of public authorities. Such laws should be enacted 'for reasons of general interest and in accordance with the purpose for which such restrictions have been established.' . . .
>
> 90 Second, the restriction . . . should respond to a purpose allowed by the American Convention. In this respect, Article 13(2) of the Convention permits imposing the restrictions necessary to ensure 'respect for the rights or reputations of others' or 'the protection of national security, public order, or public health or morals.'
>
> 91 Lastly, the restrictions imposed must be necessary in a democratic society; consequently, they must be intended to satisfy a compelling public interest. If there are various options to achieve this objective, that which least restricts the right protected must be selected . . .

94 In the instant case, it has been proved that the restriction applied to the access to information was not based on a law. At the time, there was no legislation in Chile that regulated the issue of restrictions to access to State-held information.

95 Furthermore, the State did not prove that the restriction responded to a purpose allowed by the American Convention, or that it was necessary in a democratic society, because the authority responsible for responding to the request for information did not adopt a justified decision in writing, communicating the reasons for restricting access to this information in the specific case.[63]

Questions

a Article 79 of the constitution of Colombia stipulates that "[e]very person has the right to the enjoyment of a healthy environment." To what end has the constitution of Colombia recognized the right to a healthy environment? What is the relationship between this right and the protection of public life, health and physical integrity? Would this duty be breached by activities that affect the environment but not public life, health, and physical integrity? Article 41 of the constitution of Argentina stipulates that "[a]ll inhabitants have the right to a healthy and balanced environment, fit for human development and with productive activities that meet present needs without jeopardizing future generations; in addition, all inhabitants have a duty to preserve the environment." Compare this right to the one recognized by the constitution of Colombia. What are the implications of the recognition of a right to a "healthy and balanced environment, fit for human development"?

b The recognition of nature as a subject of law raises a number of questions. The constitution of Ecuador does not provide a definition of "nature"; thus, if a broad definition is adopted, it would include "everything that makes up the universe."[64] In this context, potential clashes—for which the constitution foresees no solution—can be expected between different non-human species, as well as between humans and non-humans. How does the Provincial Court of Loja resolve conflicts between humans and non-humans? Do you think the solution would be different if a conflict arose between the rights of nature and the right to health of the inhabitants of Loja? Could measures be taken for the extermination of bacteria that are hazardous to human health?

c What tools does the judiciary have for enforcing the rights granted by the constitution in the face of the inaction of political powers?

d The constitution of Argentina states that the following persons can file writs of *amparo* for the protection of environmental rights: "affected individuals, the Ombudsman, and associations that foster such ends." Compare this approach with the decision of the Constitutional Chamber of the Supreme Court of Costa Rica. What are the advantages of broader rules of standing? What are the shortcomings of this approach? What arguments support the Constitutional Chamber's decision regarding Carlos Roberto Mejía Chacón's standing?

e With regard to the standing of environmental associations in Argentina, in the case of *Mendoza Beatriz c/ Estado Nacional* the supreme court held that:

> On August 30, 2006, the court partially authorized the intervention of the seven applicant entities, admitting only *Fundación Ambiente y Recursos Naturales*, Greenpeace Argentina, Center for Legal and Social Studies, and *Asociación Vecinos de La Boca*. The court held that the power that had been granted to the above organizations was founded on the ends they claimed to seek in their bylaws. Thus, their actions were not

aimed at general and diffuse interests related to the enforcement of the constitution and other laws, but were instead aimed at preserving collective rights, such as the right to a healthy environment.[65]

Why does Argentina only grant standing to associations that are dedicated to defending the environment? How should these associations be identified? What would happen if the lawsuit had been filed by an NGO whose mission was to protect public health? Are these criteria preferable to those of the Constitutional Chamber of the Supreme Court of Costa Rica? Why?

f As discussed in previous sections, some constitutions in the region expressly mention future generations in their texts and, in fact, some courts have forced public authorities to consider the impact of their decisions on future generations. However, to date, there has not been a single case in which the environmental issue in question only affects future generations. In that scenario, who should have standing for filing claims in their defense? Some countries have created an Ombudsman for Future Generations.[66] Is this approach preferable to granting standing to any member of the current generation to defend the rights of future generations? Why?

g Like its Colombian counterpart, the judgment of the Constitutional Court of Ecuador regarding the Mining Act touches on several of the elements of the prior consultation. However, and assuming that conditioning the judgment to the constitutional transition period was legitimate, the court's statements about the effects of the participation of indigenous communities in the formal law-making process leading to the Mining Act's enactment are not all that clear. Does the court mean to say that by participating in this process the indigenous peoples waived their right to prior consultation? Can the right to prior consultation be waived? Assuming for a moment that it can be and that, as acknowledged by both the Constitutional Court of Colombia and the Constitutional Court of Ecuador, the right to prior consultation is a collective right, who would have authority to waive that right?

Apart from this, what can be said about the right to prior consultation if, as the Constitutional Court of Ecuador seems to suggest, it can be satisfied through the notification of the bill to certain representatives of indigenous peoples that could be affected by it? In what way is that interpretation compatible with the prior consultation principles discussed before?

Notes

* This chapter was originally written in Spanish and was translated by Paula Arturo. The authors wish to thank Guillermo Holsman for his excellent research assistance and Érika Fontánez Torres for her valuable comments on the design and development of this chapter, as well as Isa M. Santori Rodríguez for her dedicated research assistance.

1 Adriana Fabra Aguilar, *Enforcing the Right to a Healthy Environment in Latin America*, 3/4 Review of European Community & International Environmental Law, 215–222, 215 (1994).

2 David R. Boyd, The Environmental Rights Revolution: A Global Study of Constitutions, Human Rights, and the Environment (2012); Orlando Rey Santos, *El desarrollo del constitucionalismo ambiental en América Latina*, in Programa de las Naciones Unidas para el Medio Ambiente, Quinto Programa Regional de Capacitación en Derecho y Políticas Ambientales, at 386–7 (2010); Álvaro García Hernández, *Derecho ambiental y garantías constitucionales*, 46/2 Revista de la Unidad Académica de la Universidad Autónoma de Zacatecas, 54 (2001).

3 Constitution of Argentina, Articles 41, 43, 75, and 124 (1994).

4 Constitution of Bolivia, Preamble and Articles 9, 30, 33–4, 80, 99, 108, 124, 135, 158, 186–9, 255, 264, 298–300, 302, 304, 309, 311–13, 316, 319, 342–92, 397, 402–3, and 406–7 (2009).

5 Constitution of Brazil, Articles 5, 20, 23–4, 129, 170, 174, 186, 200, 220, 225, and 231 (1988, as amended).
6 Constitution of Chile, Articles 19–20 (1980, as amended).
7 Constitution of Colombia, Articles 9, 49, 63, 67, 78–82, 88, 95, 267–8, 277, 289, 300, 310, 317, 330–34, 339, 360–61, and 366 (1991, as amended).
8 Constitution of Costa Rica, Articles 6, 46, 50, and 89 (1949, as amended) (environmental provisions were introduced after the 1994 reform).
9 Constitution of Cuba, Articles 11, 15 27, 39, and 105 (1976, as amended).
10 Constitution of Ecuador, Articles 12–15, 27, 31–2, 57, 66, 71–4, 83, 97, 213, 242, 250, 258, 261–4, 267, 275–8, 281–5, 288, 290–91, 304, 306, 308, and 313 (2008).
11 Constitution of El Salvador, Articles 34, 60, 63, 69, and 117 (1983, as amended).
12 Constitution of Guatemala, Articles 64, 96–7, 118–19, 121, 125–8, and 142 (1985, as amended).
13 Constitution of Haiti, Articles 52–1 and 253–8 (1987).
14 Constitution of Honduras, Articles 145, 274, 340, and 354 (1982, as amended).
15 Constitution of Mexico, Articles 2, 4, 25, 27, 73, and 121 (1917, as amended) (environmental provisions were introduced in 1987).
16 Constitution of Nicaragua, Articles 60, 102, 177, and 180–81 (1987, as amended).
17 Constitution of Panama, Articles 110, 118–21 (1972, as amended).
18 Constitution of Paraguay, Articles 6–8, 38, 47, 66, 112, 115–16, 168, and 268 (1992).
19 Constitution of Peru, Articles 2, 66–9, 192, and 195 (1993, as amended).
20 Constitution of Puerto Rico, Article VI, paragraph 19 (1952).
21 Constitution of the Dominican Republic, Articles 14–17, 50, 61, 63, 66–7, 75, 193–4, 217, and 265 (2010).
22 Constitution of Uruguay, Article 47 (1967, as amended) (environmental provisions were introduced in 1996).
23 Constitution of Venezuela, Preamble and Articles 11–12, 15, 107, 112–13, 120, 127–9, 153, 156, 178, 184, 299, 326, and 337 (1999, as amended).
24 See: the constitution of Argentina, Article 5; the constitution of Bolivia, Articles 30 and 33; the constitution of Brazil, Article 225; the constitution of Chile, Article 19; the constitution of Colombia, Article 79; the constitution of Costa Rica, Article 50; the constitution of Ecuador, Article 14; the constitution of Mexico, Article 4; the constitution of Nicaragua, Article 60; the constitution of Paraguay, Article 7; the constitution of Peru, Article 2; the constitution of the Dominican Republic, Article 66; and the constitution of Venezuela, Article 127.
25 For a summary of the general objections against submitting constitutional environmental rights to the courts, see TIM HAYWARD, CONSTITUTIONAL ENVIRONMENTAL RIGHTS (2005).
26 DAVID R. BOYD, THE ENVIRONMENTAL RIGHTS REVOLUTION: A GLOBAL STUDY OF CONSTITUTIONS, HUMAN RIGHTS, AND THE ENVIRONMENT 124 (2012).
27 Joshua J. Bruckerhoff, *Giving Nature Constitutional protection: A Less Anthropocentric Interpretation of Environmental Rights*, 86/3 TEXAS LAW REVIEW, 615–31 (2008).
28 Ibid., 631–3.
29 Ibid., 633. See, for example, the constitutions of Argentina and Brazil.
30 Antonio Herman V. Benjamin, *Introduçao ao Direito Ambiental Brasileiro*, in MANUAL PRÁTICO DA PROMOTORIA DE JUSTIÇA DO MEIO AMBIENTE, at 10 (Daniel Roberto Fink ed., 2005); constitution of Brazil, Article 225.
31 Ibid.
32 Ibid., 12.
33 Constitution of Argentina, Article 41.
34 Supreme Court of Argentina, case of "Salas, Dino y otros c. Provincia de Salta y Estado Nacional," March 26, 2009, (V. 1144. XLIV) (Decisions 332:663). Similarly, see Court of Appeals of Copiapó, case of "Comunidad de Chañaral v. Codeco División el Saldor," June 23, 1988, File No. 2052 (confirmed by the Supreme Court of Chile).
35 Ibid.
36 Alberto Acosta, President of the National Constituent Assembly of Ecuador, published on the National Constituent Assembly of Ecuador's website on February 29, 2008. Reproduced in the weekly magazine *Peripecias*, vol. 87, March 5, 2008.
37 Constitutional Court of Colombia, Decision T-092/93, February 19, 1993, case of "Monroy Céspedes c/ Municipio de Villavicencio."

38 Provincial Court of Loja, Ecuador, case 11121–2011–0010, case of "Richard Frederick Wheeler v. Director de la Procuraduría General del Estado de Loja."
39 Lesly K. McAllister, Making Law Matter 152 (2008) (internal citations omitted).
40 Samantha Namnun, Derecho a un Medio Ambiente Sano. Una Mirada hacia los Mecanismos Legales para su Defensa 68 (2008).
41 David R. Boyd, The Environmental Rights Revolution: A Global Study of Constitutions, Human Rights, and the Environment 128 (2012).
42 Sheila Abed, *Paraguay*, in The Role of Judiciary in Environmental Governance, at 310–11 (Louis J Kotzé and A. Paterson eds, 2009).
43 José Juan González Márquez, La responsabilidad por el daño ambiental en América Latina (2003).
44 Ibid.
45 David R. Boyd, The Environmental Rights Revolution: A Global Study of Constitutions, Human Rights, and the Environment 135 (2012).
46 Supreme Court of Costa Rica, Constitutional Chamber, Vote No. 3705–93, case of "Carlos Roberto Mejía Chacón," July 30, 1993.
47 Much of the case law involving these issues has focused on the recognition of indigenous peoples as subjects within national and international legal systems, their rights over their territories, and their sovereignty as indigenous peoples. See, for example, the Inter-American Court of Human Rights, case of "Kichwa Indigenous People of Sarayaku v. Ecuador," June 27, 2012; the Inter-American Court of Human Rights, case of "Saramaka People v. Suriname," November 28, 2007; and the Inter-American Court of Human Rights, case of "Yakye Axa Indigenous Community v. Paraguay," June 17, 2005. See also Juan Daniel Oliva Martínez, *Acerca de la protección de la diversidad cultural y los derechos de los pueblos indígenas en el Derecho Internacional*, 21/1 Revue québécoise de droit international, 267–316 (2008) and Frank Semper, *Los derechos de los pueblos indígenas de Colombia en la jurisprudencia de la Corte Constitucional*, 2/2 Anuario de Derecho Constitucional latinoamericano, 761–78 (2006).
48 Inter-American Court of Human Rights, case of "Kichwa Indigenous People of Sarayaku v. Ecuador," June 27, 2012, paragraph 159.
49 Ibid.
50 Daniel Bonilla Maldonado, *Democracia participativa, consulta previa y diversidad cultural: La ley general forestal y la Corte Constitucional*, in Justicia colectiva, medio ambiente y democracia participativa, at 12 (Daniel Bonilla Maldonado, coord. 2010).
51 Ibid., 14.
52 See Inter-American Court of Human Rights, case of "Kichwa Indigenous People of Sarayaku v. Ecuador," June 27, 2012; Constitutional Court of Colombia, Decision T-129/11; Constitutional Court of Bolivia, File 2008–17547–36-RAC, October 25, 2010; Constitutional Court of Peru, File 0022–2009-PI/TC, June 9, 2010; Constitutional Court of Guatemala, File 3878–2007, December 21, 2009; Constitutional Court of Ecuador, case of "Dry Marshes of Pastaza," Case 222–2004-RA, June 9, 2004; Constitutional Court of Colombia, Decision C-891/02, October 22, 2002; Constitutional Court of Colombia, Decision C-169/01, February 14, 2001; Constitutional Court of Colombia, Decision T-652/98, November 10, 1998; Constitutional Court of Colombia, Decision SU-039/97, February 3, 1997; Constitutional Court of Colombia, Decision C-139/96, April 9, 1996.
53 Inter-American Court of Human Rights, case of "Kichwa Indigenous People of Sarayaku v. Ecuador," June 27, 2012, paragraphs 180–211; Constitutional Court of Colombia, Decision C-891/02, October 22, 2002; Constitutional Court of Colombia, Decision T-652/98, November 10, 1998.
54 Constitutional Plurinational Court of Bolivia, Judgment 300–2012, June 18, 2012; Constitutional Court of Ecuador for the Transitional Period, Decision 001–10-SIN-CC, March 18, 2010; Constitutional Court of Colombia, Decision C-030/08.
55 Constitutional Court of Colombia, Decision C-030/08.
56 Constitutional Court of Ecuador for the Period of Transition, Decision No. 001–10-SIN-CC, March 18, 2010.
57 Svilana Kravchenko and John E. Bonine, Human Rights and the Environment. Cases, Law, and Policy 259 (2008).
58 Report of the United Nations Conference on Environment and Development, A/CONF.151/26/Rev. 1 Vol. I (1992).
59 See, in general: the constitution of Argentina, Article 5; the constitution of Bolivia, Article 21; the constitution of Brazil, Article 5; the constitution of Colombia, Article 20; the constitution of Costa

Rica, Article 30; the constitution of Ecuador, Articles 18 and 91; the constitution of Guatemala, Articles 30 and 35; the constitution of Mexico, Article 2; the constitution of Nicaragua, Article 66; the constitution of Panama, Articles 43–9; the constitution of Paraguay, Article 28; the constitution of Peru, Article 5; and the constitution of the Dominican Republic, Article 49.

60 Inter-American Court of Human Rights, case of "Claude Reyes y otros v. Chile," September 19, 2006:

> [T]he Court has established that, according to the protection provided by the American Convention, the right to freedom of thought and expression includes not only the right and freedom to express one's own thoughts, but also the right and freedom to *seek, receive and impart* information and ideas of all kinds.

Supreme Court of Puerto Rico, case of "Soto v. Secretario de Justicia," 112 DPR 477, 485 (1982):

> [T]here is a close relationship between the freedom of speech and the freedom of information. The premise is simple. It is impossible to pass judgment on something without knowledge of the facts; neither may redress from government damages be claimed through judicial proceedings or at the polls every four (4) years.

61 See Supreme Court of Puerto Rico, case of "Colón Cabrera v. Caribbean Petroleum," 170 DPR 582, 590 (2007) ("[A]ccess to information constitutes an important component of a democratic society, where a citizen can make an informed judgment about government actions.").

62 Inter-American Court of Human Rights, case of "Claude Reyes y otros v. Chile," September 19, 2006.

63 Inter-American Court of Human Rights, case of "Claude Reyes y otros v. Chile," September 19, 2006.

64 Diccionario de la Lengua Española (2001).

65 Supreme Court of Argentina, case of "Mendoza, Beatriz y otros, c. Estado Nacional y otros" (Decisions 331:1622).

66 HLS International Human Rights Clinic, Models for Protecting the Environment for Future Generations (2008).

References

Sheila Abed, *Paraguay*, in The Role of Judiciary in Environmental Governance at 310–11 (Louis J. Kotzé and A. Paterson eds, 2009).

Antonio Herman V. Benjamin, *Introduçao ao Direito Ambiental Brasileiro*, in Manual Prático da Promotoria de Justiça do Meio Ambiente, at 10 (Daniel Roberto Fink ed., 2005).

Daniel Bonilla Maldonado (Ed.), Justicia colectiva, medio ambiente y democracia participativa (Ediciones Uniandes, 2010).

David R. Boyd, The Environmental Rights Revolution: A Global Study of Constitutions, Human Rights, and the Environment (2012).

Joshua J. Bruckerhoff, "Giving Nature Constitutional protection: A Less Anthropocentric Interpretation of Environmental Rights", in 86Texas Law Review 615–31 (2008).

Adriana Fabra Aguilar, *Enforcing the Right to a Healthy Environment in Latin America*, 3/4 Review of European Community & International Environmental Law, 215–22, 215 (1994).

Álvaro García Hernández, "Derecho ambiental y garantías constitucionales", in 46 Revista de la Unidad Académica de la Universidad Autónoma de Zacatecas 54 (2001).

José Juan González Márquez, La responsabilidad por el daño ambiental en América Latina (2003).

Tim Hayward, Constitutional Environmental Rights (2005).

HLS International Human Rights Clinic, Models for Protecting the Environment for Future Generations (2008).

Svilana Kravchenko and John E. Bonine, Human Rights and the Environment. Cases, Law, and Policy (2008).

Lesly K. McAllister, Making Law Matter (2008).

Samantha Namnun, Derecho a un Medio Ambiente Sano. Una Mirada hacia los Mecanismos Legales para su Defensa (2008).

Juan Daniel Oliva Martínez, *Acerca de la protección de la diversidad cultural y los derechos de los pueblos indígenas en el Derecho Internacional*, 21/1 REVUE QUÉBÉCOISE DE DROIT INTERNATIONAL, 267–316 (2008).

Orlando Rey Santos, *El desarrollo del constitucionalismo ambiental en América Latina*, in Programa de las Naciones Unidas para el Medio Ambiente, Quinto Programa Regional de Capacitación en Derecho y Políticas Ambientales, 386–7 (2010).

Frank Semper, *Los derechos de los pueblos indígenas de Colombia en la jurisprudencia de la Corte Constitucional*, 2/2 ANUARIO DE DERECHO CONSTITUCIONAL LATINOAMERICANO, 761–78 (2006).

Mary Elizabeth Whittemore, *The Problem of Enforcing Nature's Rights under Ecuador's Constitution: Why the 2008 Environmental Amendments Have no Bite*, 20 PACIFIC RIM LAW & POLICY JOURNAL659–691 (2011).

Further reading

Alan E. Boyle and Michael R. Anderson (eds), HUMAN RIGHTS APPROACHES TO ENVIRONMENTAL PROTECTION (1998).

DANIEL BONILLA MALDONADO, LA CONSTITUCIÓN MULTICULTURAL (2005).

David M. Beatty (ed.), HUMAN RIGHTS AND JUDICIAL REVIEW: A COMPARATIVE PERSPECTIVE (1994).

Brian Doherty and Marius de Geus (eds), DEMOCRACY AND GREEN POLITICAL THOUGHT: SUSTAINABILITY, RIGHTS, AND CITIZENSHIP (1996).

ROBYN ECKERSLEY, THE GREEN DEMOCRATIC STATE: RETHINKING DEMOCRACY AND SOVEREIGNTY (2004).

EL CONVENIO 169 DE LA OIT Y EL DERECHO CHILENO: MECANISMOS Y OBSTÁCULOS PARA SU IMPLEMENTACIÓN (Jorge Contesse Singh, ed. 2012).

Érika Fontánez Torres, *El derecho a participar: Notas para una concreción*, 68 REVISTA JURÍDICA DEL COLEGIO DE ABOGADOS DE PUERTO RICO 631–80 (2007).

Érika Fontánez Torres, *Equality and Environmental Protection: A Constitutional Approach in the Navarro Case*, 7/1 MCGILL INTERNATIONAL JOURNAL OF SUSTAINABLE DEVELOPMENT LAW AND POLICY, 101–13 (2011).

Thomas Greiber (ed.), JUDGES AND THE RULE OF LAW: CREATING THE LINKS: ENVIRONMENT, HUMAN RIGHTS AND POVERTY (2006).

Leff, Enrique (ed.), JUSTICIA AMBIENTAL: CONSTRUCCIÓN Y DEFENSA DE LOS NUEVOS DERECHOS AMBIENTALES CULTURALES Y COLECTIVOS EN AMÉRICA LATINA (2001).

Andrew Light and Avner de-Shalit, MORAL AND POLITICAL REASONING IN ENVIRONMENTAL PRACTICE (2003).

James R. May, *Constituting Fundamental Environmental Rights Worldwide*, 23 PACE ENVIRONMENTAL LAW REVIEW 113–182 (2005–2006).

NORMAN J. VIG AND REGINA S. AXELROD (eds), THE GLOBAL ENVIRONMENT: INSTITUTIONS, LAW, AND POLICY (2010).

Gerardo Ruiz-Rico (ed.), DERECHO COMPARADO DEL MEDIO AMBIENTE Y DE LOS ESPACIOS NATURALES PROTEGIDOS (2000).

María Florencia Saulino, *Derecho a un ambiente sano, equilibrado, apto para el desarrollo*, in Julio C. Rivera (h) et al., TRATADO DE LOS DERECHOS CONSTITUCIONALES (2014).

Luis José Torres Asencio, *A las puertas del Tribunal*, 46 REVISTA JURÍDICA UNIVERSIDAD INTERAMERICANA DE PUERTO RICO, 333–73 (2012).

10 The protection of the rights of indigenous peoples

Silvina Ramírez and Nahuel Maisley[*]

Introduction

The relationship between indigenous peoples and Latin American states has been troublesome from the very beginning. Most of our countries were built in direct and explicit contraposition to the cultures and interests of the native inhabitants of our lands, who were marginalized from every instance of state construction. In some cases, this implied not only a considerable degree of neglect and discrimination, but actual persecution, torture, and even annihilation.[1]

The traces of this tragic past were built into the original constitutions of our states, many of which have lasted until our days. Of course, there have been different waves of reform, trying to adapt those texts to the theoretical progresses that have been made regarding the relationship between the state and indigenous peoples over the past 200 years. However, we will suggest in this chapter that the reforms introduced to these constitutions have not been able to modify the basic matrix that characterized those original texts, at least according to the usual interpretation made by the relevant legal operators. Specifically, we will try to focus on the impact and the implications of the reasoning carried out by judicial institutions, both at the domestic and the Inter-American level. We will also explore the kind of adaptation required to perform such a reform, which might need some pervasive cultural, institutional, and legal change. In the end, our analysis will lead us to the idea that such change is possible, and that Latin American states have some alternatives to attain it, albeit in the long run.

Our analysis will have three steps. First, we will describe the traditional constitutional structure of Latin American states, and the way in which the concerns for the situations of indigenous peoples were inserted within those structures. Secondly, we will analyze some of the practical and theoretical difficulties that have prevented Latin American states from becoming truly intercultural entities. And, finally, we will sketch some proposals to overcome these difficulties and achieve more inclusive societies. Although we will work with examples from different Latin American countries, all along the way, special attention will be paid to the case of Argentina, since it is representative of these issues, and it is the one regarding which our knowledge is most profound.

Constitutional approaches to the situation of indigenous peoples in Latin America

In the mid-nineteenth century, most Latin American countries gave themselves constitutions to regulate the functioning of their newly achieved independent states. The basic matrix of those constitutions was, according to Roberto Gargarella, the result of a pact between the liberal and conservative sectors of those societies,[2] which resulted in the establishment of limited political liberties and ample civic (economic) liberties. "The basic institutional structure that was then created," Gargarella explains, "proved enormously successful, at least with regard to two fundamental issues: (1) the diffusion that it achieved, and (2) the stability that it gained. In the end, and after 150 years of its creation, the main constitutional structure of the region appears to be basically the same."[3]

In terms of its consideration for indigenous peoples, this constitutional matrix also had some common features, which can be derived from the founding pact between liberals and conservatives: first, the traditional Latin American constitutions were all based on the establishment of individual rights and the disdain for collective rights;[4] secondly, they did not usually consider the "indigenous other" as a different entity, with specific rights that should be protected.

According to some, this relationship between the constitution and indigenous peoples changed with the later reforms of the constitutions, with the incorporation of international human rights treaties and/or with the progress in theoretical and constitutional discussions surrounding the principle of equality. However, as we anticipated in the introduction, our thesis is that the constitutional matrix that gave origin to Latin American states in the nineteenth century has not been transformed substantially, and that the reforms have influenced mostly the formal side of the constitution. This does not mean to disregard the relevant progress that has been made in terms of the definition and expansion of the rights of indigenous peoples. Instead, what we would like to point out—just as Gargarella does, with reference to the constitution in general—is that indigenous peoples have achieved some formal recognition but have never been allowed into the "engine room" of the constitution (the structuring of power), which remains an area of exclusive access for some.

We will describe the evolution of the two main attempts to reform the approach given to indigenous rights by the traditional Latin American constitutional matrix. First, we will describe the progress in the discussions surrounding the principle of equality and their impact in the three waves of Latin American constitutional reform regarding indigenous affairs. Secondly, we will take a look at the international commitments assumed by Latin American states regarding indigenous peoples. In both cases, we find that there has been significant legal progress, but that the "engine room" of the constitutions has remained intact.

The internal side of the "constitutional bloc": monist, multicultural, plurinational constitutions

The first attempt to reform the way in which the Latin American constitutions approached the issue of indigenous peoples was through evolving interpretations of the principle of equality and, eventually, constitutional reform. Specifically, the past 30 years have witnessed three cycles of constitutional reform regarding indigenous matters in Latin America: a) a first wave, in the 1980s; b) a second wave, in the 1990s; and c) a third wave, in the first decade of the new century.[5]

The first wave came in the 1980s, with the 1985 reform of the Guatemalan constitution and the 1987 reform of the Nicaraguan constitution.[6] What appeared in these cases was a first attempt at the recognition of indigenous peoples, i.e. rules that referred specifically to these peoples as such (as opposed to, for example, "disadvantaged groups"), and that granted them a set of rights. This was the first constitutional acceptance of the existence of diverse cultures within the same geopolitical state, and the result of incipient theoretical developments from scholars demanding states to adopt a "multicultural" character.[7] A good example of this first attempt are Articles 66 and 67 of the Guatemalan constitution:

> Article 66. Protection of Ethnic Groups. Guatemala is made up of various ethnic groups among which are native groups of Mayan descent. The state recognizes, respects, and promotes their form of life, customs, traditions, forms of social organization, the wearing of Indian dress by men and women, their languages, and dialects.
>
> Article 67. Protection of Indigenous Agricultural Lands and Cooperatives. The lands of the cooperatives, native communities, or any other forms of communal possession or collective agrarian ownership, as well as the family heritage and popular housing will enjoy the special protection of the State, preferential credit and technical assistance, which may guarantee their ownership and development in order to insure an improved quality of life to all inhabitants.[8]

The second wave came in the 1990s, when many countries of Latin America introduced broad reforms in their constitutions (Colombia in 1991, Paraguay in 1992, Peru in 1993, Bolivia and Argentina in 1994, and Ecuador and Brazil in 1998). By then, ideas of "multiculturalism" and "pluriculturalism" had become almost mainstream, and every state purported to include some reference to indigenous peoples in their constitutions. As a result, these states began considering themselves as multiethnic nations and incorporated some degree of legal pluralism, such as respect for indigenous justice and its authorities.[9] These normative formulations have been the object of different interpretations—giving them wider or narrower meanings—but they allowed for the advancement of indigenous movements.

An example of this second wave of constitutional reform is the inclusion of paragraph 17 into Article 75 of the Argentinian constitution. Article 75 establishes the duties of Congress, and paragraph 17 includes among them:

> To recognize the ethnic and cultural pre-existence of indigenous peoples of Argentina. To guarantee respect for their identity and the right to bilingual and intercultural education; to recognize the legal capacity of their communities, and the community possession and ownership of the lands they traditionally occupy; and to regulate the granting of other lands adequate and sufficient for human development; none of them shall be sold, transmitted or subject to liens or attachments. To guarantee their participation in issues related to their natural resources and in other interests affecting them. The provinces may jointly exercise these powers.[10]

However, the wording of the provisions and their location within the mandates of Congress have led some commentators and many legal operators to understand these as programmatic goals instead of operative rights.[11] We will deal with this in the chapter's next section.

The third constitutional cycle appears with the constitutions of Ecuador (2008) and Bolivia (2009). From the concept of multiculturalism and pluriculturalism, they move on to the notion of plurinationality. It is now not about a multiethnic nation, but about a set of nations which coexist in the same geopolitical space as the state. The new constitutions are much more appealing, the rights included are more ambitious in terms of the protection of indigenous peoples, and they intend to leave the classic state model behind in order to relaunch states with different profiles. The Ecuadorian constitution, for example, expressly states the multicultural nature of the state:

> Article 6. All female and male Ecuadorians are citizens and shall enjoy the rights set forth in the constitution. Ecuadorian nationality is a political and legal bond between individuals and the state, without detriment to their belonging to any of the other indigenous nations that coexist in plurinational Ecuador. Ecuadorian nationality is obtained by birth

> or naturalization and shall not be forfeited because of marriage or its dissolution or by acquiring another nationality.[12]

However, despite the substantive reforms promised by the new constitutions, there are questions regarding the way to achieve the effective protection of the rights of indigenous peoples when both the international instruments and the constitutions (belonging to old paradigms) have shown their insufficiency, even if they signify a relevant normative advancement, to fight for the defense of rights. The core question is whether these changes in the national constitutions can produce genuine changes in the distribution of powers within the state itself.[13] To date, with the exception of some prominent judicial decisions of the Constitutional Court of Colombia[14] (which have tried to develop the constitution's text), there has been no progress in the development of measures tending to make the recognition effective. This gap between the formal advances and the effective protection of indigenous peoples' rights led the Supreme Court of Mexico, as recently as 2013, to issue a resolution stating the need for rights to have not only a formal but also a substantive dimension that effectively results in indigenous peoples fully enjoying their rights as humans:

> Therefore the principle of equality before the law in our constitutional system protects both individuals and groups. Which leads us to consider that the human right to equality before the law needs not only a formal or legal dimension, but also a substantive or factual dimension that aims to remove or diminish the social, political, cultural or economic obstacles that keep a group of people from enjoying and practicing in a real and effective way their human rights . . .[15]

The external side of the "constitutional bloc": the impact of international human rights law on the situation of Latin American indigenous peoples

Besides constitutional reform, the Latin American states also modified the way in which their traditional constitutions tackled the issue of indigenous rights through their participation in several international mechanisms designed for the protection of human rights. Because of the importance of their impact, three of these mechanisms deserve specific attention: first, the International Labor Organization's Convention 169 on Indigenous and Tribal Peoples; secondly, the United Nations Declaration on the Rights of Indigenous Peoples; and, thirdly, the inter-American system of human rights (IASHR).

Convention 169 on indigenous and tribal peoples

The International Labor Organization's (ILO) Convention 169 is the most advanced international norm regarding indigenous rights.[16] Its content shows a change of conception with respect to the previous rule (ILO Convention 107 of 1957), since its articles overcome the idea of "integration" of the indigenous person to the bigger society, in order to capture an intercultural paradigm which recognizes the rights of indigenous individuals as members of a community.

The convention protects, among others, the indigenous peoples' right to a collective existence, to cultural identity and to their own institutions, the right to political participation, to internal self-determination, to administer justice, and the collective right to possession and property of lands. However, as we will see in the chapter's next section, firstly, Latin American (and Argentinian, in particular) legal operators have not yet fully internalized the existence of these rights, and, secondly, there has been no significant institutional reform to put them in practice.

United Nations declaration on the rights of indigenous peoples

The United Nations Declaration on the Rights of Indigenous Peoples[17] is a step forward in the consolidation of a normative framework guaranteeing these rights, as well as a consolidation of the recognition already formulated in the convention and many of the constitutions. Four differences can be noted, however, between the convention and the declaration. The first, which can be derived from the names themselves, is the fact that while the ILO instrument is a treaty—and thus mandatory under international law—the UN instrument is a declaration—lacking a binding character unless it becomes customary international law. The second difference has to do with the process of elaboration of both instruments: as opposed to what happened in 1989 with the drafting of the ILO Convention, indigenous peoples were granted significant participation rights in the drafting of the UN Declaration.[18] This participation can be seen in itself as an unequivocal sign of the recognition of indigenous peoples as legal subjects.[19] The third difference is that the declaration widens the scope of some of the rights acknowledged in the convention. For example, the declaration includes the right to prior, free, and informed consent, a step forward regarding the right of consultation included in the convention. The fourth difference has to do with the centrality given to the idea of self-determination in the declaration, key to many of the later claims of indigenous peoples.

The Inter-American System of Human Rights (IASHR)

The IASHR currently plays a fundamental role in the protection of indigenous rights in Latin America for two main reasons. First, the work of the commission and the court is meant to be respected by the states, as a result of the obligations deriving from the Inter-American Convention of Human Rights. Despite a general trend of compliance, there are some troubling cases of resistance by the states to accept the decisions made by the organs of the system, which usually result in important delays in the satisfaction of the rights claimed. For example, in the first case decided by the Inter-American Court regarding the rights of indigenous peoples, *Mayagna Awas Tingni v. Nicaragua*,[20] the court's decision dates to 2001, but implementation did not begin until 2008.[21] And, in the case of the *Lhaka Honhat*[22] community, in the province of Salta, in Argentina, the procedure before the Inter-American Commission began in 1998 and still has not ended, as a result of the use of several maneuvers by the state to prolong the dispute. As a consequence of these problems, the fundamental importance of the IASHR is probably based on its second way of impacting on reality, i.e. through its case law. The commission and the court have elaborated a solid jurisprudence that shows a protective approach to indigenous peoples, creative and novel in its analysis, with a profound reasoning behind it. In turn, this case law influences local decision makers, such as judges and politicians, who tend to follow the patterns established by the IASHR, ultimately favoring the protection of indigenous rights.

In particular, there are three standards that the case law of the IASHR has consolidated which are extremely relevant for the rights of indigenous peoples. The first is that of communal indigenous property. Both the court and the commission have adopted an expansive interpretation of the notion of the "territory" belonging to the communities, including not only those physically occupied, but also those utilized for cultural or subsistence activities, including the subsoil of the lands. In the absence of an explicit reference to indigenous property in the Inter-American Convention, the court expressly utilized ILO Convention 169 in order to interpret Article 21 of the former, concluding with a protective hermeneutic of such provision.[23] Both organs also emphasized that the relationship between the communities and the lands goes beyond the traditional concept of property, due to the special—spiritual—relationship that unites them. As the Inter-American Court stated in *Saramaka People v. Suriname*, "states must respect the special relationship that members of indigenous and tribal peoples have with their territory in a way that guarantees their social, cultural, and economic survival."[24]

In *Mayagna Awas Tingni v. Nicaragua*, the court stated that:

> Given the characteristics of the instant case, some specifications are required on the concept of property in indigenous communities. Among indigenous peoples there is a communitarian tradition regarding a communal form of collective property of the land, in the sense that ownership of the land is not centered on an individual but rather on the group and its community. Indigenous groups, by the fact of their very existence, have the right to live freely in their own territory; the close ties of indigenous people with the land must be recognized and understood as the fundamental basis of their cultures, their spiritual life, their integrity, and their economic survival. For indigenous communities, relations to the land are not merely a matter of possession and production but a material and spiritual element which they must fully enjoy, even to preserve their cultural legacy and transmit it to future generations.[25]

The second standard that the IASHR has clarified and advanced is that of the "free, informed, and prior consultation" and the "free, informed, and prior consent" of indigenous peoples regarding development and investment plans that affect their communities. In both *Saramaka v. Suriname*[26] and *Sarayaku v. Ecuador*[27] the court mentioned the importance of engaging in a consultation process with local communities before making decisions that might affect them. For instance:

> . . . the State must . . . adopt legislative, administrative and other measures necessary to recognize and ensure the right of the Saramaka people to be effectively consulted, in accordance with their traditions and customs, or when necessary, the right to give or withhold their free, informed and prior consent, with regards to development or investment projects that may affect their territory, and to reasonably share the benefits of such projects with the members of the Saramaka people, should these be ultimately carried out.[28]

The commission explained, in turn, that the consultation does not only require the supply of information, but also a real role in the decision-making process:

> It is a moment of truly intercultural dialogue in which the State is obliged to give serious consideration to the arguments made by the indigenous people and the values, principles and rights that could be infringed by the potential project, all of which must be done from a respectful and genuinely multicultural perspective.[29]

Further, in *Saramaka v. Suriname*, the court noted that:

> regarding large-scale development or investment projects that would have a major impact within Saramaka territory, the State has a duty, not only to consult with the Saramakas,

> but also to obtain their free, prior, and informed consent, according to their customs and traditions.[30]

According to the Commission, in turn, this requirement of consent must be interpreted as a "heightened safeguard for the rights of indigenous peoples, given its direct connection to the right to life, to cultural identity and other essential human rights."[31]

Meanwhile, in *Sarayaku v. Ecuador*, the court stated, in relation to the right to consultation:

> The Court observes that, in general, the close relationship between the indigenous communities and their land has an essential component, which is their cultural identity based on their specific worldviews, which, as distinct social and political actors in multicultural societies, must receive particular recognition and respect in a democratic society. Respect for the right to consultation of indigenous and tribal communities and peoples is precisely recognition of their rights to their own culture or cultural identity . . . which must be assured, in particular, in a pluralistic, multicultural and democratic society . . . Based on all the above, one of the fundamental guarantees to ensure the participation of indigenous peoples and communities in decisions regarding measures that affect their rights and, in particular, their right to communal property, is precisely the recognition of their right to consultation, which is established in ILO Convention No. 169, and other complementary international instruments.[32]

Finally, the third standard set by the IASHR is that of political participation. In *Yatama v. Nicaragua*, the court considered that

> the State should adopt all necessary measures to ensure that the members of the indigenous and ethnic communities of the Atlantic Coast of Nicaragua can participate, in equal conditions, in decision-making on matters and policies that affect or could affect their rights and the development of these communities, so that they can incorporate State institutions and bodies and participate directly and proportionately to their population in the conduct of public affairs, and also do this from within their own institutions and according to their values, practices, customs and forms of organization, provided these are compatible with the human rights embodied in the Convention.[33]

This is a right distinct from that of prior consultation, since it affects a much wider range of situations and, hence, it can have a considerable impact on the legal and political situation of indigenous peoples.

If we were to take these rights seriously there would be two consequences. First, the culture of Latin American legal operators—judges, civil servants and other officers—would change, and they would be very careful when making decisions that might affect indigenous peoples. Secondly, some institutional reforms would be put in place in order to ensure that the structure of the state is compatible with the requirements acknowledged by the IASHR. However, as we will see in this chapter's next section, none of these two developments has yet taken place.

Difficulties for the establishment of intercultural states

Having analyzed the constitutional dimension of the relation between Latin American states and indigenous peoples, we would now like to focus on the difficulties for the establishment of true intercultural states. To do so, we will look at two aspects of the problem. First, we will study the conceptual difficulties that exist in the relationship between the national state and indigenous peoples. Secondly, we will place our attention on the institutional problems beyond the constitution. In both cases, as anticipated earlier, we will focus on the particularities of the situation in Argentina.

Conceptual difficulties

All three waves of Latin American constitutional reform looked promising for indigenous peoples at first. Everything seemed as if the recognition of rights in the constitutions of the states would inevitably and imminently lead to changes in practice. However, the fact is that there were no notable actions transferring the constitutional changes to concrete actions. Either as a result of ambiguous interpretations which required secondary legislation for the application of constitutional clauses, or because there was no commitment or political will to implement the content of the constitutional rules, these recognitions have not proven completely effective to guarantee the rights of indigenous peoples.

In order to understand the difficulties of putting in practice the recognition of indigenous rights, we could mention the example of the interpretations given to Article 75.17 of the Argentinian constitution. Gregorio Badeni, an Argentinian professor of constitutional law, considers that:

> The delegates at the constitutional convention, clinging to 'constitutional snobism,' incorporated a clause whose contents are very dear and respected in many Latin American countries, considering their cultures and their historical development. However, these contents did not seem to adjust to the Argentinian reality of the eve of the twenty-first century, and even less to the noble ideal that inspired the constituents of 1853/60 when they dictated the Preamble and sanctioned Article 16 of the constitution. This is reinforced by the fact that as of the September 1, 1811 decree of the Governing Board, indigenous rights have always been recognized, since indigenous peoples were equated to every other citizen, with absolute obliviousness to their racial origins.[34]

Badeni's remarks are useful to understand the first of the two kinds of conceptual difficulties regarding the constitutional approach to the relation between the state and indigenous rights. The first of these challenges is of a cultural nature, meaning that there is a longstanding tradition within legal operators and commentators of neglecting the existence of indigenous peoples, as such, within the territories of the Latin American nation states. This culture used to be endorsed by the wording of the nineteenth-century constitutions but cannot be sustained any longer with the current constitutional bloc. Badeni's comments—and the importance of arguments of the sort within the Argentinian legal community—are useful to prevent advocates of indigenous rights from falling into a "normative fetishism,"[35] i.e. from understanding that legal reform is sufficient to change a certain legal practice. The wording of the constitution might be important, but it becomes irrelevant if the most prominent interpretations of the text are of the nature of the one proposed by Badeni. Advocates of indigenous rights still have to put up a hermeneutic fight, in order to make sure that the most protective understanding of indigenous rights becomes the standard interpretation of our constitutional bloc.

The second conceptual challenge, as we suggested earlier, has to do with the constitutional matrix, i.e. with the very structure of the state. Despite the specific institutional details that we will analyze in the next section, the fulfillment of indigenous rights requires a new conceptual understanding of the state. As opposed to what occurred before, where the state was the one and ultimate source of authority, the respect of the rights of indigenous peoples requires the state to acknowledge some other forms of political power that coexist with it within its boundaries. We will get back to this issue later on. For the moment, we will focus on the fine print of the institutional structure of the state.

Institutional difficulties

Legislative decisions and public policy

As a result of the restoration of democracy and of the revaluation of the idea of rights after a bloody dictatorship, the Argentinian state began paying attention to indigenous issues in the second half of the 1980s. During this period a law was passed to create the National Institute of Indigenous Affairs,[36] a governmental entity in charge of public policy related to indigenous peoples and the natural interlocutor of indigenous leaders and representatives. This public perspective on the matter was later reaffirmed by the 1994 reform of the constitution, which removed anti-indigenous provisions and included clauses providing for recognition and respect. For example, in the case of *Consejo Qompi*[37] (Qompi tribal leaders) there was a discussion of the validity of the laws in which the indigenous communities were recognized but their political organizations were not. The community filed a lawsuit against the Chaco Province, and the organizations obtained legal recognition. The chamber held that:

> Article 75 paragraph 17 is fully operational. Congress could not deny it recognition due to the applicable constitutional doctrine of the 'social content' which as a minimum should be considered operative even when there has not been legislative action . . . Consequently, it is necessary to reinforce the awareness of the enforceability and the operative character deriving from the rules that regulate the relationship between governments and indigenous peoples, with the purpose of avoiding that our constitutions and laws are merely a declaration of good intentions, as against a sector that demands positive and concrete actions to protect their rights.[38]

However, despite these promising changes, the state has maintained ambivalent policies towards indigenous peoples. There is recognition in terms of discourse and of norms, but in practice it still has a handout mentality towards vulnerable and disadvantaged groups (among which indigenous peoples are included), and there are some traces of an integrationist paradigm, which does not accept multiculturalism.[39]

The discussions generated around the equality principle deserve to be mentioned, because of what they mean in terms of the lack of recognition towards indigenous peoples' rights. In the *Vera de Casih*[40] case, from Córdoba province, Argentina, the debate focused on the legality of taking one's only home because of debt.

> . . . Indigenous housing, throughout the national territory, cannot be subject to a writ of attachment, whereas non-indigenous housing can, which results in a blatant violation of the equality principle (Article 16 of the National Constitution), but also in an action that perfectly falls within the prohibitions set forth in the Antidiscriminatory Law . . . It would be a case of reverse discrimination, perhaps the first case in history, against non-indigenous

> people, and in favor of indigenous peoples, even when the constitution states that there is to be no discrimination for or against anyone.[41]

Even though the explanation of this situation is broader, relating to the main theme of this chapter, there might be a specific, institutional reason for this duality. In fact, the National Institute of Indigenous Affairs (INAI) has failed to establish itself as the unique interlocutor and protector of indigenous peoples, perhaps as a result of its institutional subordination to the executive power. Consequently, several public offices have assumed responsibilities regarding these issues, and they have all been dealing with these affairs at the same time.[42] Each of these offices performs its duties within its mandate, but with no contact with each other, generating fragmentation and even contradictory decisions.

This fragmentation of the handling of indigenous affairs has two notable consequences. First, there is a dilution of responsibility.[43] Since there is a superposition of duties between several public offices, the officials in charge can elude their responsibilities by deriving the issues to other entities. As a result, indigenous communities usually have to end up going from one office to another, making huge efforts to try to get a concrete answer from the state.[44] This does not mean that the existence of multiple state instances dealing with indigenous peoples is problematic in and by itself. The problem lies in the lack of articulation between these offices and, mainly, in the absence of a centralized organ that can present itself as the representative of the state in order to make decisions alongside indigenous peoples in affairs that are relevant to them. The second consequence is that indigenous peoples are not treated as democratic subjects but, instead, as objects of public policy. Each of these offices considers their interests as part of their own scope of action only insofar as they are in line with the policies that they intend to implement. Instead of having a say in the determination of the public policies, indigenous peoples have to try to fit their demands within those that have been predetermined by the state. In other words, instead of trying to establish a truly intercultural paradigm, each office of the state tries to add "some indigenous ingredient" to its own work.

Judicial review

Since the Argentinian constitutional reform decided to handle the relation between the state and indigenous peoples through the enumeration of rights in the constitution,[45] the role of judges has become crucial with regard to this issue. As a result, the case law regarding the protection of indigenous rights can be understood as a thermometer of the evolution of the relation between the state and the communities. In general, there are four aspects that can be noted from analyzing these decisions.

First, the case law regarding indigenous peoples in Argentina is not abundant, showing that there is still a great deal of distrust on the side of the communities regarding the judicial system. In fact, there is an institutional side to this distrust, which has to do with the state's inaction regarding the cultural homogeneity of most judges. Instead of facilitating the training and election of judges who are representative of the cultural diversity of the local populations, there is an institutional silence regarding the fact that most judges are white males, from certain social classes, who have been taught by other white males at law schools.

The second feature that can be easily recognized is that the case law is not uniform: while some judges have acknowledged the constitutional changes operated in 1994, others have had a hard time accommodating their conservative paradigm with these new rights. In cases like *Comunidad Mapuche Mellao Morales*,[46] *Consejo Qompi*,[47] or *Palma Arturo*[48] the judges upheld some of the rights that were incorporated to the constitutional bloc, such as the right to free, informed, and prior consultation, or the right to land. However, there have also been cases such as *Comunidad Mapuche Paichil Antriao*,[49] in which the judicial system took no consideration of the indigenous peoples or their recently acquired constitutional rights.

In *Comunidad Mapuche Mellao Morales v. Provincia de Neuquén*, for example, the judges understood that:

> The commitment to the rights involved in this case . . . (to communal property, to be consulted; to participate in the administration of their own natural resources, and to other interests that may affect them, and to the protection and preservation of the environment in their land) make it clear that the requested protection has to be granted, so the passage of time will not make the aforementioned rights illusory.[50]

The third notable fact regarding the evolution of the judicial approach to indigenous rights in Argentina has to do with the increasing involvement of the national Supreme Court in these affairs. In 2007, the court made its first important decision regarding indigenous peoples in the case known as *Defensor del Pueblo de la Nación v. Estado Nacional y otra (Provincia del Chaco)*. On that occasion, the national ombudsman asked the court to order both the national government and the provincial government of Chaco to provide humanitarian and social aid to the indigenous communities located in the General Güemes and Libertador General San Martín departments of the said province.[51] As a result, the court took a strong stance and ordered provisional measures to alleviate the situation of the communities, in what became a landmark case. However, even if the court took into consideration arguments regarding the very existence of the communities as such, it is important to note that the core of the decision was not based on indigenous rights, but instead on broader humanitarian arguments. The court thus held:

> The gravity and urgency of the reported situation demand that this court exercises the mandated oversight over the activities of the other branches of the state and, in this context, the adoption of measures that, without infringing on these branches' constitutional powers, will ensure that the national constitution is complied with, without undermining the faculties of other branches, and irrespective of an eventual decision on the court's jurisdiction to rule in this case . . .
>
> This is so because it is the national judicial branch's task to find the ways to guarantee rights' effectiveness . . . as a fundamental and guiding principle when administering justice . . . especially when the right to life and to physical integrity are at stake. This, by no means, constitutes and inappropriate intervention of the judicial branch, which is only protecting the rights or making up for omissions in cases where this rights are violated.[52]

Besides mandating provisional measures, the court has adopted a dialogic stance in a few cases involving indigenous rights. In *Salas, Dino y Otros v. Salta y Estado Nacional*, a case in which a group of communities demanded the unconstitutionality of the authorizations given by the state to private companies to chop down trees from the local forests, the court decided to call the parties to a hearing, while dictating a provisional measure to stop the deforestation. Similar resolutions were made by the court in *Comunidad Indígena Toba La Primavera-Novogoh*,[53] and in *Comunidad Aborigen de Santuario Tres Pozos*.[54]

Finally, there is a fourth feature, which has to do with the persistence of institutional obstacles to the access of the communities to the judicial system. The first obstacle has to do with the jurisdiction to which the communities must present their claims.

Although the constitution does not say so explicitly, the Supreme Court has accepted the jurisdiction in cases concerning indigenous peoples. Even though the court justified these decisions based on the humanitarian importance of these cases, some public law scholars have argued that there were solid grounds for the court to accept all indigenous cases as a first-instance tribunal, based on a dynamic reading of the constitution. A second obstacle results from the acceptance of the legal capacity of the community to be a part of judicial conflicts related to it. A third one has to do with the language of the proceedings, which is usually Spanish and rarely translated to the indigenous languages. And, finally, there is the obvious problem related to the costs of litigation: hiring a lawyer and attending the sessions in the cities where the tribunals are located are expensive. So long as the state does not get involved in guaranteeing that indigenous peoples have sufficient resources to access the judicial system, their rights will not be entirely respected.

A pluralist constitution

In this last section, we will try to combine the conclusions drawn from the two previous ones. Hence, we will employ the constitutional mandates described at the beginning of this chapter to illuminate some alternatives available for the state in order to overcome some of the most important challenges presented above. Once again, we will divide the analysis into two parts: specific, institutional reforms on the one hand, and conceptual discussions on the other.

Institutional solutions

As it was noted throughout this chapter, the implementation gap between rights and realities is still one of the central nodes of the difficulties of configuring a different state. Even if there is certain progress—it would be absurd to deny that—these rights have not been able to change a matrix that has remained unaltered since the nineteenth century. The purpose of this section is to take a look at some of the reforms that would be needed as a result of these new, enhanced obligations to protect the rights of indigenous peoples. The aim is to show, first, that the rights discourse must be accompanied by specific institutional amendments in order to assure their fulfillment, and, secondly, that there are realist and viable alternatives to perform those reforms. In particular, we will look at the fulfillment of two types of rights: first, political rights, and, secondly, rights of access to justice.

Political rights

In terms of political rights, the case law of the Inter-American Court of Human Rights—which is now constitutive of the constitutional bloc of many Latin American countries—demands that states modify their structures in order to allow for the consultation, participation, and representation of indigenous peoples.

Firstly, the obligations of consultation and participation—as explained by the Inter-American Court in *Saramaka v. Suriname*[55] and *Sarayaku v. Ecuador*[56]—require significant institutional reform. Currently, the discussions on this topic have to do with the precise delimitation of the actual procedure for consultations. Even if there is abundant material regarding this particular issue, it is important to point out that a “consultation protocol” should be elaborated in order to standardize the conditions for the exercise of the right. According to a document elaborated by activists in indigenous rights, this protocol should include eight conditions:[57] a) consultation must be previous to the adoption of the measure in question; b) it must be mandatory; c) it should be carried out with good faith; d) the will of the indigenous communities should be expressed freely, without any sort of coercion; e) the state must provide adequate information regarding the consequences of the measure consulted; f) there must be a measure of cultural adaptation, in order to respect the traditional decision-making methods of the communities; g) it must be sufficient, allowing for diverse voices within the indigenous communities; and h) the state must guarantee accessibility, i.e., the budgetary and logistic resources to allow the participation of the indigenous peoples consulted.

Secondly, states should consider reforms in order to guarantee the right to representation of indigenous peoples, which can be derived from the court's decision in *Yatama v. Nicaragua.*[58] A way of complying with this right could consist of, for example, facilitating indigenous representation within national and local parliaments. The idea would be to establish a minimum quota of indigenous peoples in the lists of candidates to parliamentary positions, such as the one that currently exists for women.[59] The debates that would be generated by the mere fact of having indigenous representatives in Congress would make their problems visible and would raise the level of discussion of legislators, by including topics and positions that are now excluded from the deliberation. A similar measure was implemented in both Bolivia and Colombia, with some success. Another, more modest, way of enhancing the debate on indigenous affairs in Congress would be to create a specific congressional commission to discuss those issues that might affect these peoples. With this, the congressmen and women who would participate in the commission would be able to give particular consideration to these affairs, and to establish an intercultural dialogue with indigenous representatives who should be allowed to attend those sessions relevant to their communities.

Access to justice

Even if the right to access to justice is universal, and not solely applicable to indigenous peoples, the new obligations established in the constitutional bloc demand that the state give special consideration to the fulfillment of rights such as this one in the case of these communities. In order to comply with this mandate, two reforms might be needed.

The first consists of creating instances of respect towards the indigenous worldview within the current judicial system. The general idea is that the state has an obligation to instrument those procedures that are necessary to overcome the obstacles that might be created by the interaction of different cultures. In particular, this could be implemented with six specific policies. Firstly, it is very important that the state assure the existence of translation services, allowing indigenous peoples to be tried in their native tongues.[60] Secondly, it would be interesting to enhance the participation of indigenous individuals as members of judicial courts, specifically those involved in dealing with affairs related to their communities. Thirdly, the state should create public defenders' offices specializing in indigenous affairs, such as those successfully established in Chile and Guatemala. Fourthly, the communities, as collective subjects, should be allowed to take part in those cases that are relevant to them. Fifthly, judges should have an obligation to consult experts on indigenous affairs (be they anthropologists, sociologists, etc.) before making decisions that affect them, in order to ensure that they are knowledgeable of the particular culture of the community. Finally, since prisons are particularly hostile to indigenous individuals, the state should try to find alternatives to the loss of liberty as a way to reprehend criminal offenses committed by members of the communities.

The second measure that could bc taken requires some bolder changes in the current structure of the judicial system, in order to allow indigenous communities to establish and enforce their own systems of justice. The purpose, in this case, would not be to create "syncretisms" or hybrid cultures,[61] where there is one predominant culture and a subordinate culture. On the contrary, the idea would be to make efforts to create genuine dialogues between different cultures that privilege the respect for different worldviews, spiritualities, and ways to solve conflicts. With this purpose, the recognition by the state of indigenous justice mechanisms could be seen as a way of respecting their self-determination and of allowing them to strengthen their identities.

In order to achieve this acknowledgment, there are two challenges that must be overcome. The first consists of the coordination between state justice and indigenous justice. This could be performed with a specific law, as it has happened in the case of Bolivia, or directly, without a statute, as a result of the interpretation of the ILO Convention 169 and the United Nations Declaration.[62] The second challenge is the compatibility of these systems with international human rights commitments by the state. Just as it happens with an ordinary judicial system, the indigenous system should also be bounded by the fundamental rights of human beings, albeit interpreted interculturally. As has been stated by the Constitutional Court of Colombia in a famous decision, "the minimum limits which must be complied with by the indigenous authorities in the exercise of their jurisdictional functions respond, according to the court, to an intercultural consensus on what is really intolerable, as it infringes the most precious goods of man."[63] There are several institutional mechanisms that could be put in force to ensure these systems' compliance with international human rights law. Perhaps the most interesting proposal is that put forward by Raquel Yrigoyen Fajardo,[64] of creating a jury of both lay members of the communities and judges, where an intercultural dialogue can achieve a fair solution regarding the specificities of the case. This does not mean to ignore the fact that alternatives such as these are hard to implement, or that their development can require a long process; however, it might be one of the paths we must go through if we want to achieve a genuinely intercultural state.

Conceptual solutions: legal pluralism

These institutional solutions might be helpful in order to get closer to an ideal situation of respect for the rights of indigenous peoples. However, this will be impossible unless we modify the nature of the constitutional matrix, i.e. a wider change that includes some conceptual change beyond mere institutional reform.

The main conceptual problem in this regard is that the traditional structure of the state—monist in nature—has shown considerable difficulties to resolve the "range of complex legal problems"[65] created by the factual superposition of different legal systems in the same geopolitical space. For instance, the rules of the state are usually incapable of "decid[ing] when a subgroup's law applies to a particular transaction or conflict, to what group particular individuals belong, how a person can change which law is applicable to him or her,"[66] etc.

In order to solve these empirical problems, theorists have proposed alternative ways of thinking about the relation of different systems of law, in a set of theories that have been labeled "legal pluralism." This school of thought does not find its roots in theoretical abstractions but rather, on the contrary, in the pressing necessity for practical answers. The idea is to abandon the monist conception of the state, where state is equated to nation, and to admit that there can be, for instance, a state with multiple nations. There is also a rupture in the classical conception that the legislative power of the state is the only legitimate mechanism for the production of rules. Hence, the normative production located, for example, within indigenous peoples is considered legitimate as well. In sum, the adoption of ideas of legal pluralism produces a radical change in the conformation of modern states.

As we have suggested throughout the chapter, in order to be successful, the concept of legal pluralism must prevail in three different—but strongly interrelated—fields. Firstly, it must pervade the institutional structure of the state: it must appear in the distribution of functions of the different government agencies, and it must be present in the tasks carried out by every public officer. Secondly, it must achieve a certain degree of cultural hegemony: it has to become the most powerful interpretation of the wording of the constitution. And thirdly—and, to a certain degree, as a result of the previous two—it must change the constitutional matrix of the state. These are the tasks ahead of us to achieve the effective protection of the rights of indigenous peoples in Latin America.

Questions

a What is the purpose of referring to a "constitutional matrix" when analyzing the development of constitutional law? What is the appropriate way to determine whether that matrix has actually changed? Has the Latin American constitutional matrix really remained unaltered over the past 200 years? What elements could be mentioned for and against such a claim?

b The Inter-American Court of Human Rights recognized the rights of indigenous peoples to consultation, participation, and representation. Are these rights somehow different from those acknowledged by the "internal side" of the Argentinian constitutional bloc (to take an example whose constitutional provision is explained in the chapter)? If not, is the Inter-American System of Human Rights's case law still important?

c In this chapter we mention two different sorts of difficulties for the protection of the rights of indigenous peoples: institutional and conceptual. Is there really a difference between the two? If so, can they be resolved separately?

d According to the Constitutional Court of Colombia, the independent systems of indigenous justice should still respect a minimum set of basic human rights when making its decisions. Is it possible to accommodate both systems? If so, is it useful to establish standards beforehand? Which human rights should be included and excluded from those standards?

Notes

* Most of the ideas contained in this chapter were part of Silvina Ramírez's doctoral thesis at the University of Buenos Aires Law School.

1 For some general reference, see, for example. Osvaldo Bayer (coord.), HISTORIA DE LA CRUELDAD ARGENTINA. JULIO A. ROCA Y EL GENOCIDIO DE LOS PUEBLOS ORIGINARIOS (2011).

2 Gargarella mentions the constitutions of Argentina (1853), Mexico (1857), Peru (1860), Uruguay (1830), Chile (1833), and Paraguay (1870) in ROBERTO GARGARELLA, LATIN AMERICAN CONSTITUTIONALISM, 1810–2010: THE ENGINE ROOM OF THE CONSTITUTION 32 (2013).

3 Ibid., 198.

4 As explained by Charles Beitz, collective rights can be understood as constituted by individual rights: "It is important to see that a value can have a collective dimension without being non individualistic. The value of self-determination, for example, has a collective dimension because its importance to the individuals who enjoy (or wish to enjoy) it cannot be explained without reference to their group membership, but it is still an individualistic value: it is a value for the individuals who enjoy it. The same is true of whatever rights there are to cultural membership and participation." CHARLES BEITZ, THE IDEA OF HUMAN RIGHTS 113 (2009).

5 Raquel Yrigoyen, *A los veinte años del Convenio 169 de la OIT: Balance y retos de implementación de los derechos de los pueblos indígenas en Latinoamérica*, in Pueblos indígenas. Constituciones y Reformas Políticas en América Latina, at 31–7 (Raquel Yrigoyen ed., 2012).

6 The Canadian constitution of 1982 could be added to this group, if we were to consider the whole continent and not just Latin America.

7 See, for example, Thomas Carothers, *The Many Agendas of Rule of Law Reform in Latin America*, in Rule of Law in Latin America: The International Promotion of Judicial Reform (P. Domingo and Rachel Sieder eds, 2001).

8 Constitución Política de la República de Guatemala (Political Constitution of the Republic of Guatemala), 1985, Articles 67 and 68, available in English at www.right2info.org/resources/publications/laws-1/guatemala_constitution_eng.

9 Raquel Yrigoyen, *Reconocimiento constitucional del derecho indígena y la jurisdicción especial en los países andinos (Colombia, Perú, Bolivia, Ecuador)*, 4 Revista Pena y Estado: Justicia Penal y Comunidades indígenas, 129–40 (2000).

10 Constitución de la Nación Argentina (Constitution of Argentina), August 22, 1994, Article 75, available in English at http://pdba.georgetown.edu/Constitutions/Argentina/argen94_e.html#title1firstdivisionch4.

11 See, for example: Gregorio Badeni, Tratado de Derecho Constitucional 500 (2006); Néstor Sagües, Manual de Derecho Constitucional 772–5 (2007); Miguel Ángel Ekmekdjian, Tratado de Derecho Constitucional 529–31 (1999).

12 Constitución del Ecuador (Constitution of Ecuador), October 20, 2008, Article 6, available in English at http://pdba.georgetown.edu/Constitutions/Ecuador/english08.html.

13 Roberto Gargarella, *Dificultad, Inutilidad y necesidad de la Reforma Constitucional*, in Teoría y Crítica del Derecho Constitucional, at 529–30 (Roberto Gargarella coord., 2008).

14 See "A Pluralist Constitution" below.

15 Supreme Court of Mexico, Amparo directo en revisión 1464/2013, November 13, 2013.

16 Convention 169 is particularly important to the Latin American region. In fact, out of the 22 states that have ratified the convention to this date, 15 are Latin American. The ILO was the first international organization to legislate on the rights of indigenous peoples because they were a big part of the work force and were then visualized as "workers in a special situation of vulnerability."

17 United Nations Declaration on the Rights of Indigenous Peoples, UN Doc. A/RES/61/295, September 13, 2007.

18 See: Claire Charters and Rodolfo Stavenhagen (eds), El Desafío de la Declaración. Historia y futuro de la declaración de la ONU sobre Pueblos (2010); and Augusto Willemsen-Díaz, *Cómo llegaron los derechos de los pueblos indígenas a la ONU*, and Adelfo Regino Montes and Gustavo Torres Cisneros, *La Declaración de las Naciones Unidas sobre los Derechos de los Pueblos Indígenas: base de la nueva relación entre los pueblos indígenas, los Estados y las sociedades*, in El desafío de la Declaración. Historia y futuro de la Declaración de la ONU sobre Pueblos Indígenas (Claire Charters and Rodolfo Stavenhagen eds, 2010).

19 See Augusto Willemsen-Díaz, *Cómo llegaron los derechos de los pueblos indígenas a la ONU*, in El desafío de la Declaración. Historia y futuro de la Declaración de la ONU sobre Pueblos Indígenas, at 16–31 (Claire Charters and Rodolfo Stavenhagen eds, 2010).

20 Inter-American Court of Human Rights, case of "The Mayagna (Sumo) Awas Tingni Community v. Nicaragua." Merits, Reparations and Costs, August 31, 2001.

21 Furthermore, this delay added up to that required by the process before the different instances of the system, which meant that the situation had been brought to the attention of the Inter-American Commission back in 1995.

22 See the Inter-American Court of Human Rights, case of "Aboriginal Community Of Lhaka Honhat ('Our Land') v. Argentina," Report No. 78/06, Petition 12,094, Admissibility, October 21, 2006.

23 Inter-American Court of Human Rights, case of "Sawhoyamaxa Indigenous Community v. Paraguay," Merits, Reparations, and Costs, March 29, 2006, paragraph 117.

24 Inter-American Court of Human Rights, case of "Saramaka People v. Suriname," Preliminary Objections, Merits, Reparations, and Costs, November 28, 2007, paragraph 91.

25 Inter-American Court of Human Rights, case of "The Mayagna (Sumo) Awas Tingni Community v. Nicaragua." Merits, Reparations, and Costs, August 31, 2001, paragraph 149.

26 Inter-American Court of Human Rights, case of "Saramaka People v. Suriname," Preliminary Objections, Merits, Reparations, and Costs, November 28, 2007, paragraph 16.

27 Inter-American Court of Human Rights, case of "Kichwa Indigenous People of Sarayaku v. Ecuador." Merits and Reparations, June 27, 2012.
28 Inter-American Court of Human Rights, case of "Saramaka People v. Suriname," Preliminary Objections, Merits, Reparations, and Costs, November 28, 2007, paragraph 194.d.
29 Inter-American Commission on Human Rights, "Application to the Inter-American Court of Human Rights in the case of Kichwa People of Sarayaku and its members (Case 12,465) against Ecuador," April 26, 2010, paragraph 143.
30 Inter-American Court of Human Rights, case of "Saramaka People v. Suriname," Preliminary Objections, Merits, Reparations, and Costs, November 28, 2007, paragraph 134.
31 "Indigenous and Tribal Peoples' Rights over their Ancestral Lands and Natural Resources, Norms, and Jurisprudence of the Inter-American Human Rights System," OEA/Ser.L/V/II. Document 56/09, December 30, 2009, paragraph 333.
32 Inter-American Court of Human Rights, case of "Kichwa Indigenous People of Sarayaku v. Ecuador," Merits and Reparations, June 27, 2012. Series C No. 245, paragraphs 159 and 160.
33 Inter-American Court of Human Rights, case of "Yatama v. Nicaragua," Preliminary Objections, Merits, Reparations, and Costs, June 23, 2005. Series C No. 127, paragraph 225.
34 Gregorio Badeni, Tratado de Derecho Constitucional 500 (2006). For similar remarks, see Néstor Sagües, Manual de Derecho Constitucional 772–5 (2007); Miguel Ángel Ekmekdjian, Tratado de Derecho Constitucional 529–31 (1999).
35 See Alberto Binder, *La cultura jurídica entre la tradición y la innovación*, in Los actores de la justicia latinoamericana, at 38 (Luis Pásara ed., 2007).
36 Law 23,302, passed in 1989.
37 Chaco Province Judicial Administrative Appellate Court, sitting at Resistencia City, case of "Consejo Qompi-Lqataxac Nam Qompi v. Provincia del Chaco," April 21, 2006.
38 Ibid.
39 See Ana María Spadafora, Mariana Gómez, and Marina Matarrese, *Rumbos y laberintos de la política étnica: organizaciones unificadas y faccionalismos indígenas en la provincia de Formosa (pilagá y toba)*, in Movilizaciones indígenas e identidades en disputa en la Argentina, at 252–4 (G. Gordillo and S. Hirsch eds, 2010).
40 Córdoba Civil and Commercial Court, case of "Vera de Casih, Blanca S. v. Casih, Carlos E," September 11, 2006.
41 Ibid.
42 We could mention five of them: a) the Public Defender's Office, b) the Ombudsman's Office, c) the Human Rights Secretariat, d) the Environmental Secretariat, dependent on the Chief of Cabinet, and e) the National Institute against Discrimination, Xenophobia and Racism (INADI), also dependent on the Ministry of Justice and Human Rights.
43 See Aiser Martínez de Bringas, *Las políticas interculturales ante el reto de los derechos de los pueblos indígenas*, 33 Revista Internacional de Filosofía Política, Justicia Intercultural, 103–24 (2009).
44 The bright side of this institutional design is that, if certain public officials are disrespectful of indigenous rights, the communities have an actual chance of trying to enforce their liberties recurring to other officials. However, the solution for the problem of the unwilling officer should not be this fragmentation, but an adequate institutional architecture that allows for some review of the unconstitutional decisions made by these officers.
45 Despite the deficiencies in the constitutional technique that led to these rights being protected in an article devoted to the functions of Congress.
46 Neuquén Province Higher Court, "Caso Comunidad Mapuche Mellao Morales v. Corporación Minera del Neuquén", Resolución Interlocutoria 6943/09, September 29, 2009. In this case, a mining company was given permission to look for and extract natural resources within a territory that belonged to an indigenous community which had not been consulted. The Superior Tribunal of Justice of the Province of Neuquén decided to forbid the mining activities until the rights of the community had been complied with.
47 Chaco Province Judicial Administrative Appellate Court, "Consejo Quompi—Lqataxac Nam Qompi v. Provincia del Chaco", April 21, 2006. In this case, the Province of Chaco had created a registry of indigenous communities, without any sort of participation of indigenous representatives. The judge declared that the statute creating the registry was unconstitutional.
48 District Court No. 2, Secretary No. 4, Bariloche, "Palma Arturo y Ñancunao Mirta s/ usurpación", Expte. N S.4–10–224, Decision of September 6, 2011. In this case, a company was about to build

touristic cabins within a forest that was spiritually important for a nearby indigenous community. Some of the members of the community closed a local road in order to protest against the undertaking. The judge consulted an anthropologist, who presented a report on the relevance of the forest for the community, and decided to exonerate the protesters.

49 Appeals Court on Civil, Commercial, Labour, and Mining Matters, Zapala City, "Comunidad Mapuche Paichil Antriao v. Provincia de Neuquén s/acción de amparo", Decision of October 12, 2004. In this case, a judge decided to evict an indigenous community without even allowing it to be a party to the case.

50 Id.

51 The request was based on the situation of helplessness that the communities were facing, that would lead them to a slow but inexorable extermination.

52 Supreme Court of Argentina, case of "Defensor del Pueblo de la Nación v. Estado Nacional y otra (Provincia del Chaco)," September 18, 2007.

53 Supreme Court of Argentina, "Comunidad Indígena Toba La Primavera—Novogoh c. Provincia de Formosa y otros s/medida cautelar", AR/JUR/49171/2013, Decision of March 9, 2013

54 Supreme Court of Justice of Argentina, "Comunidad Aborigen de Santuario Tres Pozos otros el Jujuy, Provincia de otros s/ amparo", Expte. C. 1196. XLVI., Decision of December 18, 2012.

55 Inter-American Court of Human Rights, case of "Saramaka People v. Suriname," Interpretation of the Judgment of Preliminary Objections, Merits, Reparations, and Costs, August 12, 2008, paragraph 16; Inter-American Court of Human Rights, case of "Saramaka People v. Suriname," Preliminary Objections, Merits, Reparations, and Costs, November 28, 2007, paragraph 194(c).

56 Inter-American Court of Human Rights, case of "*Kichwa Indigenous People of Sarayaku v. Ecuador*," Merits and Reparations, June 27, 2012.

57 Document elaborated by the "Grupo de Apoyo jurídico para el acceso a la tierra" (GAJAT) and the "Centro de incidencia y análisis politico" (CIAP), both members of the "Centro de Políticas Públicas para el Socialismo (CEPPAS)."

58 Inter-American Court of Human Rights, case of "Yatama v. Nicaragua," Preliminary Objections, Merits, Reparations, and Costs, June 23, 2005, paragraph 225.

59 See Marcela Rodríguez, *Igualdad, Democracia y Acciones Positivas*, in TEORÍA Y CRÍTICA DEL DERECHO CONSTITUCIONAL (Roberto Gargarella coord., 2009).

60 See Saqutiw Jesús Gómez (coord.), DEL MONISMO AL PLURALISMO JURÍDICO EN GUATEMALA. COMPENDIO SOBRE PAUTAS DE COORDINACIÓN ENTRE DERECHO MAYA Y DERECHO ESTATAL 160 (2003).

61 See RACHEL SIEDER AND CARLOS FLORES, DOS JUSTICIAS: COORDINACIÓN INTERLEGAL E INTERCULTURAL EN GUATEMALA 22 (2012).

62 In any event, there are three broad jurisdictional issues that must be solved: a) the scope of the personal jurisdiction, i.e. the cases of which individuals will be resolved by the communities' justice system; b) the scope of the material jurisdiction, i.e. which kinds of conflicts should be solved by each judicial system; and c) the scope of the territorial jurisdiction, i.e. whether the actual location of the event under judicial scrutiny is relevant to determine which judge will hear the case. The determination of these standards should be the result of an open and genuine dialogue between the communities and the state.

63 Colombian Constitutional Court, Decision T-523/97, October 15, 1997.

64 See RAQUEL YRIGOYEN, PAUTAS DE COORDINACIÓN ENTRE EL DERECHO INDÍGENA Y EL DERECHO ESTATAL (1999).

65 Sally Engle Merry, *Legal Pluralism*, 22/5 LAW & SOCIETY REVIEW, 869–96, 871 (1988).

66 Ibid.

References

GREGORIO BADENI, TRATADO DE DERECHO CONSTITUCIONAL (2006).

Osvaldo Bayer (coord.), HISTORIA DE LA CRUELDAD ARGENTINA. JULIO A. ROCA Y EL GENOCIDIO DE LOS PUEBLOS ORIGINARIOS (2011).

CHARLES BEITZ, THE IDEA OF HUMAN RIGHTS (2009).

Alberto Binder, *La cultura jurídica entre la tradición y la innovación*, in LOS ACTORES DE LA JUSTICIA LATINOAMERICANA, at 38 (Luis Pásara ed., 2007).

Thomas Carothers, *The Many Agendas of Rule of Law Reform in Latin America*, in RULE OF LAW IN LATIN AMERICA: THE INTERNATIONAL PROMOTION OF JUDICIAL REFORM (P. Domingo and Rachel Sieder eds, 2001).

Claire Charters and Rodolfo Stavenhagen (eds), El Desafío de la Declaración. Historia y futuro de la declaración de la ONU sobre Pueblos (2010).

Miguel Ángel Ekmekdjian, Tratado de Derecho Constitucional (1999).

Roberto Gargarella, *Dificultad, Inutilidad y necesidad de la Reforma Constitucional*, in Teoría y Crítica del Derecho Constitucional (Roberto Gargarella coord., 2008).

Roberto Gargarella, Latin American Constitutionalism, 1810–2010: The Engine Room of the Constitution (2013).

Inter-American Commission on Human Rights, "Aboriginal Community of Lhaka Honhat ('Our Land') v. Argentina." Report, No. 78/06, Petition 12,094, Admissibility," October 21, 2006.

Inter-American Commission on Human Rights, "Application to the Inter-American Court of Human Rights in the case of Kichwa People of Sarayaku and its members (Case 12,465) against Ecuador," April 26, 2010.

Inter-American Commission on Human Rights, "Indigenous and Tribal Peoples' Rights over their Ancestral Lands and Natural Resources, Norms and Jurisprudence of the Inter-American Human Rights System." OEA/Ser.L/V/II. Doc. 56/09, December 30, 2009.

Aiser Martínez de Bringas, *Las políticas interculturales ante el reto de los derechos de los pueblos indígenas*, 33 Revista Internacional de Filosofía Política, Justicia Intercultural, 103–24 (2009).

Sally Engle Merry, *Legal Pluralism*, 22/5 Law & Society Review, 869–96 (1988).

Saqutiw Jesús Gómez (coord.), Del Monismo al Pluralismo Jurídico en Guatemala. Compendio sobre pautas de coordinación entre Derecho Maya y Derecho Estatal (2003).

Adelfo Regino Montes and Gustavo Torres Cisneros, *La Declaración de las Naciones Unidas sobre los Derechos de los Pueblos Indígenas: base de la nueva relación entre los pueblos indígenas, los Estados y las sociedades*, in El desafío de la Declaración. Historia y futuro de la Declaración de la ONU sobre Pueblos Indígenas (Claire Charters and Rodolfo Stavenhagen eds, 2010).

Marcela Rodríguez, *Igualdad, Democracia y Acciones Positivas*, in Teoría y Crítica del Derecho Constitucional (Roberto Gargarella coord., 2009).

Néstor Sagües, Manual de Derecho Constitucional (2007).

Rachel Sieder and Carlos Flores, Dos justicias: coordinación interlegal e intercultural en Guatemala (2012).

Ana María Spadafora, Mariana Gómez, and Marina Matarrese, *Rumbos y laberintos de la política étnica: organizaciones unificadas y faccionalismos indígenas en la provincia de Formosa (pilagá y toba)*, in Movilizaciones indígenas e identidades en disputa en la Argentina, (G. Gordillo and S. Hirsch eds, 2010).

Augusto Willemsen-Díaz, *Cómo llegaron los derechos de los pueblos indígenas a la ONU*, in El desafío de la Declaración. Historia y futuro de la Declaración de la ONU sobre Pueblos Indígenas (Claire Charters and Rodolfo Stavenhagen eds, 2010).

Raquel Yrigoyen, Pautas de coordinación entre el derecho indígena y el derecho estatal (1999).

Raquel Yrigoyen, *Reconocimiento constitucional del derecho indígena y la jurisdicción especial en los países andinos (Colombia, Perú, Bolivia, Ecuador)*, 4 Revista Pena y Estado: Justicia Penal y Comunidades indígenas, 129–40 (2000).

Raquel Yrigoyen, *A los veinte años del Convenio 169 de la OIT: Balance y retos de implementación de los derechos de los pueblos indígenas en Latinoamérica*, in Pueblos indígenas. Constituciones y Reformas Políticas en América Latina, at 31–7 (Raquel Yrigoyen ed., 2012).

Further reading

Bruno Baronnet, Mariana Mora and Richard Stahler-Sholk, Luchas "muy otras." Zapatismo y autonomía en las comunidades indígenas de Chiapas (2011).

Miguel Angel Benedetti, *Algo más que reubicar y reescribir un inciso de la Constitución*, in La Constitución en 2020, 48 propuestas para una sociedad igualitaria (Roberto Gargarella coord., 2011).

Santos Boaventura de Sousa, Refundación del Estado en América Latina. Perspectivas desde una epistemología del sur (2010).

Santos Boaventura de Sousa, *Cuando los excluidos tienen derecho: justicia indígena, plurinacionalidad e interculturalidad*, in Justicia indígena, plurinacionalidad e interculturalidad en Bolivia (Santos Boaventura de Sousa and Jose Luis Exeni, 2012).

Inter-American Commission on Human Rights, Derechos de los Pueblos indígenas y tribales sobre sus tierras ancestrales y recursos naturales. Normas y jurisprudencia del sistema Interamericano de Derechos Humanos (2009).

Héctor Díaz-Polanco, Elogio de la Diversidad. Globalización, multiculturalismo y etnofagia (2006).

Silvina Ramírez, *Igualdad como Emancipación: los Derechos Fundamentales de los Pueblos indígenas*, in El Derecho a la Igualdad, aportes para un Constitucionalismo Igualitario (Alegre Marcelo and Gargarella Roberto coords, 2012).

Rachel Sieder, Multiculturalism in Latin America: indigenous rights, diversity and democracy (2002).

Rodrigo Uprimny Yepes, *Modernización del Estado y reformas constitucionales en América Latina: encuentros y desencuentros*, in Los Procesos de control estratégico como pilares de la modernización del Estado (VV.AA., 2007).

11 Constitutional limits on the power of the executive

Agustín Grijalva, Elsa Guerra Rodríguez, and Dunia Martínez Molina[*]

This chapter examines how states of emergency, referendums, and reelections influence presidents' power in several countries in Latin America, and the role courts have had on this subject matter. This is analyzed through a comparative and critical study of several examples of constitutional case law from a host of Latin American countries. The limits of the power of presidents, as heads of the executive branches, and the presidents' relationship with legislatures and judiciaries, are an ongoing discussion in constitutional law and political studies, especially in Latin America. This discussion intensified after the start of a wave of new constitutions and constitutional reforms in the 1980s in several Latin American countries. The debate revolves around whether, when concentrating power, the president undermines the rule of law or whether, to the contrary, strong leadership is essential for promoting urgent social changes in the region.

Many of the new constitutions enacted in Latin America have strengthened the power of presidents while extending and broadening the bill of rights. As we will see, the growth of presidential power has been expressed in various ways. This includes the scope of the presidents' authority to declare states of emergency, to carry out legal and constitutional reforms, and to institute or enhance his or her capacity to be reelected.

This chapter discusses three institutions that directly relate to this issue: a) states of emergency; b) referendums; and c) presidential reelection. If misused, these three institutions can lead to a strong concentration of power in the executive and even to the violation of both citizens' rights and the separation of powers. Hence, they are usually subject to constitutional review.

The executive and states of emergency

States of emergency are legal or political institutions that allow a country's executive branch to implement measures of constitutional exception when extraordinary, serious, and imminent circumstances arise that cannot be resolved by resorting to the ordinary legal framework.[1] Among other things, these circumstances involve economic, institutional, and social emergencies, armed conflicts, or natural disasters. However, governments can be abusive in their resort to emergency powers. For example, when Peru, Colombia, and Ecuador underwent serious political instability, it served as an excuse for the implementation of several longstanding states of emergency.

In Peru, there were profound human rights violations resulting from the implementation of states of emergency, many of which were aimed at eliminating subversive groups such as "Sendero Luminoso" ("Shining Path"). The internal persecution increased significantly between 1983 and 1985, during the administration of Fernando Belaunde Terry, and continued through Alberto Fujimori's regime in the 1990s. The abuse of the state of emergency declaration was such that ". . . in the mid-1990s, 65 provinces and one district were in a state of emergency."[2] Episodes such as this have revealed the need to establish mechanisms for limiting states of emergency in order to endow them with a certain degree of legitimacy. These mechanisms stem from both the states' own legislation and international human rights law.

Limits to states of emergency within the laws of each state

Each country has imposed regulatory limits on states of emergency, some of them based on international human rights instruments, by setting ". . . minimum requirements for, on the one hand, the demonstration and implementation of extraordinary measures by states in exercise of their sovereignty, and, on the other, preventing arbitrariness and abuse arising from the measures imposed to avert a crisis."[3]

Latin American states have opted for one of two ways to examine the constitutionality of decrees declaring or regulating states of emergency:

- Judicial review of states of emergency triggered by plaintiff action. This type of review is enabled through writs of *amparo*[4] or similar writs when, in a particular case, the court finds a violation of a fundamental right after the implementation of a state of emergency. Another example is abstract judicial review of a constitutional claim submitted by citizens against a state of emergency decree. These systems, with some variation, are found in countries like Bolivia, Argentina, Guatemala, Brazil, Paraguay, Chile, Uruguay, Costa Rica, El Salvador, Panama, and Mexico, among others.
- Immediate and *ex officio* judicial review of states of emergency. This review is automatically conducted by the constitutional review body after a state of emergency is declared by the executive. The aim is to restrict any unnecessary or unlawful manipulation of the measure on behalf of the executive and, thus, to safeguard the effective exercise of fundamental rights from arbitrariness.

Countries like Venezuela, Ecuador, and Colombia have established in their constitutions the *ex officio* judicial review of decrees of states of emergency, yet courts in Venezuela and Ecuador have not effectively conducted such a review. However, the Constitutional Court of Colombia[5] has contributed with a singular model of judicial review in Latin America.[6]

An example among many of how the Constitutional Court of Colombia has rigorously implemented judicial review of states of emergencies can be found in the grounds of its ruling in Decision C-070/09 of 2009 regarding the Decreto Declaratorio de Estado de Conmoción Interior No. 3,929 (Declaratory Act of State of Internal Commotion No. 3,929). Based on arguments contained in Decision No. C-820/02, the court elaborately analyzed the constitutionality of the measure in question (a strike by public employees) and issued a ruling that limited the excessive use of emergency declarations through a comprehensive and objective review of compliance with constitutional principles.

The event that led to the Declaratory Act was a strike by public employees in the judiciary, which had brought it almost to a halt. The conflict began in 2006, when employees and officials of the judicial council went on strike to protest the gap in salaries within the judiciary. This measure suspended much of the judicial activity for 37 days, which, according to presidential Decree No. 3,929 from October 9, 2008, caused the following damage:

> The National Police . . . indicates that in the last 35 days over 2,720 people, arrested for the commission of crimes such as homicide, aggression, theft, and drug trafficking, amongst others, have been released, causing a great harm to the common good, the public order, state security and the social harmony . . .
>
> [T]he judiciary has over 120,751 pending lawsuits, 36,986 pending *tutela* decisions, and 25,284 pending hearings . . .[7]

When conducting its review, the Constitutional Court first said that the decree satisfied the procedural requirements linked to the principles of territoriality, temporality, and legality.[8] The court then intended to verify whether the judicial gridlock and cessation of judicial activities gravely and imminently reverberated on the administration of justice. To conduct this substantive review, the Colombian court resorted to a three-prong test.[9]

The first level consisted of a factual determination of the occurrence of the events alleged in the decree. The court was satisfied that most of the events alleged in the decree had actually happened:

> . . . the government proved in an objective and verifiable manner the occurrence of the majority of the alleged factual conditions: the congestion of courts, the abnormal suspension of activity that lasted 37 days, and the various effects of this suspension . . . The verification of these facts allows us to continue with the constitutional examination of the declaratory decree of internal commotion.[10]

The second level consisted of an evaluation to determine both the gravity and imminence of the situation that led to the declaratory act and its importance for restoring institutional stability, state security and peaceful coexistence, whereby the court ruled that:

> . . . the government failed to meet the minimum assessment required by the constitution and the Statutory Law on States of Emergency concerning the serious and extraordinary nature of those facts, and its likelihood of disturbing public order.[11]

According to the court, this resulted in an arbitrary use of the power to declare states of emergency by the president, due to the failure to objectively prove the gravity and imminence of the events contained in the declaratory action.

The court went on to analyze the third level, which consisted of assessing whether the ordinary faculties of the police were insufficient to confront the situation. The Constitutional Court ruled that the executive ultimately manipulated the power to declare states of emergency.

> . . . In the preamble of Decree 3,929 the executive only states that the ordinary powers of the police are insufficient to keep criminals in jail and to solve the grave perturbation created by the judicial paralysis, as well as the necessity to include in the National Budget new expenses . . . for solving the crisis. These affirmations do not constitute an assessment by the national government on the police powers at its disposal and their precariousness for addressing these grave circumstances originated by the strike, but are only an assertion of the insufficiency of those police powers.[12]

Based on these arguments, the Constitutional Court of Colombia struck down the decree, limiting the power of the government to use this mechanism only for times when such conflict cannot be resolved with ordinary legal devices. The court also reminded the executive of its duty to bear the burden of argumentation, based on verifiable data, in compliance with the procedural and substantive provisions for the measure to be constitutional. Although parts of the ruling can be subject to criticism, the ruling constitutes a more rigorous review than others regarding similar claims by the executive.

An example of a less rigorous review can be found in Ecuador. There, despite having a constitution that seeks to uphold human rights by limiting the manipulation of states of emergency through "*ex officio* and immediate" judicial review,[13] its main review body has most likely failed to ensure proper use of states of emergency by the president. Out of the 21 decrees of states of emergency issued by the president from October 2008 to December 2010, all have been ruled constitutional,[14] though many of them did not seem to comply with the procedural and substantive rules imposed by domestic law and international human rights law. Furthermore, there appeared to be a breach of the principle of temporality. After the first decree, the subsequent decrees were simply a renewal of the former. It is also arguable that the court has failed to conduct the *ex officio* review of all decrees of states of emergency. The Constitutional Court ". . . only ruled on 4 of the 14 decrees, covering only 28 percent of the decrees that were issued."[15] All of these situations denote that there is either loose or poor judicial review of such measures.

Limits to the implementation of states of emergency imposed by international human rights law

International human rights law has attempted, from two related fronts, to prevent human rights violations stemming from an abusive use of states of emergency by the executive: firstly, by establishing boundaries in international human rights instruments and, secondly, by issuing decisions and recommendations through its bodies.

As far as the former is concerned, both the International Covenant on Civil and Political Rights (Article 4) and the American Convention on Human Rights (Article 27) require that the contents of the declaration of states of emergency comply with the principle of inviolability of human rights, as well as with the principles of proclamation, notification, legality, timeliness, territoriality, proportionality, exceptional threat, respect for the provisions of international law, and non-discrimination.[16] As far as the latter is concerned, the Inter-American Court of Human Rights in particular has clearly drawn out the limits of states of emergency. In its Advisory Opinion OC 09/87, the court said that:

> . . . the judicial guarantees essential for the protection of the human rights not subject to derogation, according to Article 27(2) of the Convention, are those to which the Convention expressly refers in Articles 7(6) [*habeas corpus*] and 25(1) [any effective remedy before competent judges or tribunals], . . . and also those necessary to the preservation of the rule of law, even during the state of exception that results from the suspension of guarantees.[17]

In the case of *Gómez Paquiyauri Brothers v. Peru*, the court ruled that Peru was internationally responsible for human rights violations stemming from the declaration of a state of emergency:

> 67 e) On the morning of June 21, 1991, Rafael Samuel and Emilio Moisés Gómez Paquiyauri were going to their mother's workplace in the province of El Callao, when they were intercepted and detained by agents of the Peruvian National Police

who were searching for the persons involved in alleged terrorist acts, in the course of implementation of the 'Cerco Noventiuno' plan . . .

67 g) The brothers Rafael Samuel and Emilio Moisés Gómez Paquiyauri were then taken, under police custody, to a place called 'Pampa de los Perros,' where they were beaten with the butt of a shotgun and subsequently shot to death in the head, thorax, and other parts of the body.[18]

According to the court, Peru failed to comply with the obligations outlined in Article 1.1 of the American Convention on Human Rights because, in addition to violating the protection of honor and dignity, the right to personal liberty, judicial guarantees, and judicial protection, the excessive use of the state of emergency infringed intangible rights such as the right to life, personal integrity, the prohibition of torture, and the rights of children,[19] and these rights cannot be suspended in the implementation of a state of emergency.[20] In the case of the violation of the right to personal liberty, the Inter-American Court of Human Rights noted that the suspension of certain rights and/or guarantees must still conform to the principle of necessity and proportionality, requirements that were not met in this case.

The court noted that states have an obligation to develop effective mechanisms for monitoring the implementation of these measures:

> Even though it was argued that, at the time of the facts, there was a state of emergency in the Constitutional Province of El Callao, pursuant to which [the right to personal liberty and safety] had been suspended, the Court has pointed out before that suspension of constitutional liberties cannot exceed what is strictly necessary and that 'any action on the part of the public authorities that goes beyond those limits, which must be specified with precision in the decree promulgating the state of emergency, would also be unlawful.' In this regard, the limitations imposed on acts by the State answer to 'the general requirement that in any state of emergency there be appropriate means to control the measures taken, so that they are proportionate to the needs and do not exceed the strict limits imposed by the Convention or derived from it.' Therefore, the emergency cannot be considered a justification in the face of acts such as those examined here.[21]

Moreover, the court said that:

> Immediate judicial oversight is a measure that tends to avoid arbitrariness or unlawfulness of detentions, taking into account that in a State in which the rule of law prevails, a judge must guarantee the rights of the detainee, authorize adoption of precautionary or coercive measures, when strictly necessary, and generally seek to ensure treatment that is consistent with the presumption of innocence that protects the accused until his responsibility has been established . . .[22]
>
> Regarding the right of every detainee to recourse to a competent judge or court, set forth in Article 7(6) of the Convention, the Court has considered that the "writs of habeas corpus and of 'amparo' are among those judicial remedies that are essential for the protection of various rights whose derogation is prohibited by Article 27(2) and that serve, moreover, to preserve legality in a democratic society."[23]

Finally:

> The Court has stated that torture is strictly forbidden by International Human Rights Law. Prohibition of torture is absolute and non-revocable, even under the most difficult

> circumstances, such as war, the threat of war, 'the struggle against terrorism,' and any other crimes, state of siege or emergency, domestic conflict or upheaval, suspension of constitutional liberties, domestic political instability, or other public calamities or emergencies.[24]

Another example is the Case of *Zambrano Vélez et al. v. Ecuador.* On September 3, 1992, Sixto Durán Ballén, President of the Republic of Ecuador, enacted Executive Order No. 86, which ordered the intervention of the armed forces throughout the country in order to fight crime and "safeguard the security of the persons and of the public and private property."[25] On March 6, 1993, in the midst of an operation in a suburban sector of the city of Guayaquil, members of the armed forces killed Wilmer Zambrano Vélez, Segundo Caicedo Cobeña, and José Caicedo Cobeña. These individuals were said to be members of a subversive group called "Sol Rojo" ("Red Sun").

In addition to determining Ecuador's international responsibility, the Inter-American Court of Human Rights, taking into account Article 27 of the American Convention on Human Rights, held that:

> It is the obligation of the State to determine the reasons and motives that lead the domestic authorities to declare a state of emergency and it is up to these authorities to exercise appropriate and effective control over this situation and to ensure that the suspension decreed is limited 'to the extent and for the period of time strictly required by the exigencies of the situation,' in accordance with the Convention. States do not enjoy unlimited discretion; it is up to the Inter-American system's organs to exercise this control in a subsidiary and complementary manner, within the framework of their respective competences. In this case, the Court analyses the conformity of the State actions within the framework of the obligations enshrined in Article 27 of the Convention, in conjunction with other provisions of the Convention under dispute.[26]

Moreover, the Inter-American Court of Human Rights stressed that states of emergency must conform to the principle of exceptional threat, insomuch as this principle requires states to use a measure of constitutional exception when strictly necessary, that is, when there are serious and imminent events that cannot be resolved under ordinary legal provisions:

> In time of public emergency which threatens the life of the nation and the existence of which is officially proclaimed, the States Parties to the present Covenant may take measures derogating from their obligations under the present Covenant to the extent strictly required by the exigencies of the situation . . .[27]

Other mechanisms of exception from ordinary law used by the executive

Declaring states of emergency is not the only mechanism to which the executive has resorted in several Latin American countries in order to endow itself with emergency powers. Instruments such as "necessity and urgency" decrees and decrees of delegated powers enable the president to increase its faculties and legislate in certain cases. An example of the controversial use of this mechanism of constitutional exception took place in Argentina in December 2001. As a measure to lessen the negative effects of a very prolonged financial crisis,[27] the president issued Decree 1570/2001. The decree stated that, in order to face the economic downturn and avoid a bank run, cash withdrawals from personal accounts would be limited, and that the need for the measure was such that it was impossible to subject it to the legislative process:

> . . . nevertheless, in situations such as the present one, it is possible to limit, for a brief period of time, cash withdrawals and the transference of funds to other countries, which in no way will influence the economy's performance . . .
>
> This eliminates the risk that a financial crisis will affect the system and harm all savers, which will be unequivocally protected by [the law] and the economy in general.[29]

These measures exacerbated the political and social crisis.[30] People affected by this decree sought to legally defend themselves. The position of the Supreme Court of Argentina regarding this measure varied from case to case. In *Carlos Antonio Smith v. Poder Ejecutivo Nacional*, decided on February 1, 2002, the court highlighted the difference between a state of emergency and a state of siege (subject to a stricter regulation). Only in the latter can constitutional guarantees, such as property rights, be suspended. Hence, the limitation and suspension of fundamental rights was found to be unconstitutional.

> The restriction imposed by the state on the regular exercise of property rights must be reasonable and have an established time frame. It has to be a remedy and not a material alteration of the essence of the right acquired either by a ruling or a contract. It is also subject to judicial review, since the state of emergency, as opposed to the state of siege, does not suspend constitutional guarantees.
>
> The right to dispose freely of funds deposited or invested in financial entities derives not from legislation but from the constitution; furthermore, it is clear that by conditioning or limiting this right the intangibility of property is violated and the purpose of obtaining justice is harmed as well. Given the seriousness of this violation and the absence of decisive reasons for that limitation, the rule cannot be construed as a reasonable regulation of those principles and is not in line with Article 28 of the constitution.[31]

However, on October 26, 2004, the court contradicted its decision in *Smith* by dismissing the writ of *amparo* filed by Alberto Roque Bustos and others. The court recognized that the original measure did not result from the explicit powers given to the executive branch in the constitution but that it was rendered valid given the delicate situation of the country and a subsequent series of decisions made by the executive:

> . . . the first steps taken, both in the onset of the severe crisis in the financial system as well as in its critical point, may be subject to censure from a legal standpoint due to the degree of infringement of individual rights, [but. . .] the government gradually adopted measures that allowed the resolution of a crisis of unprecedented proportions . . .
>
> In emergency situations such as the one that has originated the legal rule in question, the imperious necessity of coping with the circumstances justifies a broader interpretation of the constitutional powers attributed to Congress. Against this background, legal solutions or procedures that may be regarded as invalid in normal circumstances tend to survive a constitutionality test. Even if the emergency does not create powers that do not exist, or diminish the restrictions imposed on those previously conferred, it makes it possible to find a reason to sustain those that do exist [Home Building & Loan Association v. Blaisell, 290 U.S. 398, 440/48 [1934]], so that, in the face of extraordinary events, the exercise of the police power constitutionally bestowed in Congress is able to satisfy the

> needs of a deeply disturbed community, and that, if not attended to, would compromise social peace and the general interest, which are among the essential purposes of the state.[32]

Referendums and constitutional reforms

Since the 1980s, there has been a significant increase in the number of referendums and plebiscites in Latin America. Most of these public consultation processes have been driven driven by the incumbent president, although their ostensible objectives and purposes varied from country to country.[33] A significant number of these referendums sought to strengthen the president's powers. The cases of Peru, Colombia, Ecuador, and Venezuela exemplify how the referendum can be used to modify the constitutional order and often even upset the separation of powers. In 1992, Alberto Fujimori, as president of Peru, dissolved Congress and took over the judiciary. Afterwards, he held a referendum to enact a new constitution and legitimize the breakdown of the constitutional order. In Venezuela there were two public consultations in 1999: one on April 25 to convene a Constituent Assembly for drafting a new constitution, and again on December 15 to approve the new constitution drafted by the assembly.

Colombia is an especially interesting case regarding the problematic relationship between referendums and constitutional amendments. One decision announced by the Constitutional Court in 2010, concerning judicial review of a referendum attempting to amend the constitution, stands out.[34] In 2005, the court had held that an amendment authorizing presidential reelection for one term was constitutional. This allowed the popular President Uribe to be reelected.[35] Four years later, an attempt was made through a referendum to pass another amendment allowing for a second presidential reelection. This time around, however, the court halted the process. The court ruled that the law calling a referendum was unconstitutional due to very serious procedural violations but also because, according to the court, presidential reelection for a third term violated and replaced what it saw as essential constitutional principles. The court held that, by transgressing such principles as the separation of powers, equality, and democracy, this reform practically replaced the entire constitution.[36]

In the court's view:

> Of the mechanisms established in Article 374 of the constitution [amendment process], the only one that is not subject to . . . limits is the National Constituent Assembly, whenever it is expressly summoned to enact another constitution. Therefore, a referendum is not the proper way to reform the constitution's original structuring principles.
>
> To sum up, the substitution [of the constitution] implies a direct opposition between the old and the new, to the extent that, under the pretext of the reform, the constitution is transformed into a 'completely different' one that, for example, serves as the basis for a completely different form of political organization, such as abandoning democracy in order to create a dictatorship or a totalitarian regime.
>
> According to what has been stated by this Constitutional Court regarding the substitution of the constitution, this substitution can either be total, when the constitution 'as a whole is replaced by another one,' or partial, when 'a defining trait of the constitution's identity' is 'replaced by an opposite or entirely different trait.' From another point of view, it has also been pointed out that Congress is forbidden from substituting the constitution either in a 'permanent or transitory' way, given that the change, partial or total, cannot be of such a magnitude that it is no longer possible 'to recognize in the constitution the essential elements that define its original identity.'[37]

Thus, even though no single clause of the constitution is beyond amendment, the depth of this amendment cannot be such that the constitution is replaced by a different constitution. Particularly, the court said, when the attempt was made through a referendum, not a constitutional assembly. The court added:

> In the contemporary world, because of the development of democratic principles and of the concept of popular sovereignty, the constituent power belongs to the people, who have and keep the power to give themselves a constitution. This original constituent power has no legal limits, and represents above all else a complete exercise of the political power of each party [in the social contract]. Because of this, both this Constitutional Court and the Supreme Court of Justice [the most important constitutional adjudicator under the 1886 constitution] have invariably asserted that the acts of original constituent power are of a foundational nature, because they establish the legal order and as such they escape judicial review.
>
> In turn, the power to amend (or derived constituent power) is the capacity that certain organs of the state have, subject to prior consultation of the people, to modify an existing constitution, but within the previously determined limits established by the constitution itself. This implies that the constitution establishes this power, and that it is exercised under the terms set by it. These terms include matters of competence, procedure, and so forth. It is a power to amend the constitution, and in that sense it is constituent; but it is rooted in the existing constitution, and because of this is derivative and limited.
>
> Because [of this], the power of reform has limits and is subject to controls. So, in the Colombian case, Article 374 and subsequent articles of the constitution establish this power of reform, since they regulate the ways in which the constitution can be amended: through a legislative act, a referendum, and a constituent assembly. These norms set the rules and the procedures to which these mechanisms of constitutional reform are subject. Thus, the court does not hesitate to state that in such events one is facing an exercise of derived power and, as such, this power is limited by the constitution itself.[38]

The court stated that presidential reelection for more than one additional term implied a substitution of the constitution and as such it was contrary to the republican form of government, alternation, and democracy.

> The republican form of government is characterized by the temporality of the chief of state and by the existence of periodical, free, and competitive elections, in which several candidates in equal conditions fight for office and submit themselves to the electorate's verdict that it is generated when free citizens exercise their right to universal suffrage. The republican form of government's temporal limits make it possible, from time to time, for several citizens to run for office with an equal opportunity, and also enable the intervention of an electoral body made up of every citizen, which happens to be endowed with equal rights to choose their favorite candidate.[39]

Below we will concentrate on a case discussing a referendum and constitutional reform in Ecuador in 2011. Since returning to democracy in 1978, Ecuador has held numerous referendums and public consultations ("consulta popular") on different topics. In February 2011, the president of Ecuador, Rafael Correa, simultaneously called for both a referendum and a public consultation. While the former involves a constitutional reform, the latter involves a consultation on issues that the president deems of great public importance.[40] There were a total of 10 questions on very diverse issues submitted to the people. However, the core issue was a constitutional reform involving the procedure to become a member of the Judicial Council.

The Judicial Council is an administrative and disciplinary body of the judiciary. In Ecuador and several Latin American countries, this body is responsible for the appointment, promotion, and disciplining of judges. These councils were an important part of the process of judicial reform in the region, because they were created for the appointment and removal of judges to be conducted with little or no interference from the president and Congress, so that the administration of justice was not subject to partisan political influence.

Questions four and five of President Correa's referendum consisted of a reform of both the constitution and the Código Orgánico de la Función Judicial (Organic Code of the Judiciary). The main change involved dissolving the Judicial Council and appointing a transitional Judicial Council for a period of 18 months, made up of three members appointed by the executive, the legislative, and the Transparency and Social Control power.[41] After the transitional period, a final Judicial Council was to be appointed on the basis of the new rules in the constitution following the reform.

Arguably, this reform changed the institutional design conceived in the 2008 Ecuadorian constitution for the Judicial Council. Article 441 of the constitution of Ecuador establishes that the president can only submit to referendum constitutional reforms that do not alter the fundamental structure and constitutive elements of the state. As a result, there was a debate between those who opposed the public consultation, arguing that the reform involved the composition of the Judicial Council and thus altered the structure of the state, and the executive, which claimed that the reform had no such scope.[42]

This division also arose within the Constitutional Court, where most judges sided with the executive.[43] The court's minority, instead, argued that the proposed reform constituted a structural change as it affected the relationship between state powers and posed a threat to judicial independence. In their view, instead of resorting to referendum, the president had to convene a new constituent assembly if he wished to push forward with the reform. In the end, the court's decision favored the government in all questions, although the margin by which the president won in those questions regarding the Judicial Council was small.

What happened in Ecuador reveals how plebiscitary democracy may erode judicial independence. In fact, partly as a result of this process, serious questions and concerns have emerged about the independence of judges in the country.

Presidential reelection

Over the last decade, several constitutional reforms involving presidential reelections have taken place in Latin America. All of these reforms were directly or indirectly driven by presidents whose terms were coming to an end, like the cases of Fujimori in Peru in 1993, Menem in Argentina in 1994, Cardoso in Brazil in 1998, and Uribe in Colombia in 2005—Uribe's attempt to seek a second reelection was discussed above. Similarly, in Venezuela, then President Chávez submitted a constitutional reform to a referendum in both 2007 and 2009, promoting consecutive and indefinite presidential reelection. The reform was narrowly rejected in 2007 but approved in 2009.

In the specific cases of Bolivia and Ecuador, the discussion revolved around the question of whether or not the term in office of the incumbent president at the time of the reform should be considered the first term. While many argued that it should and, hence, that only one reelection should be allowed, the president's supporters claimed instead that the president could stand for two more terms.

Nicaragua

In Nicaragua, constitutional limits have also been removed to allow for presidential reelection, though in a peculiar way. In 2009, Nicaragua's constitution stipulated:

> Article 147. The following persons may not run for President or Vice President of the Republic:
>
> a Persons who have exercised the full powers of the presidency at any time during the period when the election for the following term is held, nor anyone who has exercised them for two presidential terms.
> b The Vice President of the Republic or the one called to replace him/her if he/she has exercised the full powers of his/her office or that of President in the two months prior to the [presidential] election for the following term . . .
>
> Article 178. The Mayor, the Vice Mayor, and the Councilors shall be elected by the people by means of a universal, equal, direct, free, and secret suffrage in accordance with the law. Those candidates who have obtained the relative majority of the votes shall be elected Mayor and Vice Mayor. The Councilors shall be elected on the basis of proportional representation, in accordance with the electoral quotient. The Mayor and Vice Mayor may be reelected only for one term. The reelection of the Mayor and Vice Mayor cannot be for the immediately subsequent term.[44]

In addition, Articles 27, 48, 50, and 51 of the constitution established the principle of equality, particularly in the enjoyment of political rights.[45]

President José Daniel Ortega Saavedra—together with the vice president and a host of city mayors and deputy mayors—filed a writ of petition in Nicaragua's Supreme Electoral Council requesting authorization to participate in the 2011 and 2012 elections with no additional requirements to those imposed on any other citizen. The request was based on the direct application of the constitutional principle of unconditional equality for all citizens. In the request, the plaintiffs asked for the removal of the electoral ban against immediate reelection. According to Ortega, the constitution violated his right to be eligible for the same public office in the next presidential election.

The Supreme Electoral Council denied the request, saying that it had no jurisdiction to adjudicate alleged constitutional contradictions between a constitutional principle (equality) and a constitutional rule (ban on immediate reelection). President Ortega filed a writ of *amparo* to appeal that decision. According to appellant, Article 147 of Nicaragua's constitution generated an unequal situation because the ban against consecutive reelection was only applicable to the election of the president, the vice president, the mayor, and the deputy mayor, but not to other elected officials.

On October 19, 2009, only three days after the writ was filed, a divided Constitutional Chamber of the Supreme Court ruled in favor of President Ortega's petition.[46] The narrow majority of members of the chamber who sided with President Ortega's position were politically identified with the president's party.

In the court's view, ". . . the constitutional principles described in the constitution's preamble and bill of rights ["parte dogmática"] trumped any other constitutional clause."[47] The principle of equality thus had to prevail. The court also said that the so-called "electoral prohibition" for the president, the vice president, the mayor, and the vice mayor had not been established by the original drafters of the constitution in an assembly but by a partial constitutional amendment (Law No. 192). This second argument attempted to reinforce the first one, according to which there were different levels of constitutional norms. Thus, norms issued by the original drafters in the exercise of original constituent power prevailed over, or were superior to, those issued in the exercise of derivative constituent power.

In the end, the court ordered the Supreme Electoral Council to acknowledge that the appellants were eligible for the 2011 and 2012 elections, and that no restriction other than age or disability were applicable to the exercise of their rights as citizens. As a result, the supreme court in practice held Articles 147 and 148 of Nicaragua's constitution regarding the immediate reelection ban inapplicable.

Ecuador

In Ecuador, a new constitution entered into effect in 2008. After drafting the new text, the constitutional assembly, controlled by President Rafael Correa, dismissed the legislature, then controlled by the opposition (it also changed the name and composition of the legislature, now called the "assembly"). Also, the constitutional assembly ratified President Correa, who had submitted his resignation to it, and determined that elections for all elected officials would be held in 2009, before the terms were completed. President Correa won the election, and many former legislators were also returned to office. While the original term Correa was serving was supposed to end in 2011, the new election changed this, since the term was extended to 2013.

In September, 2010, the Constitutional Court of Ecuador was asked by a citizen to interpret Article 114 of the constitution.[48] Article 114 reads as follows:

> Article 114. The authorities elected by the people can be reelected only once, whether consecutively or not, to the same office. The authorities elected by the people who submit their candidacy for a different office shall resign from the one they are currently holding.[49]

The court had to determine whether the 2009 election of Correa amounted to a new term of office, thus banning a future immediate reelection, or whether it did not. Again, notice that the 'new' term would end two years later than the first term would have ended. As stated by the court, the central question in this decision was the following:

> 1 Should it be understood that the citizens who access an elective office through the succession mechanisms set up in the constitution serve a regular and independent term to be considered as the first term in the event of a future reelection?
> 2 Should that subsequent election of authorities be understood as a second term because those authorities have previously held the same position?
> 3 Finally, if in the event of the assembly's dissolution the former officials were elected again to complete their respective terms, should we understand this particular situation as a second term and therefore that a future consecutive reelection would be banned by the constitution?[50]

The constitutional court said that a term must be served in full (four years) to count as a first term, and stated that:

> . . . there is no doubt that the intention of the drafters of the Constitution of Ecuador was that elected officials (assembly members as well as president for the purpose of this ruling)

> should complete their full four-year term[; it] is absolutely clear that officials or authorities who were dismissed from their office [because of the early elections] and were later reelected are not serving a second term, nor accordingly, a new regular term, because their functions end when their term expires, which, by constitutional mandate, is after four years of the people's ratification in this way (as a culmination or complement of the period they were initially elected for). This does not constitute a reelection.[51]

As a result of that constitutional interpretation, reelection in the case of Correa (and many legislators) was extended to three terms instead of two. In 2013, Correa run for a third time and won.[52]

Bolivia

The case of Bolivia is remarkably similar to that of Ecuador. Evo Morales took office in 2006 and was reelected in 2009. However, due to a decision of the Constitutional Court in 2013, he was reelected for a third term in 2014. Like in Ecuador, a constituent assembly had drafted a new constitution in 2009. Another similarity was that Morales's first term had been shorter as a result of the enactment of the new constitution.

On April 25, 2013, the Constitutional Court, with a majority of members appointed by the incumbent president, decided on the constitutionality of a draft bill called "Ley de Aplicación Normativa" (Normative Application Act). The government alleged that the bill was needed to clarify the constitution, though its main purpose was likely to allow for a second presidential reelection. One of its clauses touched upon the issue of presidential reelection; its article 4 read:

> I In accordance with the provisions of Article 168 of the Political Constitution of the State, the president and vice president elected for the first time since the enactment of the constitution can stand for one consecutive reelection.
>
> II The requirement in the First Transitory Provision, paragraph II of the Political Constitution of the State, is applicable to the authorities who, as of January 22, 2010, continued to hold public office without being reelected, nominated or appointed.[53]

The draft bill was submitted for prior judicial review in order for the Plurinational Legislative Assembly to continue with the enactment process. The question of the draft bill's constitutionality revolved around the two articles of the constitution of Bolivia mentioned in the bill—Article 168 and the First Transitory Provision. The former reads: "The period of the mandate of the President or Vice President is five years, and they may be reelected once for a continuous term."[54] In turn, the latter establishes:

> I Within a term of 60 days from the promulgation of the present Constitution, the Congress of the Republic shall approve a new electoral regime for the election of the Pluri-National Legislative Assembly, the President, and the Vice President of the Republic. The election shall take place on December 6, 2009.[55]
>
> II The mandates prior to the time this Constitution enters into force shall be taken into account for purposes of computing the new terms of office.

Regarding Article 168, the court ruled that, even if the article states that there can only be a single consecutive reelection, the power vested in the president and vice president comes directly from the people:

> . . . [B]ecause of the legal nature of [the president's and the vice president's] term in office, which derives from popular vote, in the context of the form of government adopted by the Plurinational State of Bolivia, featured in Article 11 of the constitution, . . . it is possible to conclude that there is not any incompatibility between the normative development of the clause through the bill that is now being analyzed . . . and the constitution.[56]

Regarding the transitory provision which ordered that prior terms in office be taken into account for the purposes of computing new terms, the court considered that terms should only be taken into account for that purpose if the individual was elected *after* the entry into force of the new constitution, and not before then. In the court's view, the constituent assembly had created a new political and legal order. According to the court, this meant that:

> . . . it is absolutely reasonable and consistent with the constitution to compute the term for the exercise of the office of the president and vice president of the Plurinational State of Bolivia from the moment that the constituent assembly refounded the state and, thus, created the new political and legal order.[57]

It is up to the reader to decide whether this interpretation of the constitution exceeds or violates the constitutional text.

Conclusion

Although seemingly unrelated, the issues of states of emergency, constitutional reform, and presidential elections share the common trait of being institutional mechanisms that can strengthen the already strong presidential rule in Latin America. Improper regulation of these mechanisms and weak judicial review of them thus tend to further concentrate power in the executive branch and weaken and subordinate the other state branches. These reforms, it is worth noting, have often been supported by the majority of the electorate, either by way of referendum or by a legislative majority in support of the president.

In short, states of emergency, referendums, and elections can lead to true constitutional mutations. These constitutional mutations most often occur under the ward of a plebiscitary democracy and in the absence of adequate judicial review.

Questions

a When are states of emergency truly necessary and consistent with citizens' rights?

b Are there other institutional mechanisms with effects similar to those of states of emergency?

c Is it necessary and democratic for referendums to be subject to procedural and content-related review by constitutional courts?

d What is the relationship between states of emergency, referendums, and presidential reelections?

e In a democratic regime, should there be constitutional limits to presidential reelection?

f What do you think of the doctrine of the "substitution of the constitution" defended by the Colombian Constitutional Court?

Notes

* Translated into English by Paula Arturo. This research was supported by the Research Fund of Universidad Andina Simón Bolívar, Ecuador. The authors wish to thank José María Saravia for editing assistance.

1 See, e.g., Constitución Política del Perú (Constitution of Peru), December 12, 1993, Article 137.I; Constitución Política de los Estados Mexicanos (Constitution of Mexico), February 5, 1917, Article 29; Constitución Política de Colombia (Constitution of Colombia), July 21, 1991, Article 213; Constitución de la Nación Argentina (Constitution of Argentina), December 15, 1994, Article 99.3.

2 Comisión de la Verdad y Reconciliación (Peru), Los actores políticos e institucionales, vol. 3, 19–60 (2001–2003), available at www.usip.org/sites/default/files/file/resources/collections/commissions/Peru01-Report/Peru01-Report_Vol3.pdf.

3 Carlos Parra and María Palacios, *Los estados de excepción y el control judicial de la Corte Constitucional*, in Teoría Constitucional (Cristina Pardo et al. eds, 2006).

4 A writ of *amparo* is a judicial guarantee that allows a judge, either of the constitutional court, supreme court, or first-instance court, to rule on a case where there has been a violation of constitutional rights for appropriate protection and full compensation. This term is generic, as there are countries where the legal institution has specific names; for example, in Ecuador it is known as *acción de protección* (protective action) and in Colombia as *acción de tutela* (tutelage action). See the book's introduction for a brief explanation of the writ's origin.

5 Colombia is one of the Latin American countries that has most often declared states of emergency, which is the reason that the 1991 constitution imposed limits on the executive—to ensure the use of this legal and political institution in accordance with not only formal but also substantial limitations—and an automatic, comprehensive, and final exercise of judicial review of states of emergency.

6 Although judicial review by the Constitutional Court of Colombia is the most rigorous in Latin America, the transition from a weak review to a stronger review of the constitutionality of states of emergency has been a complex and highly criticized task. See Mauricio García Villegas, *Constitucionalismo perverso. Normalidad y anormalidad constitucional en Colombia 1957–1997*, in El Caleidoscopio de las Justicias en Colombia, at 355 (Santos Boaventura de Sousa and Mauricio García Villegas eds, 2001), and Rodrigo Uprimmy Yepes, The Constitutional Court and control of presidential extraordinary powers in Colombia, available at www.dejusticia.org/index.php?modo=interna&tema=sistema_judicial&publicacion=320.

7 Constitutional Court of Colombia, Decision C-070/09, February 12, 2009.

8 The territoriality principle requires that the declaratory action specify the geographical area where the state of emergency is to be implemented. The time limitation principle requires that states of emergency last only the time needed to solve the crisis. Lastly, the principle of legality involves the existence of rules governing the use of states of emergency and the presence of mechanisms to review compliance with these standards.

9 These levels of analysis are contained in Article 213 of the Political Constitution of Colombia, as well as in the Ley Estatutaria de Estados de Excepción (Statutory Law on States of Emergency Act).

10 Constitutional Court of Colombia, Decision C-070/09, February 12, 2009.

11 Ibid.

12 Ibid.

13 Constitución de la República del Ecuador (Constitution of the Republic of Ecuador), October 20, 2008, Article 436.8.

14 See Angélica Porras and Johanna Romero, Guía de jurisprudencia constitucional ecuatoriana 257–348 (2012).

15 See Gina Benavides, *Estados de excepción en 2012*, in Horizonte de los Derechos Humanos en Ecuador, at 85–6 (Gina Benavides and Gardenia Chavez eds, 2013).

16 The conceptual details of each principle can be found in Angélica Porras and Johanna Romero, Guía de jurisprudencia constitucional ecuatoriana, Período octubre (2012).

17 Inter-American Court of Human Rights, Advisory Opinion OC-9/87, 9, paragraph 38, October 6, 1987.

18 Inter-American Court of Human Rights, case of "Gómez Paquiyauri Brothers v. Peru," July 8, 2004, paragraph 67.

19 Ibid.
20 Ibid. See also Carlos Parra and María Palacios, *Los estados de excepción y el control judicial de la Corte Constitucional*, in Teoría Constitucional, at 335 (Cristina Pardo et al. eds, 2006).
21 Inter-American Court of Human Rights, case of "Gómez Paquiyauri Brothers v. Peru," July 8, 2004, paragraph 85.
22 Ibid., paragraph 96.
23 Ibid., paragraph 97.
24 Ibid., paragraph 111.
25 Presidency of the Republic of Ecuador, Decree No. 86, September 3, 1993, signed by the President of the Republic, Sixto Durán Ballén, and the Minister of National Defense, José Gallardo.
26 Inter-American Court of Human Rights, case of "Zambrano Vélez et al. v. Ecuador," July 4, 2007, paragraph 47.
27 International Covenant on Civil and Political Rights, March 23, 1976, Article 4.1.
28 The banking crisis that led to the bank account freeze was the result of, among other factors, an economic downturn caused by the convertibility law imposed in Argentina, as well as external debt, capital flight, and the International Monetary Fund's refusal to refinance the debt.
29 Decree 1570/2001, December 1, 2001, decree's motivation (translated by Mariana Acevedo).
30 These measures had a negative impact on ". . . an estimated 5 million people with savings accounts (thereby affecting almost all of Argentina), 90 percent of whom had savings below 50,000 dollars, indicating they belonged to middle and lower classes, thus these social classes were the most affected by current policies and, ultimately, by Argentina's decline." Antonio María Hernández, *La inconstitucionalidad del "Corralito" financiero y bancario*, 8/2 Ius et Praxis (online) (2002), available at www.scielo.cl/scielo.php?script=sci_arttext&pid=S0718–00122002000200005.
31 Supreme Court of Argentina, case of "Smith, Carlos Antonio C/ Poder Ejecutivo Nacional o Estado Nacional S/ Sumarisimo," February 1, 2002.
32 Supreme Court of Argentina, case of "Bustos Alberto Roque y otros c/ Poder Ejecutivo Nacional o Estado Nacional s/ sumarisimo," October 26, 2004.
33 Yanina Welp, *El Referendo en América Latina. Diseños Institucionales y Equilibrios de Poder*, Revista Nueva Sociedad, 26–42 (July–August 2010). See also Daniel Zovatto, *Las Instituciones de la Democracia Directa a Nivel Nacional en América Latina: Un Balance Comparado: 1978–2007*, in Democracia Directa en Latinoamérica (Alicia Lissidini, Yanina Welp, and Daniel Zovatto eds, 2008).
34 Constitutional Court of Colombia, Decision C-141/10, February 26, 2010. Referendums are one of the amendment methods described in the constitution. Oversimplifying what is a complex issue, the other two ways to amend the constitution are a statute passed by Congress under strict conditions (such as approval in two consecutive legislative periods) and a constitutional assembly. Constitución Política de Colombia (Political Constitution of Colombia), July 7, 1991, Articles 374–380.
35 Constitutional Court of Colombia, Decision C-1040/05, October 19, 2005.
36 Angélica Durán, *Referendos en América Latina: ¿Una Herramienta que Fortalece o Debilita las Instituciones Democráticas?*, 21 Revista Perspectiva, 32–5 (2009). In Colombia, the notion of the replacement or substitution of the constitution had featured for the first time in a decision from 2003 concerning a referendum to amend several constitutional articles about the political process. Constitutional Court of Colombia, Decision C-551/03, July 9, 2003.
37 Constitutional Court of Colombia, Decision C-141/10, February 26, 2010.
38 Constitutional Court of Colombia, C-141/10, February 26, 2010.
39 Ibid.
40 Constitución de la República del Ecuador (Constitution of the Republic of Ecuador), October 20, 2008, Articles 147.14 and 441.1.
41 This power is contained in the 2008 constitution, and is composed of the Ombudsman, the Comptroller General, and a citizen participation council, among others. Its main function is accountability, corruption control, and participation promotion.
42 Questions one and two of the public consultation submitted by President Correa made reference to restrictions on the power of judges for granting restraining orders, such as urgent measures for the protection of rights. With regards to these kinds of reforms, Article 441 of the constitution also limits presidential power, as it indicates that the president may not propose constitutional reforms that restrict rights or constitutional guarantees.
43 Constitutional Court of Ecuador, Case No. 0001–11-RC, February 15, 2011.

44 Constitución Política de la República de Nicaragua (Constitution of Nicaragua), January 9, 1987, Articles 147 and 178. Available in English at: www.constituteproject.org/constitution/Nicaragua_2005.pdf.
45 Article 48 clearly states that the state has an obligation "to remove obstacles that impede the actual equality among Nicaraguans and their effective participation in the political, economic and social life of the country." Id.
46 Supreme Court of Nicaragua, Judgment No. 504. Dossier No. 602–09 of the Constitutional Chamber, October 19, 2009.
47 Id.
48 According to the Constitutional Court's interpretation of the constitution, the court is allowed to issue interpretative decisions.
49 Constitución de la República del Ecuador (Constitution), October 20, 2008, Article 114. Available at http://pdba.georgetown.edu/Constitutions/Ecuador/english08.html.
50 Constitutional Court of Ecuador, Decision No. 4 0020–09-IC, September 9, 2008.
51 Constitutional Court of Ecuador, Decision No. 002–10-SIC-CC, September 9, 2010. The court did not take into account Article 10 of the new constitution's Transitional Regime (Régimen de Transición), adopted by the constitutional assembly, which establishes: "The term of office of officials elected according to the Transitional Regime shall be considered the first for all legal purposes."
52 As of 2015, a new constitutional amendment was being considered to extend reelections indefinitely.
53 Ley de Aplicación Normativa (Normative Application Act), May 20, 2013, available at www.lexivox.org/norms/BO-L-N381.pdf.
54 Constitución Política del Estado Plurinacional de Bolivia (Constitution), February 7, 2009, Article 168, available at www.constituteproject.org/constitution/Bolivia_2009.pdf. According to the government, the new constitution's clauses regarding the structure of government entered into effect on January 22, 2010.
55 Id., First Transitory Provision.
56 Constitutional Plurinational Tribunal, Constitutional Declaration 0003–2013, 16, April 25, 2013.
57 Ibid.

References

Gina Benavides, *Estados de excepción en 2012*, in HORIZONTE DE LOS DERECHOS HUMANOS EN ECUADOR, at 85–6 (Gina Benavides and Gardenia Chavez eds, 2013).

COMISIÓN DE LA VERDAD Y RECONCILIACIÓN (PERU), LOS ACTORES POLÍTICOS E INSTITUCIONALES, vol. 3, 19–60 (2001–2003), available at www.usip.org/sites/default/files/file/resources/collections/commissions/Peru01-Report/Peru01-Report_Vol3.pdf.

Angélica Durán, *Referendos en América Latina: ¿Una Herramienta que Fortalece o Debilita las Instituciones Democráticas?*, 21 REVISTA PERSPECTIVA, 32–5 (2009).

"Subversivos inspirados en Sendero Luminoso detectados a tiempo en Ecuador," *Diario El Hoy*, 18 March 18 1993, available, at www.explored.com.ec/noticias-ecuador/subversivos-inspirados-en-sendero-luminoso-detectados-a-tiempo-en-ecuador-43776.html.

EDUARDO GARCÍA DE ENTERRÍA, LA CONSTITUCIÓN COMO NORMA Y EL TRIBUNAL CONSTITUCIONAL (1994).

Mauricio García Villegas, *Constitucionalismo perverso. Normalidad y anormalidad constitucional en Colombia 1957–1997*, in EL CALEIDOSCOPIO DE LAS JUSTICIAS EN COLOMBIA, at 355 (Santos Boaventura de Sousa and Mauricio García Villegas eds, 2001).

Antonio María Hernández, *La inconstitucionalidad del "Corralito" financiero y bancario*, 8/2 IUS ET PRAXIS (online) (2002), available at www.scielo.cl/scielo.php?script=sci_arttext&pid=S0718–0012200200020 0005.

Carlos Parra and María Palacios, *Los estados de excepción y el control judicial de la Corte Constitucional*, in TEORÍA CONSTITUCIONAL (Cristina Pardo et al. eds, 2006).

Pásara, Luis, "La Experiencia Comparada de los Consejos," REFORMA JUDICIAL, 18 (July-December 2011): 107–135.

ANGÉLICA PORRAS AND JOHANNA ROMERO, GUÍA DE JURISPRUDENCIA CONSTITUCIONAL ECUATORIANA PERÍODO OCTUBRE 2008–DICIEMBRE 2010 (2012).

Rodrigo Uprimmy Yepes, The Constitutional Court and control of presidential extraordinary powers in Colombia, available at www.dejusticia.org/index.php?modo=interna&tema=sistema_judicial&publicacion=320.

Yanina Welp, *El Referendo en América Latina. Diseños Institucionales y Equilibrios de Poder*, Revista Nueva Sociedad, 26–42 (July–August 2010).

Daniel Zovatto, *Las Instituciones de la Democracia Directa a Nivel Nacional en América Latina: Un Balance Comparado: 1978–2007*, in Democracia Directa en Latinoamérica (Alicia Lissidini, Yanina Welp, and Daniel Zovatto eds, 2008).

Further reading

Giorgio Agamben, Estado de Excepción (2007).

Aguirre, Vanesa, *El derecho a la tutela judicial efectiva: una aproximación a su aplicación por los tribunales ecuatorianos*, Foro: Revista de Derecho, No. 14 (Quito: Universidad Andina Simón Bolívar, Corporación Editora Nacional, 2010).

Con Súperpoderes para Maduro, Venezuela se va a complicar más, Urgente24.com, 8 October 2013, available at www.urgente24.com/219578-con-superpoderes-para-maduro-venezuela-se-va-a-complicar-mas

Sebastián Elías, *Urgencia, necesidad, y decretos. Los DNU nuevamente sobre el tapete*, Revista Jurídica de la Universidad de San Andrés, 24 (2010), available at http://revistajuridica.udesa.edu.ar/?p=24.

Mauricio García Villegas, *Constitucionalismo perverso. Normalidad y anormalidad constitucional en Colombia 1957–1997*, in El Caleidoscopio de las Justicias en Colombia, at 355 (Santos Boaventura de Sousa and Mauricio García Villegas eds, 2001).

Agustín Grijalva, Courts and Political Parties: The Politics of Constitutional Review in Ecuador (2010).

Florentín Meléndez, La Suspensión de los Derechos Fundamentales en los Estados de Excepción según el Derecho Internacional de los Derechos Humanos (1998).

Mario Midón, *La mayor estafa del siglo en Argentina. El aniquilamiento del derecho a la propiedad y su garantía jurisdiccional a la luz del llamado corralito financiero*, in Defensa de la Constitución: Garantismo y Controles (Víctor Bazán ed., 2003).

30-S insubordinación policial, El Comercio, 30 September 2010, available at http://especiales.elcomercio.com/2011/09/30s/.

Rodrigo Uprimmy Yepes, *The Constitucional Court and Control of Presidential Extraordinary Powers in Colombia*, in Democratization and the judiciary: the accountability function of courts in new democracies (Roberto Siri Gloppen, Roberto Gargarella, and Elin Skaar eds, 2004).

Daniel Zovatto, *Las Instituciones de la Democracia Directa a Nivel Nacional en América Latina: Un Balance Comparado: 1978–2007*, in Democracia Directa en Latinoamérica (Alicia Lissidini, Yanina Welp, and Daniel Zovatto eds, 2008).

12 Economic regulation and judicial review

*Mariana Mota Prado and René Urueña**

Introduction

In the 1980s and 1990s a series of neoliberal reforms profoundly transformed Latin American economic, legal, political, and social systems.[1] A significant part of these reforms comprised the privatization of public utility services, such as electricity, telecommunications, and water. During this period, privatization often took the form of the sale of shares of state-owned companies to private investors, who became responsible for the delivery of essential services in the region.[2] Along with privatization, many Latin American countries adopted new regulatory frameworks, i.e. a complex set of rules and norms intended to govern the relationship between privatized companies, consumers, the government, and other companies operating in the same sector. This set of rules and norms is often referred to as "economic regulation." In most Latin American countries, this economic regulation is embedded in a series of legal instruments: constitutional provisions, congressional statutes, executive decrees, and administrative norms, and in some countries they also include contractual instruments such as concession contracts. In the sections below, the reader will find a selection of cases decided by the Brazilian, Colombian, and Mexican supreme courts after the privatization of public utility companies. The last section turns to Argentina, but it is not related to a particular case. Instead, it points to a relevant issue that may be discussed in national courts in the near future. The selection presented here is not representative of the breadth of issues or the content of judicial decisions related to economic regulation in Latin America. Instead, the purpose of this chapter is to highlight some of the tensions and dilemmas that the privatization reforms created by promoting legal transplants into Latin American legal systems.

Regulatory agencies, independence, and the separation of powers

Privatization reforms have introduced a new actor into the structure of administrative states in Latin America: the regulatory agencies.[3] Regulatory agencies, as the name suggests, are entities responsible for the creation, application, and adjudication of matters related to the economic regulation of public utility sectors. In many countries they were designed to have a significant level of autonomy from elected bodies.[4] In Brazil, for instance, regulatory agencies have institutional guarantees of independence, such as fixed and staggered terms of office for commissioners, congressional approval of presidential nominations, and alternative sources of funds to ensure their financial autonomy.[5] These guarantees of independence were designed to prevent an elected government from opportunistically modifying the regulatory framework after privatization had taken place.[6] They were, therefore, an instrument used by Latin American governments to signal to investors a credible commitment to the reforms.[7]

While these guarantees of independence may be necessary to protect investors, they raise some interesting questions regarding the accountability of regulatory agencies. In a democratic system, where the government derives its legitimacy from regular elections, to whom would such "independent" agencies be responding? What is the constitutional status of regulatory agencies, considering the principle of separation of powers? Are they part of the executive branch and therefore should be subordinate to the president? If not, which branch of the government do they belong to, and are therefore controlled by?

These questions are not exclusive to Latin American countries that have independent regulators. Some of these issues were raised before the US Supreme Court, and it is not surprising that such precedents were cited when the same issue came up in Brazil (see case below). There are benefits and costs of insulating agencies from fluctuation of policies that result from electoral cycles in democratic regimes. One of the benefits is to secure the system against political opportunism, which can scare off private investors.[8] One of the costs is to create a "democratic deficit" in the regulatory state. The second issue—the accountability of independent regulators—has raised numerous concerns in Europe,[9] where the creation of regulatory agencies happened at around the same time as in Latin America.[10]

In a case decided in 1999, the Supreme Court of Brazil[11] addressed a challenge against two mechanisms designed to guarantee the independence of regulatory agencies. The governor of the state of Rio Grande do Sul challenged the constitutionality of two provisions governing the state's regulatory agency (AGERGS), which stated that: a) appointments of AGERGS's commissioners should be approved by the legislative assembly of the state of Rio Grande do Sul; and b) the appointed commissioners of such an agency could only be dismissed before the end of their term in office by the same assembly.

In the petition to the Supreme Court, the governor argued that these provisions conflicted with Article 84, Paragraph II, of the 1988 constitution, which established that the president had the exclusive power to execute statutes by enacting decrees and regulation. Also, these provisions challenged Article 37, Paragraph II, of the constitution, which supposedly indicated that appointed civil servants could be appointed and dismissed at will (*ad nutum*) by the president. The governor claimed that the same powers, i.e. to enact regulation, applied to him as chief of the executive branch at the state level, or that he could delegate this function to civil servants, appointed and dismissed by him. If the challenged mechanisms were declared unconstitutional, the decision would also be applicable to federal regulatory agencies.[12] Thus, the decision could potentially revert a great deal of the regulatory reforms implemented in the 1990s.

The Federal Supreme Court of Brazil quickly dismissed the constitutional challenge to the first provision, arguing that the jurisprudence of the court had consistently affirmed the constitutionality of such a requirement (legislative approval of appointments by the chief of the executive) in other cases, such as state-owned companies, which followed a different legal regime (closer to private law), and appointments regulated by the constitution.[13] By contrast, the second provision, which established the legislature's exclusive power of dismissal of AGERGS's commissioners, generated a heated debate among the justices of the Federal Supreme Court of Brazil.

On one side of the debate, there was Justice Sepulveda Pertence, who voted in favor of declaring such a provision unconstitutional. To support his opinion, he cited the vast jurisprudence of the court in the matter,[14] which established that "appointments for term for commissioners in *autarquias*[15] do not impede dismissal at will by the President of the Republic." He argued:

> I acknowledge that in the same decade when this jurisprudence was consolidated . . . this court exempted from it the Reitores [university provosts] during their terms in office—due

to a constitutional provision guaranteeing academic autonomy. Moreover, the 1988 constitution created a new form of dismissal of the head of the prosecutor's office, who is appointed for each term, by subordinating the decision to Congress at the federal level and to state legislatures at the state level. These exceptions to the rule . . . however, are related to sectors—universities and the prosecutor's office—that are constitutionally placed outside the vertical hierarchy of the executive branch. This is obviously not the case of the regulatory agencies. In a democratic system, one government cannot subordinate its successor to its agenda.

It is reasonable—according to contemporary principles of presidential systems—to subordinate the appointments of the chief of the executive branch to legislative approval. However, the logic of such a system would be clearly subverted if appointees from the previous government were allowed to stay in power, as this would create significant obstacles for a newly elected government to pursue its agenda.[16]

On the other side of the debate, Justice Nelson Jobim argued that the provision was constitutional, extensively quoting in his opinion the dissenting vote in the main precedent[17] of the court. The dissent by Justice Vitor Nunes Leal, cited by Jobim, stated:

> . . . Our debate should be focused on the expression 'according to the law,' which is in the same constitutional provision: 'appoint public administration officials, according to the law.' . . . What becomes clear, then, is that the power of the president to appoint officials to the public administration should be exercised according to the law. Thus, the legislature can make this power conditional, as long as it does so in a way that is compatible with the constitution . . . The idea that the legislature cannot impose conditions on the appointment power of the president—if accepted by this court—would nullify most of the Civil Servants Statute . . . It would establish an unbounded presidential power, which we have not seen for a long time, at least since most legal systems around the world adopted merit-based systems for the public administration . . . The constitution does not support this Napoleonic interpretation offered by our executive branch in this case.[18]

Regarding autonomous bodies, the dissent by Justice Nunes stated:

> . . . the appointment of a public official for a fixed term is a natural component of the system of administrative autonomy that is granted by law to certain bodies. This fixed term in office aims at guaranteeing policy continuity and the independence of these autonomous entities. It does so to guarantee that these public officials are protected from short-term concerns, begin able to fully carry on and execute the policies established by the legislature, which created this body and assigned its functions. In the current political system in our country, it is the legislature that should determine the economic and administrative policies of the country . . .[19]

After citing US precedents *Humphrey* (295 US 602, 1935) and *Wiener* (357 US 349, 1958), Justice Nunes concludes that one needs to distinguish between:

> officials that belong to the direct administration [*administração direta* in Portuguese, and executive establishment in English] and therefore can be dismissed at will; and those that belong to an entity created to exercise its judgment independently of any authorization or obstacle by any other official or any other governmental department, which can only be dismissed if Congress grants the power to do so. This distinction stems from the different

> functions performed by bodies of the direct administration and those whose responsibilities require complete independence from the executive branch. These entities are equivalent to our economic and administrative *autarquias*.[20]

Turning to the problem of the democratic deficit, Nunes states:

> There was also an argument that appointments from the previous government will not be aligned with the policies of the new government, imposing obstacles to the implementation of its agenda . . . The alignment of the chief of the executive branch with the officials managing and executing public policies is, in theory, an asset for the public administration. However, this only refers to the convenience for managers, not to the language of the law. The legislature certainly weighed the costs of a possible misalignment against the benefit, regarded more relevant, of guaranteeing the independence of this body and secure the continuity in the performance of its functions. The branch that should be evaluating the advantages and drawbacks of each of these two arrangements is not the judiciary, because we do not create law, but it is the legislature . . .[21]

Considering that regulatory agencies are *autarquias*, Justice Jobim states that they should be treated in the way prescribed by Nunes. Jobim then concludes his opinion:

> . . . my conclusion is that [the jurisprudence] does not apply to this case . . . [A]gencies are an arm of the regulatory state, and should perform the functions defined in law. The objective of AGERGS is to guarantee the efficacy of the policy of the law . . . The agency is not supposed to implement the policies of the government.[22]

Justice Pertence then responds to Justice Jobim, sustaining his initial vote for the unconstitutionality of the provision:

> It is important to note that none of the cases analyzed referred to the possibility of transferring, through a statute, the dismissal power from the executive branch to the legislature. The cases have not even discussed the possibility of subordinating the dismissal by the president to the approval of the legislature . . . Thus, I think we can conclude that neither in the United States, according to the analysis of Vitor Nunes Leal, nor in Brazil, there has ever been a case in which the Senate was granted the power to authorize a dismissal just because it had the power to approve it in the first place . . .
>
> The statute in the state of Rio Grande do Sul denies the executive even the power to keep an official with fixed term in office, given that the legislative assembly can dismiss the official—and this is explicitly the rule stated in this statute—without any request from the governor. This is more than a violation to the principle of separation of powers. This is a mechanism that belongs to parliamentary systems . . .[23]

In light of this, Justice Jobim then decides to revise his opinion, but sustains his concern regarding the guarantees of independence of regulatory agencies:

> In this case, the statute of the state of Rio Grande do Sul ascribed a unilateral decision [to the legislative assembly], which I did not notice previously . . . I will follow [Justice Sepulveda Pertence's] opinion, in principle . . . But one should not conclude from his opinion or the decision of this court that we are authorizing governors or the president to dismiss at will commissioners in any of these agencies . . .

In the end, the court decided to declare the second provision unconstitutional,

> . . . without striking down any restrictions to the governor's power to dismiss commissioners at will, considering that commissioners of AGERGS are appointed for a fixed term in office, and also without striking down any supervening legislation on this matter.[24]

Interestingly, the court never addressed the significant trade-offs involved in securing this type of independence to regulatory agencies.[25]

Economic regulation and socioeconomic rights

The adoption of an economic regulatory framework in Latin America occurred as several other transformations were changing the legal landscape of the region. Along the wave of privatization, new constitutional texts underscoring socioeconomic rights opened room for a different kind of debate concerning distributive choices throughout the region. The language of rights became the vehicle of choice for crucial discussions, and courts became the primary forum for distributive claims.[26] In this context, courts had to discuss how best to integrate the new economic regulation in this process of judicial disputes over distributive issues.

The tension between these two sets of transformations in the legal systems in the region is clear. On the one hand, a regulatory framework was necessary as infrastructure sectors were not fully competitive and therefore required a structure of incentives to move prices closer to what they would be under a free and competitive market. But, on the other, economic regulation was needed not only to correct market failures and promote efficient allocation of resources, but also to promote redistribution and reduce inequality. The latter was a pressing concern in developing countries in general, and in Latin America in particular. Indeed, some scholars argued that, in contrast with regulatory reforms in OECD countries, economic regulation in developing countries should address redistributive issues.[27] In line with that, there is evidence associating privatization and regulatory reforms with a sharp increase in poverty and inequality in the region.[28]

Such a debate between efficiency and distribution partly overlaps with the disciplinary divide between economists and lawyers in Latin America during the 1990s.[29] Such transnational disciplinary tension found varied outlets in the different states of the region, following institutional particularities and cultural idiosyncrasies. In Colombia, for example, a group of elite US-trained economists led the neoliberal reform that set the basic institutional framework for economic regulation,[30] including the introduction of the independent regulatory agency as the cornerstone of efficiency-based regulation.[31] Against this view, a group of elite foreign-trained lawyers, who gained access to the inner circles of power in the mid-1990s[32], fostered legal reforms to modify a legal system that was perceived as too formalistic and unresponsive to the harsh socioeconomic reality of the country and its bloody spiral of violence.[33] This group created a new constitution (adopted in 1991) and a new constitutional court[34], establishing a new legal and institutional framework often called "neo-constitutionalism."[35] What both groups had in common was the belief that Congress was better avoided. However, their institutions of choice were rather different: while neoliberal economists championed the advantages of the independent regulatory agency, neo-constitutional lawyers held the virtues of a strong constitutional court.

It took a decade for the tensions between these two projects to come before the Constitutional Court of Colombia. Case C-150/03 was a challenge against several sections of Law 142 of 1994, the central piece of legislation concerning public utilities in Colombia. The legislation defined as the guiding principles of public utility regulation the notions of "economic efficiency," "financial sufficiency," and the recovery of a rate of return for private investors. The plaintiff claimed that the law emphasized the protection of the market and entrepreneurship, in stark opposition to the framework of the "social state grounded on the rule of law" ("Estado Social de Derecho") as enshrined in the constitution. The court was thus faced with the challenge of integrating public utilities regulation (of undeniable neoliberal inspiration) with the public law framework of a progressive constitution.[36]

> . . . [T]he court moves forward to solve the following legal questions: (i) Are the provisions on tariffs for public utilities, contained in Law 142 of 1994, an impediment for the regulatory intervention of the state in such sector and, therefore, in contravention of Articles 334 and 365 of the constitution?[37] (ii) Is it in accordance with the constitution the provision according to which economic efficiency and financial sufficiency are part of the criteria used to determine the tariffs of public utilities? Is the establishment of priority for these criteria, when defining the tariff regime, a violation of the principles of solidarity and redistribution contained in Article 367 of the constitution, in relation with Articles 1 and 365 thereof? . . .[38]

In analyzing these questions, the Constitutional Court of Colombia first stated that the goal of efficiency in the regulatory framework of public utilities does not contradict the constitution:

> . . . State intervention is justified when the market lacks competitive conditions, or to protect the market from those who engage in activities aimed at breaking its balance; both are phenomenon that can be understood by the concept of 'market failures.' Indeed, the analysis of this phenomenon shows that market regulation by the respective agencies is one of the mechanisms available to the state to respond rapidly to the needs of sectors, such as public utilities, that are subject to permanent variations. The adjustment of the market through regulation is a task that has as one of its functions, besides pursuing basic conditions of equality and solidarity . . . the search for adequate conditions of competitiveness . . .
>
> . . . The court finds that the efficiency criterion established in the challenged norm develops the mandate contained in Article 365 of the constitution, according to which 'it is a duty of the state to ensure the efficient supply [of public services] to all inhabitants of the national territory.' Even though the legislator could have defined the notion of efficiency in different terms, this is a matter that falls within the legislator's margin of discretion, and Congress is free to do so following economic theories of efficiency in a competitive market . . . In addition, the legislative definition of efficiency is aimed at avoiding distortions of the market that would allow free competition to cease being a right in benefit of all. Therefore, this provision is declared constitutional . . .[39]

Then it addressed the question of whether the "financial sufficiency" criteria to determine rates for public services violated the state's obligation to guarantee the provision of public services to all inhabitants of the national territory (Article 365 of the constitution) and other constitutional provisions. Here, the court also answers in the negative

> [I]f a norm establishes a rate of return that is inferior to the one established by the market, the private enterprise would not be motivated to participate in the activity, rendering useless Article 365 of the constitution, which determines that any individual may provide public services. On the other hand, if the norm establishes a rate of return, for public utility

> companies, higher than the one obtained by enterprises under similar conditions and risks, it would be in violation of the principle of efficiency regarding the provision of public services, also contained in Article 365 of the constitution.
>
> . . . the definition of the financial sufficiency criterion adopted by Law 142 of 1994 establishes the parameters needed for ensuring that the formula used to determine the tariffs includes the costs and expenses of the provision of public services, including those of expansion, with the objective of gradually covering all inhabitants in the territory; achieving a profit level for the enterprises which guarantees both the rights of users and the effective exercise of private enterprise; and making possible that the enterprises have enough resources to guarantee further improvements in the quality, continuity and security indicators of the service.
>
> Therefore, the financial efficiency criterion defined by the legislator responds to the mandate of Article 365 of the constitution, which establishes that the tariffs regime should take into account, among others, the cost criterion.[40]

Finally, the court ponders whether efficiency should have priority over other considerations when designing the regulation of public utilities, distinguishing between a technical and a legal analysis of the provision.[41]

> The first part of [the challenged provisions] establishes that 'the efficiency and financial sufficiency criteria will be given priority when defining the tariff regime'. This court finds that such expression results from a technical perspective that considers that both criteria are instrumental to determine the cost of the service . . . However, all provisions should be interpreted in such a way as to be effective and have a normative meaning, and not simply describe the practical steps of a technical process. Therefore, it is the legal meaning, not the technical one, of the prioritization of efficiency and financial sufficiency, which will be reviewed by this court.
>
> From a technical perspective . . . this court observes that the efficiency and financial sufficiency are not necessarily incompatible with solidarity. According to the efficiency criterion, public services should be produced as affordably as possible under adequate standards of quality. In turn, the criterion of financial sufficiency seeks to include all costs of service in the tariff formula (including costs, expenses, and returns on investment) according to the needs of the target population, and the objectives and parameters set forth in the constitution and the law. On the other hand, the criterion of solidarity is concerned with the way in which the cost of services is distributed among society's members, taking into account their economic capacity, so that all may have access to services, and such access will not depend exclusively on their capacity to pay, but will also respond to the principle of necessity, according to which persons without the resources for access to basic consumption will be benefited by measures in their favor which will allow such access.
>
> The criterion of solidarity entails the full application of the constitutional mandate according to which the state must ensure the efficient supply of public services for all inhabitants of the national territory. This criterion allows the fixing of a variable tariff scale, in accordance with the economic conditions of different users, which facilitates access for persons of low income and demands a greater burden of persons with higher income, a burden that is equitable under these conditions, without conflicting with the principles of efficiency and financial sufficiency.
>
> The court will review the challenged rule in its juridical sense, and not as the steps of a technical process. The expression 'shall have priority' has a legal meaning insofar as it

establishes the prevalence of some criteria over others. Indeed, when two legal criteria are in conflict in a concrete case, this conflict may be resolved in different ways by the legislator. One such way is to seek the harmonization of principles in conflict, and another is to set a scale of priorities. In the challenged legal norm, the legislator decided to give priority to the criteria of efficiency and financial sufficiency over others, that is, over the criteria of neutrality, solidarity, redistribution, simplicity, and transparency.

> Thus, a legal interpretation of the first sentence of the norm under review may entail the idea that in case of contradiction between the principles of efficiency and financial sufficiency, with the principle of solidarity, the latter might be sacrificed to ensure the effectiveness of the first two principles. This provision conflicts with Article 367 of the constitution, which expressly establishes solidarity as one of the constitutive criterion of the tariff regime for public utilities, without subordinating it to any other criteria.
>
> Thus, the court will declare the unconstitutionality of the first sentence of [the challenged provisions], according to which 'the criteria of efficiency and financial sufficiency shall have priority over the definition of the tariff regime.'[42]

Then the court proceeds to review the second part of the provision: "If any contradiction exists between efficiency and the financial sufficiency criteria, due account should be taken of the fact that, for an efficient enterprise, the economically efficient tariffs should be defined based on financial sufficiency."[43] The court decided it was constitutional:

> . . . [T]he formula set forth by the legislator, in which public services must obey the criterion of sufficiency in efficient conditions, protects the interests of users insofar as conditions are established for the supply of public services to be financially sustainable in the long run, and for them to have adequate standards of quality. The legislator does not confer primacy on the criterion of financial sufficiency per se. In the challenged rule, the legislator was simply demanding that economic efficiency is not measured in light of a static situation in which an enterprise comfortably remains within its market niche without improving the quality of the service. The aim is to understand efficiency as an improvement of the quality of the supplied service, and a will to bring the service to more users, so that the constitutional mandate of enjoyment of services for all, especially those of marginal sectors and low income, is fulfilled. In this sense, the norm under review does not contradict constitutional principles. Rather, it sets a parameter for its application in case of conflict between two economic criteria.[44]

It is interesting to note that the two sets of concerns addressed here—companies unfairly appropriating rents from consumers, and poor people having access to these services at a reduced (or at no) cost—are in the backdrop of many of the consumer movements that arose in the region in the 1990s.[45]

Judicial review of regulatory agencies

Regulatory provisions often govern the behavior and the relationship between privatized companies and other companies operating in the sector. Some regulatory agencies are also in charge of solving disputes among regulated companies and/or among companies and consumers. Often, a regulated company may challenge a regulatory rule or decision before the judiciary, asking it to modify what the regulator initially determined. Then, faced with these challenges, courts have to decide the acceptable and desirable level of judicial interference in economic regulation. The question is even more pressing in the case of regulation established by the newly created regulatory agencies, as courts are dealing with such entities for the very first time.

Should there be deference to agencies? If not, on what grounds could a court strike down the regulation set up by technocrats? Some argue that courts lack expertise to analyze regulatory issues, and therefore should limit themselves to procedural review of regulation. On the other hand, there are those who support substantive judicial review of regulation, to secure that democratic values and the protection of minorities are not violated by regulatory provisions. The debate is fierce and the US Supreme Court itself has gone back and forth on this issue.[46]

In May 2011 the Supreme Court of Mexico had to address one particular dimension of this debate on judicial review of administrative agencies: injunctions. Mexico has an instrument called *amparo*, a special type of judicial review, which allows courts to suspend the effects of a regulation until a final decision has been issued by a court of law. Previous precedents had established that courts could strike down regulation imposed on service providers, in this case by the Mexican regulatory authority for telecommunications, COFETEL. The question in this case was whether courts could temporarily suspend the application of such a regulation before a final judicial decision had been reached.[47]

This question was particularly relevant in the Mexican context. Since the privatization of telecommunications services, the dominant company in the sector, Telcel, has used the judiciary to have regulatory decisions struck down and avoid regulatory compliance.[48] The *amparo* allows a court to suspend regulatory decisions of COFETEL until a judicial decision has been reached. By using this mechanism, Telcel was able to opportunistically use the judiciary to circumvent most of the obligations imposed by COFETEL's regulations, undermining competition in the sector.[49]

In this particular case, the Supreme Court of Mexico was prompted to address this issue because there was conflicting jurisprudence in lower courts regarding interconnection rules.[50] These are rules that apply to two telecommunications operators when calls are placed between consumers in each of their networks. COFETEL imposed mandatory interconnections between one or more service providers, and adjudicated disputes related to the value of interconnection fees. While some courts stated that the COFETEL's adjudicatory decisions (and the payment determined by the agency) could be suspended with injunctions, others declared that it could not.

The court started by stating what was required for the Supreme Court to forbid other courts from granting an injunction:

> the first question before the Plenary Chamber of the Supreme Court of Justice of the Nation is whether the suspension of the COFETEL's resolution, which settles issues that were not agreed upon by the licensees, and orders the interconnection between them, affects social interest and contravenes public order provisions.[51]

Some courts in Mexico believed that the suspension of COFETEL's resolution neither affected social interest, nor did it contravene public order provisions. By contrast, other courts argued the opposite, as quoted by the Supreme Court:

> . . . All these factors, when analyzed together, show that the judge erred in deciding that the suspension could be granted; as can be gathered from the reasoning above, the interconnection of networks is not enough to safeguard public order and social interest sought by the rule of law; to achieve that aim, it is also necessary to guarantee that such interconnection will be provided under efficient conditions, in an environment of competition between licensees, taking into account the interest of the users by guaranteeing the best price, variety and quality in the service.

> To grant the requested provisional measure would prevent the Commission from exercising its powers regarding interconnections, which seek to safeguard the public order and social interest . . . thus harming the society of users of telecommunication services.[52]

Regarding these two criteria, the Supreme Court determined the following:

> First, it is necessary to determine the scope to be given to the concepts 'social interest' and 'public order provisions,' since there is no established definition . . .
>
> [I]n principle, there is a detriment to social interest and a contravention of a public order provision when the community is deprived of a benefit granted by the law, or when a damage is caused that would otherwise not have been inflicted; the latter, to be sure, on the basis that each of these concepts should be analyzed on a case-by-case basis.[53]

The court then proceeded to the first issue in dispute, COFETEL's mandatory interconnections:

> . . . The Plenary Chamber of the Supreme Court of Justice of the Nation finds that, when the COFETEL orders the interconnection of telecommunication networks between parties that were unable to reach an agreement, it is in fact preserving the establishment, continuity, and efficiency of the provision of public services, in this case, telephone service; thus, a possible suspension of this kind of resolutions would deprive the community of a benefit granted by the law, and causes a damage that would otherwise not have been inflicted. Suspending a possible interconnection would have as a result that one or more operators in the market could not operate, or that one of them would be at a disadvantage compared to other competitors, which would in turn affect final users, since they would either not be able to communicate with a specific point, whose interconnection was ordered by the regulatory organ, or else they would be constrained to contract with particular operators in order to be able to reach the interconnection. This affects the conditions of free competition that, according to the law, should prevail in the telecommunications market.
>
> . . .
>
> Therefore, since the suspension of a COFETEL resolution establishing the interconnection of telecommunication networks may deprive the community from a benefit granted by the law, or cause a damage that would otherwise not have been inflicted, the court concludes that neither the requirements of the Federal Law of Administrative Procedure, nor those of the Law of Writ of Protection ['*amparo*'] are fulfilled. Thus, if one such measure is challenged, it cannot be provisionally suspended.[54]

The Supreme Court of Mexico then proceeded to analyze the second issue in dispute: COFETEL's mandatory rates for interconnections. Does an injunction suspending the regulatory decision affect social interest and contravene public order provisions? The answer is in the negative, according to the court.

> . . . the COFETEL resolution, which establishes the rate that a licensee must pay to another for interconnection, is a matter that fails to concern the community, since it only affects the licensees; thus, the suspension of this resolution fails to affect the community, and neither does it deprive the latter from a benefit granted by law, since, as has been established, the interconnection is maintained, regardless of whether the licensees can reach an agreement on an aspect such as rates.
>
> Now, the Plenary Chamber of the Supreme Court of Justice of the Nation is aware that the variation in interconnection rates between licensees may affect the cost of service for

> the final users, because the COFETEL establishes the rise or decrease of rates—in preexistent interconnections—in the first case, because the interconnected licensee could shift the burden of the rise of the rates to its users; or, in the second case, because the cost of the public service could decrease.
>
> However, the increase or decrease of the cost of the public services for the final user resulting from the modification of interconnection rates between public network telecommunications licensees, is not a direct and necessary consequence of the COFETEL resolution, since the Commission is not in charge of determining the final rates that should be collected from the users. Therefore, whether the increase or decrease in interconnection rates affects the final charge to the users will be determined by the economic and commercial policies of providers of telecommunication services.[55]

Despite allowing courts to grant injunctions suspending COFETEL's mandatory interconnection rates, the Supreme Court of Mexico emphasized that there are strict requirements that need to be met before an injunction can be issued:

> . . . it is important to underscore that . . . the entity to which the request of this provisional measure is addressed must be especially careful in verifying that the requirements of the law for such measure are fulfilled, including the requirement that the suspension be requested by the injured party.
>
> This last requirement is relevant, since if there was no previous rate agreed upon between the licensees, the rate determination by the COFETEL only affects the enterprise that is trying to interconnect with another enterprise's preexistent public network, since it is the former enterprise that will be obliged to pay the COFETEL rate; thus, the entity in charge of deciding the suspension must make sure that such provisional measure was request by the enterprise that is trying to interconnect, and, therefore, obliged to pay. This is important, since the enterprise that has the right to be paid is not affected in any way by the determination of a rate that was not charged before. Its only possible interests are the amount of the rate—if it considers that it should be higher than the one set by the COFETEL—or the interconnection in itself, a concern that may be subject to a discussion in the merits of the challenge, but give no grounds for suspension.[56]

This seems to be the first decision in which the Supreme Court imposed clear limits to judicial interventions in regulatory decisions. This decision was followed in 2013 by a new law regulating the *amparo*,[57] which seemed to generally forbid regulated companies from asking for injunctions against decisions by regulatory agencies.[58] This has the potential to have a negative impact on Telcel, while possibly benefiting smaller competitors in the Mexican market. Whether such results will be achieved, however, remains to be seen.

Regulatory change and international investment arbitration

Governmental expropriation has often been a paramount concern for private investors. The state's power to seize private property is one way in which such expropriation may happen. Another, more subtle, way is by changing the regulatory framework. After investors have sunk their money into a sector, it is more costly to remove that investment than to continue operating with a reduced margin of profit than initially expected. In this context, sometimes governments change the regulatory framework opportunistically, generating losses by simply modifying the rules that govern the sector.[59] Allowing investors to seek compensation for the losses incurred as a result of such changes could prevent the government from acting opportunistically.

However, in some cases, such changes are principled and/or necessary instead of opportunistic. Thus, a rule that protects investors against any type of change could potentially undermine the government's or the regulator's ability to bring much-needed modifications to the regulatory framework. In sum, it is hard to determine whether regulatory changes should entitle private investors to some type of compensation and, if so, under what circumstances.[60]

This possibility has become a concern in the context of foreign investment law, particularly under the rules pertaining to indirect expropriation, and the fair and equitable treatment standard. Under certain conditions, changes in domestic regulatory frameworks can be interpreted by an international arbitration tribunal as being an indirect expropriation of a foreign investment, or as unfair or unequitable treatment of foreign investors. In such cases, the state hosting the investment, responsible for changing the regulatory framework, will be held financially liable for such unlawful acts. In this sense, international investment tribunals perform, in effect, a judicial review of domestic regulations, which has an impact in the domestic regulatory state.

This was the case in Argentina, where massive privatization was used in the late 1980s and 1990s to help deal with the adverse macroeconomic conditions faced by the government. Similarly to most of Latin America, there was a delicate balance between "the political stability that made reform possible, and the flexibility needed to adapt contracts to changing circumstances and technology. To be successful in attracting private capital, the reform had to be credible and sustainable to the eyes of investors."[61] In the case of Argentina, some argue that the government was more focused on making public enterprises look attractive for privatization (in order to attract much-needed capital to deal with adverse macroeconomic conditions) than on building an effective and sustainable regulatory framework.[62]

Given that the Argentina's judicial system was not "seen as either truthful or skilled" to perform the task of avoiding administrative expropriation, "foreign investors sought additional protection from international agreements."[63] Thus, Argentina signed the ICSID (International Center for Settlement of Investment Disputes) Convention in May 1991 and deposited its instrument of ratification in October 1994. By signing the ICSID Convention and a number of other bilateral investment agreements, Argentina abandoned its previous policy that required contractual disputes to be submitted to local courts[64] and allowed the use of international investment arbitration without resorting to domestic courts.[65] "This was a strong signal that the government was willing to show commitment to reform."[66]

In 2001, the Argentinian economy collapsed and the government started to unilaterally review several contractual obligations with private investors. In regulated sectors, utility rates were originally pegged to the American dollar, but in 2002 they were converted into pesos (which was largely devalued at the time) and frozen. Foreign and domestic companies suffered significant losses, but foreigners could resort to ICSID arbitration for compensation.[67] As a result, more than 40 claims have been brought against Argentina in the ICSID by foreign investors for breach of bilateral investment treaties,[68] mostly due to the country's adoption of emergency measures enacted after the financial crisis of 2001.[69] Despite having won six of the 10 resolved cases, by February 2012 the awards Argentina had lost amounted to US$400 million.[70]

This process of arbitration had important impacts on the Argentinian regulatory state. Water supply regulation is a case in point. The province of Tucumán (the Republic of Argentina is a federation) awarded in 1995 a 30-year concession of water supply to the Compañía de Aguas del Aconquija S.A. (CAA), an Argentinian company mostly owned by French multinational Vivendi.[71] The concession failed. CAA delivered turbid water in at least two occasions and government officials pressured CAA to reduce tariffs. After several failed negotiations, CAA terminated the contract in August 1997 and was required by provincial authorities to provide the service until October 1998.[72] In 1997 the dispute was brought to an investment tribunal, constituted under ICSID as the investor claimed that Argentina had failed to fulfill its obligations under the 1991 bilateral investment treaty with France. The tribunal agreed and awarded US$105 million to the investor. It is beyond the scope of this chapter to discuss the details of the litigation, which included two awards,[73] two annulment procedures[74] and has been widely analyzed by investment-law scholars. It is clear, though, that such arbitration triggered political mobilization[75] and became an important variable in further developments of the Argentinian regulatory framework.

A similar situation of effective international judicial review of domestic regulation was the dispute between Argentina and the American natural gas company CMS Energy, involving the conversion to pesos of tariffs charged for public utilities, which were originally calculated in US dollars. In the CMS case, the decision was not favorable to Argentina[76]. As Goodman explains:

> . . . although the tribunal in CMS recognized that Argentina had not singled out foreign investors for discriminatory treatment, it found that the government had denied such investors the stable regulatory framework advertised to foreigners throughout the 1990s, which they say induced them to invest into the country. This failure to ensure stability and predictability amounted to a breach of the treaty requirement to give foreign investors 'fair and equitable treatment.'[77]

After the first decision in this case, Argentina applied to annul the CMS award, but the ad hoc committee upheld only one of Argentina's complaints and did not annul the award as a whole.[78] One final dimension related to judicial review of regulation is enforcement of investment awards by local courts. Argentina insists it is open to honoring investment awards. "The only delay, it says, is that the claimants have not brought their rulings to a local court for collection."[79] In this regard, a distinction should be made between ICSID and non-ICSID awards. On the one hand, ICSID awards are domestically enforceable, even without domestic judicial review. As Palacio describes:

> Faced with a large number of claims, Argentina chose to draw out the process by systematically using annulment proceedings against any unfavorable decision, and linked any payment to domestic judicial review—a procedure that violates the language and intent of the ICSID Convention and the BITs themselves. The strategy worked; Argentina has avoided making any payments to its creditors.
>
> But Argentina's short-term gain came at a steep price. A perceived lack of enforceability weakens compliance with investment treaties and rewards repeat offenders, such as Argentina, which has appeared in more ICSID cases than any other state. Indeed, Argentina has developed a general attitude of impunity . . .[80]

Non-ICSID awards, on the other hand, can be reviewed domestically. The US Supreme Court, for example, has reviewed one investment arbitration award concerning Argentina, confirming its jurisdiction to perform such review, but adopting a deferential standard to do so.[81] There are two questions that remain unanswered at this point: one is whether Argentina is able to satisfy all the claims, and the other is whether its insistence on enforcement by local courts is a wise strategy.[82]

As a result of these dynamics, judicial review of the regulatory state in Latin America has become a complex multilevel undertaking: domestic regulation adopted by countries in the region (for example, Argentina) is not only reviewed by domestic courts, but also might be reviewed by international investment tribunals, whose awards can be, in turn, also reviewed by domestic courts (in the case of non-ICSID awards), or by international annulment panels (in the case of ICSID awards).

Conclusion

This chapter sought to highlight some of the tensions and dilemmas that privatization reforms have created in Latin American legal systems. The cases selected and discussed here focused on problems related to regulatory agencies' independence from other branches of government, the tensions between economic regulation and socioeconomic rights, and the dilemmas related to expropriation and the loss of future investment. The judicial decisions presented here try to tackle these issues by determining the priorities and boundaries of both economic regulation and regulatory agencies within Latin American legal regimes.

While bringing attention to these decisions, and making them accessible to an English-speaking audience, this chapter did not seek to discuss their normative underpinnings. In other words, the chapter has not discussed how legal transplants associated with neoliberal reforms could or should be integrated and harmonized with legal systems in the region. Within this broader theme, three topics can be identified.

Questions

a Were independent regulatory agencies properly integrated into Latin American presidential systems and their separation of powers? How? Were courts equipped to deal with questions related to the adequate level of control of agencies and tensions arising from guaranteeing regulatory independence at the expense of democratic accountability?

b Was the new economic regulatory framework harmonized with the constitutional provisions related to socioeconomic rights that are common in Latin America? Were the tensions between the concerns with efficiency in economic regulation and distributive goals in socioeconomic rights resolved? How? Are courts the right forum to sort out such tensions? Should courts be invited to decide whether efficiency should have priority over other considerations in the regulation of public utilities?

c Was the new regulatory framework designed to accommodate the dynamics of Latin American markets? Did the regulatory framework take into consideration the particularities of the legal systems of the region and the potential for opportunistic use of legal mechanisms (such as injunctions) by private actors? Are courts equipped to evaluate and decide when the regulator is abusing its power and when private actors are abusing the use of the legal system to their own advantage and to the detriment of the public interest?

d How did the new regulatory framework interact with pre-existing and emerging international legal obligations acquired by countries in the region? Investment protection treaties, for example, or human rights instruments, impose an external limit to the domestic regulatory process, which is often enforced by courts—domestic, as was the case in Colombia, or international, as the Argentinian experience evidences. How is judicial review of domestic regulation in Latin America affected by these transnational forces? Should policymakers start thinking about a multilevel process of judicial review in the regulatory state?

These four topics illustrate some of the most promising avenues for future research on regulation in Latin America. We hope this chapter contributes to spark even more interest in these themes, especially in the English-speaking world.

Notes

* We are extremely grateful to the comments and suggestions made by Juan F. Gonzalez-Bertomeu, Alejandro Madrazo Lajous, Santiago Montt, Luz Helena Orozco y Villa, and Jose Roldan Xopa. We are also very grateful to Julia Cadaval Martins and Maria Prada for their valuable research assistance.

1 For an overview of these reforms in this book, see Gargarella and Alvarez Ugarte. See also John Williamson (ed.), LATIN AMERICAN READJUSTMENT: HOW MUCH HAS HAPPENED (1989). Moises Naim, *Fads and Fashion in Economic Reforms: Washington Consensus or Washington Confusion?*, 21/3 THIRD WORLD QUARTERLY, 505–28, 505 (2000).

2 D.A.C. Smith and M. Trebilcock, *State-Owned Enterprises in Less Developed Countries: Privatization and Alternative Reform Strategies*, 12/3 EUROPEAN JOURNAL OF LAW AND ECONOMICS, 217–52 (2001). For a concrete overview of the experiences, see Alberto Chong and Florencio Lopez-de-Silanes (eds), PRIVATIZATION IN LATIN AMERICA: MYTHS AND REALITY (2005).

3 Jacint Jordana and David Levi-Faur, *Towards a Latin American Regulatory State? The Diffusion of Autonomous Regulatory Agencies across Countries and Sectors*, 29/4–6 INTERNATIONAL JOURNAL OF PUBLIC ADMINISTRATION, 335–66 (2006). Jacint Jordana and David Levi-Faur, *The Diffusion of Regulatory Capitalism in Latin America Sectoral and National Channels in the Making of New Order*, 598/1 THE ANNALS OF THE AMERICAN ACADEMY OF POLITICAL AND SOCIAL SCIENCE, 102–24 (2005).

4 David Levi-Faur, *The Politics of Liberalization: Privatization and regulation-for-competition in Europe's and Latin America's Telecoms and Electricity Industries*, 42 EUROPEAN JOURNAL OF POLITICAL RESEARCH, 705–40 (2003) (showing that, while Latin America had more full privatizations, it ended up with fewer independent regulatory bodies: Latin American countries had 13 independent agencies against 25 in European countries in 2000).

5 For a detailed description, see Mariana Mota Prado, *The Challenges and Risks of Creating Independent Regulatory Agencies: A Cautionary Tale from Brazil*, 41/2 VANDERBILT JOURNAL OF TRANSNATIONAL LAW (2008), available at http://ssrn.com/abstract=983807.

6 See Warrick Smith, *Utility Regulators: The Independence Debate*, VIEWPOINT, Note No. 127 (The World Bank October 1997). See also OECD, *Reviews of Regulatory Reform: Brazil*, STRENGTHENING GOVERNANCE FOR GROWTH SERIES (2008), available at www.regulacao.gov.br/publicacoes/livros/oecd-reviews-of-regulatory-reform-brazil.

7 Brian Levy and Pablo T. Spiller, *The Institutional Foundations of Regulatory Commitment: A Comparative Analysis of Telecommunications Regulation*, 10/2 JOURNAL OF LAW, ECONOMICS, & ORGANIZATION, 201–46 (1994).

8 Ibid.

9 Giandomenico Majone, *The Regulatory State and its Legitimacy*, 22/1 WEST EUROPEAN POLITICS, 1–24 (1999). See also Colin Scott, *Accountability in the Regulatory State*, 27/1 JOURNAL OF LAW AND SOCIETY, 38–60 (2000).

10 David Levi-Faur, *The Politics of Liberalization: Privatization and regulation-for-competition in Europe's and Latin America's Telecoms and Electricity Industries*, 42 EUROPEAN JOURNAL OF POLITICAL RESEARCH, 705–40 (2003).

11 Supreme Federal Court of Brazil, Decision ADIN 1949–0—RS, November 11, 1999.

12 An important difference between federal and state agencies, which is not relevant for the case, is that federal agencies were exclusive of specific sectors (telecommunications, electricity, oil, transportation, etc.) and state agencies were cross-sectoral, i.e. one agency regulating different services in the same state.

13 Ibid., 9–10, Justice Pertence's opinion. But see the dissenting vote of Marco Aurélio, who argued that this violated the principle of separation of powers.

14 These decisions were consolidated in the Súmula, No. 25. Súmula is "a collection of rules of law that have become firmly settled by decisions of the Supreme Federal Tribunal. Its provisions are summarily cited to dispose of those issues in future litigation." Keith S. Rosenn, *Brazil's Legal culture: the Jeito revisited*, 1/1 FLORIDA INTERNATIONAL LAW JOURNAL, 2–43 (1984).

15 *Autarquias* is a term that will not be translated, and therefore deserves an explanation. The Brazilian bureaucracy can be divided into bodies of the *administração direta* (direct administration) and bodies of the *administração indireta* (indirect administration). *Autarquia* refers to some bodies of the indirect administration that have a higher degree of autonomy, such as public universities. However, regular *autarquias* are not equivalent to independent regulatory agencies, which are classified as special *autarquias* as they have particularly strong guarantees of independence.

16 Supreme Federal Court of Brazil, Decision ADIN 1949–0—RS, November 11, 1999, 11–12, Justice Pertence's vote.
17 Supreme Federal Court of Brazil, Decision MS 8693, November 17, 1962.
18 Dissenting vote of Justice Nunes, quoted by Justice Jobim in Decision ADIN 1949–0—RS.
19 Ibid. It is worth noting that Vitor Nunes Leal issued his opinion in a time when Brazil had a parliamentary system of government. It is not fully clear, however, whether the idea that agencies are agents of the legislatures is compatible with strong presidential systems, such as the ones that exist in Latin America. See Mariana Mota Prado, *Presidential Dominance: the Relationship between the Executive Branch and Regulatory Agencies in Brazil*, in Comparative Administrative Law (S. Rose-Ackerman and P. Lindseth eds, 2010).
20 Ibid.
21 Ibid.
22 Supreme Federal Court of Brazil, Decision ADIN 1949–0—RS, November 11, 1999, opinion of Justice Jobim.
23 Ibid., opinion of Justice Pertence.
24 Ibid. Except for the dissenting vote of Justice Marco Aurelio, who favored simply striking down Article 8.
25 For a discussion of these trade-offs, see Martino Maggetti, *Legitimacy and Accountability of Independent Regulatory Agencies: A Critical Review*, 2 Living Reviews in Democracy (2010), available at www.livingreviews.org/lrd-2010–4.
26 See Julieta Rossi and Leonardo Filippini, *El Derecho Internacional en la Justiciabilidad de los Derechos Sociales: El caso de Latinoamérica* in Derechos Sociales: Justicia, Política y Economía en América Latina at 195 (Pilar Arcidácono, Nicolas Espejo, and César Rodríguez Garavito eds, 2010).
27 Diogo R. Coutinho, *Developing countries in the wake of liberalisation: big challenges ahead*, 4/6 This Century's Review (2006). Diogo R. Coutinho, *Entre eficiência e equidade: a universalização das telecomunicações em países em desenvolvimento*, 2 Revista Direito GV, 137–60 (2005). Bronwen Morgan, Water on Tap: Rights and Regulation in the Transnational Governance of Urban Water Services (2011).
28 For a nuanced analysis of the main distribute issues in the region, based on case studies, see John Nellis and Nancy Birdsall (eds), Reality Check The Distributional Impact of Privatization in Developing Countries (2005).
29 See Yves Dezalay and Bryant G. Garth, *The Internationalization of Palace Wars: Lawyers, Economists, and the Contest to Transform Latin American States*, The Chicago Series in Law and Society (2002).
30 César Rodríguez-Garavito, *Towards a Sociology of the Global Rule of Law Field: Neoliberalism, Neoconstitutionalism, and the Contest over Judicial Reform in Latin America*, in Lawyers and the Rule of Law in an Era of Globalization, at 155–81 (Yves Dezalay and Bryant Garth eds, 2011).
31 See Vivien Foster, Ten Years of Water Service Reform in Latin America: Toward an Anglo-French Model (The International Bank for Reconstruction and Development/The World Bank 2005).
32 César Rodríguez-Garavito, *Towards a Sociology of the Global Rule of Law Field: Neoliberalism, Neoconstitutionalism, and the Contest over Judicial Reform in Latin America*, in Lawyers and the Rule of Law in an Era of Globalization, at 165 (Yves Dezalay and Bryant Garth eds, 2011).
33 See Julieta Lemaitre Ripoll, El Derecho Como Conjuro: Fetichismo Legal, Violencia Y Movimientos Sociales (2009).
34 The court later became instrumental in a massive effort of social transformation, appealing to the language of socioeconomic rights to solve distributive problems, especially through the formula of the Estado Social de Derecho (social state grounded on the rule of law): Rodrigo Uprimny Yepes, *The Enforcement of Social Rights by the Colombian Constitutional Court: Cases and Debates*, in Courts and Social Transformation in New Democracies: An Institutional Voice for the Poor?, at 127–52 (Roberto Gargarella, Pilar Domingo, and Theunis Roux eds, 2006).
35 César Rodríguez-Garavito, *Towards a Sociology of the Global Rule of Law Field: Neoliberalism, Neoconstitutionalism, and the Contest over Judicial Reform in Latin America*, in Lawyers and the Rule of Law in an Era of Globalization, at 158 (Yves Dezalay and Bryant Garth eds, 2011).
36 For a discussion of the underlying theories of justice in this dispute that are, however, not expressly discussed by the court, see Jeremy Waldron, *Socioeconomic Rights and Theories of Justice*, New York University School of Law Public Law & Legal Theory Research Paper Series, No. 10–79 (2010).

37 The relevant articles of the constitution of Colombia:

> Article 334. The general management of the economy is the responsibility of the state. By means of the law, the state will intervene in the exploitation of natural resources, land use, the production, distribution, use, and consumption of goods, and in public and private services in order to streamline the economy with the purpose of achieving an improved quality of life for the inhabitants, the equitable distribution of opportunities, and the benefits of development and conservation of a healthy environment.
>
> The state will make a special effort to ensure full employment and to ascertain that all individuals, especially those of low income, may have effective access to basic goods and services, and to promote productivity and competitiveness and the harmonious development of the regions.
>
> Article 365. Public services are inherent to the social purpose of the state. It is the duty of the state to ensure their efficient provision to all the inhabitants of the national territory.
>
> Public services will be subject to the juridical regime determined by the law, may be provided by the state directly or indirectly, by organized communities, or by individuals. In any case, the state is responsible for the regulation, control, and application of such services. If for reasons of sovereignty or social interest, the state, by means of a law approved by the majority of the members of both chambers upon the initiative of the government, should decide to assign to itself specific strategic or public service activities, it must first indemnify fully those individuals who by virtue of the said law are deprived of the exercise of a lawful activity.

38 Constitutional Court of Colombia, Decision C-150/03, February 25, 2003.
39 Ibid.
40 Ibid.
41 For an interesting discussion about the court as an insider or an outsider of the regulatory process see Manuel José Cepeda Espinosa, *The Judicialization of Politics in Colombia: The Old and the New*, in The Judicialization of Politics in Latin America, at 67 (Alan Angell, Line Schjolden, and Rachel Sieder eds, 2005). See also David Landau, *Political Institutions and Judicial Role in Comparative Constitutional Law*, 51/2 Harvard International Law Journal, 319–65335–42 (2010).
42 Ibid.
43 Ibid.
44 Ibid.
45 For an interesting analysis of the differences in these movements in Latin America, see Sybil Rhodes, Social Movements and Free-Market Capitalism in Latin America: Telecommunications Privatization and the Rise of Consumer Protest (2006). In Brazil there is actually a special consumer protection system established by Statute No. 8,078/90, the Sistema Nacional de Defesa do Consumidor (SNDC) (National System for Consumer's Protection). As a consequence, in Brazil some of these issues are raised as contractual disputes that violate consumer protection clauses.
46 Robert B. Horwitz, *Judicial Review of Regulatory Decisions: The Changing Criteria*, 109/1 Political Science Quarterly, 133–69 (1994). See also Richard J. Pierce, Administrative Law Treatise 1217–400 (2010) (discussing reviewability doctrines).
47 The term in Spanish is *juicio de amparo* and it is regulated by Articles 103 and 107 of the Mexican constitution.
48 OECD, Review of Telecommunication Policy and Regulation in Mexico, 13 (2012):

> the unsatisfactory performance of telecommunications market in Mexico is due in part to the relentless use of injunctions, in particular by the fixed [Telmex] and mobile incumbent [Telcel], which cannot be addressed by a dysfunctional legal system and has replaced, to a large extent, the right and responsibility of the government to implement economic policy and regulation.

49 Ibid. See also *Let Mexico's moguls battle: Mexico suffers from two near-monopolies. It should let them fight each other*, The Economist, February 4, 2012.
50 For a careful analysis of the importance of these rules and the problem of opportunistic use of the judiciary long before this particular case, see Martha Garvia-Murillo and James B. Pick, *Interconnection Regulation: Explaining Dominance by the Incumbent in Mexico,* 53 Communications & Strategies, 17–52 (2004).

51 Supreme Court of Mexico, Thesis Contradiction 268/2010, May 3, 2011.
52 Ibid.
53 Ibid.
54 Ibid.
55 Ibid.
56 Ibid.
57 Nueva Ley de Amparo, April 2, 2013 (regulating Articles 103 and 107 of the Mexican constitution).
58 Article 129, III establishes: "It will be considered that an injunction [against a declared act by the government] negatively affects the social interest and contravenes the public order when . . . it allows the continuation or consummation of wrongs and their effects.
59 Brian Levy and Pablo T. Spiller, *The Institutional Foundations of Regulatory Commitment: A Comparative Analysis of Telecommunications Regulation*, 10/2 Journal of Law, Economics, & Organization, 201–46 (1994).
60 In the United States, this is known as "regulatory takings" and it is a widely disputed issue. In general, some argue that the Fifth Amendment takings clause protects against regulatory takings, but critics argue that the clause applies exclusively to the protection of physical property. Nevertheless, "there seems to be a growing recognition that takings claims are not limited to the land-use context, for regulatory takings claims are being raised in an increasingly broad range of circumstances." Andrea L. Peterson, *The Takings Clause: In Search of Underlying Principles—Part I—A Critique of Current Takings Clause Doctrine*, 77/6 California. Law Review, 1299–1364 (1989). See also Holly Doremus, *Takings and Transitions*, 19/1 Journal of Land Use, 1–46 (2003) and Michael Rapport, *Originalism and Regulatory Takings: Why the Fifth Amendment May Not Protect Against Regulatory Takings, But the Fourteenth Amendment May*, 45 San Diego Law Review, 729–60 (2008).
61 Manuel A. Abdala, *Institutions, Contracts and Regulation of Infrastructure in Argentina,* IV/2 Journal of Applied Economics, 217–54, 220 (2001).
62 Ibid., 222. But see Sunil Tankha, *Lost in Translation: Interpreting the Failure of Privatisation in the Brazilian Electric Power Industry*, 41/1 Journal of Latin American Studies, 59–90 (2009) (arguing that many privatisation policies and the economic stabilization programmes within which they were embedded were not mutually reinforcing in the way that policymakers had expected, and that in their application much of what privatisation theories had claimed was lost in translation).
63 Ibid., 225.
64 This is known as the *Calvo* Doctrine:

> "Named for the Argentine diplomat and jurist, Carlos Calvo, the Calvo Doctrine states that legal disputes involving private individuals conducting business in a foreign country should be resolved by local remedies rather than by international legal remedies . . . Argentina subscribed to the theory that inserting Calvo Clauses into treaties and contracts was necessary to preserve sovereignty and independent authority over its investment interests," Charity L. Goodman, Comment, *Uncharted Waters: Financial Crisis and Enforcement of ICSID Awards in Argentina*, 28/2 University of Pennsylvania Journal of International Law, 449–84, 469–70 (2007).

65 Ibid.
66 Manuel A. Abdala, *Institutions, Contracts and Regulation of Infrastructure in Argentina,* IV/2 Journal of Applied Economics, 217–54, 235 (2001).
67 See Kathryn Khamsi and Jose Alvarez, *The Argentine Crisis and Foreign Investors: A Glimpse into the Heart of the Investment Regime*, in Yearbook on International Investment Law & Policy 2008–2009 (Karl P. Sauvant ed., 2009).
68 ICSID, https://icsid.worldbank.org/.
69 Charity L. Goodman, Comment, *Uncharted Waters: Financial Crisis and Enforcement of ICSID Awards in Argentina*, 28/2 University of Pennsylvania Journal of International Law, 449–84, 452 (2007).
70 *Foreign Investment Disputes: Come and get me*, The Economist, February 18, 2012, available at www.economist.com/node/ 21547836.
71 ICSID, case of "Compañía de Aguas Del Aconquija S.A. and Vivendi Universal S.A. v Argentine Republic," No. ARB/97/3, August 20, 2007.
72 ICSID, case of "Compañía de Aguas Del Aconquija SA and Compagnie Générale Des Eaux v Argentina, Award," No. ARB/97/3, November 21, 2000.
73 Ibid.

74 ICSID, case of "Compañía de Aguas Del Aconquija S.A. and Vivendi Universal S.A. v. Argentine Republic, Decision of the Ad Hoc Committee on the Application for Annulment of the Award," No. ARB/97/3 (Viviendi I), July 3, 2002. ICSID, case of "Compañía de Aguas Del Aconquija S.A. and Vivendi Universal S.A. v. Argentine Republic, Decision of the Ad Hoc Committee on the Application for Annulment of the Award," No. ARB/97/3 (Viviendi II), October 8, 2010.

75 Bronwen Morgan, *Comparative Regulatory Regimes in Water Service Delivery: Emerging Contours of Global Water Welfarism?*, 4 COMPARATIVE RESEARCH IN LAW & POLITICAL ECONOMY RESEARCH PAPER SERIES (2008).

76 ICSID, case of "CMS Gas Transmission Co. v. Argentine Republic," No. ARB/01/8, Award, May 12, 2005.

77 Charity L. Goodman, Comment, *Uncharted Waters: Financial Crisis and Enforcement of ICSID Awards in Argentina*, 28/2 UNIVERSITY OF PENNSYLVANIA JOURNAL OF INTERNATIONAL LAW, 449–84, 478 (2007).

78 John R. Crook, *CMS Gas Transmission Company v. Argentine Republic (ICSID Case No. ARB/01/8) (Annulment Decision, September 25, 2007)*, 22/2 ICSID REVIEW, 455–65 (2007).

79 *Foreign Investment Disputes: Come and get me*, THE ECONOMIST, February 18, 2012, available at www.economist.com/node/ 21547836.

80 Ana Palacio, *How to Boost Foreign Investment*, PROJECT SYNDICATE, April 22, 2013, available at www.project-syndicate.org/commentary/strengthening-international-investment-protection-by-ana-palacio.

81 US Supreme Court, case of "BG Group, PLC v. Republic of Argentina." 134 S. Ct. 1198, 1203 (2014).

82 Charity L. Goodman, Comment, *Uncharted Waters: Financial Crisis and Enforcement of ICSID Awards in Argentina*, 28/2 UNIVERSITY OF PENNSYLVANIA JOURNAL OF INTERNATIONAL LAW, 449–84 (2007). See also SANTIAGO MONTT, STATE LIABILITY IN INVESTMENT TREATY ARBITRATION: GLOBAL CONSTITUTIONAL AND ADMINISTRATIVE LAW IN THE BIT GENERATION (2009).

References

Manuel A. Abdala, *Institutions, Contracts and Regulation of Infrastructure in Argentina,* IV/2 JOURNAL OF APPLIED ECONOMICS, 217–54 (2001).

Alberto Chong and Florencio Lopez-de-Silanes (eds), PRIVATIZATION IN LATIN AMERICA: MYTHS AND REALITY (2005).

Diogo R. Coutinho, *Developing countries in the wake of liberalisation: big challenges ahead*, 4/6 THIS CENTURY'S REVIEW (2006).

Diogo R. Coutinho, *Entre eficiência e equidade: a universalização das telecomunicações em países em desenvolvimento*, 2 REVISTA DIREITO, 137–60 (2005).

John R. Crook, *CMS Gas Transmission Company v. Argentine Republic (ICSID Case No. ARB/01/8) (Annulment Decision, September 25, 2007)*, 22/2 ICSID REVIEW, 455–65 (2007).

Yves Dezalay and Bryant G. Garth, *The Internationalization of Palace Wars: Lawyers, Economists, and the Contest to Transform Latin American States*, THE CHICAGO SERIES IN LAW AND SOCIETY (2002).

Holly Doremus, *Takings and Transitions*, 19/1 JOURNAL OF LAND USE, 1–46 (2003).

Foreign Investment Disputes: Come and get me, THE ECONOMIST, February 18, 2012, available at www.economist.com/node/ 21547836.

Martha Garvia-Murillo and James B. Pick, *Interconnection Regulation: Explaining Dominance by the Incumbent in Mexico,* 53 COMMUNICATIONS & STRATEGIES, 17–52 (2004).

Charity L. Goodman, Comment, *Uncharted Waters: Financial Crisis and Enforcement of ICSID Awards in Argentina*, 28/2 UNIVERSITY OF PENNSYLVANIA JOURNAL OF INTERNATIONAL LAW, 449–84 (2007).

Robert B. Horwitz, *Judicial Review of Regulatory Decisions: The Changing Criteria*, 109/1 POLITICAL SCIENCE QUARTERLY, 133–69 (1994).

Jacint Jordana and David Levi-Faur, *The Diffusion of Regulatory Capitalism in Latin America Sectoral and National Channels in the Making of New Order*, 598/1 THE ANNALS OF THE AMERICAN ACADEMY OF POLITICAL AND SOCIAL SCIENCE, 102–24 (2005).

Jacint Jordana and David Levi-Faur, *Towards a Latin American Regulatory State? The Diffusion of Autonomous Regulatory Agencies across Countries and Sectors*, 29/4–6 INTERNATIONAL JOURNAL OF PUBLIC ADMINISTRATION, 335–66 (2006).

Kathryn Khamsi and Jose Alvarez, *The Argentine Crisis and Foreign Investors: A Glimpse into the Heart of the Investment Regime*, in YEARBOOK ON INTERNATIONAL INVESTMENT LAW & POLICY 2008–2009 (Karl P. Sauvant ed., 2009).

Julieta Lemaitre Ripoll, El Derecho Como Conjuro: Fetichismo Legal, Violencia Y Movimientos Sociales (2009).

David Landau, *Political Institutions and Judicial Role in Comparative Constitutional Law*, 51/2 HARVARD INTERNATIONAL LAW JOURNAL, 335–65 (2010).

Let Mexico's moguls battle: Mexico suffers from two near-monopolies. It should let them fight each other, THE ECONOMIST, February 4, 2012.

David Levi-Faur, *The Politics of Liberalization: Privatization and regulation-for-competition in Europe's and Latin America's Telecoms and Electricity Industries*, 42 EUROPEAN JOURNAL OF POLITICAL RESEARCH, 705–40 (2003).

Brian Levy and Pablo T. Spiller, *The Institutional Foundations of Regulatory Commitment: A Comparative Analysis of Telecommunications Regulation*, 10/2 JOURNAL OF LAW, ECONOMICS, & ORGANIZATION, 201–46 (1994).

Martino Maggetti, *Legitimacy and Accountability of Independent Regulatory Agencies: A Critical Review*, 2 LIVING REVIEWS IN DEMOCRACY (2010), available at www.livingreviews.org/lrd-2010–4.

Giandomenico Majone, *The Regulatory State and its Legitimacy*, 22/1 WEST EUROPEAN POLITICS, 1–24 (1999).

Santiago Montt, State Liability in Investment Treaty Arbitration: Global Constitutional and Administrative Law in the BIT Generation (2009).

Bronwen Morgan, *Comparative Regulatory Regimes in Water Service Delivery: Emerging Contours of Global Water Welfarism?*, 4 COMPARATIVE RESEARCH IN LAW & POLITICAL ECONOMY RESEARCH PAPER SERIES (2008).

Bronwen Morgan, Water on Tap: Rights and Regulation in the Transnational Governance of Urban Water Services (2011).

Moises Naim, *Fads and fashion in economic reforms: Washington consensus or Washington confusion?*, 21/3 THIRD WORLD QUARTERLY, 505–28 (2000).

John Nellis and Nancy Birdsall (eds), Reality Check The Distributional Impact of Privatization in Developing Countries (2005).

OECD, *Reviews of Regulatory Reform: Brazil*, STRENGTHENING GOVERNANCE FOR GROWTH SERIES (2008), available at www.regulacao.gov.br/publicacoes/livros/oecd-reviews-of-regulatory-reform-brazil.

OECD, Review of Telecommunication Policy and Regulation in Mexico, 13 (2012).

Ana Palacio, *How to Boost Foreign Investment*, PROJECT SYNDICATE, April 22, 2013, available at www.project-syndicate.org/commentary/strengthening-international-investment-protection-by-ana-palacio.

Andrea L. Peterson, *The Takings Clause: In Search of Underlying Principles—Part I—A Critique of Current Takings Clause Doctrine*, 77/6 CALIFORNIA. LAW REVIEW, 1301–62 (1989).

RICHARD J. PIERCE, ADMINISTRATIVE LAW TREATISE 1217–400 (2010).

Michael Rapport, *Originalism and Regulatory Takings: Why the Fifth Amendment May Not Protect Against Regulatory Takings, But the Fourteenth Amendment May*, 45 SAN DIEGO LAW REVIEW, 729–60 (2008).

Sybil Rhodes, Social Movements and Free-Market Capitalism in Latin America: Telecommunications Privatization and the Rise of Consumer Protest (2006).

César Rodríguez-Garavito, *Towards a Sociology of the Global Rule of Law Field: Neoliberalism, Neoconstitutionalism, and the Contest over Judicial Reform in Latin America*, in LAWYERS AND THE RULE OF LAW IN AN ERA OF GLOBALIZATION, at 155–81 (Yves Dezalay and Bryant Garth eds, 2011).

Keith S. Rosenn, *Brazil's Legal culture: the Jeito revisited*, 1/1 FLORIDA INTERNATIONAL LAW JOURNAL, 2–43 (1984).

Julieta Rossi and Leonardo Filippini, *El Derecho Internacional en la Justiciabilidad de los Derechos Sociales: El caso de Latinoamérica* in DERECHOS SOCIALES: JUSTICIA, POLÍTICA Y ECONOMÍA EN AMÉRICA LATINA, at 195 (Pilar Arcidácono, Nicolas Espejo, and César Rodríguez Garavito eds, 2010).

Colin Scott, *Accountability in the Regulatory State*, 27/1 JOURNAL OF LAW AND SOCIETY, 38–60 (2000).

D.A.C. Smith and M. Trebilcock, *State-Owned Enterprises in Less Developed Countries: Privatization and Alternative Reform Strategies*, 12/3 European Journal of Law and Economics, 217–52 (2001).

Warrick Smith, *Utility Regulators: The Independence Debate*, Viewpoint, Note No. 127 (The World Bank October 1997).

Sunil Tankha, *Lost in Translation: Interpreting the Failure of Privatisation in the Brazilian Electric Power Industry*, 41/1 Journal of Latin American Studies, 59–90 (2009).

Rodrigo Uprimny Yepes, *The Enforcement of Social Rights by the Colombian Constitutional Court: Cases and Debates*, in Courts and Social Transformation in New Democracies: An Institutional Voice for the Poor?, at 127–52 (Roberto Gargarella, Pilar Domingo, and Theunis Roux eds, 2006).

Jeremy Waldron, *Socioeconomic Rights and Theories of Justice*, New York University School of Law Public Law & Legal Theory Research Paper Series, No. 10–79 (2010).

John Williamson (ed.), Latin American Readjustment: How Much has Happened (1989).

Michael Wilson, *The Enron v. Argentina Annulment Decision: Moving a Bishop Vertically in the Precarious ICSID System*, 43/2 University of Miami Inter-American Law Review, 347–76 (2012).

Further reading

Stephen G. Breyer, Economic Reasoning and Judicial Review (2004).

Manuel José Cepeda Espinosa, *The Judicialization of Politics in Colombia: The Old and the New*, in The Judicialization of Politics in Latin America (Alan Angell, Line Schjolden, and Rachel Sieder eds, 2005).

Vivien Foster, Ten Years of Water Service Reform in Latin America: Toward an Anglo-French Model (The International Bank for Reconstruction and Development/The World Bank 2005).

Giandomenico Majone, *The Regulatory State and its Legitimacy*, 22/1 West European Politics, 1–24 (1999).

Levi-Faur, David and Jacint Jordana, *The Diffusion of Regulatory Capitalism in Latin America Sectoral and National Channels in the Making of New Order*, 598 The Annals of the American Academy of Political and Social Science, 102–124.

Levi-Faur, David and Jacint Jordana, *Towards a Latin American Regulatory State? The Diffusion of Autonomous Regulatory Agencies across Countries and Sectors*, 29/4–6 International Journal of Public Administration, 335–66 (2006).

Mariana Mota Prado, *The Challenges and Risks of Creating Independent Regulatory Agencies: A Cautionary Tale from Brazil*, 41/2 Vanderbilt Journal of Transnational Law (2008), available at http://ssrn.com/abstract=983807.

Mariana Mota Prado, *Implementing Independent Regulatory Agencies in Brazil: The Contrasting Experiences in the Electricity and Telecommunications Sectors*, 6/3 Regulation & Governance, 300–26 (2012).

Mariana Mota Prado, *Presidential Dominance: the Relationship between the Executive Branch and Regulatory Agencies in Brazil*, in Comparative Administrative Law (S. Rose-Ackerman and P. Lindseth eds, 2010).

Colin Scott, *Accountability in the Regulatory State*, 27/1 Journal of Law and Society, 38–60 (2000).

Rene Urueña, *The Rise of the Constitutional Regulatory State in Colombia: The Case of Water Governance*, 6/3 Regulation & Governance, 282–99 (2012).

13 International law and domestic adjudication

*Fernando Basch and Jorge Contesse**

Introduction

The last 25 years in Latin America have witnessed constitutional reforms strengthening the standing of international human rights law, many in response to prior authoritarian regimes.[1] Countries have adopted these reforms at a time in which constitutional review has also risen to prominence. In some countries, constitutions expressly construe international human rights treaties in relation to domestic law, whereas in others they lay silent. Regardless of the constitutional stance, however, courts throughout Latin America have had to articulate doctrines giving application to human rights treaties within domestic legal systems.

In the next section, this chapter examines the particular interaction between constitutional law and international human rights law in Argentina, Chile, and Colombia. We chose these countries as exemplary because they reveal the varying levels of integration between domestic and international law in Latin America. In Argentina and Colombia, courts rely extensively on international human rights treaties in local adjudication; in Chile, however, the use of international human rights standards is inconsistent. Several Latin American countries have adopted Colombia's "constitutional bloc" doctrine, whereby national judges must not only consider domestic norms when deciding cases involving fundamental rights, but also international treaties and the interpretation of such treaties by international courts. In other countries, such as Argentina, constitutional amendments specifically incorporate a large number of international human rights treatises into the constitution. The final part of this chapter offers our conclusions.

Domestic legal systems and international human rights law

Argentina

Since its inception, the Argentinian constitution has been permeable to international law. Inspired by the constitution of the United States, the constitution of 1853–60 recognized as the "supreme law of the nation" not only the constitution and domestic laws, but also international treaties.[2] It also referenced treaties in the spirit of its constitutional principles as the means by which the federal government would strengthen peaceful relations and trade with other countries,[3] and as a source of law governing court cases.[4]

Constitutional interpretations about the status of international law vis-à-vis domestic law oscillated during much of the twentieth century, which was marked by political instability and multiple interruptions to the rule of law. Only in the 1990s did a body of case law, together with a constitutional reform, bring human rights treaties to the forefront of Argentina's constitutional system and begin to build a more stable, although still dynamic applicable framework.

The rights provided for in international treaties: from programmatic to operational

In June 1988, after a well-known Argentinian writer referred to Jesus and Mary on a TV show in a potentially offensive way, an equally well-known and religious legal scholar filed an action against the show's host, requesting that the latter respond by publicly reading aloud a proposed letter. The request was grounded on Article 14.1 of the American Convention on Human Rights (ACHR), to which Argentina had been a party since 1984, which establishes the right to a reply or correction for the benefit of anyone injured by inaccurate or offensive statements or ideas disseminated to the public by a legally regulated media.

After lower courts dismissed the case, it reached Argentina's Supreme Court of Justice, which accepted the claimant's request and ordered his letter to be read on the TV show.[5] In doing so, the court reversed its traditional jurisprudence,[6] whereby rights contained in treaties but not enshrined in domestic legislation were non-enforceable.[7] By holding that immediately applicable treaty provisions were enforceable, the Supreme Court's decision sparked a remarkable evolution in the reception of international law at the domestic level. The court also noted that the normative hierarchy of treaties vis-à-vis domestic law was governed by Article 27 of the Vienna Convention on the Law of Treaties, which confers primacy to conventional international law over domestic law: the incorporation of the American Convention on Human Rights (ACHR) into Argentinian law necessarily involved acknowledging that primacy.[8] Lastly, the court held that any interpretation of the ACHR must be guided by the Inter-American Court of Human Rights' case law.[9] The court also cautioned against the danger of "international responsibility" for breach of international agreements.

This judgment marked the governing principles of the Supreme Court's case law regarding the incorporation of international human rights law to the domestic legal system for the late twentieth and early twenty-first centuries. The advancement of international law and its impact on national sovereignty would from there forward join central discussions in Argentinian constitutionalism regarding the supremacy of the constitution and of the Supreme Court.

The constitutional reform of 1994 and the constitutional status of human rights treaties

In response to the political violence and state terrorism of the twentieth century, Argentina's 1994 constitutional reform conferred constitutional status to more than a dozen human rights treaties already part of Argentinian law, while also establishing a simpler mechanism by which Congress could endow new human rights treaties with constitutional status—by a qualified legislative majority instead of by constitutional amendment.[10]

Article 75, subsection 22, of the constitution of Argentina stipulates that:

> The American Declaration of the Rights and Duties of Man; the Universal Declaration of Human Rights; the American Convention on Human Rights; the International Covenant on Economic, Social and Cultural Rights; the International Covenant on Civil and Political Rights and its Optional Protocol; the Convention on the Prevention and Punishment of the Crime of Genocide; the International Convention on the Elimination of All Forms of Racial Discrimination; the Convention on the Elimination of All Forms of Discrimination against Women; the Convention against Torture and other Cruel, Inhuman or

> Degrading Treatment; the Convention on the Rights of the Child; subject to the conditions of [their] validity, have constitutional status, without repealing any Article of the first part of this constitution, and must be understood as complementing the rights and guarantees therein enshrined . . .
>
> Other treaties and conventions on human rights, after being approved by Congress, shall require the vote of two thirds of all the members of each House to attain constitutional rank.[11]

Because of this norm, all remaining international treaties to which the state is party are hierarchically inferior to the constitution, but superior to legislative statutes ("[T]reaties and concordats take precedence over laws . . .")[12]

In *Monges*, the Board of the School of Medicine of the University of Buenos Aires (UBA) created a different enrollment system than that of the university's other academic units. The Higher Council ("legislative" body) of the UBA requested in court that the federal law legalizing the School of Medicine's action be declared unconstitutional. Such federal law established that "[i]n universities with over fifty thousand (50,000) students systems for admissions, retention, and passing shall be established by each school or equivalent academic unit."[13] The Higher Council believed that this law violated the principle of academic autonomy at university level contained in Article 75.19 of the constitution, which granted to the university, rather than to its individual units, autonomy over such decisions. In response, the School of Medicine pointed to the International Covenant on Economic, Social and Cultural Rights, which also had constitutional status and stipulated that "[h]igher education should be made equally accessible to all, on the basis of capacity, by every appropriate means" (Article 13). After the lower courts rejected the university's claim, the case reached the Supreme Court, which also dismissed the challenge. Most members of the court held that Article 75, subsection 22, of the constitution, which stipulates that treaties "do not repeal any Article" of the constitution, is evidence that "drafters of the constitution made an evidence-based judgment, collating treaties and constitutional provisions, and found that there is no such repeal; and this conclusion cannot be disregarded or challenged by the established powers."[14]

The opinion yielded the doctrine that courts must seek to permanently "harmonize" the constitution with treaties, giving meaning to both while violating neither in the event of apparent inconsistencies. The goal was to prevent a system of "double constitutional status" whereby the constitution took primacy over the treaties contained in Article 75, subsection 22.

Justice Augusto Belluscio, however, alone at first, defended double constitutional status. In the case of *Petric*, in which the right of reply granted by Article 14.1 of the ACHR was also invoked, the dissenting judge noted that human rights treaties constitute "second-rank constitutional rules that prevail over ordinary laws but are valid only to the extent they do not affect the rights enshrined in the first part of the constitution."[15] Justice Fayt reassumed this position almost 20 years later in his dissenting opinions in different cases related to the criminal prosecution of the crimes of the last dictatorship, maintaining that treaties should be subordinated to the constitution pursuant to Article 27, which stipulates that the federal government has the duty to strengthen relations of peace and trade with "foreign powers" by way of "treaties in accordance with the principles of public law established in this constitution." Justice Fayt believed that this norm not only required that treaties be consistent with constitutional principles, but also their subordination to these principles:[16] "constitutional reform merely changed the relationship between treaties and laws that had previously been established in the case of *Ekmekdjian* on the basis of Article 27 of the Vienna Convention, but not that of the treaties—regardless of status—and the national constitution . . ."[17]

The minority positions expressed by Justices Fayt and Belluscio warned about the danger of limiting national sovereignty and sought to prevent "the extension of colonial sovereignty hidden behind apparent legal humanism."[18]

The interpretive authority of the Inter-American Court of Human Rights

The Supreme Court of Argentina has ruled that international treaties must be applied according to a treaty body's interpretation of the treaty's norms.[19] After some oscillation, courts concluded that this standard requires not only that judgments of the Inter-American Court against Argentina are enforced, but also that decisions against other countries serve as guidelines for the interpretation of treaty provisions.

In *Giroldi*,[20] a person who had been convicted and sentenced to one month in prison appealed to the National Court of Cassation in Criminal Matters, the highest criminal court in the country, requesting a ruling on the constitutionality of a procedural norm preventing those who had been sentenced to less than three years from appealing their convictions. The claim was based on Article 8.2.h of the American Convention on Human Rights, which provided a right to appeal in criminal cases. After the court of appeals rejected his claim, the case reached the Supreme Court, which declared the law in question unconstitutional after reviewing Inter-American Court of Human Rights case law on the right to appeal. The court noted that "international treaties to which the country is bound" had to be applied following the decisions of authoritative bodies, "otherwise, the nation could be held accountable by the international community."[21]

However, in the case of *Cantos*, after the Inter-American Court ruled against the Argentinian government for violating the right of access to justice,[22] the Supreme Court rejected a request for the enforcement of the Inter-American Court's judgment. In reaching its conclusion, the Argentinian court first described the two major problems that could arise from the enforcement of judgments of an international tribunal against the state: possible violations of the *res judicata* principle, because already-closed cases could be reopened; and potential violations of the right to defense of persons who, without having participated in the international process, could suffer its consequences.

The majority then held that executing the Inter-American Court's decision meant

> complying with a duty emanating from a treaty with constitutional status . . . leading to the nefarious—and paradoxical—situation of having the Argentinian state incur international responsibility for affecting recognized guarantees and rights . . . arising precisely from the instrument invoked.[23]

In the *Espósito* case the court once again faced a conflict between an Inter-American Court decision and the constitutional rights of those not participating in the inter-American process.[24] The court heard an appeal challenging the dismissal, on the grounds of the application of statute of limitations, of a case accusing a police agent of murdering a young man. In this case, while the Supreme Court's decision was pending, the Inter-American Court issued a ruling against the Argentinian state,[25] ordering, among other remedies, that the investigation continue in order to hold accountable those who were guilty (case of *Bulacio*).[26] The Inter-American Court held that statute of limitation norms could not affect the victim's right to have the offenders prosecuted and punished.

Surprisingly, just one month after *Cantos*, the Supreme Court changed course and ordered the enforcement of a judgment of the Inter-American Court. As in *Cantos*, the Argentinian court stressed "the paradoxical situation of only being able to enforce the duties of the Argentinian state within international human rights jurisdiction [by] strongly restricting the right to defense." But, unlike *Cantos*, it then concluded that it had a duty to comply with the judgment, because "such restrictions, however, were imposed by the international court in charge of ensuring the effective compliance of the rights recognized by the Convention."[27]

The Argentinian court consolidated this doctrine several years later in the case of *Derecho*.[28] At last, the highest court of Argentina seems to have gotten its message through to the Inter-American Court. Following the *Bulacio* case, the Inter-American Court toned down some of its more radical ideas pertaining to the inapplicability of statute of limitations norms and the right of the offender to a defense, reducing the scope of the "duty to punish" doctrine that had been established in the *Bulacio*[29] case, apparently as a result of the criticism levied against it by the Argentinian court.

The highest court of Argentina also established the legal status of the Inter-American Court's decisions on cases decided against other states.

The *Simón*[30] case (2005) questioned the constitutionality of the so-called "impunity laws" that prevented the prosecution of crimes committed during the 1976–83 dictatorship. The Supreme Court had already found such laws constitutional in the case of *Camps*[31] (1987) and several subsequent cases.[32] In *Simón*, however, the court overruled those precedents due to the recent "irruption" of international human rights law and, particularly, of the decisions of the Inter-American Court in the case of *Barrios Altos*, where the latter court had found massive human rights violations committed by the state of Peru.

Barrios Altos held primarily that:

> provisions of amnesty and statutes of limitations and measures designed to eliminate responsibility and hinder the investigation and sanction of those responsible for serious human rights violations such as torture, summary, extrajudicial or arbitrary executions, and enforced disappearances are inadmissible.[33]

The Inter-American Court stated that its judgment was applicable not only to the case's specific violations in Peru, but to all similar amnesty legislation.[34] It consistently applied this doctrine in several and diverse subsequent cases.[35]

Although the self-amnesty laws examined in *Barrios Altos* differed significantly from the "impunity laws" issued by the democratically elected congress of Argentina, the majority of the Argentinian court believed that the *Barrios Altos* doctrine was applicable, stressing that if it were not, the state would incur international liability.[36]

The Supreme Court had already noted the importance of the *Barrios Altos* case in *Arancibia Clavel*[37] and would reiterate it later in the case of *Mazzeo*, where the doctrine of *Barrios Altos* was applied with respect to pardon decrees in favor of persons charged with or convicted of crimes against humanity.[38]

Chile

Like other countries in Latin America where monist legal systems are prevalent, once an international human rights treaty in Chile is ratified by the president and approved by Congress it becomes part of Chile's domestic law.[39] In the specific case of international human rights treaties, in 1989, after Pinochet lost the plebiscite to remain in power for another 10 years, his supporters and the political opposition agreed on 54 amendments to the constitution that the

Chilean people would later approve by referendum. Among these amendments was the addition of a decisive paragraph to Article 5, subsection 2, of the constitution, committing to human rights. The country wanted to cleanse its reputation for human rights violations and thus sought to enhance the position of fundamental rights within its constitutional structure.[40]

The original Article 5, subsection 2, in the 1980 constitution stated that "[t]he exercise of sovereignty is limited by the respect for essential rights originating from human nature." The following was added: "All branches of government, and all public offices, must respect and promote such rights, as guaranteed by this constitution as well as by international treaties ratified by Chile that have entered into force."

As Cumplido observes, there were two reasons for this addition. On the one hand, courts were used to enforcing and interpreting statutes, rather than the constitution. Courts saw the constitution as a political program, not a legal norm that they must enforce. On the other hand, courts often demanded that domestic legislation explicitly look to international treaties before giving full application to constitutional law.[41]

A decision by the Constitutional Court in 1987 largely motivated the 1989 amendment. In a case concerning Clodomiro Almeyda, a prominent socialist political leader who went into exile after Pinochet's coup and returned to Chile secretly, the Constitutional Court stripped Almeyda of his political rights,[42] applying the infamous Article 8 of the constitution, which banned organizations and individuals who disseminated Marxist ideas.[43] Almeyda argued in defense that his conviction constituted a breach of several international human rights instruments that Chile had ratified, but that the executive had nonetheless failed to publish in the *Official Gazette*, the nation's official repertoire of laws.[44] The court closed the debate by declaring that, "within the domestic realm, constitutional norms prevail over international treaties . . ."[45]

The amendment to Article 5 supplements the scope of rights guaranteed by the constitution: individuals were to be protected not only by the bill of rights established in the constitution, but also by the rights enshrined in international treaties.[46] The first step was to fully integrate some of the core international human rights treaties, namely the International Covenant on Civil and Political Rights,[47] the International Covenant on Economic, Social and Cultural Rights,[48] and the American Convention on Human Rights.[49] Eventually, the Pinochet regime published the presidential decrees enacting the international covenants in the *Official Gazette* (except for the American Convention on Human Rights, which only came into force after the new democratic regime took office in 1991) only months before the presidential election that followed his loss in the plebiscite.

International human rights case law after 1990

The new Article 5 has given rise to a bulk of cases in which courts use international human rights norms to adjudicate domestic disputes. However, Chilean courts have not developed a fully consistent theory of the implementation of international human rights law. In some cases courts give constitutional rank to international human rights provisions, whereas in other instances—particularly in decisions by the current constitutional court—they grant merely statutory rank. To analyze this disparity, it is useful to first divide the relevant case law into three subject categories: first, we find decisions on gross and massive human rights violations committed during the dictatorship (1973–90); secondly, decisions involving violations of rights established by both the constitution and international law that do not amount to such systematic violations; and, thirdly, decisions involving violations of rights that are not established by the constitution but solely by international law.

The first group of decisions looks to international human rights treaties to resolve domestic cases concerning gross and massive violations committed by the state during the dictatorship. Here is where the most judicial consistency can be found. For many years, in cases involving forced disappearances, individuals were reported dead and, as a result, courts applied the five-year statute of limitations for murder, thus granting *de jure* impunity for the most egregious human rights violations. However, in 1998, the Supreme Court of Chile changed its stance, ruling that cases of disappearances were not instances of murder but rather of kidnapping, insofar as the individuals (or their bodies) were never found.[50] The court also applied the Chilean-ratified Geneva Conventions, the international human rights treaties that addressed war crimes and listed certain violations as crimes against humanity, to conclude that the crimes against humanity committed during the dictatorship had in fact no statute of limitations. This doctrine, giving preeminence to international human rights treaties, has remained in place with only minor variations for the past decade.

Furthermore, in 2006, the Supreme Court took another step forward in the integration of international law by making use of the 1970 Convention on the Non-Applicability of Statutory Limitations to War Crimes and Crimes Against Humanity, a treaty that Chile had not even ratified. The court deemed the treaty part of international customary law and its norms therefore peremptory (*jus cogens*).[51] More significantly, the court endorsed the doctrine that international norms prevailed over domestic provisions.[52] In the Supreme Court's words: "for years, the court's case law as well as expert opinions have acknowledged that whenever a conflict arises, international law trumps municipal law."[53]

A second group of Chilean decisions concerns third-party human rights violations in a democracy. In these cases, spanning such areas as criminal law,[54] family law,[55] constitutional law (e.g., freedom of expression or non-discrimination), and debtors' prisons,[56] courts have turned to international human rights law to supplement domestic rights. For instance, the constitution of Chile establishes in Article 19, subsection 12, the right to freedom of information. Courts have interpreted such a right in connection with Article 13 of the American Convention and Article 19 of the International Covenant on Civil and Political Rights in order to articulate more sophisticated legal doctrines,[57] in what Gerald Neuman would call "convergence and harmony" between different legal orders.[58]

Finally, a third group of decisions relates to cases in which courts maintain that some rights not explicitly recognized in the text of the constitution are nonetheless protected by Chilean law through Article 5, subsection 2, and thus are domestically enforceable. This is the closest to the situation in other countries, like Colombia, where scholars and courts refer to a " constitutional bloc," whereby, as explained below, international human rights law and constitutional law integrate a common body of applicable law.[59]

The Constitutional Court provides some useful examples.[60] In a 2009 decision the court argued that the child has a right to identity, according to the Convention on the Rights of the Child, notwithstanding that such a right cannot be found in the text of the Chilean constitution,[61] reasoning that "the right to identity is paramount to the right to citizenship—a right that is essential to individuals," and that "[a]s a result . . . the right to identity is among the essential rights that Article 5, subsection 2, recognized for all human beings . . ."[62] The court's decision was preceded by scholars arguing that, despite the fact that certain rights may not be listed in the bill of rights of the Chilean constitution, courts are entitled to enforce them precisely through Article 5, subsection 2.[63]

International human rights law provisions absent from domestic law, however, are not always enforceable by Chilean courts. Arguably, the main feature of this state's case law is its inconsistency: more than two decades after the amendment of Article 5 it remains unclear how international human rights interact with domestic law, particularly in a comparison of decisions by the

Supreme Court with those of the Constitutional Court (a tribunal that is separate from the judiciary and deals only with constitutional questions). The Supreme Court has in fact developed a body of case law increasingly turning to international human rights law in the adjudication of domestic disputes, suggesting that the rights enshrined in international human rights treaties are part of the constitutional scheme of rights.[64] The Constitutional Court nevertheless rejects this trend by reinforcing the notion that international human rights treaties do not trump domestic law. Consequently, the Constitutional Court distances itself jurisprudentially from other jurisdictions.[65] While the Constitutional Court still utilizes international human rights law in its decisions,[66] it has gone so far as to declare that "international treaties are ranked below the constitution because this court may exercise constitutional review of the treaty's norms . . . which would not be possible to do if treaties had a rank equivalent, or superior, to the constitution."[67]

Colombia

Colombia is an excellent example of the transformation of Latin American legal systems resulting, at least in part, from the effect of human rights treaties on domestic law.[68] Pursuant to international conventions, countless decisions of the Constitutional Court of Colombia have expanded in an unprecedented way the scope of rights, and reviewed public policies with the strictest standards, leading to great transformation on not only a legal, but also a political and social level.

The biggest turning point in Colombian legal practice concerning the implementation and application of international human rights law was the adoption of a new constitution in 1991. Before then, during the long period in which the 1886 constitution was effective, the Supreme Court—which until the constitutional reform was the highest authority of judicial review—systematically rejected the idea that a domestic standard could be declared "unenforceable" (or unconstitutional) for breaching a human rights treaty.

The constitution of 1991

The constitution of 1991 radically changed this state of affairs. It established a "social state under the rule of law" ("*estado social de derecho*") organized on the basis of the basic principle of guarantee of and respect for fundamental rights. In keeping with this maxim, the new constitution broadened the catalog of constitutional rights by subjecting state action to a) treaties adopted by the state and b) constitutional rights as interpreted in accordance with such treaties.

The reasons for the enormous transformative power of the constitutional reform are found in the diverse make-up of the Constitutional Assembly, which consisted of not only the traditional liberal and conservative political parties, but also the political and social forces that had been historically excluded from political elections[69] such as leftist parties, demobilized former guerrilla groups, and indigenous and ethnic groups. This multirepresentative composition was the result of the country's special circumstances: prolonged political instability and violence of increasing intensity resulting from the war on drugs.[70]

In addition to explicit rights recognition, the new constitution incorporated the following rules of internalization of international human rights law:

- The principle of non-limitation or non-exhaustiveness of enumerated rights (formula for implicit recognition of the rights in Article 94);
- A rule according to which "duly ratified international labor treaties are part of domestic law" (Article 53);

- The principle that the state's foreign affairs are founded on national sovereignty, respect for the self-determination of peoples, and recognition of the principles of international law accepted by Colombia (Article 9); and
- Priority in the domestic order of certain human rights treaties and their role as guidelines for mandatory constitutional hermeneutics (Article 93).

Human rights treaties in the Colombian constitutional system: the constitutional bloc

Article 93 of the constitution of Colombia stipulates that:

> International treaties and conventions ratified by Congress that recognize human rights and prohibit their limitation in states of emergency prevail in domestic law.
>
> The rights and duties enshrined in this Charter must be interpreted in accordance with international human rights treaties ratified by Colombia.[71]

With this norm, the constitution distinguished two kinds of human rights treaties. On the one hand, those that protect core rights, which cannot be limited even in states of emergency or siege[72] and, on the other hand, the remaining human rights treaties adopted by the state. The constitutional text seems to indicate that the first group prevails over domestic law, whereas the second group is limited to aiding in the interpretation of constitutional standards.

However, the notion of prevalence of the first group of international treaties in the domestic order required greater precision—for example, do the rules mentioned prevail only over statutes, or also over the constitution itself?—as more precision was also needed over the scope of the incorporation of the second group of norms as an interpretive tool.

The Constitutional Court interpreted Article 93 consistently with Article 214 of the constitution. The latter stipulates that: "The states of emergency referred to in the preceding Articles shall be subject to the following provisions . . . II. Human rights and fundamental freedoms may not be suspended. International humanitarian law shall be applicable to all cases . . ."[73]

The Colombian court noted that the treaties mentioned in Article 93 are part of the "constitutional bloc," a concept that originated in French law and that the court has used since 1995.[74] The constitutional bloc was defined as being

> composed of those standards and principles that, without formally appearing in the body of the constitution, are used as parameters for reviewing the constitutionality of laws, for they have been normatively integrated into the constitution, via various channels and constitutional mandates. Thus, these principles and rules of constitutional value hold true, that is, these rules are at a constitutional level, even if they may sometimes contain reform mechanisms that vary from *stricto sensu* constitutional standards.[75]

The court has articulated two different interpretations of this concept. In a narrow sense, the constitutional bloc consists of rules that the constitution itself ranks with constitutional status; in a broader sense, however, the constitutional bloc also includes rules that do not have constitutional status yet but are ranked above domestic laws and must be taken into account by courts when exercising judicial review.[76]

The incorporation of the concept of the constitutional bloc into the Colombian legal system solved the problem of the hierarchy of norms contained in human rights treaties adopted by the state. The constitutional case law immediately following the 1991 reform highlighted that such treaties prevail as long as they do not breach the standards contained in the constitution.[77]

The court made use of the constitutional bloc concept to solve the apparent conflict between the standard contained in Article 93, according to which certain human rights treaties prevailed in the domestic order, and that in Article 4, which stipulates that "the constitution is the norm of norms. In the event of incompatibility between the constitution and statute or other legal norms, constitutional provisions shall prevail."

The apparent conflict between the supremacy of the constitution on the one hand and human rights treaties on the other was solved by placing both at the same hierarchical level, as part of the same constitutional bloc. In the words of the Colombian court:

> [T]he Constitutional Court agrees that the only reasonable interpretation of the notion of prevalence of human rights treaties and international humanitarian law . . . is that, together with the rest of the constitution, they make up a 'constitutional bloc' that must be enforced by law. This, in fact, fully harmonizes the principle of constitutional supremacy as the norm of norms (constitution of Colombia, Article 4) with the prevalence of treaties that have been ratified by Colombia, which recognize human rights and prohibit their limitation except in states of emergency (constitution of Colombia, Article 93).[78]

The court noted that, if pursuant to the first paragraph of Article 93, the constitution should incorporate all rights and principles not expressly recognized by the constitution but still meeting the requirement of illimitability during states of emergency, then the second paragraph of said article would enhance the rights already enshrined in the constitution by conforming them to the treaties ratified by Colombia. On the other hand, by emphasizing the binding nature of the *pro homine* clause contained in human rights treaties, the court noted that the second paragraph "constitutionalizes all human rights treaties ratified by Colombia and relating to rights already enshrined in the constitution."[79]

Thus, the Constitutional Court abandoned its literal interpretation of Article 93, subsection 2. Not only do human rights treaties prohibiting the limitation of rights during states of emergency in Colombia have constitutional hierarchy, but so do ratified human rights treaties to the extent that they relate to rights already enshrined in the constitution.

Authority of decisions by treaty supervisory bodies

The interpretation of the second paragraph of Article 93 of the constitution of Colombia led the Constitutional Court to state that the jurisprudence of the supervisory bodies of international human rights treaties was "an important hermeneutical criterion for establishing the meaning of constitutional provisions with respect to fundamental rights."[80]

According to the Constitutional Court, "insofar as Article 93 of the constitution provides that constitutional rights and duties are to be interpreted in accordance with international human rights treaties ratified by Colombia," it is clear that the case law of international bodies in charge of interpreting those treaties are an important hermeneutic criterion for establishing the meaning of constitutional provisions with respect to fundamental rights."[81] According to the judgment of the Constitutional Court, this category includes not only the case law of international courts, but also the recommendations of the supervisory bodies of the human rights treaties ratified by Colombia.[82]

However, Colombian case law is still not sufficiently clear as to whether the decisions of international courts and other treaty bodies that make up the constitutional bloc are binding or merely guiding. While the Constitutional Court has referred to the binding nature of decisions by the Inter-American Court,[83] it has only done so when citing precedent that merely confirms its relevance as an interpretational guideline, without establishing precise criteria for determining in which cases a decision of an international body is binding.

In conclusion, the incorporation of international human rights law to the Colombian constitutional scheme gave legal basis to many major decisions of the Constitutional Court that, by direct application of international treaty standards or formulation of generous interpretations based on international case law, significantly broadened the scope of rights, for example in the application of international humanitarian law,[84] criminal and procedural guarantees,[85] social rights,[86] personal rights,[87] indigenous rights,[88] and women's rights.[89] Inter-American case law was also relevant to the debates on reduced sentences in the peace process with paramilitary groups in Colombia,[90] among other political issues of significance.

Conclusion

By examining how the international law of human rights has been incorporated to the domestic legal systems of Argentina, Chile, and Colombia, we were able to reveal the various patterns common to different Latin American countries. Both the Argentinian and the Colombian cases are examples of strong integration, developed as a consequence of constitutional engineering expressly determined to incorporate human rights treaties into domestic law. Both countries' courts have also taken the lead, as well, in articulating the duty to follow the case law of international human rights tribunals.

On the other hand, the Chilean case shows a more moderate path in the process of integration. In Chile, debate continues as to the meaning of constitutional clauses regarding obligations under international treaties, with courts less consistent than those in Argentina and Colombia regarding the hierarchy of human rights treaties and the authority of international or regional human rights case law. Nonetheless, international human rights law has still impacted Chile's legal system, producing surprising legal transformations.

Finally, the recent doctrine of conventionality control is at the core of the current constitutional debate in Latin America. It has significant potential to strengthen the protection of human rights within domestic legal systems. However, it requires further refinement in order to avoid conflict with the domestic distribution of judicial review authority.

Questions

a In some Latin American countries the use of international human rights standards is pervasive (e.g., Argentina and Colombia) whereas in others, such as Chile, it is more limited. Do you think the integration of international human rights norms enhances or weakens the national democratic processes?

b Did the court go too far in the case of *Gelman v. Uruguay* (reviewed in chapter 7)? If a national law is supported by a popular referendum, should a regional court defer to the domestic decision? Is the case of gross and massive violations of human rights distinct? Should a regional court strike down domestic legislation that, for instance, bans same-sex marriage in a conservative country?

c The European Court of Human Rights has articulated the doctrine of the "margin of appreciation," whereby the court defers to states regarding how rights ought to be protected on the grounds that the states are in a better position to decide. Some commentators think the inter-American human rights system should also embrace such a doctrine, while others argue that such a doctrine is foreign to inter-American law. Which position do you agree with?

Notes

* This chapter was translated into English by the authors in collaboration with Paula Arturo.

1 Thus, for instance, new constitutions were adopted in Brazil (1988), Colombia (1991), Venezuela (1999), and Peru (1993), and significant constitutional reforms were passed in Argentina (1994) and Chile (1989).

2 Constitución de la Nación Argentina (National Constitution of Argentina), August 22, 1994, Article 31.

3 Ibid., Article 27.

4 Ibid., Article 116.

5 Supreme Court of Argentina, case of "Ekmekdjian, Miguel A. c. Sofovich, Gerardo y otros," July 7, 1992.

6 Supreme Court of Argentina, case of "E.F.E." (Decisions 310:1081). In that case, the court held that Article 17.5 of the American Convention on Human Rights, which provides for the right to equal treatment of children born out of wedlock, was programmatic.

7 The court also overturned a precedent in an analogous case: Supreme Court of Argentina, case of "Ekmekdjian, Miguel A. c/ Neustadt, Bernardo y otros s/amparo," December 1, 1988.

8 Ibid., paragraph 18.

9 Ibid., paragraph 21.

10 To date, this procedure was applied to give constitutional status to two instruments: the Inter-American Convention on Forced Disappearance of Persons and the Convention on the Non-Applicability of Statutory Limitations to War Crimes and Crimes against Humanity.

11 Constitución de la Nación Argentina (National Constitution of Argentina), August 22, 1994, Article 75, subsection 22.

12 Ibid.

13 Ley Nacional de Educación Superior (National Law of Higher Education), Article 50.

14 Supreme Court of Argentina, case of "Monges, Analía M. c/ U.B.A.," December 26, 1996, paragraph 20.

15 Supreme Court of Argentina, case of "Petric, Domagoj A. c/ diario Página 12" April 16, 1998, paragraph 7.

16 This doctrine is grounded on the notion that treaties enjoy constitutional status "subject to the conditions of [their] validity," that is, that treaties have been incorporated into domestic law as they are effectively applied on the international plane, "taking particularly into account their effective jurisprudential application by competent international courts in their interpretation and enforcement." See Supreme Court of Argentina, case of "Arancibia Clavel, Enrique Lautaro y otros s/asociación ilícita, intimidación pública y daño y homicidio agravado," August 24, 2004, opinion of Justice Fayt in dissidence, paragraph 15.

17 Ibid.

18 Ibid., paragraph 16.

19 Supreme Court of Argentina, case of "Giroldi, Horacio David y otro s/ recurso de casación," April 7, 1995, paragraph 11.

20 Ibid.

21 Ibid., paragraph 12.

22 Inter-American Court of Human Rights, case of "Cantos v. Argentina," November 28, 2002 (Merits, Reparations, and Costs), paragraph 77.

23 Supreme Court of Argentina, case of "Cantos, José María c/ Santiago del Estero," August 21, 2003, paragraph 4.

24 Supreme Court of Argentina, case of "Espósito, Miguel Ángel s/ incidente de prescripción de la acción penal promovido por su defensa," December 23, 2004.

25 Inter-American Court of Human Rights, case of "Bulacio v. Argentina," September 18, 2003 (Merits, Reparations, and Costs).

26 Ibid., paragraph 105.

27 Ibid., paragraph 16.

28 Supreme Court of Argentina, case of "Derecho, René Jesús s/ incidente de prescripción de la acción penal—Case No. 24,079," November 29, 2011.

29 See Inter-American Court of Human Rights, case of "Albán Cornejo et al. v. Ecuador," November 22, 2007 (in this case, the Inter-American Court restricted the applicability of the principle of

imprescriptibility of criminal prosecution to those recognized in international law, as claimed by the Argentinian court in the case of *Espósito*).

30 Supreme Court of Argentina, case of "Recurso de hecho deducido por la defensa de Julio Héctor Simón en la causa Simón, Julio Héctor y otros s/ privación ilegítima de la libertad, etc.—causa No. 17,768," June 14, 2005 (Decisions 328:2056).

31 Supreme Court of Argentina, case of "Camps, Ramón Juan Alberto y otros," June 22, 1987 (Decisions 310:1162).

32 Supreme Court of Argentina, Decisions 311:401, 816, 890, 1085 and 1095; 312:111; 316:532 and 2171, and 321:2031, among others.

33 Inter-American Court of Human Rights, case of "Barrios Altos (Chumbipuma Aguirre et al. v. Peru)," March 14, 2001, paragraph 41.

34 Inter-American Court of Human Rights, case of "Barrios Altos (Chumbipuma Aguirre et al. v. Peru)," September 3, 2001.

35 This argument contains the rationale behind the "conventionality control" doctrine, in light of which all national judges have a duty to contrast local legislation not only with the constitution, but also with the American Convention on Human Rights.

36 Supreme Court of Argentina, case of *Simón*, particularly the opinion of Justice Boggiano, paragraphs 30–31, Justice Zaffaroni, paragraphs 30–35, Justice Highton de Nolasco, paragraph 30, and Justice Lorenzetti, paragraph 29.

37 Supreme Court of Argentina, case of "Arancibia Clavel, Enrique Lautaro s/ homicidio calificado y asociación ilícita y otros," August 24, 2004.

38 Supreme Court of Argentina, case of "Mazzeo, Julio Lilo y otros s/ rec. de casación e inconstitucionalidad," July 13, 2007.

39 See Robert Goldman et al., The International Dimension of Human Rights: A Guide for Application in Domestic Law 95–5 (Inter-American Development Bank 2001) (discussing Latin American constitutions that establish monist systems of incorporation). On the monist and dualist theories, see Rosalyn Higgins, Problems & Process: International Law and How To Use It 209 (1994): "Monists contend that there is but a single system of law, with international law being an element within it alongside all the various branches of domestic law . . . Dualists contend that there are two essentially different legal systems, existing side by side within different spheres of action—the international plane and the domestic plane."

40 On the history of this amendment, see Francisco Cumplido, *La reforma constitucional de 1989 al inciso 2o del artículo 5o de la Constitución: sentido y alcance de la reforma. Doctrina y Jurisprudencia*, 9/1 Ius et Praxis, 365–74 (2003). Cumplido's account is particularly relevant as he led the political opposition's negotiation team with the military junta.

41 Ibid., 369. During the Pinochet dictatorship courts were particularly obsequious with the executive's violations of basic rights. See Lisa Hilbink, Judges Beyond Politics in Democracy and Dictatorship: Lessons from Chile (2007) (discussing the structure and ideology of the Chilean judiciary and its failure to take stands in defense of rights and rule of law principles). See also Human Rights Committee, Consideration of Reports Submitted by States Parties Under Article 40 of the Covenant, CCPR/C/95/Add.11 (December 2, 1998), paragraph 44 ("The aim of the reform was to strengthen the position of human rights in the domestic legal order.")

42 Constitutional Court of Chile, Decision 46/1987, December 21, 1987.

43 Former Article 8 of the constitution established: "Any action by an individual or group intended to propagate doctrines attempting against the family, or which advocate violence or a concept of society, the State or the juridical order, of a totalitarian character or based on class warfare, is illegal and contrary to the institutional code of the Republic. The organizations and political movements or parties which, due to their purposes or the nature of the activities of their members, tend toward such objectives, are unconstitutional . . ."

44 According to Chilean law, statutes are fully valid only when published in the *Official Gazette* (Article 7 of the civil code). This provision also applies to international treaties: they can only be cited as valid legal rules once they have been fully incorporated into domestic law. The process of incorporation is not complete with the treaty's ratification, but its publication. See M. Verdugo, E. Pfeffer, and H. Nogueira, II Derecho Constitucional 79 (2003).

45 Constitutional Court of Chile, Decision 46/1987, December 21, 1987, paragraph 27. The court's doctrine can be traced back to the first half of the twentieth century. In a case decided in 1920, the Supreme Court (a court that is different from the Constitutional Court) stated that international

treaties must be subject to the same regulations as domestic statutes to enter into force; that is, a presidential decree of enactment and its subsequent publication in the *Official Gazette*. See Santiago Montt, *Aplicación de los Tratados Bilaterales de Protección de Inversiones por Tribunales Chilenos. Responsabilidad del Estado y Expropiaciones Regulatorias en un Mundo Crecientemente Globalizado*, 32/1 REVISTA CHILENA DE DERECHO, 19–78 (2005).

46 HUMAN RIGHTS COMMITTEE, CONSIDERATION OF REPORTS SUBMITTED BY STATES PARTIES UNDER ARTICLE 40 OF THE COVENANT, CCPR/C/95/ADD.11 (December 2, 1998), paragraph 16: "It is almost universally understood that, in order to reinforce respect for and protection of human rights in Chile, the legislative force of the international conventions embodying those rights has been altered to give them constitutional status and create an important distinction between them and international conventions on other subjects. As a result, the fundamental rights, responsibilities and guarantees contained in the international conventions ratified by, and in force in, Chile, must be understood to augment and supplement the list of rights embodied in Article 19 of the constitution [where the bill of rights is contained], and to have the same constitutional status."

47 December 16, 1966, 999 UNTS 171; S. Exec. Doc. E, 95–2 (1978).

48 December 16, 1966, 993 UNTS 3; S. Exec. Doc. D, 95–2 (1978).

49 November 21, 1969, OAS TS No. 36; 1144 UNTS 143.

50 Supreme Court of Chile, Decision 469–98, September 9, 1998. According to the Chilean penal code, someone cannot be charged with murder if there is no dead body. And, as long as the body is not found, the crime of kidnapping is still in progress, therefore no statute of limitations can be applied.

51 Dinah Shelton, a US law professor and current president of the Inter-American Commission on Human Rights, explains that "[t]he theory of *jus cogens* or peremptory norms posits the existence of rules of international law that admit of no derogation and that can be amended only by a new general norm of international law of the same value." See Dinah Shelton, *Normative Hierarchy in International Law*, 100/2 AMERICAN JOURNAL OF INTERNATIONAL LAW, 291–323, 291 (2006).

52 Supreme Court of Chile, Decision 559–2004, December 13, 2006.

53 Ibid., paragraph 23. This decision cites at least three decisions by the Inter-American Court of Human Rights: *Blake*, *Godínez Cruz*, and *Barrios Altos*. Ibid., paragraphs 19–20. See also Supreme Court of Chile, Decision 907/2004, March 13, 2007 and Supreme Court of Chile, Decision 4183/2006, April 18, 2007.

54 The Rules of Criminal Procedure establish that the Supreme Court shall have the power to annul a given decision if the rights of the defendant, as recognized by both the constitution and international treaties, are breached. See Article 373, subsection a, of the Rules of Criminal Procedure.

55 Family law courts must interpret notions such as "the best interest of the child" according to international human rights law. See, for example, Article 225 of the civil code.

56 Constitutional Court of Chile, Decision 519/2007, June 5, 2007.

57 See Felipe González (ed.), LIBERTAD DE EXPRESIÓN EN CHILE (2006) (discussing cases on access to information where courts have followed the interpretation of Organization of American States's bodies).

58 See Gerald Neuman, *Human Rights and Constitutional Rights: Harmony and Dissonance*, 55/5 STANFORD LAW REVIEW, 1863–1900, 1863 and 1866 (2003).

59 There are, in fact, scholars who claim that the constitutional bloc is a reality in Chile. See Miguel Ángel Fernández González, *La aplicación por los tribunales chilenos del derecho internacional de los derechos humanos*, 8/1 ESTUDIOS CONSTITUCIONALES, 425–42 (2010) and Humberto Nogueira, *El uso del derecho convencional internacional de los derechos humanos en la jurisprudencia del Tribunal Constitucional chileno2006–2010*, 39/1 REVISTA CHILENA DE DERECHO, 149–87 (2012). The Constitutional Court, however, has explicitly rejected the notion of a constitutional bloc. See Constitutional Court of Chile, Decisions 2387/12 and 2388/12, January 23, 2013.

60 Nogueira cites at least 15 decisions by the Constitutional Court adopted in a rather short period of time (2006–10). Ibid., 183.

61 Constitutional Court of Chile, Decision 1340/09, September 29, 2009.

62 Ibid., paragraph 10.

63 See ANGELA VIVANCO, II CURSO DE DERECHO CONSTITUCIONAL 239 (2006). See also JOSÉ LUIS CEA, II DERECHO CONSTITUCIONAL 49 (2004) and Marisol Peña, *La aplicación del derecho internacional de los derechos humanos por el Tribunal Constitucional chileno*, 6/1 ESTUDIOS CONSTITUCIONALES, 205–22 (2008).

64 Such a doctrine has gained some track with cases regarding indigenous peoples' rights. See Jorge Contesse and Domingo Lovera, *El Convenio 169 de la OIT en la jurisprudencia chilena: prólogo del incumplimiento*, 1/5 1 Anuario de Derecho Público, 127–51 (2011).

65 Constitutional Court of Chile, Decision 2387–12 and 2388–12, January 23, 2013, 31. Interestingly, the court cites Argentina and Colombia to show the differences with the Chilean system.

66 Perhaps the most notorious case is the decision on the constitutionality of heterosexual marriage. In this decision, the court did not address the merits of the problem, rejecting the petition on formal grounds. However, all justices wrote separate opinions in which they all used international human rights law to either justify the constitutionality of the definition of marriage as the union of a man and a woman or to reject that definition as unconstitutional. See Jorge Contesse, *Matrimonio civil y Constitución Política: la sentencia del Tribunal Constitucional sobre matrimonio para parejas del mismo sexo*, 8 Anuario de Derechos Humanos, 155–64 (2012).

67 Constitutional Court of Chile, Decision 2387–12 and 2388–12, January 23, 2013 32. The court has held such doctrine in at least five decisions (Decisions 346/2002, 1050/2008, 1288/2008, 1307/2009, and 1988/2011).

68 New trends in the Colombian legal system should also be attributed, among other things, to the creation—and the great activism—of a Constitutional Court that places special emphasis on the adjudication of constitutional issues and a true "revolution in access to justice" that was made possible thanks to the creation of procedural instruments for the guarantee of rights, such as protection measures and public action of unconstitutionality. Francisca Pou Giménez, *Justicia constitucional y protección de derechos en América Latina: el debate sobre la regionalización del activismo* in El Derecho en América Latina: un mapa para el pensamiento jurídico del siglo XXI, at 231 (César Rodríguez Garavito ed., 2012).

69 Rodrigo Uprimny Yepes, *La judicialización de la política en Colombia: casos, potencialidades y riesgos*, 6/3 Sur-Revista Internacional de Derechos Humanos, 53–70 (2007).

70 César Rodríguez Garavito, La Globalización del Estado de Derecho 48–9 (2009).

71 Article 17 of the constitution of Ecuador of 1998 contains a similar provision to that found in Guatemala and Honduras.

72 The Constitutional Court included in this group the four Geneva Conventions on international humanitarian law, on the basis that they are *ius cogens* standards whose purpose is precisely to regulate the protection of fundamental rights in states of emergency such as military conflicts: Constitutional Court of Colombia, Decision C-488/09, July 22, 2009.

73 Constitución Política De Colombia (Constitution of Colombia), July 21, 1991, Article 214.

74 Constitutional Court of Colombia, Decision C-225/95, May 18, 1995.

75 Ibid., paragraph 12.

76 Ibid. This view has prevailed to date. See Constitutional Court of Colombia, Decision C-307/09, April 29, 2009.

77 Constitutional Court of Colombia, Decision C-295/93, July 29, 1993.

78 Constitutional Court of Colombia, Decision C-225/95, May 18, 1995, paragraph 12.

79 Constitutional Court of Colombia, Decision T-1319/01, December 17, 2011, paragraph 12.

80 Constitutional Court of Colombia, Decision C-376/10, May 19, 2010, paragraph 4, among many others.

81 Constitutional Court of Colombia, Decision C-370/06, May 18, 2006, paragraph 4.6. See also Decisions: C-406/96, August 23, 1996, and C-010/00, January 19, 2000, among others.

82 Alejandro Ramelli Arteaga, Jurisprudencia penal Internacional aplicable a Colombia (2011).

83 The constitutional court has held that "on several occasions, this court has ruled on the compulsory and binding nature of the decisions of the Inter-American Court of Human Rights, whose jurisdiction has been accepted by Colombia and this court pursuant to Article 93 above, as this court is the competent body for interpreting the American Convention on Human Rights" (Constitutional Court of Colombia, Decision C-715/12, September 13, 2012, paragraph 4.3).

84 Constitutional Court of Colombia, Decisions T-409/92, June 8, 1992, and C-574/92, October 28, 1992.

85 Rodrigo Uprimny Yepes, Bloque de constitucionalidad, derechos humanos y nuevo procedimiento penal, available at www.dejusticia.org/index.php?modo=interna&tema=estado_de_derecho&publicacion=73.

86 As noted by César Rodríguez Garavito, "Colombia's Constitutional Court in general and its jurisprudence on social rights in particular, have become one of the icons of progressive neoconstitutionalism" (César Rodríguez Garavito, La Globalización del Estado de Derecho 40 (2009)). See

Constitutional Court of Colombia, Decisions T-568/99, August 10, 1999; C-551/03, July 9, 2003; T-642/04, July 1, 2004; T-666/04, July 9, 2004; T-697/04, July 22, 2004; and T-827/04, September 29, 2004.

87 Constitutional Court of Colombia, Decision T-447/95, October 23, 1995, in which the right to a person's identity was recognized as an inherent right.

88 Convention 169 of the International Labor Organization was included by the Constitutional Court among the treaties that made up the constitutional bloc, and more than 40 cases have been resolved on this normative basis. See Christian Courtis, *Notes on the implementation by Latin American countries of the ILO Convention 169 in indigenous peoples* 10/3 SUR-INTERNATIONAL JOURNAL ON HUMAN RIGHTS, 53–82, 58 (2009). Other conventions, such as Conventions 87 and 88, were also included in the constitutional bloc. Decisions T-568/99, August 10, 1999; T-304/04, March 29, 2004; T-615/04, June 26, 2004; and T-891/04, September 15, 2004, considered Conventions 87 and 88. Decision T-606/01, June 7, 2001, considered Convention 169.

89 Constitutional Court of Colombia, Decision T-622/97, November 27, 1997.

90 Víctor Abramovich, *From massive violations to structural patterns: new approaches and classic tensions in the inter-American human rights system*, 6/11 Sur-International Journal on Human Rights, 7–38 (2009).

References

Víctor Abramovich, *From massive violations to structural patterns: new approaches and classic tensions in the inter-American human rights system*, 6/11 SUR-INTERNATIONAL JOURNAL ON HUMAN RIGHTS, 7–38 (2009).

JOSÉ LUIS CEA, DERECHO CONSTITUCIONAL (2004).

Jorge Contesse and Domingo Lovera, *El Convenio 169 de la OIT en la jurisprudencia chilena: prólogo del incumplimiento*, 1/5 1 ANUARIO DE DERECHO PÚBLICO, 127–51 (2011).

Jorge Contesse, *Matrimonio civil y Constitución Política: la sentencia del Tribunal Constitucional sobre matrimonio para parejas del mismo sexo*, 8 ANUARIO DE DERECHOS HUMANOS, 155–64 (2012).

Christian Courtis, *Notes on the implementation by Latin American countries of the ILO Convention 169 in indigenous peoples* 10/3 SUR-INTERNATIONAL JOURNAL ON HUMAN RIGHTS, 53–82 (2009).

Francisco Cumplido, *La reforma constitucional de 1989 al inciso 2o del artículo 5o de la Constitución: sentido y alcance de la reforma. Doctrina y Jurisprudencia*, 9/1 IUS ET PRAXIS, 365–74 (2003).

Miguel Ángel Fernández González, *La aplicación por los tribunales chilenos del derecho internacional de los derechos humanos*, 8/1 ESTUDIOS CONSTITUCIONALES, 425–42 (2010).

Robert Goldman et al., THE INTERNATIONAL DIMENSION OF HUMAN RIGHTS: A GUIDE FOR APPLICATION IN DOMESTIC LAW (Inter-American Development Bank 2001).

Felipe González (ed.), LIBERTAD DE EXPRESIÓN EN CHILE (2006).

ROSALYN HIGGINS, PROBLEMS & PROCESS: INTERNATIONAL LAW AND HOW TO USE IT (1994).

LISA HILBINK, JUDGES BEYOND POLITICS IN DEMOCRACY AND DICTATORSHIP: LESSONS FROM CHILE (2007).

Human Rights Committee, *Consideration of Reports Submitted by States Parties Under Article 40 of the Covenant*, CCPR/C/95/Add.11 (December 2, 1998).

Santiago Montt, *Aplicación de los Tratados Bilaterales de Protección de Inversiones por Tribunales Chilenos. Responsabilidad del Estado y Expropiaciones Regulatorias en un Mundo Crecientemente Globalizado*, 32/1 REVISTA CHILENA DE DERECHO, 19–78 (2005).

Gerald Neuman, *Human Rights and Constitutional Rights: Harmony and Dissonance*, 55/5 STANFORD LAW REVIEW, 1863–1900 (2003).

Humberto Nogueira, *El uso del derecho convencional internacional de los derechos humanos en la jurisprudencia del Tribunal Constitucional chileno2006–2010*, 39/1 REVISTA CHILENA DE DERECHO, 149–187 (2012).

Marisol Peña, *La aplicación del derecho internacional de los derechos humanos por el Tribunal Constitucional chileno*, 6/1 ESTUDIOS CONSTITUCIONALES, 205–22 (2008).

Francisca Pou Giménez, *Justicia constitucional y protección de derechos en América Latina: el debate sobre la regionalización del activismo* in EL DERECHO EN AMÉRICA LATINA: UN MAPA PARA EL PENSAMIENTO JURÍDICO DEL SIGLO XXI, at 231 (César Rodríguez Garavito ed., 2012).

ALEJANDRO RAMELLI ARTEAGA, JURISPRUDENCIA PENAL INTERNACIONAL APLICABLE A COLOMBIA (2011).
CÉSAR RODRÍGUEZ GARAVITO, LA GLOBALIZACIÓN DEL ESTADO DE DERECHO (2009).
RODRIGO UPRIMNY YEPES, BLOQUE DE CONSTITUCIONALIDAD, DERECHOS HUMANOS Y NUEVO PROCEDIMIENTO PENAL, available at www.dejusticia.org/index.php?modo=interna&tema=estado_de_derecho&publicacion=73.
Rodrigo Uprimny Yepes, *La judicialización de la política en Colombia: casos, potencialidades y riesgos*, 6/3 SUR-REVISTA INTERNACIONAL DE DERECHOS HUMANOS, 53–70 (2007).
M. VERDUGO, E. PFEFFER, AND H. NOGUEIRA, DERECHO CONSTITUCIONAL (2003).
ANGELA VIVANCO, CURSO DE DERECHO CONSTITUCIONAL (2006).

Further reading

ALLAN R. BREWER-CARÍAS, CONSTITUTIONAL PROTECTION OF HUMAN RIGHTS IN LATIN AMERICA. A COMPARATIVE STUDY OF AMPARO PROCEEDINGS (2009).
Daniel M. Brinks and William Forbath, *Commentary: Social and Economic Rights in Latin America: Constitutional Courts and the Prospects for Pro-poor Interventions*, 89/7 Texas Law Review, 1943–55 (2011).
José Antonio Cheibub, Zachary Elkins, and Tom Ginsburg, *Latin American Constitutionalism in Comparative and Historical Perspective*, 89/7 Texas Law Review, 1707–39 (2011).
Diego García-Sayán, *The Inter-American Court and Constitutionalism in Latin America*, 89/7 Texas Law Review, 1537–55 (2011).
Roberto Gargarella, *No place for popular sovereignty? Democracy, rights and punishment in Gelman v. Uruguay,* November 30, 2012, available at www.law.yale.edu/documents/pdf/sela/SELA13_Gargarella_CV_Eng_20121130.pdf.
Gretchen Helmke and Julio Rios-Figueroa (eds), COURTS IN LATIN AMERICA (2014).
Alexandra Huneeus, *High courts and the inter-American court: judicialization, human rights and a tenuous relationship*, in CULTURES OF LEGALITY: JUDICIALIZATION AND POLITICAL ACTIVISM IN LATIN AMERICA (Javier A. Couso, Alexandra Huneeus, and Rachel Sieder eds, 2013).
Gerald Neuman, *Import, Export, and Regional Consent in the Inter-American Court of Human Rights*, 19/1 EUROPEAN JOURNAL OF INTERNATIONAL LAW, 101–23 (2008).
César Rodríguez-Garavito, *Beyond the Courtroom: The Impact of Judicial Activism on Socioeconomic Rights in Latin America*, 89/7 TEXAS LAW REVIEW, 1669–98 (2011).
Rodrigo Uprimny Yepes, *The Recent Transformation of Constitutional Law in Latin America: Trends and Challenges*, 89/7 TEXAS LAW REVIEW, 1587–609 (2011).

Index